MW00811623

Cervantes, the Golden Age, and the Battle for Cultural Identity in 20th-Century Spain

Cervantes, the Golden Age, and the Battle for Cultural Identity in 20th-Century Spain

Ana María G. Laguna

BLOOMSBURY ACADEMIC
NEW YORK · LONDON · OXFORD · NEW DELHI · SYDNEY

BLOOMSBURY ACADEMIC
Bloomsbury Publishing Inc
1385 Broadway, New York, NY 10018, USA
50 Bedford Square, London, WC1B 3DP, UK
29 Earlsfort Terrace, Dublin 2, Ireland

BLOOMSBURY, BLOOMSBURY ACADEMIC and the Diana logo are
trademarks of Bloomsbury Publishing Plc

First published in the United States of America 2021
This paperback edition published 2023

Copyright © Ana María G. Laguna, 2021

For legal purposes the Acknowledgments on pp. xi–xii constitute
an extension of this copyright page.

Cover design: Namkwan Cho
Cover image: Photograph © Roger Viollet / Universal History Archive /
Katsumi Murouchi / Getty Images

All rights reserved. No part of this publication may be reproduced or
transmitted in any form or by any means, electronic or mechanical,
including photocopying, recording, or any information storage or retrieval
system, without prior permission in writing from the publishers.

Bloomsbury Publishing Inc does not have any control over, or responsibility
for, any third-party websites referred to or in this book. All internet addresses given in this book
were correct at the time of going to press. The author and publisher regret any inconvenience
caused if addresses have changed or sites have ceased to exist, but can accept no responsibility
for any such changes.

Library of Congress Cataloging-in-Publication Data
Names: Laguna, Ana María G., 1971- author.
Title: Cervantes, the Golden Age, and the battle for cultural identity in
20th-century Spain / Ana María Laguna.
Other titles: Cervantes, the Golden Age, and the battle for cultural identity
in twentieth-century Spain
Description: New York : Bloomsbury Academic, 2021. | Includes bibliographical
references and index.
Identifiers: LCCN 2021006803 (print) | LCCN 2021006804 (ebook) | ISBN 9781501374920
(hardback) | ISBN 9781501374937 (ebook) | ISBN 9781501374944 (pdf)
Subjects: LCSH: Spanish literature–20th century–History and criticism. | National characteristics,
Spanish, in literature. | Cervantes Saavedra, Miguel de, 1547-1616–Influence. | Literature and
society–Spain. | LCGFT: Literary criticism.
Classification: LCC PQ6073.N3 L34 2021 (print) | LCC PQ6073.N3 (ebook) | DDC 860.9–dc23
LC record available at https://lccn.loc.gov/2021006803
LC ebook record available at https://lccn.loc.gov/2021006804

ISBN: HB: 978-1-5013-7492-0
          PB: 978-1-5013-7491-3
          ePDF: 978-1-5013-7494-4
          eBook: 978-1-5013-7493-7

Typeset by Integra Software Pvt. Ltd.

To find out more about our authors and books visit www.bloomsbury.com
and sign up for our newsletters.

To Abhi

CONTENTS

FIGURES

PREFACE

This book offers a major shift in the scholarly perception of two periods of Spanish cultural history: the 1500s to the 1600s and the first four decades of the 1900s, the so-called Golden and Silver Ages of Spanish literature.[1] Recovering uncharted literary works, critical commentary, and historical records, this study celebrates the provocative cultural landscape that inspired by the Golden Age flourished in the Spain of the 1920s and 1930s and in the diaspora thereafter.

Inquiries that connect the Spanish Golden Age to the twentieth century usually do so through a highly conservative lens, assuming that the blunt imperialism of the early modern era endlessly glorified by Franco's dictatorship was a constant in the Spanish imaginary. In contrast, this monograph presents a moment in the twentieth century when the connection between the two periods hinged on antihegemonic values. The recuperation of the humanistic and dynamic vision of the early modern age embraced by liberal Spanish thinkers, writers, and artists in the decades prior to the establishment of the Francoist Regime in 1939 reinstates a progressive view of the past that preceded Franco's obsession with the two cultural stages, Renaissance and Baroque, included in the Golden Age designation.[2]

While fascist distortions of the Spanish early modern age are starting to receive proper critical attention, the fascinating dialogue with the Golden Age that preceded Franco's ascent to power remains largely overlooked. There is an urgent need to fill that void, examining the ambitious, modern design of a country that uniquely incorporated the literary and political legacies of the Spanish Renaissance into its wager on a forward-thinking, democratic future. Spaniards of the early 1900s seemed to embrace a hybrid understanding of modernity that is earning new respect in the twenty-first century as a "habitat of multiple temporalities that braid together a complex and plural *now* that is internally self-divided, and contaminated by pre-modern time."[3] In my exploration of the complex understanding of Spanish modernity as "contaminated" by references to the premodern, the figure of Miguel de Cervantes (1547–1616) emerges as a pivotal presence, not only as a canonical literary authority, but as an embodiment of the humanistic and secular values that unorthodox reformers believed could shape a new Spanish society. Precisely because it traces so revealingly the different outlooks on Cervantes at play during the first half of the twentieth century, this research opens up new comparative possibilities among the various schools of Cervantine criticism that were consolidated throughout that long century.

The modernizing, secular vision of the 1500s and 1600s that I discuss in the following chapters is thus incompatible with the traditionalist and authoritarian view of the early modern period reinforced, first, by traditional thinkers and, later, by the Francoist regime during its almost forty years in power (1939 to 1975). Both perspectives, the progressive/unorthodox and traditional/(ultra)conservative, highlight the polarized political positions that led to the violent clashes of the Spanish Civil War but were also evident both before the war and in the decades following the fascist victory.[4] In the 1920s through the 1940s particularly, both liberal and conservative camps projected in often blunt and anachronistic ways their own values onto the early modern period. Yet, only one of those visions is broadly known today. By recovering the progressive dream of incipient and future Spanish modernities—a dream that has been ignored for almost a century—this book provides a more balanced understanding of both historical stages, and casts into doubt the idea of a consistent conservatism in both Golden Age literature and its critical appraisals.

Cervantes, the Golden Age, and the Battle for Cultural Identity in 20th-Century Spain explores why Cervantes and his peers became touchstones for the unconventional worldview and ambition of the 1920s through to the 1940s, why a "modern" Spain felt the need to go back three hundred years in order to carry out its political and artistic experiments, and why the vindication of a humanist legacy played such a pivotal role in the long-lived battle to define Spain's cultural identity. Ultimately, this study asks Spanish studies to recognize a crucial chapter in its critical history, a chapter that, precisely because of its power, was systematically erased by the Francoist regime.

ACKNOWLEDGMENTS

Since this book took eleven years to complete, it owes its existence to eleven thousand people. I first and foremost thank Haaris Naqvi and Amy Martin at Bloomsbury Academic for giving this project a home in their Literary Studies list, a space unusually attentive to the social and political repercussions of creative texts, critical trends, and reading cultures.

With the same diligence, I thank the countless librarians, curators, and interns at the Rutgers Library system and the Biblioteca Nacional of Madrid. Their archivists have over the years endured thousands of requests with unmatched patience and professionalism. I have been incredibly lucky with almost all elements of the book chain, having had the opportunity to collaborate with and learn from some of the most outstanding figures of Cervantes studies. At the executive board of the Cervantes Society of America, I received immense inspiration, feedback, and encouragement from Mercedes Alcalá Galán, Luis Avilés, Laura Bass, Susan Byrne, Bruce Burningham, David Boruchoff, David Castillo and Moisés Castillo, William Childers, Marsha Collins, Frederick de Armas, Steven Hutchinson, Paul Johnson, Ignacio López, Howard Mancing, Adrienne Martin, Carolyn Nadeau, Cory Reed, Christina Lee, Julia Domínguez, James Iffland, and Steven Wagschal, among others. My good fortune also allowed me to collaborate with other illustrious and cherished specialists, such as Michael Armstrong-Roche, Marina Brownlee, Israel Burshatin, Anne Cruz, Diana de Armas Wilson, William Egginton, María Antonia Garcés, Enrique García Tomás, Mary Gaylord, Isabel Lozano-Renieblas, Jesús Maestro, José Manuel Martín Morán, Christina Quintero, John Slater, Rachel Schmidt, Michael Solomon, Alison Weber, and Bill Worden. Their work, presence, and sense of humor have inspired some of my best days and hopeful lines.

The curse of the *Cervantista* is believing you have discovered a "true" and/or "novel" dimension of Cervantes's writing, only to hear someone suggest one or two dozen studies on the subject. In this case, a major reference has been Aurora Hermida Ruiz, who generously shared with me an article that immediately became a cornerstone for my argument. Other inspiring and validating references that I only know in print, such as José Carlos Mainer, Enric Bou, Joan Ramon Resina, and Sebastiaan Faber, I hope to thank in person soon. Scholars like Carroll Johnson, Amy Williamsen, and John J. Allen I can sadly only address in this printed fashion; they are gone too early but not completely, since we all keep citing their brilliant insights. I continue to allude to Anthony Close on a daily basis, almost invariably to diverge from his views, acutely aware, however, of the mark that he (and these other scholars) has left on the Cervantine world in general, and on my own critical outlook in particular.

In a much more terrestrial manner, I am fortunate to thank for their guidance and patience my heaven-sent editorial advisors, Audra Wolfe first, Christianne Mariano, and Alison Howard. Barbara Tessman and Katherine Aid deserve some form of cosmic recognition for reading almost every draft of this manuscript, identifying in each pass promising leads and lingering inconsistencies. As I wandered through the circles of drafting purgatory, colleagues like Patricia Akhimie, Henry Turner, and Anjali Nerlekar, and fellow writers like Concha Alborch helped me sharpen my comparativist lens. My research assistant, Aliza Levenson, aided me in compiling this book's bibliography with a concerning meticulousness. My deepest gratitude to them all.

The long journey here would have never been possible without the various forms of institutional support that I received at Rutgers and beyond, most notably through the Rutgers University Research Council Program and the Chancellor's Institutional Equity and Diversity Grant Program of Rutgers Camden. Generous assistance has also come from the International Fund for the Cooperation and Promotion of Spanish Culture of the Spanish Ministry of Foreign Affairs, and from the Institute of Research in the Humanities at the University of Wisconsin–Madison.

Equally essential has been the logistic support of the Lagunas' and Pathaks' foundations, my family. As I celebrate the memory of my parents, I realize that they would have probably disagreed with almost every aspect of this book, which would not have stopped them from recommending it to surrounding acquaintances, relatives, and friends. Their generosity of spirit has been passed to the members of my physical and extended family, who graciously forgave my absence from countless events and celebrations. I have been concerned about the example that this behavior could set for the Laguna children, but our youngest writer, Olivia, has the good sense to only consider writing bestsellers. Generation Z will save the world, the climate, and our bank accounts, hopefully in that order.

Finally, this book is dedicated to the most patient husband in the universe, partner in countless transatlantic adventures, and healer of all the homesickness they leave behind.

Introduction:
A Tale of Two Modernities

In April of 1521, the Austrian absolutism that had settled in Spain obliterated the comuneros—*representatives of municipal democracies—in Villalar. In 1931, the Spanish town governments lawfully defeated the absolutist monarchy and instituted the Republic.* We thus close a great historical cycle. A deep and peaceful revolution has been accomplished, a revolution that in its etymological sense implies a return to its origin. We return to 1521, to the supreme popular sovereignty. *It's been four centuries and ten years. Many centuries and many years ... A patient Spain— not dead, like many believed—has provided the world with a magnificent example of historical dignity.*

LUIS ARAQUISTÁIN, "VOLVEMOS A 1521" (1931)[1]

In this epigraph, Luis Araquistáin (1886–1959), one of the co-writers of the 1931 Spanish constitution, celebrates the proclamation of the country's Second Republic (1931–9), characterizing it as the pinnacle of a peaceful Spanish "revolution" that had lasted more than four centuries. Araquistáin's triumphant "We return to 1521" (Volvemos a 1521) illustrates the deep-seated belief of progressives of his generation that, by amending the missteps of its past, Spain was finally able to actualize and fulfill the promise of its future.

Araquistáin's proud, if anachronistic, return to the Spanish Golden Age to vindicate the unconventional, democratic modernity of both periods advances the main tenet of this book.[2] For progressive thinkers like him,

Spanish modernity had originated at the onset of Golden Age, a period that rather than representing an Inquisitorial interim, encapsulated the insurgence of daring humanists such as Cervantes and proto-democratic institutions like the Medieval Castilian Councils. In Araquistáin's eyes, it was thanks to this humanist culture, and to the memory of such local councils—despite their destruction by Charles V in 1521—that Spain had managed to preserve for four hundred years its desire for popular sovereignty. The success of that silent, dignified, and "patient" country was finally able to refute the traditional image of Spaniards as "caught in time warp that prevented them from embracing modernity of any sort."[3]

Although the contagious optimism of Araquistáin's words vanished after 1939 (once Francisco Franco's army claimed its victory over Republican forces in the Spanish Civil War, ushering in a dictatorship that endured till Franco's death in 1975) the cultural emphasis on Spain's early modern period did not fade. Quite to the contrary, the assumption that the 1500s and 1600s contained the seeds of Spain's greatness and were likewise the genesis for its contemporary troubles intensified, as writers on both sides of the political divide—Republicans and other progressives, versus conservatives and proto-fascists—continued to return to the Golden Age in their efforts to either oppose or justify Spain's restoration of an authoritarian and imperial-like order.

After 1939, one of such competing views—Araquistáin's proto-democratic and rebellious early modern past—would completely disappear from public view for more than forty years. Once declared victorious over the Republican government, the Francoist regime would turn the Golden Age into the golden age of Spanish imperialism, a period full of "totalitarian and warlike values ... perfectly in tune with their own historical moment."[4] By erasing from the public stage the innovative ideas of the 1500s and 1600s vindicated by left-wing artists and intellectuals, Francoism satisfied its own political needs, reinforcing in the process an understanding of the age that was completely fictitious. As Filipe Ribeiro de Meneses summarizes:

> The vision of Spain heralded by Franco's propaganda machine represented a romantic return to a Golden Age that never existed, which resulted from a very selective and nationalistic reading of the country's history. The intellectuals at Franco's service proposed to recreate, in the twentieth century, Spain's imperial age, the reigns of Ferdinand and Isabella, of Charles V and Philip II which had seen the expulsion of the Moors from Granada and the sudden and massive expansion of Spanish power around the world.[5]

Paraphrasing Duncan Wheeler, we could say that if progressive Republicans such as Araquistáin used the Golden Age past to shape a democratic, modern future, Francoist ideologues stretched the orthodoxical impositions of that past to lock the country into an archaic and immobile present.[6] As the sweeping dictatorial establishment took root in Spain, this fictitious understanding of an "invincible" Golden Age became a ubiquitous reference (and justification) for a "timeless" authoritarian order. As a side effect, few unorthodox or secular ideas would appear to be compatible with Cervantes's age.[7]

An Old but Not New Relationship: On (Neo)Baroque, Cervantes, Modernity, and Critical Historiography

At the other side of the Atlantic, in Latin American letters, the link between the early modern age and a progressive twentieth-century culture continued to thrive. Writers as disparate as Jorge Luis Borges (1899–1986), José Lezama Lima (1910–76), Haroldo de Campos (1929–2003), and Octavio Paz (1914–98) argued that the early modern period—what they usually addressed as the Baroque—constituted from its early arrival in Latin America "a fitting channel of resistance against orthodoxy."[8] In their view, despite being the artistic style imposed by the *conquistadores*, the Baroque soon started functioning as a liberating aesthetic rather than a channel of domination, eliciting what Gonzalo Celorio calls an "art of Counter Conquest" rather than the art of the Counter Reformation.[9] For de Campos, the subversive application of this aesthetic idiom can be attributed to the intrinsic allegorical *pathos* of the Baroque, often too complex to convey the straightforward messages of conquest and cultural domination.[10] Latin American authors believed that in the gaps, breaks, and fissures of this Baroque form, early modern and contemporary writers and artists could assert the "difference of the different," forging with that formula "an anti-tradition" from which to rewrite a local experience and historiography.[11] Twentieth-century Latin American reinventions of this spirit—what has been called the "Neobaroque"—thus affirmed the subversive nature of this early modern heritage, believing that it was completely unrelated to the cultural impositions of its source, Spain.[12]

If scholars have traditionally considered such a combative view of the Baroque inapplicable to Spain, this is likely because in the Peninsular context, the interactions between modern Spain and its Baroque or Golden Age have generally focused on the distorted Francoist portrayal of the period. The continued oversight of any other moments of Spanish history where the country looked back on its past with more progressive intentions (as in the 1920s and 1930s) prolonged the silence of critics and historians that witnessing the Francoist perversion of that early modern legacy in real time did little to contest it. One of the most consequential protagonists of this process was José Antonio Maravall (1911–86), a historian who, unlike his Latin American counterparts, not only refused to consider the Baroque a liberating force, but proclaimed it to be a hegemonic instrument, a monolithic artistic expression of "unanimous opinions in favor ... of the ruling minority."[13] Despite the lingering perception in some circles of the deep debt that Spanish scholarship continues to owe to Maravall,[14] *Cervantes, the Golden Age, and the Battle for Cultural Identity in 20th-Century Spain* uncovers the disruptive impact of the scholar, who—being clearly sympathetic to the fascist regime—succeeded in silencing the humanist legacy of figures such as Erasmus and Cervantes, who had been enthusiastically celebrated by progressive intellectuals, social critics, and politicians up to 1939.

While most of Maravall's conservative ideas of Golden Age genres such as the *Comedia* have by now been debunked, literary criticism has not yet thoroughly examined his misrepresentation of Cervantes.[15] This omission has been particularly damaging for our understanding of the author, since in *Humanismo en las armas de* "Don Quijote" (1948), and its late sequel, *Utopía y contrautopía en* "Don Quijote" (1976), Maravall used Cervantes to assert the inherently traditional and imperialistic nature of the Golden Age. To date, this is one of the first books to uncover the alignment of Maravall's views of Cervantes with unmistakable elements of a Francoist ideology.

Here, I also reexamine the impact of another monumental pillar in the field, the British Hispanist Anthony Close, whose seminal study *The Romantic Approach to "Don Quixote"* (1978) demonstrated minimal awareness of the progressive critical culture that had flourished in Spain from the 1920s through the 1940s. If the myths Maravall propagated about Cervantes and the conservative character of the Spanish Golden Age have only recently begun to be consistently disputed, Close's theories about the Spanish Cervantism of the last century, meanwhile, remain in full force.[16]

For Close, Spanish Cervantes criticism from the mid-1800s to the late 1900s was characterized by a "simplifying and philistine [theoretical] reductionism," which he identified as the "Romantic Approach (28)." For novels such as *Don Quixote,* this approach comprised a total disregard of the text ("novel's artistic texture"), since critics following this paradigm focused instead on contextual facts about "the author's life, Spanish history," and even "disputes of Renaissance poetics, Renaissance philosophy, and other such esoteric patterns," which then became the main bases for their interpretations.[17] For Close, this Romantic school had become so successful in Spain that it sanctified this "adolescent state of historically-conscious literary study" for more than a century.[18] Part of its long-term success was due to the high stature of its practitioners, writers such as Miguel de Unamuno (1864–1936), Angel Ganivet (1865–98), Azorín (1873–1965), Maeztu (1874–1936), Francisco Navarro Ledesma (1905–36), and José Ortega y Gasset (1883–1955), all, apart from Ledesma and Ortega y Gasset, members of the reputed Generation of 1898.[19] Few could argue against the fact that these '98 scholars, being almost unable to read *Don Quixote* independently of the "problem of Spain," had indeed used the novel "as a vessel which distill the essence of his [their] philosophy."[20] As a result, these writers, rather than advancing a deeper understanding of the novel, erected a nationalist and heavily philosophical filter with which many subsequent authors and readers approached not only Cervantes's opus, but almost any other work from the Spanish Golden Age tradition.

While it is hard to contest this particular view of the generation's legacy, it may be difficult to accept the validity of Close's Romantic Approach as a whole, given the limited parameters on which it rests. When attempting to understand an entire critical landscape as complex as that of Cervantine studies in Spain during the 1800s and 1900s, Close's monograph relied on a minuscule number of Spanish critics, mainly '98 writers and a few other critics such as Américo Castro (1883–1955). Operating within this reductive sample of Spanish intellectual tradition, Close reached the conclusion that for almost 150 years of Spanish critical history, from the 1830s to the late 1970s, "academics resident in Spain did not produce any Quixotic criticism which could be regarded as a really significant landmark."[21] To him, the Spanish Cervantism of the twentieth century was so homogeneous and static that all the work produced between the "1940s and 1965 period resembles its counterpart between 1833 and 1859."[22] Ignoring the 1920s through 1940s, as if those decades were even less noteworthy, Close reinforced the assumption that Spanish criticism from the nineteenth and twentieth centuries had produced a sterile and "fairly coherent tradition," an assertion my rehabilitation of a diverse and untraditional Cervantine strand firmly contradicts.[23]

Complementary to Close's analysis, some Spanish studies in the past two decades have mapped out the twentieth century's vibrant and engaging interest in Cervantes. Monographs such as Maria Angeles Varela Olea's *Don Quijote como mitogenema nacional* (2003), and volumes such as Jenaro Talens's *La Generación del 27 visita a Don Quijote* (2005), and Francisco Layna and Antonio Cortijo Ocaña's *Cervantes, política nacional y estética nacionalista, 1920–1975* (2014) have illustrated the enormous and complex intellectual attention that Cervantes received outside of the Generation of '98. Indispensable as these studies are, documenting the attention that twentieth-century Spanish authors paid to *Don Quixote* without fully acknowledging how the writers' different ideological perspectives influenced their views of Cervantes, can emphasize the confusion surrounding this convoluted period. By recuperating the unifying threads—in this case, political and ideological—that structure this cultural panorama, we may find clear patterns that articulate the multiple divides of these years (the 1920s and 1930s).

Some of those threads are more apparent than others. Christopher Britt Arredondo's book *Quixotism: The Imaginative Denial of Spain's Loss of Empire* (2004) provides a formidable examination of the imperialistic myths that the authors and critics of the influential Generation of 1898 built around *Don Quixote*, and of the unfortunate usefulness of this legacy to Francoist ideology. This valuable study is less concerned with the rejection of these myths by the members of a group of younger and more progressive intellectuals, often associated with the Generation of '27.[24] The implication of this perspective is that all twentieth-century "Quixotists" are to be identified with the right-wing thinkers and '98 ultra-conservative writers such as Azorín and Ganivet, and with proto-fascist theorists, such as Ernesto Giménez Caballero, who later adopted and developed their views.

Here, I not only explore Maravall's bias and counter the symbolic picture of a "fairly coherent" body of Cervantes's criticism painted by Close, but also examine other, less evident dynamics of this cultural spectrum, such as the differences between nonconventional writers, mostly associated with the Generation of 1927, and their conservative predecessors, largely identifiable with the Generation of 1898. By establishing well-defined reasons for these differences, this book challenges the notion that the cultural panorama of the twentieth century in Spain is too fragmented and confusing to permit the identification of any common patterns among its participants. The abundant critical output published from the 1920s to the 1940s (in Spain and then in the diaspora) makes it clear that, without negating unavoidable self-contradictions and disagreements within and among authors, we can recognize major literary trends and sensibilities in this period. One of the most obvious points of reference involves the alignment of each artist, writer, and philosopher with right- or left-wing political beliefs, an indication that allows us to identify Quixotes of left and the right, so to speak—the former encompassing complex networks of liberal, socialist, and Republican thinkers and supporters, and the latter a traditional, monarchic, ultra-conservative, and, ultimately, fascist conglomerate. In doing so, *Cervantes, the Golden Age, and the Battle for Cultural Identity in 20th-Century Spain* insists on recognizing the major and divergent political strains that have deeply affected Spain, and the field of Spanish and Cervantine studies, thus providing a larger context for the captivating dialogue of past and present that articulates the Spanish twentieth century.

The recovery of a polychronic chapter of Spanish history that looked so elastically backward in order to look forward may illustrate the reasons why, as Aubrey Bell put it almost ninety years ago, we have "failed to appreciate the more generous outlook of those more spacious [and flexible] times," including the twentieth century.[25] Indeed, in the "spacious" 1920s, 1930s, and 1940s, both in Spain and in exile, a multidimensional generation of artists, writers, philosophers, and politicians often associated with the Generation of 1927 continued to apply a progressive view of the early modern past to praise, (re)build, and mourn the elusive modernity of their country. Ultimately, this study explores why, for them, the political and artistic innovations of Golden Age literary culture provided an essential reference for the initially promising and eventually disappointing conditions and opportunities of their own age.

Addressing a Dual Modernity: The Organization of this Book

Chapter 1, "Mining the Golden Age: The Spanish Avant-Garde and Visions of Modernity," traces how, in the 1920s and 1930s, the irreverent and prolific Spanish avant-garde facilitated a cultural return to the Golden Age, and examines the ambivalent outcomes produced by this return. While the avant-garde's dialogue with Golden Age authors and genres produced highly liberating innovations in the arts, it resulted in a less-constructive synergy in intellectual realms, where radical experimentation contributed to a hostile polarization of political sensibilities. At a purely artistic level, the avant-garde produced an astonishingly rich legacy. Unlike other moments in the evolution of science or the arts, where the achievement of one trend is predicated on the elimination or rejection of others, the avant-garde consolidated its success by juxtaposing old and new models in a complementary fashion. The resulting inclusive artistic experimentation of the 1920s benefited from invigorating the "fusion of codes" (*fusión de códigos*) of Renaissance arts, which blurred distinctions between the visual and verbal domains (word and image) and distant chronologies (present and past).

Within this aesthetic revolution, ultra-conservative and progressive views of a modern Spanish identity started to consolidate their presence in the country's cultural scene. While these disparate visions of modernity would agree about the importance of considering the Golden Age a guiding light for progress, they worked from divergent understandings of that period and the idea of modernity it implied. In general terms, for progressive thinkers, the Golden Age reflected a tolerant, humanistic, and at its core, counter-hegemonic Spain; conservative and proto-fascist ideologues, on the other hand, saw in the same period a supposed Spanish propensity for order, authority, and conformity, which led to the glorification of imperial structures which ultra-conservative thinkers were intent on recovering. As tensions escalated and the public cultural discourse deteriorated, both visions would invoke the figure of Cervantes to justify their positions. Among progressive thinkers, the author, whom they considered a sophisticated humanist, would emerge as a champion of Spain's incipient modernity; in conservative ranks, Cervantes—and, more specifically, his magnum opus, *Don Quixote*—would often embody the political weakness and secular propensities that the country needed to eliminate to rise again as a messianic power.

It has been said that only "repressive, authoritarian regimes take literature seriously,"[26] and the Francoist charges against Cervantes and Cervantism, which I explore in Chapter 2, "The Empire Strikes Back: Cervantes, Enemy of the State," sadly exemplify that claim. In the late 1920s, Giménez Caballero and other proto-fascists became increasingly frustrated by the rising popularity of Cervantes. The recognition of the author as a full-fledged humanist concerned such critics, who sought to characterize the Golden Age as an ultra-orthodox, triumphant period, irreconcilable with the secular humanism that Cervantes represented. Positing a mythical age of never-ending *conquistas* and *reconquistas*, the manufactured fascist idea of a messianic Golden Age managed to corrupt the already troubling axiom of the sixteenth-century monarch Philip II—"to God through the empire"—with the even more unholy "to the empire through God" (Por el imperio hacia Dios, o Por Dios hacia el imperio).[27]

In the ultra-conservative camp, Cervantes's humanistic perspective would then earn the novel the title of "most anti-national, dangerous, immoral, and tragic ... book" in Spanish history.[28] Even before Ernesto Giménez Caballero was named vice-secretary of education in the first Francoist government, he would pronounce himself not only the nemesis of Cervantes, but "the cure against Quixotism" and the "secular plague" it represented.[29] Such fascist "cure" would be directed not only at Cervantes, but also at the vibrant Cervantine culture that developed in the 1920s and consolidated through the educational investments of the Second Republic. Although the fascist rush to dismantle the Cervantine resurgence of these decades was only one of the many cultural calamities caused by Francoist order, it is one that has sadly been overlooked. Chapter 2 illustrates the nature, scale, and long-term impact of this cultural tragedy.

Chapter 3, "A Generational Shift: Riding Away from the Empire," explores how Republican supporters and progressive exiles—largely associated with the members of the Generation of '27—reacted to the staggering cultural and political changes occurring in the 1930s and 1940s. Their unfaltering defense of Cervantes reveals the nature of the intellectual debates of this period, and the reasons a seventeenth-century author (and the critical discourse surrounding him) came to acquire such political significance in those years.

Authors associated with the '27 group initially approached Cervantes and Cervantism from a purely literary perspective, manifesting enormous disapproval of the critical traditions that had preceded them—Restoration critics, Romantics, and the Generation of '98. While willing to commend these critical forebears for some of their contributions, crediting the Romantic critics, for example, with rescuing Cervantes from neglect, they denounced just as clearly the insidious effects of their deficient analyses. For their younger counterparts, the Generation of '98, with their overtly symbolic enunciations on Cervantes, had constructed an imperial fantasy that easily could be—and was—co-opted by Falangist and Francoist demagoguery. Demanding historical accountability from those '98 critics, a brave Luis Cernuda, writing in the 1950s, wondered why they continued to be held in such reverence, despite these "irresponsible" opinions.[30]

From the perspective of the '27 group, rather than promoting authoritarian discourses and imperial dreams, Cervantes warned against the devastating effects of both. Thus, just as Giménez Caballero came to define the fascist approach to Cervantes, writers and critics such as María Zambrano, Pedro Salinas, Luis Cernuda, and Max Aub came to embody a progressive understanding of Cervantes and his age. In reconstructing an active, inventive, and invested critical landscape very different from the homogeneous and static one assumed by traditional criticism, this chapter recovers the critical controversies that, in the 1940s, led members of the Generation of '27 to rebel against the dictates of a hegemonic critical tradition (that of the Generation of '98) and the draconian distortions of the Francoist regime.

While anachronism is generally anathema in current cultural and critical analysis, it is prominent in the political and literary developments of the 1920s, 1930s, and 1940s. Embracing this anachronistic logic, Chapter 4, "Anachronism as Weapon and Resistance (Quixotes Left and Right)" explores how Cervantes scholarship became an ideological battlefield, especially in the 1940s. Despite the initial Francoist disregard for the writer seen in Chapter 2, the regime's pragmatic officials soon latched onto Cervantes's growing international stature, particularly in the context of the 1947 celebrations of the four-hundredth anniversary of his birth. Realizing the great propagandistic opportunity presented by the occasion, the dictatorship launched a powerful celebratory campaign aimed at capitalizing on Cervantes's repute as one of the country's greatest writers, in the process representing Cervantes and his most famous character as unquestioning proponents of empire.[31]

Progressive authors and critics, meanwhile, adopted a strategic anachronism of their own, redoubling their efforts to present Cervantes as an agent of modernity. Determined to defeat the Francoist attempts to assimilate Cervantes to their cause, Spanish exiles dedicated all means available in their newly adopted homelands to this objective: new curricula, special issues of periodicals, and thematic events centered on figures such as Don Quixote all emphasized the degree to which Cervantes's hero and life illustrated the miseries rather than the glories of war, heroism, and empire, the three tenets of fascist ideology. By highlighting significant episodes of *Don Quixote* and of Cervantes's life, the writers of the diaspora briefly succeeded in protecting their revered author from the fascist rebranding.

Sadly, exiled writers won a battle only to lose a cultural war. After 1948, they would be silenced and defeated by the very kind of discourse and environment that was supposed to protect them: academia. The presumably "neutral" historian, José Antonio Maravall, carrying out "unbiased" historical analysis, would quietly yet powerfully delegitimize the once-thriving humanist and Erasmist scholarship that progressive intellectuals, politicians, and researchers had produced in the decades prior to 1936 and maintained afterward in the diaspora. Thanks to Maravall's calculated spin, Cervantes and his age would come to be seen as inherently religious, orthodox, and even imperial. It took more than fifty years for specialists to question the soundness of some of Maravall's historical and literary criteria; even then, this questioning has not been fully applied to his views on Cervantes—until now. This chapter addresses this oversight, demonstrating that, while Maravall was surely not the only one responsible for the almost surgical excision of progressive thought from Golden Age studies, he was one of the most important figures wielding the scalpel.

Chapter 5 inquires into how Spanish progressives reaffirmed their cultural perspective on Cervantes and the Golden Age in exile when everything else had apparently failed them. Unable to reinstate a democracy in Spain, and seeing their own influence (and that of Cervantes) being rapidly forgotten in the Francoist cultural climate, displaced writers would turn to Cervantes's prose as they tried to remain hopeful about Spain's—and their own—future. In this context, *Don Quixote* emerges as "an exiled book" (*un libro exiliado*), while its *ex-libris* dictum "Post tenebras spero lucem" ("In darkness, I await the light") appears as the unofficial motto for the diaspora.

Despite the bleak tone of the adage, the exiles' return to Cervantes and *Don Quixote* provided more than an indulgent platform for despair: it was also an opportunity for resistance and rebirth. In this context, Cervantes's humanist perspective is constantly invoked by diaspora writers, cognizant that this humanism provided them the best opportunity to counter Spain's imperial past, and to demonstrate an alignment, furthermore, with the counter-colonialist views of their newly adopted Latin American homes. Salinas succinctly voiced the hope for a reconciliation between Spain and the Americas arguing that despite their obvious differences "[i]n *Don Quixote,* we all can understand one another."[32] Yet rejecting the imperial delusions of their homeland by invoking Cervantes became another unfeasible dream for these émigrés, whose criticism of the Spanish empire was not always considered consistent or sincere. This last chapter reconnects the anti-imperialistic positions that progressive writers had already expressed in Spain (before the complete victory of Franco) with their counter-colonial reflections in exile. It pays special attention to the role that Cervantes played in these anti-imperialist formulations.

The epilogue considers some of the reasons for the suppression or disregard of the progressive and humanistic perspectives on both early modern and modern Spanish culture and criticism, as well as the consequences of this loss.

1

Mining the Golden Age:
The Spanish Avant-Garde and
Visions of Modernity

Nothing at the beginning of the twentieth century suggested that Spain desired to use the Golden Age as an inspiration for modernity. After the loss of the last Spanish colonies overseas in 1898, old icons such as Don Quixote would be famously associated with the nostalgic laments of the Generation of '98, which urged the country to look inward and to the far past of the sixteenth century to recover the national soul, now as lost as its empire.[1] During the early 1900s, however, the "politics of despair" associated with the Generation of '98 would coexist with much more optimistic aspirations to move the country forward into the modernity of the new century.[2] This desire for progress materialized into a series of policies that by the 1930s had started to produce some encouraging results, albeit with considerable delays. From 1910 to 1930, the population grew by 10 percent, life expectancy improved from forty-one years to fifty, the proportion of the population that lived in cities increased from 15.8 percent in 1910 to 26.5 percent in 1930, and salaries (especially in urban areas) rose a staggering 29 percent.[3] Not surprisingly, the improvement in the standard of living translated into a dramatic rise in the country's literacy rate, evolving from an embarrassing 48 percent in 1900 to a more respectable 73 percent by the late 1920s, which made Spain's once lagging cultural standards comparable to those of other developed nations.[4] Other indicators of progress also dramatically improved, despite constant political volatility: domestic production tripled, a timid tax reform was accomplished, and the number of railways miles doubled.[5] The country was certainly on a new path.

These advances occurred during the so-called Spanish Restoration (1874–1931), a period that saw the re-establishment of a constitutional monarchy under the Bourbon dynasty and an electoral system that deliberately alternated liberal and conservative governments, hoping to bring stability to an otherwise turbulent political scene.[6] In reality, the differences between the liberal and conservative programs were so dramatic that both factions dedicated large portions of their time in power to reversing the policies instituted by the previous legislature.

It was therefore only a matter of time before this counterproductive political system resulted in massive domestic and international failures, such as the disastrous Spanish-American War of 1898, the long military conflict with the Moroccan Protectorate, and the inability of the government to reconcile regional disparities and combustible social discontents (exemplified by the tragic civil conflict of Barcelona in 1909).[7] The growing unrest, deepened by military and financial pressures, precipitated a coup in 1923 by Genral Primo de Rivera, who remained in power until 1931.[8] While Primo de Rivera's "technocratic regenerationist" reform—aided by King Alfonso XIII—was genuinely invested in continuing and even accelerating the timid reform of the country begun by his predecessors, the nature and corruption of the regime set an uneven pace for such modernizing process, limiting it mostly to urban areas.[9]

This complex political scenario posed obvious challenges for Spain's emerging but fragile modernity, leading several schools of thought to negate its existence altogether. Indeed, when modernity is measured by the specific benchmarks and indicators that most European powers had reached in the 1800s (national debt, gross domestic product, and so on), by the early 1900s, Spain's battle for development could be considered already lost. However, when modernity is understood as a more dynamic endeavor, dependent on the fluid development of major interlocking dimensions—economic, political, social, and cultural—Spain's quest for progress appears more promising and less unique, even when plagued by the extreme inconsistencies built into the development of the country.[10] Thus, as the Spain of the late 1920s, struggled to make overdue technological and financial improvements, it also witnessed extraordinary developments in its cultural and social spheres. By 1931, with the birth of the Second Republic, this uneven evolution had positioned the country at a critical turning point: While its lingering structural deficiencies could very well torpedo the most carefully drafted development programs, its new demographic strength and political will could launch it to the spectacular, national success it had dreamed of.

This juncture, with its tension between historical limitations and an exciting, if hesitant, leap into the future, provides the context from which we can best understand Spain's fixation with the past. If the explicit nexus between the 1521 *Comuneros*' revolt and the 1931 Republican revolution was foundational for the progressive agenda, it was just one of the many inspirational references that progressives took from early modern Spain. Other events, artists, and authors—from Cervantes to Erasmus—would also acquire a place of honor in their outlooks and programs. The practice was not limited to left-wing thinkers; a wide array of political theorists, writers, and philosophers of every ideological inclination would turn to the 1500s for inspiration or justification for their views and aims. The influential José Ortega y Gasset is a case in point. In 1914, appearing particularly well positioned to identify the reasons for the country's stalling on the road to modernity, the philosopher censured the errors and inconsistencies of the Restoration with multiple comparisons to the early modern period:

> The Restoration period lacks nothing. There are great state men, great thinkers, great generals, great parties, great wars: Our army battles the Moors in Tetuán just as in the times of Gonzalo de Córdoba, and goes after the Northern enemy—finding death at sea—just as in the times of Phillip II; Pereda is Hurtado de Mendoza, and from Echegaray, a Calderón can emerge. But all of this occurs within the realm of nightmare; it is the appearance of a life where the only thing real is the act of imagining it. The Restoration period was, in short, a ghost act, and [Antonio] Cánovas [del Castillo] the man responsible for this phantasmagoria.[11]

Ortega's reluctance to assess the Restoration in and of itself, choosing instead to contrast it with the more distant realities of the 1500s and 1600s, implies an obvious respect for the Golden Age and a marked interest in keeping a safe distance from his country's more immediate past.[12] By portraying the Restoration's flawed statesmen, diplomats, and playwrights as nightmarish shadows of brilliant earlier figures such as Gonzalo de Córdoba (1453–1515), Hurtado de Mendoza (1535–1609), and Calderón de la Barca (1600–81), Ortega paints a somber picture of Spain's inability in the late 1800s to meet modernity's challenges and dreams. At the same time, he obliquely suggests that modern Spain might benefit from a dive further back into its own history, to the great figures of the Golden Age.

Exasperation with the Restoration was not the only reason thinkers such as Ortega turned their attention to the Golden Age. A new cultural force, the avant-garde entered Spain with an unforeseen strength in the early 1920s, highlighting a new association between present and past, with the Golden Age as a primary point of reference. While a return to the past may at first sight seem incompatible with vanguardist anti-traditionalist experimentation, a closer look at the movement explains its paradoxical interest in early modern models and sources.

A Golden Avant-Garde

One of the most idiosyncratic attitudes of avant-garde artists was their well-known animosity toward the "traditionalism" of art, which they rebelled against passionately. They often expressed their rebellion through a return to artistic "primitivism," that is, to the aesthetic parameters of African and pre-Columbian cultures that were considered too "remote in space and time" to have fallen prey to the constrictive expectations of Western art and conservative criticism.[13] The primitivism cherished by experimental artists in turn served to channel their aesthetic rejection of "European mediateness," since all reference to the Western artistic tradition had to "be destroyed."[14] However, as avant-garde movements evolved, they started to incorporate recognizable elements or technical features of European artistic production—for example, the specific kinds of paint and brushstrokes of Renaissance masters.[15] It soon became apparent that the avant-garde's wrath was not directed toward just *any* kind of past, but only the recent one, marked by Romantic painters, bourgeois taste, and traditional academic norms. Thus, the avant-garde, somewhat ironically, embraced the influence of more distant inspirations, such as the Renaissance old masters.

As the avant-garde progressed, a return to the early modern past would become more intimately connected to radical and modern experimentation. As André Malraux noted, "at the beginning of the twentieth century, it was the painters who wished to be the most modern, which means most committed to the future, who rummaged most furiously in the past."[16] This contorted journey forward toward the innovation of modernity echoes the assessment of Ortega y Gasset quoted above, where the return to a distant early modern reference involves not only a rejection of an immediate precedent, but also a search or longing for a better—more modern—future.

In tracing and assessing the unexpected return to the 1600s that occurred in the early 1900s, this chapter explores the avant-garde's productive dialogue between the early and late modernities of these two centuries. This dialogue, however, had a mixed long-term effect. On the one hand, thanks in part to the multitalented group of artists, writers, and professionals born around the 1890s or early 1900s—many eventually known as, or associated with, the Generation of 1927—the vanguard would re-energize the synergetic relationship characteristic of Renaissance arts at a caliber and scale unseen since the 1500s. On the other hand, this hybrid aesthetic revolution, while productive in the arts, brought a very different outcome in other cultural and intellectual contexts, since its radicalization of sensibility and thought contributed to the increasing polarization of left and right ideologies in the late 1920s and early 1930s.

The antagonistic political poles that developed inside and outside the avant-garde agreed on aesthetic principles—hybrid artistic experimentation, inspiration from the past—but differed on pretty much everything else. While liberal thinkers and experimental artists would generally view the Golden Age as a dynamic catalogue of artistic and intellectual techniques and perspectives, conservatives would focus on the doctrinal and political frameworks erected to reign in such heterogeneity. This increasingly polarized approach to the past would enhance early modern references with an additional—seldom recognized—significance for the country's present. Thus, while in literary discussions of the connections between twentieth-century and early modern writers, scholars have almost exclusively focused on the attention paid by the Generation of '27 to the towering poet Luis de Góngora—whose rediscovery in 1927, the tercentenary of his death, gave the group its name[17]—it is the attention to Cervantes that epitomizes the widening gaps, frictions, and fears of the moment. Unlike the fatigue with Góngora that soon followed his revival during that intense 1927, the evocation of Cervantes only continued to grow over the decades, if not always in positive ways. Reflecting the ideological schism of the literary and cultural environment, Cervantes would become a painful symbol of the competing ideas of Spanish modernity that emerged in these decades.

A Blended, Modern Revolution

Spain's return to the early modern past in the 1920s and 1930s was not unique. On the preoccupation of Western avant-garde movements with early modern art forms, Wendy Steiner notes that "[u]nlike such moments in scientific history where one paradigm directly supplants another, the avant-garde model was instead superimposed upon the Renaissance norms, and carried with it not only meaning and power but the marker of newness and success."[18] Spain was clearly at the forefront of this practice; Pablo Picasso, for example, the most revolutionary painter of the Spanish avant-garde (and, arguably, of twentieth-century art) demonstrated a deep interest in Renaissance and Baroque art though his "devouring preoccupation" with Golden Age "traditions."[19] Beyond the obvious influence of the Spanish pictorial vernacular in his opus, the artist paid constant explicit homage to his Golden Age predecessors by painting forty-four renditions of Velázquez's *Las Meninas*, dedicating a collection of poems—*Entierro del Conde de Orgaz* (1969)—to Domenico Theotokopoulos, El Greco (1541–1614) (Figures 1.1 and 1.2), and publishing a collection of twenty illustrations of Góngora's sonnets in *Vingt poèmes de Góngora* (1948) (Figures 1.3 and 1.4).[20]

Like other experimental artists, Picasso gravitated toward Cervantes's main opus, *Don Quixote* (Figure 1.5). During the 1920s to 1950s, a period that witnessed the failures of economic, political, and social systems at local and global levels, a wide range of abstract artists like him—including José De Creeft (1884–1982), Julio González (1876–1942), Salvador Dalí (1904–89), Jackson Pollock (1912–56), his brother Charles Pollock (1902–88), David Smith (1906–65), and Hans Hoffman (1880–1966)—who considered themselves as rebellious and unorthodox as Cervantes's solitary hero produced captivating renditions of the protagonist.[21] Picasso's engagement with

FIGURE 1.1 *Rafael Alberti shows the book "Diez sonetos romanos" to Pablo Picasso. Mougins, 1966. Fons Roberto Otero. Museu Picasso, Barcelona. © 2020 Estate of Pablo Picasso/Artists Rights Society (ARS), New York.*

Cervantes—beyond his famous rendition of Don Quixote—is only starting to be explored, as it also included an intended translation (with Guillaume Apollinaire) of the short-novel "The Glass Graduate," and a homage to the tragedy *The Siege of Numancia* in the impactful *Guernica* (1937).[22] The latter is little surprising if we consider that both works, *Numancia* and *Guernica*, explore the cruel destruction of the Spanish "pueblo" at the hands of a foreign (Roman/ Nazi) invading army (Read 43).

Far better recognized is the influence that Spanish Baroque poetry provided for the polychronic, aesthetic innovation pioneered by artists like Picasso. Góngora's reappraisal in the late 1920s, characterized by Rafael Alberti "an act of faith to make up for three hundred years of misunderstanding," was highly defining of this unconventional spirit since it illustrated two fundamental avant-garde attitudes shared by Spanish poets and artists:[23] the protest against the academic establishment, and the celebration of new poetic languages. Considered a "bold creator of images and metaphors, a 'pure' poet who had been unfairly treated ... by his contemporaries and posterity," Góngora was thus credited with inventing in the 1600s an artistic language that, being "difficult, but not impossible" was particularly attractive to the new breed of Spanish painters, poets, and prose writers.[24]

FIGURE 1.2 *Picasso*. El entierro de del Conde de Orgaz (*1969*) © *2020 Estate of Pablo Picasso/Museu Picasso, Barcelona.*

Jorge Guillén—a poet of the Generation of 1927—describes Góngoran poetry as being able not only to duplicate but also to surpass its classic referents, "producing in the process an unexpectedly modern result."[25] Four plus four was not eight in the non-mimetic world of Góngoran poetics, and modern writers and artists celebrated this rare early escape from realism.[26]

FIGURE 1.3 *Picasso*. Góngora *(1948)* © *2020 Estate of Pablo Picasso/Artists Rights Society (ARS), New York.*

This might have been the quality most appreciated by surrealist painters, who got to know Góngora a bit later than their literary counterparts but celebrated him with the same enthusiasm in their rejection of figurative art. Attributing Góngora's aesthetic sensibility to his Andalusian origins, Picasso would humorously claim that "all Andalusians are a bit surrealist ... like

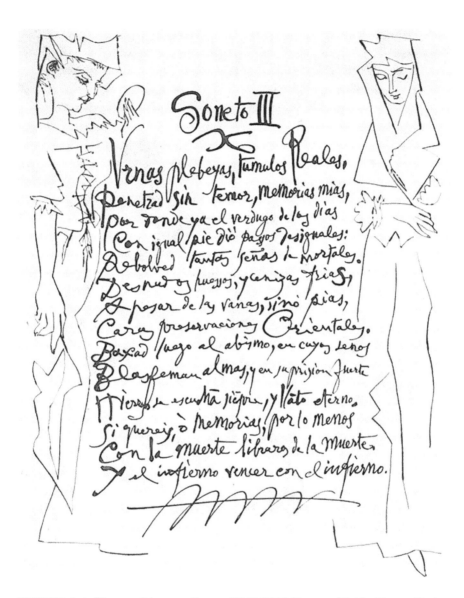

FIGURE 1.4 *Picasso. Góngora. Soneto III* © *2020 Estate of Pablo Picasso/Artists Rights Society (ARS), New York.*

Don Luis de Góngora and Argote."[27] Andalusian or not, most surrealist artists would end up hailing Góngora "as one of their patron saints," believing that he had already invented in the seventeenth century the rapid form of association that ruled their experimental compositions.[28]

FIGURE 1.5 *Picasso.* Don Quixote *(1955)* © 2020 Estate of Pablo Picasso/Artists Rights Society (ARS), New York.

The impeccable cross-pollination of verbal and visual content in avant-garde painters such as Picasso extended to other contemporaneous Spanish artists. Alberti, recipient of the National Literary Award of 1924, was first known as a visual artist, and the inspiration for much of his poetry came from his artistic collaborations with painters—Maruja Mallo first, and Picasso later. The multi-dimensional creativity that Alberti represented illustrated the *ut pictura poesis* formula (as is painting so is poetry) defended four hundred years earlier by Golden Age writers such as Lope de Vega, Francisco de Quevedo, Calderón de la Barca, and Góngora. Indeed, as Cervantes argued, "the painter and the writer [are] one and the same."[29] The avant-garde not only reaffirmed this symbiosis of word and image, of visual and verbal expression, but expanded it to include other artistic domains, such as music. As Guillermo de la Torre—one of the most accomplished avant-garde theorists—posited, "if music is the language of ultra-sensations, poetry must be a language of ultra-images."[30] This artistic relationship was exemplified by other 1927 authors such as Gerardo Diego, whose symphonic poetic compositions were collected in a volume titled *Image* (*Imagen*, 1919). In such poetry, obviously invested in pictorial and musical overtones, Diego would speak of a "green silence," and describe objects like a guitar as "a well with wind in place of water."[31] Diego's good friend Jorge Guillén published a similar blended media poetic collection titled *Cántico* (1928).

Blended poetic experiments would become the norm. Federico García Lorca, cherished by Pedro Salinas as both "poet and painter," and unanimously recognized as a piano virtuoso, would be perhaps the most accomplished musical poet, given the strong flamenco rhythms that he incorporates in collections like the *Poems of Deep Song* (*Poemas del Cante Jondo*) (1921).[32] Lorca's poetry is delightfully dependent on music rather than meter and form, which results in the impression that the poem reads more like "a sung prose" piece.[33] In the midst of this extraordinary creative experimentation and environment, Lorca proudly confided in the rising poet Miguel Hernández that "at that moment [the 1920s], Spain produced the most beautiful poetry in Europe."[34] Clearly, Lorca could have boasted about this poetry also being one of the most multi-dimensional.

Collaborations between peer artists, musicians, and poets were productive, common, and welcome; Salvador Dalí designed Lorca's costumes for his play *Mariana Pineda* (1927), and Lorca and the greatest Spanish musician of his time, Manuel de Falla, organized the first international flamenco festival in 1922, which resulted in recognition of the genre as a valid musical form. Luis Buñuel, the filmmaker who proudly affirmed, later in life, his membership in the Generation of '27, produced numerous films deeply imbued with literary references, including *L'Age d'Or* (*The Golden Age*, 1930), where he fused Renaissance and contemporary mores with his surrealistic critique of modernity.[35]

Since it had taken more than three hundred years for this symbiotic mindset to return to the methods for creating and understanding Western art, it is easy to wonder why such blended artistic expressions came back in the twentieth century with such vigor, especially after the extreme compartmentalization of disciplines in the eighteenth century. Attempting to craft an answer, the poet Wallace Stevens had hypothesized that, in the twentieth century, especially in a post-war environment, artists and writers had embraced the particular relation between painting and literature as a "compensation for what has been lost, ... a vital assertion of self in a world where nothing but the self remains, if that remains" (171).[36] However, in the Spain of the 1920s, where no national or international disasters (world or civil wars) seemed to be looming, this artistic symbiosis appears to have been more intrinsic to the experimental and freeing atmosphere in which it took shape.

An iconic illustration of such atmosphere was the *Residencia de estudiantes*, one of the most sophisticated European cultural and scientific centers of the 1920s, an institution that regularly hosted figures such as Marie Curie, Albert Einstein, Paul Valéry, Le Corbusier, Severo Ochoa, and Falla, and where students stayed or studied.[37] The spirit of the *Residencia* pervaded the artistic centers of the country, especially in Madrid and Barcelona. For a time at least, it appeared that the Golden Age was productively influencing the last years of the Restoration (i.e., up to 1931) through its legacy of interdisciplinary creation and humanist values, and that Spain's modernity would be formed in that mold.[38]

Avant-Garde Politics

While the artistic avant-garde defined itself through this open, cross-disciplinary, and liberating ethos that incited collaborations of all forms and domains, the political and social structures emerging in this context had a much more conflicted path forward. After all, as José-Carlos Mainer has indicated, Spain's technical, political, and social hunger for progress in the 1930s still coexisted with powerful, lingering anti-modern structures and influences that, increasingly defiant, insisted on holding on to the sempiternal specter of Spain's imperial dream.[39] The absence of a positive, modern, and less-hegemonic national culture in the Spain of the 1930s is evident in the fascination among young progressive artists for the Soviet Union. The idea that Russia "conjured up" in this public as "a powerful image of political and cultural modernity" was for the most part almost impossible to find in Spanish public life.[40] While progressive young intellectuals, artists, and writers looked up to countries such as the USSR for cultural and political inspiration, right-wing supporters despised foreign models, craving domestic inspiration instead. The impasse helped nurture the extraordinary frictions that would tear apart artistic and political worlds just a few years later.

In the meantime, if right- and left-wingers disagreed on the appropriateness of emulating foreign models, they agreed, at least temporarily, on one homegrown source of inspiration—Góngora. The provocateur Giménez Caballero did not exaggerate, for once, when he claimed in 1927 that "[a]ll current literature, the young and the old (currently under renovation) is, in one way or another, unavoidably steeped in Gongorism. Góngora's fragmentary and juggling poetic technique reigns supreme."[41] For at least a couple of years after 1927, this assessment was still valid, although by the 1930s, most poets and thinkers were less enthralled by Góngora's "juggling technique." Some, like the influential Ortega, had never fallen for it. Ortega distrusted the formal experiments associated with Gongorine poetics, regarding them as "dehumanized," since this artistic praxis eliminated for him "all 'human, all too human' ingredients from the work of art to allow its pure artistic essence to emerge and manifest itself."[42] While the emphasis on formal experimentation had certainly displaced emotional expression, the real trouble with such artistic practice came out of a human dimension, when increasingly radicalized critics such as Giménez Caballero started to value and interpret poetic forms and figures such as Góngora through a nationalistic lens.

Nationalism had penetrated Spanish letters in the late 1920s, and Giménez Caballero had been at the forefront of that trend; in a 1927 editorial from the magazine that he had founded, *La Gaceta literaria*, Giménez Caballero insulted Latin American writers, claiming that Madrid continued to be the intellectual epicenter ("el meridiano intelectual") of Latin America, an accusation that predictably provoked tense reactions on both sides of the Atlantic.[43] The same year, in a no less notorious move, the agitator published an "imagined interview" with a fellow poet and former colleague, the timidly conservative Gerardo Diego, that put openly fascist slogans into his subject's mouth. Giménez Caballero had anachronistically characterized the iconic Góngora as a bellwether of the dictatorial nature of Spanish society, arguing that "Gongorine literature is richly developed in dictatorial regimes, because dictators respect pure literature."[44] Giménez Caballero puts these controversial judgments on a fictional Diego that characterizes Góngora as a "nationalist and 'fascist' essence," arguing even that "the return to rhymes like the décima stanza, the sonnet, and the silva," some of Góngora's favorites, "constitutes a return to the oldest nationalism" and that such verses even convey the germ "of the Revolution from above defended by Mussolini."[45] The attack forced Diego—who did have conservative leanings—to defend himself in his own magazine, *Lola,* arguing that he "did not support *fascist art or politics ... nor was he encouraging any revolution* from above or below."[46]

By projecting his own ideological positions on a Golden Age author and a contemporary colleague, Giménez Caballero inflamed political polarization within the strictly literary realm. Furthermore, by adding an anachronistic authoritarian veneer to respected classic figures such as Góngora, Giménez Caballero and other proto-fascist theorists were starting to create an alternative, right-wing "high culture" with which they could vindicate a despotic form of Spanish "greatness" by identifying the Golden Age as its root. As a result, at the time when the Golden Age poet Góngora was being rediscovered by progressive poets and artists and celebrated as a visionary innovator—the father of pictorial surrealism—his legacy was being branded by ultra-conservative actors as representative of the vertical culture characteristic of a dictatorial regime such as Mussolini's.

Giménez Caballero's loud fascist evolution ran parallel to the deterioration of Spanish political life and was sadly indicative of the contradictory legacy left behind by the avant-garde. In advocating for a freeing and experimental environment, the vanguard might have also fed the rise of fascist culture by embracing within its purview a wide variety of ideologies, all welcome as long as they were radical. In a sweeping survey that *La Gaceta* organized and published in 1930, where many of Spain's most highly reputed artists and writers were asked to reflect on the imminent death of the avant-garde, almost all interviewed subjects characterized the movement in openly belligerent terms, as a reactive artistic opposition to all archaic facets of Spanish public and cultural life.[47] Although such "archaic facets" were, supposedly, clearly recognizable to all its participants—"we all knew what we should step away from," claimed the writer Esteban Salazar y Chapela—they in fact varied dramatically for each artist or author.[48] Guillermo de la Torre, a collaborator of *La Gaceta,* did not consider that sort of polarization a problem but, rather, an asset indicative of the rich and solid aesthetic and political legacy of the movement. In his mind, such extremism was linked to an innovating spirit: "[t]hese opposing sides seem equally legitimate to me," he claimed, speaking of the right- and left-wing poles emerging out of this context, adding that "they [both] are valid positions, as long as they respect, rather than attack, the supremacy of intelligence."[49]

Yet, intelligence, and, by extension, education and critical thinking, would be among the first victims of the fascist ideology that was brewing. The famous anecdote in which, in 1936, an indignant General José Millán Astray, offended by the words of a lecture by Miguel de Unamuno, interrupted his speech with the battle cry of the Legión, "Long live death!" and "Down with intelligence!" offered a sad foreshadowing of the relentless persecution of intellectuals and educators that instituted the infamous cultural desert of the Francoist regime.[50] Francoist ideologues demonized those who "call themselves arrogantly 'intellectuals,'" charging them with a "corruption campaign aimed at destroying the purest ethical values [of the country] in order to consummate an apocalyptic, black epilogue of a hellish, antipatriotic environment."[51] The massive and indiscriminate condemnation of education, as María Zambrano painfully reminds us, is indicative of how "fascism uses [this scorn for] intelligence very aptly, in order to mask itself, in order to show its contempt for the world" so that it can justify its violent elimination of difference and dissidence.[52]

While it is impossible to know how aware de la Torre was of the consequences of the anti-intellectual pressures he saw forming in 1930, his passing reference conveys a telling preoccupation with the increasing assault on knowledge and learning among conservative writers. Works by Victor Pradera, Vicente Marrero, Constancio Eguía Ruiz, and Pedro Laín would soon develop the anti-intellectual thesis to a national level.[53] Tellingly, some of these proto-fascist ideologues, such as Ledesma, Maeztu, and of course Giménez Caballero, would advance these ideas within the avant-garde context.

The 1930 survey on the state of the vanguard by the *Gaceta* would indicate another point of contention among liberal and (ultra)conservative thinkers and artists in these years: the desire to foster diverse and democratic viewpoints in contrast to the aspiration to cancel equality and freedom through the imposition of a specific ideology. Ledesma, for example, disparaged the inclusive and democratic aims of progressive writers and artists, considering their egalitarian parading inconsequential, historically speaking, when compared to the great, national ambitions that ultra-conservative authors like him were pushing forward. "[S]*ome little* avant-garde groups," Ledesma stated, simply wanted to "be liberal and democratic," while "we"—he argues, showing a clear collective consciousness—"vindicate something they all have ignored, the secret of a Spain that affirms itself in its *nationalism and hunger for power* [*voluntad de poderío*]."[54] This rejection of liberal and democratic thought, combined with the explicit intent to violently impose a nationalist creed (or will), offers another somber prelude to the national state of affairs less than a decade later.[55]

One of the first consequences of this dialectical radicalization was the push to force artists and writers declare their political or ideological affiliation, just as Gerardo Diego had been forced to do a couple of years earlier. "To be frank," admits Buñuel in his memoir, "[m]ost of us did not fully awake [politically] until 1927–28, just before the proclamation of the Republic [1931]. Up to that moment, we paid only minimal attention to the infant Communist and anarchist publications."[56] In the factionalized context of the late 1920s, and in the face of the ultra-conservative Giménez Caballero, Maeztu, and Ledesma, poets such as Alberti, Cernuda, and Altolaguirre would commit themselves passionately to communist ideology, declaring themselves—as Salinas privately notes—"revolutionary writers," seemingly "absorbed by this thing they call 'the social issue'" (lo que ellos denominan lo social).[57] Others, like Salinas himself, would stay publicly but less passionately committed to the Republic, admitting privately to be "a Republican of little faith but fierce anti-monarchical conviction."[58] In the "days of constant struggle" that surrounded the declaration of the new democratic government of 1931, an increasingly hostile feud between progressive and conservative writers was ignited.[59]

Turning the Golden Age into the Age of Iron

Before a clearly recognizable fascist ideology took hold in the mid-1930s, Giménez Caballero would come to be generally considered by contemporary historians as "the closest thing to a fascist leader in Spain."[60] Right-wing ideology needed a powerful organizing narrative to counter worrying ideas of Spanish decline and the energized ideas of the left.[61] Giménez Caballero was able to provide Spanish fascism with a much-needed "grand mythological apparatus," an imperial mythology.[62] Until this astute concoction of literary referents and imperial paradigms, ultra-conservative authors attempting to use Golden Age literature as a way to conjure the great Spanish empire often faced an unsurmountable historical problem: the fact that the decline, even the "destruction" of the country (which, according to them, had been consolidated in 1648 with the Treaty of Westphalia) had been attested much earlier, in the literary texts from the mid- to late 1500s.[63] Although it was at Westphalia where Spain—forced to recognize the independence of the Dutch—was presumed to be an "exhausted" power both "economically and demographically," Spain's weakened international standing had actually been in full display decades earlier.[64] Authors such as Ledesma and Maeztu feared that literary works of the Golden Age highlighted this national frailty. Cervantes was a prime example; despite the literary admiration of these two conservative critics for *Don Quixote,* they considered it "the best book on political decline ever written in any literature," an observation that consequently turned Cervantes as the most painful illustrator of how "Spain had lost its historical initiative" in the 1600s.[65]

Agreeing that Cervantes had formidably illustrated the deficiencies of his age, Giménez Caballero chose to discard the author and his opus viciously and completely. Thus, in 1932, he published an article that characterized *Don Quixote* not as an aging classic but as the worst "national danger" of his day, and the "most anti-national, dangerous, immoral, and tragic Spanish book," and indeed the country's "most punishable literary work" for spreading the "most alarming and corrosive ... secular poison."[66] To Giménez Caballero, Cervantes, with that novel, not only had dismantled the national myth of empire and glory, but also—by avoiding explicit religious allusions in his work—had presented the declining Spanish empire as a secular domain. While Giménez Caballero saw some other Golden Age writers such as like Lope de Vega and Fray Luis as redeemable—since they were much more aligned with the "myth" of "national power" that he was working so hard to bring back—Cervantes was not.[67]

Obviously, even at this early stage, Spanish classics were being read very differently on this side of the ideological spectrum. In contrast to Giménez Caballero's assessment of the "toxic" secularism of *Don Quixote,* Antonio Machado celebrated the universality and hopefulness of Cervantes's humanistic, non-dogmatic, views. In a letter to a Russian confidante and friend, the poet states that a humanistic and empathetic spirit (what he calls "sentido fraterno del amor") is "deeply present in the Spanish soul, not in the *Calderonian* soul—Baroque and ecclesiastic—but in the *Cervantine* one—that of our generous Don Quixote, which is in my opinion genuinely popular, and non-Catholic, understood here as truly human and universally Christian" (emphasis is Machado's).[68] The vastly differing perspectives and assessments of Machado and Giménez Caballero demonstrate how the ideological polarity of their own time was being extrapolated to sixteenth- and seventeenth-century authors by thinkers across the political divide.

On the ultra-conservative side, by combining the nostalgic logic of the Generation of '98 with the radical intolerance of the avant-garde, Giménez Caballero's imperialistic ideas on Spanish historical and literary references would deliver a fascist take not only on Góngora but on the entire Golden Age. This performance would earn the provocateur Giménez Caballero the title of "corruptor of the avant-garde" from those who held him responsible for the "loss of innocence" of the movement; the grave consequences of such corruption would unfortunately be far greater than poisoning a literary sphere, a sphere, it should be reminded, that at least initially had been able to absorb ideological differences in its dialogue.[69]

Alarmed by Giménez Caballero's "canalladas" (caddish tricks, as Salinas called them), former colleagues and collaborators of the '27 group developed an uncomfortable antipathy toward the crude and manipulative proto-fascist theorist, reacting viscerally to the multiple affronts he committed against classic writers and former colleagues.[70] By 1929, once Giménez Caballero had announced his official conversion to fascism, writers such as Dámaso Alonso and Gerardo Diego agreed on the need to "break any interaction with [him] and his *Gaceta*, taking him out of any public collaboration, and putting into our own hands the publication of our own 'anti-literary journal.'"[71] But no one was able to stop Giménez Caballero from advancing his ideological agenda in the most creative and reprehensible ways. Even his mentor, the powerful Ortega y Gasset, after unsuccessfully trying to rein him in several times, ended up painfully disavowing his former student, announcing a solitary future for him: "from now on, you can only walk alone."[72]

Ortega was right, for a while at least. By 1931, most members of the editorial board of the *Gaceta* had resigned, forcing Giménez Caballero to produce the magazine entirely by himself. By that point, the journal had become a completely different kind of publication, and Giménez Caballero produced six more issues under a different title, the *Literary Robinson*, emphasizing—and apparently, not minding—the solitary nature of the endeavor.[73] Even more defiant than before, he embraced the rupture that he had instigated, declaring that he could not "declare support for people from my generation who fight in the other trench."[74] A poet like Lorca, not generally prone to political statements, would energetically contest this exclusionary, self-serving nationalist view. In one of his last public interviews, the Granadan poet noted: "I am genuinely Spanish, and, for me it would be completely impossible to live outside a Spanish geography, and yet, I hate those who identify themselves as Spanish and only Spanish. I am a brother to any Spaniard, and detest those who sacrifice their humanity for the sake of an obtuse nationalistic idea, just because they love their homeland."[75] The friction between these incompatible viewpoints and sensibilities tore the literary community apart. As Salinas observed, "each day [is] more poisonous and more filled with hated and resentment ... and I have a feeling that it is only going to get worse."[76] By the early 1930s, it was clear to any perceptive intellectual that no movement or literary figure would be able to reconcile the leftish-anarchist and traditional-(ultra)conservative ideological camps that had fully solidified in Spain and had contaminated its cultural and literary traditions and atmospheres.

As both left- and right-wing critics gained strength in the Spanish cultural scene of the 1930s, both stimulated by the energy associated with the proclamation of the Second Republic, "two opposite quests for a modern Spanish identity" started to solidify: "rediscovering the power of the people [pueblo] and popular culture" in the case of the left, and the "great ideal of nation," on the right. Despite their conflicting beliefs, both of these "aesthetic visions" of culture and politics began to allude to "mythical, quasi-sacred rhetorical constructs" of the early modern period in order to fortify their visions.[77] It is easy to agree with Schammah Gesser that both of these political formulae and cultural readings of the past became almost "equally essentialized."[78]

If Spanish avant-garde thinking in the 1920s had splintered over the model of avant-garde, experimental poetics, questioning whether modern literary expression should prize form or subjectivity, by the 1930s the debate had shifted. Progressive intellectuals, whether they favored formal or humanist methods of reading, interdisciplinary experimentation, or adherence to traditional genres, found it necessary to counter nationalism and imperialism with an insistence on the humanist legacy of Golden Age literature. Aware of the transcending literary and political dimensions of the Golden Age legacy, both sides, fascist and Republican, appropriated the authors and works of the early modern period, identifying them as markers of the "true national identity" that they were willing to go to war for.

2

The Empire Strikes Back: Cervantes, Enemy of the State

We must bring the Anti-Quixote to Spain! ... We must use criticism, irony, resentment, and sarcasm to go back and corrode Spain's Quixotic spirit! ... Let's murder criticism with another form of criticism!

GIMÉNEZ CABALLERO[1]

The [Spanish Civil] war left those who lost without a future, but those who won were left without a past; they know nothing about it and continue to educate without any awareness of it.

ROSA REGÀS[2]

As seen in the preceding chapter, by the early 1930s, the proto-fascist pronouncements and aggressive tactics of avant-garde dissident Ernesto Giménez Caballero had isolated him from practically all his literary and artistic collaborators. However, after the fascist victory in the Civil War, his trials were rewarded by the Francoist government when he was appointed Vice-Secretary of National Education.[3] His "educational" labor had started much earlier, of course, in the avant-garde circles where his bias had been instrumental in preventing Cervantes from enjoying the almost unanimous appreciation that other Golden Age figures (such as Góngora) received at that time. Ironically, despite his efforts, reverence for or repudiation of Cervantes would turn out to be far more significant than fascination with any other Golden Age figure, since reactions to and interpretations of Cervantes came to define the expansion and contraction that Spanish cultural life experienced from the 1920s to the end of Francoist dictatorship in 1975.

By the late 1920s, Giménez Caballero and other proto-fascist thinkers such as Pedro Laín Entralgo and Rafael Calvo Serer had become increasingly frustrated by the rising popularity and recognition of *Don Quixote*'s author.[4] Cervantes was by then beginning to be considered a full-fledged humanist, and the secular ring of that label did little to support the ultra-conservative campaign that sought to characterize the 1500s and 1600s as the period of never-ending *crusades* and *reconquistas,* the "peak of Spanish military and cultural power."[5] Equally worrisome for the proto-fascist contingent was another major cause for Cervantes's return to prominence: his centrality in the reading habits and print culture of the new century. Although improved literacy levels do not always translate into socioeconomic mobility and cultural change, in the Spain of the 1930s, the sustained demand for a text like *Don Quixote* evidenced not only the existence of new consumers of books, but the fact that those consumers counted on better literacy skills. Both cultural accomplishments had been the result of solid and continued educational investments during the 1920s and 1930s.[6] *Quixote*'s popularity in that moment would emblematize not only the democratizing thrust of Republican education, "para todos," but also its ultimate success in eroding the enduring division between high and low cultures that had traditionally surrounded classic texts of this nature (still evident during the tercentenary publication anniversaries of Parts I and II of *Don Quixote* in 1905 and 1915).

Since the neutralization of social and cultural distinctions posed an inadmissible threat to the vertical order demanded by Francoist ideology, once proto-fascist critics gained official sanction under the dictatorship in 1939, all traces of this democratizing cultural thrust, and the humanistic Cervantine learning associated with it, would be erased. This chapter traces this cultural "evolution," outlining first the elements of the Cervantine splendor that bothered Giménez Caballero so much, to detail later how such vibrant, intellectual and educational developments were quickly dismantled by the fascist establishment. Although the Francoist obsession with removing Cervantes from his privileged place in the Spanish cultural pantheon was only one of the many programs that the fascist order would take on in 1939, it would be one of greatest and most overlooked Spanish cultural disasters of the twentieth century. Unfortunately, with this magnitude of destruction, the regime managed to return the country to the inferior cultural standards of nineteenth century.[7]

"He Has Not Always Been This Popular": The Rediscovery of a Modern(izing) Cervantes in Twentieth-Century Spain

Giménez Caballero's anti-Cervantine manifesto "A National Danger: The Return to *Don Quixote*" (1932) opens with the proud reminder that

Cervantes "had not always been this popular" (no siempre ha estado a la moda).[8] Unable to deny the cultural relevance of the author, or the success of the Republican educational policies that were highlighting this relevance, fascist ideologues could only emphasize that it had not always been so. While Giménez Caballero was right in characterizing it Cervantine rediscovery as a recent development, he was of course wrong to characterize this as a fortuitous event.

Not even the sweeping educational reform undertaken by the Republic could be solely credited for the vibrant, renewed interest in Cervantes in the 1930s. After the publication anniversaries of *Don Quixote* in the first two decades of the century in 1905 and 1915, the novel had become mandatory reading in most primary and secondary curricula.[9] Regardless of the doubts that some of Spain's most prominent thinkers—such as Miguel de Unamuno and José Ortega y Gasset—held about the benefits or effectiveness of a reading mandate, the measure did start to bring the average student closer to Cervantes. Students even appeared to gain a considerable understanding of the text, since the novel began to be used not only for grammar instruction but also as a tool for civic and moral education. The army of well-qualified and well-paid teachers of the Republic would maximize this ongoing engagement with the classic by incorporating it into their own courses in new and creative ways, in part thanks to the wide array of school editions— loaded with innovative didactic resources—that were starting to become available in the 1930s.[10]

The gradual institutional investment in Cervantes and the growing demand for *Quixote*'s educational editions would dramatically incentivize the Spanish publishing industry in these decades. As a result, Cervantine print culture exploded, making *Don Quixote* a highly profitable enterprise for all parties; the general public, the emerging editorial, industry, and the educational world. Juan Suñé Benages counted more than 400 new editions of the novel between 1917 and 1939, in addition to the 966 already existing worldwide.[11] Such editorial expansion is impressive, considering that the bicentenary of *Don Quixote*'s publication in 1805 had left behind very few, and rather expensive editions (one in Madrid, and two abroad, in Berlin and Burdeos).[12] Rather than luxurious reprints, the large majority of the editions produced around and after the tricentenary were educational adaptations intended to facilitate the reading of the novel both "in school and at home."[13]

Furthermore, the educational gains of this Cervantine explosion transcended traditional environments and expanded curriculums and sales. Thanks to the experimental didactic initiatives supported by the Republic, Cervantes also hit the road. Educational itinerant programs like *La Barraca* (the shack) and the *Misiones Pedagógicas* (Pedagogical Missions), formed by emerging educators, artists, poets, and scholars, were asked to travel through Spain's rural areas with the aim of improving the literacy of rural populations through lectures, dramatic readings, and interactive exhibits and performances. In both *La Barraca* and the *Misiones*, the curriculum was mainly composed of Spanish classic authors from the sixteenth and seventeenth centuries such as Cervantes, Lope de Vega, and Calderón de la Barca.[14]

La Barraca was particularly notable for being led by Federico García Lorca. He had repeatedly asserted the ability of rural and working-class audiences to be deeply moved by complicated sacramental plays (*autos*) and *comedias* like Calderón's *Life Is a Dream*. However, as a director of these performances, Lorca ended up relying more often on Cervantes than on Calderón, since his company performed Cervantes's interludes more than any other plays.[15] Lorca's awareness of "the forgotten rhythm, wisdom, and grace" of Cervantes's interludes seems to have inclined him to think that a heavily illiterate rural population could connect most easily with these short, dramatic pieces.[16] It was perhaps because of this trust in Cervantes's text that Lorca repeatedly expressed, throughout his time at *La Barraca*, the belief that all Golden Age plays should be performed in an unmodified form.[17]

By contrast, Maria Teresa de León, a well-known theater director and Republican activist, considered that the educational programs of *La Barraca* and the *Pedagogical Missions* could have been much more effective if some texts had been more freely adapted to serve the social and political needs of the moment. In her view, a Cervantine interlude such as *El juez de los divorcios* (The Divorce Court Judge), for example, could have allowed educators to deconstruct the rampant misconceptions that church officials and moralists in rural regions had built around the 1932 legislation that approved divorce. De León laments that,

> While Congress approved a law favorable to women, divorce, the Pedagogic Missions performed *The Divorce Court Judge* by Cervantes, where a marital problem is solved in the traditional way [forced reconciliation] that is forged in the patriarchal disdain [for women's rights]. The performance should have revised this ending, using it instead to popularize the law just passed by the Republic in order to inform Spanish villages of a new kind of justice.[18]

Against Lorca's opinion that the educating force of Spanish classics was (and should remain) independent of the "political orientation of the country's government," thinkers such as de León believed that excessive faithfulness to the original text wasted important opportunities to make Cervantes's works even more useful in supporting the Republic's titanic effort to modernize the country.[19]

De León's view is not an isolated anecdote. The regard for Cervantes as a resource or ally in the modernization process took on a host of forms and variations in these years, and did not rely only on school curriculums or theaters' repertoires. In 1931, for example, the respected journalist Dionisio Pérez published an article entitled "Resurrection of Cervantes in the World," where he praised Cervantes for providing the "modern man" with an escape from the "barbarous" and "materialist" trappings of the time.[20] Censuring dated Romantic perceptions of *Don Quixote,* Pérez contended that the key to Cervantes's enduring appeal was his ability to "understand the truth of a humanity that feels increasingly restricted and oppressed by the very societies it creates."[21] The article characterizes *Don Quixote* as an accurate—and much appreciated—expression of the "current state of consciousness of mankind," offering the theory that,

> in a world troubled by a full array of new worries and concerns, an old soldier from Lepanto, defeated by the Spanish life, brings solace to this century through his humorous wisdom, a wisdom that, although badly misunderstood as a whining sadness by Byron and Chateaubriand, people enjoy today with a good belly laugh.[22]

Pérez would probably have agreed with his contemporary Emilia Pardo Bazán when she noted a few years earlier that, in Cervantes, "melancholy is around the corner from laughter" (la melancolía está a la vuelta de la broma);[23] like her, and unlike the Romantic critics who saw only grief, Pérez believed that this mix of emotions is inseparable in *Don Quixote.* In arguing that the novel's philosophical method was better understood in the twentieth century than in the nineteenth, especially by average readers than by the aristocratic figures like Byron and Chateaubriand, Pérez underlined the palatable moral guidance that Cervantes's text provided to contemporary readers: that is, to receive with both humor and gravity whatever the modern world throws at them.

Pérez's article provides a reliable indication of the popularity of the novel in the early 1930s, and of the ways it was read by non-specialist audiences, both dimensions that highlight Cervantes's general accessibility. Pérez's tribute to the writer seems to have been the final straw for Giménez Caballero, who wrote his anti-Cervantine manifesto, "The Return to *Don Quixote,*" as a direct response to Pérez's article. At the beginning of his own essay, Giménez Caballero thus notes that "A little over a month ago, in an article that appeared on December 16th at the Madrid's paper *ABC* the writer Dionisio Pérez published an essay, 'Resurrection of Don Quixote in the World' that cited some bibliographic references that should be completed right away."[24] Obviously, the kind of "completion" that the ideologue was eager to undertake entailed a demolishing critique of both Pérez and those critics who Giménez Caballero believed had been his sources.

Notably, while Giménez Caballero's response attempts to discredit and invalidate Pérez's views, both authors appeared to agree on one main thesis: the intimate connection between Cervantes and the modern world. Even in his adversarial response, Giménez Caballero reluctantly acknowledged the contemporary relevance of Cervantes, attacking Pérez for giving an incomplete analysis of such relevance while blaming a professional Cervantine critic, Américo Castro (and his seminal *El pensamiento de Cervantes* [1925]) for not going "far enough in modernizing Cervantes: not far enough in identifying the consequences of his modernity."[25] Giménez Caballero elaborates this admission by stating that:

> Some people characterize Castro's Cervantes as the founder of the Free Educational Institution, as the illustrious predecessor of Francisco Giner, as the embodiment and most obvious national figure of Spanish liberalism (of Spanish reformism) in our literature, a service to the cause of a democratic Spain, for which the Republic would offer fair compensation.
> I am one of those who believe it.[26]

Giménez Caballero's surprising admission is not meant as a compliment to Castro or Cervantes. From his perspective, the premise that Castro's study "did not modernize Cervantes enough" serves as a complaint that Castro did not "foresee the national danger that this, its best writer, posed to Spain," given the cultural, secular, and communal revolution that Cervantes had inspired.[27] For fascist thinkers such as Giménez Caballero, the recognition of this kind of modernity in Cervantes only sealed their renewed vows to eradicate the author from Spain's cultural history.

The abrasive provocateur would go so far as to declare himself the nemesis of Cervantes and the ultimate executioner of his "corrupting" influence, promising to become

> the cure against Quixotism; identifying that secular plague affecting our spirit as a doctor recognizes an unspoken, hereditary defect .... This is what I am responsible for, in this critical hour for Spain, in which Don Quixote, that doomed and damned Quixote ... is raising his cardboard weapons in a new sally and becoming once again fashionable in Spain.[28]

Giménez Caballero's "cure" would affect not only Cervantes, but also the educational plans, editorial expansion, and theatrical outreach programs that popularized and energized the author among the diverse audiences of the 1930s. Once supported by the fascist establishment, Giménez Caballero would target the democratic, "plebeian background" ("el fondo plebeyo") that he saw portrayed in the novel in the sixteenth century, which had clearly been rediscovered in the text and Cervantes in the twentieth.[29] For Giménez Caballero, Spain's fascist hour, the time to act to disrupt the "poisonous" and "infectious" spread of Cervantism, could not come fast enough.[30]

The Birth of Twentieth-Century Spanish Cervantism: Transcending Old Labels

Fortunately, before Giménez Caballero was able to impart his "cure" an emerging Cervantism was able to spread its wings. If the dissemination of Cervantes's broadly defined humanism had disturbed ultra-conservative theorists so deeply, their outright hatred of the enthusiastic specialized academic attention given to Cervantes did not lag behind. Despite the lack of solid precedents in Cervantine criticism—what Castro had, in the mid-1920s, characterized as an embarrassing "shortage of scientific [serious] scholarship" (verdadera penuria de trabajo científico)—a new, professionalized phase in the field of Cervantism had started to timidly open in 1925 with a commitment to focus on the humanistic dimensions of Cervantes, a subfield of growing importance throughout the next decade.[31]

The development of a humanistic scholarship of Cervantes and his age had started then, in the 1920s, delayed by the long-lasting impact of symbolic approaches in Cervantes's studies. Decades later, Anthony Close had scrupulously studied the impact of this symbolic method in his *Romantic Approach to "Don Quixote."*[32] As noted earlier, Close argued that this kind of allegorical, interpretative praxis had dominated literary thinking unopposed for the greater part of the nineteenth and twentieth centuries, throughout the different stages of Spanish criticism such as the esoteric, Romantic, and Regenerationist schools. Close defined the symbolic method or Romantic approach as a form of interpretation that considers the "persons and events in *Don Quixote* as deliberate, figurative embodiments of abstract ideas."[33] Those ideas could be hidden messages (according to esoteric criticism), philosophical views (Romantic), or nationalist claims (Regenerationist), all of which had in common a departure from the text, a free license to project onto the novel the concerns and preoccupations of its critics.[34]

Close issued his famous assessment of this Romantic/symbolic approach—I will refer to it by alluding instinctively to either one of these designations—in the late 1970s, with the implicit understanding that the damaging effects of this form of criticism had not been recognized in Spain, apparently unaware that some Spanish authors had expressed, early on, similar denunciations;[35] Manuel de la Revilla, for example, had noted in the 1880s that "what we call today the Symbolic interpretation of *Don Quixote*" constituted "a vain and petty form of Cervantism that has been with us for too long," a Cervantism that was fueled by the "vain and reckless" motives of its practitioners.[36] De la Revilla wished, moreover, that such an "absurd" critical exercise would only be a temporary transition toward a more solid form of scholarship, and wished that "just like looking for the philosopher stone led to the birth of chemistry, perhaps trying to decipher the supposed symbolism of *Don Quixote* would lead us to reconstruct the dark and little-known biography of Cervantes."[37]

Even Ortega y Gasset had blamed Romantic and Regenerationist critics (as stated, a variant of the Symbolic approach) for their inability to recognize Cervantes's sound humanism and modernity. "Read Menéndez Pelayo and [Juan] Valera closely," Ortega had noted, "And you will clearly notice the lack of [intellectual] perspective [in their approaches]. In good faith, those men—being unable to experience any [critical] depth—could only applaud mediocrity .... In such circumstances, how could we expect them to give Cervantes his due credit?"[38] Despite Ortega's harsh estimation of his predecessors, and his apparent intent in giving Cervantes's proper recognition, he would not particularly advance our understanding of the author. Rather than the cogitations of an iconic metaphysics professor such as Ortega, what the Cervantine field needed was the clear textual, cultural, and literary articulations of a historian and critic such as Castro. By the mid-1920s, Castro had obviously understood that Cervantes's true recognition could come only through a new, solid understanding of the author and opus that eradicated the inherited myths about his work and persona endlessly perpetuated by Symbolic criticism, and by earlier generations of critics who had not understood the depth of Cervantes's insight, and the wide range of the literary influences that he was recalibrating.

Historians such as José Carlos Mainer Javier Varela, and Aurora Hermida Ruiz believed that Castro was able to develop such a transforming critical innovation aided, at least in part, by the work that the *Centro de Estudios Históricos*—Center for Historical Studies—had taken on in the 1920s.[39] For Mainer the *Centro* had tackled with unprecedented weight an old scholarly accusation against the Spanish Golden Age reignited in those years: the allegation by "erudite Protestant voices that a proper Renaissance had never reached Spain."[40] This controversial hypothesis, usually referred to as the "Klemperer's theory" (since it was formulated in 1927 by the German literary scholar Victor Klemperer), revived the old claim that the specific conditions of Spain (the Arab invasion, Catholic orthodoxy, the Inquisition, and so on) had prevented the country from fully experiencing core trends of Renaissance thought and art, such as humanism.[41] In questioning whether Spain had experienced a Renaissance, Klemperer also debated if Spanish writers such as Cervantes could be considered humanists, at least the kind of humanists produced by the secular, northern schools.

As the 1930s unfolded, the efforts of Spanish researchers attempting to dispel the theory of Iberian exclusion from European humanism intensified. Castro appeared to have realized by then that rebranding Cervantes as a humanist required not only a dramatic historiographical shift from symbolic Spanish approaches to the author, but also a broader refutation of the preconceived ideas about the Spanish early modern context itself, since such ideas made the Spanish Golden Age incompatible with various other trends affecting European cultural traditions.

Ironically, it was Giménez Caballero who, in his 1932 anti-Cervantine manifesto, identified three of the major misconceptions—he called them "ghosts"—that criticism needed to address to fully establish Cervantes's intellectual stature in domestic and European environments: the assumption that "a) that Cervantes was an illiterate genius .... b) That Cervantes was a Counter-Reformationist and a reactionary .... c) That Cervantes was a humanist and a liberal."[42] The first claim alludes to the myth of the "ingenio lego"—a lingering, baseless misconception that assumed Cervantes to have been illiterate, and yet somehow able to write *Don Quixote*. The idea that was first suggested by Tamayo de Vargas in 1624 "and has been applied to him [Cervantes] ever since" constitutes an obvious mischaracterization of Cervantes's intellectual stature that had indeed hindered comprehension of his works.[43]

The second assumption refers to another famous thesis formulated in 1924 by an Italian professor, Cesare De Lollis, which considered Cervantes a "reactionary," that is, a proponent of the Counter-Reformation exemplary ideals.[44] De Lollis's assumption was widely and almost immediately discredited; as Helmut A. Hatzfeld noted a few years later, and Marina Brownlee has recently reaffirmed, De Lollis's "preconceived" counter-reformist allegiance immediately "ran into great difficulties," when having to "interpret the humorous, ironical, lively Don Quixote," and even when facing the complexity of an allegorical romance like *Persiles*.[45] In both cases, De Lollis's counter-reformist characterization of Cervantes's fiction was considered "a failure."[46]

Giménez Caballero does not miss the opportunity to establish a false equivalence between these two obviously flawed ideas—the myth of Cervantes's "ingenio lego" and the "Counter-reformist" thesis—and the humanist attribution of Cervantes. His anti-Cervantine manifesto argues that any secular identifications, humanism, or rationalism associated with Cervantes (such as Castro's), were as fallacious as the most traditional ones (*ingenio lego*, counter-reformism). Taking aim at Castro once again, Giménez Caballero notes:

> Castro soaked up all Cervantes, and his conclusion was that Cervantes was not an illiterate author, nor a reactionary or liberal one, *he was simply one of those great thinkers of the time*: a genius hypocrite, like contemporaries such as Descartes Galileo, Erasmus, and all of those great figures that Ortega y Gasset had characterized as infused with— that sentence so valuable for Castro—"the heroic hypocrisy of the men of the 1600s." He [Cervantes] was a spirit in between two sensibilities, what I have called—in a pretty precise way—when talking about Goya (a delayed Cervantes of the visual arts) a pinnacle [vertex].[47]

Giménez Caballero goes to great lengths here trying to deny Cervantes's "liberal" and progressive perspective. His critical distortion leads him to characterize Cervantes as a "pinnacle [vertex]," which for him refers to "a figure between two worlds: one that dies and one that is born. The dogmatic world, and the *individualistic*. The world of absolutism and that of freedom. The Medieval and the Renaissance one. The Catholic and the nationalist."[48] Note Giménez Caballero's explicit effort not to say "humanist," using the term "individualistic" instead. Anything that could describe or locate Cervantes within a humanist world is off limits for Giménez Caballero. The fascist theorist complains that Castro, instead of leaving Cervantes in this limbo, dares to characterize his world as ultimately secular: "According to Castro," complains Gimenez Caballero, "Cervantes's life will be spent in the secular realm, dying as a [humanist] wise man, not as a mystic or devoted [Christian]."[49]

Ultimately, Giménez Caballero's efforts to establish false equivalences among these cultural labels and to euphemistically mischaracterize them are a response to the critical vitality of those decades (1920s–1940s) in which the application of historical and cultural designations such as "humanistic," "secular," and "non-dogmatic" to Cervantes and his age was first under serious consideration. Despite Giménez Caballero's complaints about Castro's seminal study, it was clear to him that if the myth of the *ingenio lego* appeared defeated—although only temporarily—in the early 1930s, this accomplishment was largely the result of Castro's work. Castro—Gímenez Caballero admits—had given the author "something that has been consistently denied in him [Cervantes]: the existence of his own form of thought, a *Weltanschauung*, a Cervantine world."[50] Castro certainly demonstrated the uniqueness and sophistication of Cervantes's thought and of his worldview, attributes that would have been impossible for an *ingenio lego*.

Furthermore, by contextualizing Cervantes within the European aesthetic and literary trends of his time and with contemporaneous writers—from Tasso and Montagne to Erasmus and Castiglione—Castro had indeed shown that Cervantes was not only a mere collector of sources, but one of their most accomplished reformulators. According to Castro, then, the focus of Cervantes's research should revolve around the ways in which he presented current trends, theories, and scholarship in his writing. Castro continues:

> We should proceed inside out ... Culture in Cervantes is a working and constitutive element of his fiction; for this man, so many times characterized as a mediocre and vulgar thinker, as a regular man indistinguishable from those around him, there is not one aspect of his writing that has not been carefully constructed .... [T]he little care we have shown towards our intellectual history (at times overstated, at others completely disregarded) has made us ignore issues of this nature, which are so acutely present in Cervantes.[51]

There is no better indication of the success of Castro's new consideration of Cervantes than the appearance of his thesis in 1930s educational and popular editions of *Don Quixote*. These new releases started to include brief clarifications of the author's intellectual stature that noted that Cervantes "was called an *ingenio lego*, which, in the language of the time, referred to those who had never had a university education; however, we assume that in a cultivated, urban environment, his contact with learned, prominent intellectuals, and his personal reading, study, and reflection, nourished his spirit."[52] The advances of the new Cervantine criticism, then, were clearly applied to the educational front, planting the seeds for a new generation of readers and critics.

There was, in fact, such an enthusiasm for Cervantes in the generation of readers and critics of these years (late 1920s and early 1930s) that specialists like James Fitzmaurice-Kelly warned about the possibility of developing an opposite misconception, a sort of Cervantine "idolatry." For Fitzmaurice-Kelly, an overtly exaggerated admiration for the writer could be ultimately detrimental for a true understanding of his literary merit:

> Cervantes was unlucky in life, nor did his misfortunes end with his days. Posthumous idolatry seeks to atone for contemporary neglect, and there has come into being a tribe of ignorant fakirs, assuming the title of "Cervantophiles," and seeking to convert a man of genius into a common Mumbo-Jumbo. A master of invention, a humourist beyond compare, an expert in ironic observation, a fellow meet for Shakespeare's self: all that suffices not for these fanatical dullards. Their deity must be accepted also as a poet, a philosophic thinker, a Puritan tub-thumper, a political reformer, a finished scholar, a purist in language, and—not least amazing—an ascetic in private morals. A whole shelf might be filled with works upon Cervantes the doctor, Cervantes the lawyer, the sailor, the geographer, and who knows what else?[53]

As Cervantine criticism evolved and professionalized itself in response to the unprecedented popularity of the author, critics such as Fitzmaurice-Kelly grew uncomfortable with overly enthusiastic approaches to the author, finding it necessary to assert the authority that specialized readings held over the "proper" demarcations of his influence.[54]

Fitzmaurice-Kelly was only one of the many specialists who were laboring in the 1920s to develop an appropriate critical framework able to fully appreciate Cervantes's literary and cultural innovation. Other important critical figures who published Cervantine criticism in these years include Adalberto Hämel (1926), Rodríguez Marín (1927), G. K. Chesterton (1927), Marcel Bataillon (1928), Flacomio Rosaria (1928), Maurice Bardon (1931), Pierre Perrault (1931), and Esther Crooks (1931)—most of whom are mentioned in Giménez Caballero's account of the "alarming" rebirth of critical interest in Cervantes.[55] Yet Giménez Caballero remained silent about emerging scholars in Spain, fellow avant-garde writers (such as the members of the Generation of '27), and female scholars (e.g., Pardo Bazán), acknowledging works by only three traditional Spanish critics besides Castro: Unamuno (1905), Ortega (1914), and Menéndez Pidal (1921 and 1924).

While Giménez Caballero's bibliographical summary ignores much of the progressive scholarship that Cervantine criticism was generating among Spanish and foreign scholars in the early 1930s, other critics would eventually provide a more balanced assessment of the period. In 1947, Helmut Hatzfeld provided an informative account of the field in his article "Thirty Years of Cervantes Criticism (1917–1947)"; three years later, Victor Oelschläger expanded on that report in his bibliographical article "More Cervantine Bibliography," which lists more than two hundred research titles in several languages and traditions.[56] Both articles attest to the flurry of critical activity in the 1920s through the mid-1930s; both inside and outside of Spain, a wide range of scholarly approaches were considering Cervantes through a multitude of approaches that declared him to be a reactionary, secular, conservative, counter-reformist, counter to the Counter-Reformation, Baroque, relativist, medieval, and revolutionary author.[57] Of all such positions, two would receive prominent attention in the next few decades: Cervantes as a humanist and as an orthodox writer.

Humanism or Dogmatism, the Erasmist Question

One of the reasons Castro's humanist analysis was so compelling and influential was its attention to Cervantes's text. Castro had highlighted two traits in Cervantes's writing that made his work comparable to that of other Renaissance humanist writers: the rationalist nature of his thought process, and the Erasmist sensibility of his moral perception.[58] Castro claimed that "Cervantes is a rationalist who provides us the limits of what is rationally manageable," arguing, in other words, that Cervantes's rationalism was aware of its own limits, even when such limits were constantly put to the test by characters such as Tomás Rodaja, "Licenciado Vidriera," Cardenio, and Don Quixote, which came to embody the attrition between rationality and logic, will, and emotion.[59] For Castro, this narrative ambivalence was one of the engines of Cervantes's fiction, a feature that allowed him to consider the various (sometimes simultaneous) possibilities of what the world was for each of those characters, and how it could or should be.[60]

Certainly, other progressive critics and thinkers had similarly recognized this Cervantine ambiguity as an idiosyncratic quality of the author's opus. "Without taking out or adding a comma to his text," Azaña pointed out in 1930, "Cervantes could have been benevolent or envious, cheap or generous, social or taciturn, well-behaved or a trouble-maker."[61] What Castro did beyond articulating these impressions was to identify an authorial strategy underlying this structural feature (ambivalence). If Castro initially and famously characterized this strategy as an indication of Cervantes's hypocrisy—believing that Cervantes fearfully concealed a deep critique of Spanish society through this vagueness—he later conceded that the societal pressures of Cervantes's age surely justified this tactic, which reflected an effort at self-preservation rather than self-interest.[62]

While much attention has been paid to Castro's brief characterization of Cervantes as hypocritical, less consideration has been given to his association of Cervantes's conscious ambiguity to the philosopher Erasmus of Rotterdam (1466–1536). By connecting the author's ambivalence to the Dutch humanist, Castro validated the pivotal thesis of the young French scholar Marcel Bataillon, whose ideas about Erasmus in the Golden Age would eventually be published in the monumental *Erasme et l'Espagne* in 1937.[63] Castro's claim that "without Erasmus, Cervantes would never have been who he is" (*sin Erasmo Cervantes no hubiera sido lo que es*) was a game changer for the study and understanding of the author and his age.[64] As Francisco Márquez Villanueva remembered years later, "[Castro's] idea of situating Cervantes with the other great minds of the Renaissance constituted a liberating breath of fresh air, scandalous for some, since it exposed Cervantes's creative familiarity with Erasmus, which became the central axis of a new critical vision."[65]

The characterization of Cervantes as not only a humanist but also an Erasmist would be almost disturbing for conservative critics and thinkers. The Dutch humanist, one of the most admired and despised moralists of his generation, maintained a tremendously conflicted relationship with the Catholic Church in general, and with the Spanish Catholic orthodoxy of the sixteenth and seventeenth centuries in particular.[66] In his critique of the corruption, violence, and allegiance of the Catholic Church to political power, Erasmus had morally delegitimized the two greatest institutions of his time, the church and the empire, and all their "greatest" enterprises— wars, conquests, and crusades. For Erasmus, all wars reflected an abhorrent Christianity too often tied to political interests; "We [Christians]," he complains, "are willing to annihilate Asia and Africa with the sword."[67] It would be "by far less evil," in his opinion, "to be an honest Turk or a Jew, than this kind of fake Christian."[68] As an inconvenient reformist in his own time, Erasmus was a particularly sore reference for the right-wing defenders of Spain in the twentieth century. Along with Erasmus's historical confrontations with the sixteenth-century Spanish church, they noted that some of Spain's most progressive intellectuals of the twentieth century, such as Fernando de los Ríos, had been alluding to him for decades to justify their intellectual opposition to Catholic authoritarian principles, such as those promoted by the most prominent conservative leaders of the day, like Primo de Rivera.[69]

The influence of Erasmus ran so deep among some Republican theorists and supporters—especially those influenced by Krausean reformism, such as de los Ríos—that they proudly termed themselves the "new Erasmists" of the twentieth century.[70] As de los Ríos proclaimed, "[W]e, the heterodox Spanish thinkers, ... are the children of Erasmus ... carrying the scars from the sixteenth century ... the spiritual children of those whose dissident consciousness was strangled for centuries."[71] For progressive intellectuals like himself, Erasmism constituted an essential antecedent to Spanish Catholic dissidence, one that they were proud to reintroduce into the twentieth-century political and educational scene, wrapped in the prestige of this Renaissance referent.

It is within the context of this fight against an orthodox Spain of the present and past that the diachronic fight against writers such as Erasmus or Cervantes can be understood. Given its political reverberations, a rediscovered Erasmist valence in Cervantes and his age transcended a purely literary sphere. Erasmus's influence, which had powerfully stimulated the aims and ambitions of Republican reformists and educators, disputed from its core the purity of a Christian nation, mission, and empire that Francoism so heavily relied on. Hence, it needed to be eliminated. At first, conservative thinkers aggressively questioned the historicity of an Erasmist influence in Spain. Their doubts were partially justified, since despite the enormous initial popularity of the Dutch moralist in the Spanish court, the death of his great protectors in Iberia—the inquisitor general Alonso Manrique (1471–1538), for example, and most especially Charles V (1500–56)—had put Erasmus and his thought in a precarious situation. The humanist's reputation deteriorated so quickly after the loss of these supports that his work was soon afterward banned by the Inquisition, partially in the index of 1559, and completely in the 1612 expanded index of *auctores damnati* (forbidden authors).[72]

Traditional early modern specialists considered the celebration of the Council of Trent (1563)—convened by the Roman Catholic Church as a response to the "heresies" of the Reformation—to ultimately entail the triumph of Catholic orthodoxy and the crushing defeat of almost every value Erasmus believed in: tolerance, Christian unity, and religious interiority.[73] Few scholars questioned the assumption that the same "forces that triumphed at Trent," and engaged in a "relentless effort to rid Spain of humanism," were apparently able to erase this humanist (Erasmist) influence from Iberia. The arrest, imprisonment, and demotion of major Spanish humanists such as Luis de León (1527–91) and Bartolomé Carranza (1500–71) supposedly proved it.[74] As a result, critics had generally assumed that Erasmism had enjoyed too brief a flourishing in Spain to have been culturally or ideologically significant.

In contrast, Bataillon's seminal study demonstrated the diffuse yet persistent way in which "Erasmian reference still lingers" in authors such as Cervantes.[75] The French critic taught an entire generation of specialists how to find Erasmist traces in the language in which writers including Cervantes had coded it, since authors like him had been forced to learn to "speak" in ways that enabled them to elude heavy Inquisitorial surveillance. Bataillon allowed those critics to see how, probably more than any other Golden Age writer, Cervantes's gentle irony adapted some of Erasmus's most ferocious and demolishing critiques against imperialism, ignorance, and church corruption.

Uncovering an Erasmist, anti-imperialistic perspective—and deep criticism of the church—in twentieth-century Spain meant not only vindicating a pacifist and humanist strain in Spanish literature, but also providing a historical foundation for a whole culture of dissidence supposedly extinct in the sixteenth century. Castro and Bataillon did not realize that, as the international transcendence and repute of Cervantes grew (in part thanks to this humanist dimension of his opus), the resentment of proto-fascist ideologues such as Giménez Caballero about the author deepened accordingly. For such ultra-conservative ideologues, an enriched defense of a Cervantine rationalism and humanism would be taken as further proof of the need to remove the author from a "legitimate," Catholic national tradition. Conservative literary critics more measured than Giménez Caballero would try to contain the enthusiastic reception of the Erasmist thesis by either ignoring Bataillon's and Castro's contributions altogether, or by acknowledging that while their work was well crafted, it was also "ideologically motivated" (de sesgo tendencioso).[76] For critics and thinkers attempting to remain in the middle, the only possible position was Hatzfeld's careful recognition that while with respect to a writer like Cervantes, born in the first half of the sixteenth century, "[n]othing seems more natural ... than the question of whether he is a late Erasmian humanist," nothing was "more difficult to answer."[77] Hiding behind Cervantes's ambiguity, a number of specialists chose to avoid the humanist question altogether.

This litany of animosity and controversy surrounding Cervantes's Erasmism and humanism appears to have been forgotten in contemporary criticism. When in 1982, Alban Forcione updated Castro's and Bataillon's Erasmist thesis in his influential study of Cervantes (*Cervantes and the Humanist Vision*), he assumed that Cervantes's humanism was perfectly compatible with the Christian dogmatism of the seventeenth century. Forcione's study aimed "to illuminate the exemplary vision of Cervantes's short stories" situates this fiction "within the spiritual climate [of the Golden Age]" in which Cervantes was supposedly and comfortably recognized as the "most influential spokesman [of] Erasmism."[78] While Forcione explicitly connected his book to "the tradition in Cervantine studies initiated by Castro's *El pensamiento de Cervantes*," he was apparently unaware of how contested Castro's humanist thesis had been in the Spain of the mid-century.[79] For Forcione, a better understanding of the Erasmist question in the Spanish context simply necessitated "a more sophisticated method of comparative study than that which has limited traditional studies of sources and influences."[80]

In a pointed review of Forcione's fundamental study, Márquez Villanueva discreetly reminds Forcione, that if Cervantes's humanism was stripped of its controversy, and his critical spirit deemed able to "coexist with an Inquisitorial Spain," then his Erasmism would be deprived of the dissidence ("no tendría así nada de polémico") that conservative critics so deeply resented. Márquez Villanueva warned against the error of reducing Erasmus to "an edifying and Christian author," which "surely he is to Cervantes, but not to the official Spain of his time."[81] He then adds:

> In this book [Forcione's], there is no Inquisition or inquisitorial spirit, everything happens within the realm of an *unconflicted Spain*. Nothing is [forced] to compromise, there is nothing of the self-inhibition or self-censorship of creative minds. Given the uneasiness among certain critical sectors with regard to the Erasmist question in Cervantes, F.'s book will have a cathartic or liberating effect in them. *The opportunity to reduce to a technical dimension what before constituted the core of Cervantes's awareness of dissidence, or awareness of being "at the other side," will* be undoubtedly well-received among those critical factions, working on them like a soothing balm.[82]

Here, Márquez Villanueva reminds us of the longstanding conservative animosity toward Erasmus from the 1930s to the 1970s. Having been forced into exile in the 1950s, Márquez Villanueva, unlike Forcione, was keenly aware that Erasmus, Cervantes, and the dissident sensibility that they represented had been harshly marginalized and suppressed by (ultra) conservative critics, who had deemed them as "those at the other side." Dissidents and heirs of this unorthodox ideological strain would be treated as belligerent antagonists under Francoism, which ultimately considered them to be "anti-Spain." The fact that Márquez Villanueva alluded to this marginalization, forty-plus years later, in 1985, proves how persistently this anxiety about the ostracism of humanists resonated in Spanish letters.

The Triumph of Fascist Hegemony: Shaping the "Anti-Spain"

The enemy that Francoist forces were eager to face in 1936 had been a long time in the making. The Francoist national campaign against a "corruptive" antagonist, an enemy within that needed to be systematically eradicated, evoked distant Medieval theories of purity of blood (*limpieza de sangre*) and military clashes such as the Reconquest. In a way, such heretical antagonisms had never stopped being conjured by ultra-conservative thinkers such as Marcelino Menéndez Pelayo, whose monumental *History of the Spanish Heterodox* (*Historia de los heterodoxos españoles* [1880–2]) continued to use an Inquisitorial reference to invoke the spirit of the "true" Spain, a Catholic nation always at war with the infidel.

Menéndez Pelayo, however, made a major contribution to the idea of a national antagonist that his book historicizes: expanding the traditional definition of *the* "Spanish" enemy to include not only the "infidel" and "heretic," but also the "rationalist," the intellectual dissident.[83] The addition was particularly welcomed in the early 1900s, as ultra-conservative oligarchies were starting to viscerally attack progressive thinkers and liberal reformists first, and communists later. The abrupt social and economic change of the new century had given rise to trade unions, left-wing parties, and regional conflict over demands for better conditions for the average laborer, which drove conservative layers of Spanish society against the entire spectrum of the left. During the first decades of the 1900s, that left-wing spectrum would be conveniently compressed by several ultra-conservative conspiracy theories into a secret conglomerate "of Jews, freemasons, and Communists" supposedly aiming "to destroy Christian Europe, with Spain as a principal target."[84] The ideologues of the government of Primo de Rivera in the 1920s were particularly masterful at exacerbating the anxiety against this hybrid construct of a Jewish, freemason, and Communist "axis of evil," which aggravated the frictions between liberals and conservatives.

Francoist ideologues, and Franco himself, would ultimately capitalize on these ideological tensions with a savvy juxtaposition of sacred and profane symbols portraying him as a God-chosen leader (see Figure 2.1).[85] With extraordinary official support of the church, Franco astutely avoided the use of the term "civil war," instead referring to the conflict as a crusade.[86] Francoism then could paint its opponents not only as enemies but as the profaning foes of a sacred mission summarized in the official slogan "With empire toward God" [*Por el imperio hacia Dios*], in which the leader and his quest for empire are to be seen as both the channel and manifestations of God's will.[87] From such political references, which so freely drew from religious and pagan elements to assert a Catholic military imperialism, emerged the specific form of authoritarianism of the Francoist regime.

On the other side of this sacred mission was the "anti-Spain," which included anyone who opposed it.[88] As Hoyos Puente argues, figures as disparate as the nineteenth-century educational reformer Francisco Giner de los Ríos and the anarchist Buenvanetura Durrit were tarred with the

FIGURE 2.1 *Arturo Reque Meruvia.* Allegory of Franco's Crusade *(1948–49).* *Archivo Histórico Militar, Madrid.* ©*Artists Rights Society (ARS), New York.*

same brush: to Nationalists, these disparate figures "represented the same ideal" and "would be caricaturized and minimized in the same systemic way, as dangerous beings that, favoring a foreign influence, were interested only in the eradication of the Spanish tradition."[89] Enemies of Francoism representing the anti-Spain were stripped of not only their humanity but also their right to historical existence.[90]

When considered within this context, it is no surprise that Giménez Caballero's attack on *Don Quixote* as an "anti-national" novel is so deeply infused in violence: it is a "sadistic book," he states, one "that would not stop strangling us, and that intended to let us die slowly without any ability to come back and be resurrected."[91] The assessment is ironic, given Cervantes's humanist vision, which destroys callous constructions of enmity from the very start of the novel. In the Prologue to the first part, for example, when an anonymous friend of the author's reminds Cervantes's alter ego that "when speaking of enemies," one must observe at all costs the divine command "Ego autem dico vobis: diligite inimicos vestros" (Matthew 5:44; "But I say to you, love your enemies").[92] The biblical command invoked by Cervantes at the beginning of the knight's journey, stands in contrast to the sinister moral distortion that shapes the fascist agenda as a divinely ordained position. This kind of contrast epitomizes why Giménez Caballero developed such a deep-seated hatred for the secular leanings of the author and the novel.

Cervantes, Enemy of the People

The quick dismantling of Republican educational initiatives and structures, which had generated such impressive cultural gains prior to 1939, had been planned even before the fascist victory. As early as November 11, 1936, the Francoist army had issued an official decree mandating the "purification" of the Spanish school system, a horrifying process that would be carried out in the following years by investigating, suspending, and/or murdering up to a third of the teaching corps employed by the Republic.[93] As fascist troops gained control of Republican zones, all educational programs were immediately suspended and replaced by fascist "educational" agendas (more accurately described as propagandistic campaigns) that imposed a heavily constricted Francoist view of Spanish history, dominance, and power. Even earlier, in April 1936, in the areas that they controlled, the fascists had begun censorship of all books and materials containing the "secular" and humanist "poison" denounced by Giménez Caballero in 1932. As María Josefa Villanueva Toledo has shown, the censorship of Cervantes and Cervantism dating from this time continued to exist—albeit rarely enforced—until 1983.[94]

The progressive thinkers whose support and work had been so instrumental for the Republican cultural revolution had now been exiled, murdered, or heavily silenced. An exceptional young witness, Juan Goytisolo (1931–2017), details in his memoirs the effects of this cultural repression: "the performance of Lorca's dramas was prohibited ... Ortega and Baroja were harshly censored in church circles ... [and] [o]ther more hostile writers remained ... on the regime's black lists and direct access to their writings was nigh impossible."[95] In the case of Cervantes, reading *Don Quixote* would still be required in Francoist school programs—in fact, it would be the only surviving title from Republican curricula—but the novel would, once again, be used primarily for teaching language and grammar, and would be framed by explicitly fascist slogans.

If, under Republican educational guidelines, young students had been encouraged to "meditate on the difficulties and anxieties of [Cervantes's] life" as an example of how, despite those obstacles, knights and writers could reach or create "luminous destinies,"[96] from 1939 on, the rare introductions to the novel in fascist textbooks emphasized the values of Cervantes's supposedly "fervent patriotism" and interjected so many allusions to the generalissimo that it is often difficult to identify whether the text is referring to Cervantes or Franco. Both were often praised for their "exact fulfillment of the call of duty, which is the most noble and elevated trait gifted to the giant spirit of illustrious *caudillos* [military leaders]."[97] In the 1950s, "children's" editions of the classic disappeared altogether. While teachers—as revealed in a rare pedagogy poll conducted in 1954—continued to consider *Don*

Quixote the most useful literary text in their classes,[98] it is not clear how the state directed these educators to teach the novel in their lessons.[99]

The scholarly world underwent a similarly insidious suppression. As Giménez Caballero had vowed it would be (as illustrated in the first epigraph to this chapter), independent criticism was replaced with an official, unintellectual version that set a very different critical tone, decrying Cervantes with "resentment, and sarcasm." The specific study of Cervantes became both implicitly and explicitly "discouraged" as the field was targeted by Francoist surveillance. Villanueva Toledo has documented more than nine hundred investigative files opened by the fascist intelligence services on Cervantist specialists, projects, and editions of any sort, including educational studies of Cervantes's life or works.[100] Most studies of Cervantes were censored and thus withdrawn from public access for reasons—as adduced by the officials evaluating them—that were rarely intellectual, literary, or "moral." The censor only had to bluntly refer to the topic of the study—Cervantes—or to the personal or ideological leanings of the author or editor to disqualify a book from open circulation. In condemning a seemingly harmless work entitled *Cervantes's Thought Seen by a Lawyer* by Niceto Alcalá Zamora (1947), for example, the Francoist official argued that "given the pernicious personality of the author of this study, which on the other hand has no literary value, the circulation of this work should not be permitted."[101]

It's little wonder, then, that when José Montero Reguera studied post-Civil War Cervantist criticism in Spain, he concluded that "[t]hose [philologists and writers] who stayed in Spain after 1936 have *Don Quixote* in their head, but write little about it. In general, the themes of those specialists follow other paths, concentrating on other authors or themes, such as Góngora, Valle-Inclán, Garcilaso de la Vega, San Juan de la Cruz, dialectology, or language history."[102] Even the still-prominent Center for Historical Studies (Centro de Estudios Históricos) "did not often concentrate on Quixote" anymore.[103] At first, Montero Reguera surprisingly argues that, after all, "there was little that could be added to everything Castro had said," but he ends up admitting that "these [Cervantine] ideas were not well-regarded [by the authorities] and, hence, it was better not to approach the subject."[104]

The lack of a greater critical acknowledgment of—let alone uproar over— the fascist censorship of Cervantes explains to some degree why subsequent criticism has focused so little on the effects of this chapter of Spanish history on the development of its literary criticism. As Castro wrote, the evolution of Cervantes's critical field was already "abnormal" in the mid-1920s Spain. Within a mere decade and a half, after a subsequent brief flowering of the editorial and scholarly worlds, major fascist disruptions would reinstitute and intensify the dysfunctionality of the field. Cervantes enthusiasts and scholars, witnessing fascist assaults from exile, did not bear them quietly, as I will demonstrate in the next three chapters. Through numerous and incisive denouncements, they attempted, using all the media at their disposal, to reverse the proscriptions against Cervantes and other authors of his stature.

In 1947, for example, Ramón J. Sender, a former avant-garde peer of Giménez Caballero, denounced from Mexico the particular hatred that Francoist ideologues felt for the classical author:

> Those who betrayed Spanish democracy could never be loyal to its culture, and if Cervantes could talk to them from the golden heavens where he must rest, he would surely utter those words of Cide Hamete, "Careful, careful, worthless idlers!" with a mix of empathy and disdain. They know it, and they hate it. They hate him today as much as they did then.[105]

"Careful, careful, worthless idlers" is, of course, the warning of the Moorish character Cide Hamete Benengeli, issues at the end of *Don Quixote* Part II to the future historian or novelist who might dare "to write with a coarse and badly designed ostrich feather about the exploits of my valorous knight."[106] Fittingly, Sender extends that quote to fascist historians and ideologues. With such defiance, Sender and his contemporaries would declare an open critical war against the political and cultural oppression of the regime. Meanwhile, in official Spain, the response to such protests was to nationalize literary criticism, canceling out exiled voices and delegitimizing the opinion of foreign critics. A constrained form of literary and cultural studies was thus instituted in this dark stage of Spanish history.

Con permiso de los cervantistas: Murdering Cervantine Criticism

The tenets of Francoist culture would be imposed not only by official policies and editorial practices; other more subtle and seemingly more "personal" choices would effectively contribute to the repression. Take the influential input of José Martínez Ruiz ("Azorín"), then the oldest surviving member of the Generation of '98, whose open collaboration with the Francoist regime allowed his domestic prestige to be harnessed by the government to minimize the vacuum left by exiled writers.[107] Azorín, someone still highly regarded today as the "master of writers and patriarch of Spanish letters," chose a curious title for his 1948 homage to Cervantes: *Con permiso de los cervantistas.*[108] That sarcastic gesture represents a damning invalidation of the professional ethos of Spanish criticism that specialists such as Castro had attempted to institute.

Castro had referred to Azorín by name decades earlier in his *Pensamiento de Cervantes* (1925) as a detractor of criticism that sought new depths in *Don Quixote.* "Azorín had noted," Castro says, that "the greatest damage that we could inflict on *Don Quixote* is to keep approaching the novel from this [position of] Cervantist mysticism."[109] However, Castro goes on to show that Azorín's reservations about more profound explorations of the Cervantine oeuvre were ultimately motivated by Azorín's own prejudiced views of Cervantes, and his anticipation that his claims would be refuted. Castro believed that the powerful "fetishist culture built around the author"—a bastion of received notions that refused all new interpretation—was the ultimate reason for the "absence of technical studies of Cervantes."[110] The subjective criticism produced and nurtured by this "fetishist" imaginary was largely responsible for the esoteric, "naïve," and "unsubstantiated" (Close would call them "Romantic") commentaries at the turn of the century, and for the "lamentable" positivist approaches of the early 1900s.[111] "Shouldn't it be time," Castro had wondered in 1925, "to approach a text-based study of Cervantes's works serenely [i.e., rationally], without prejudices, and [guided by] clear and specific intents?"[112] Little could Castro have imagined, as he penned these words, that the professional, text-bound, and historically contextualized Cervantism that his book proposed—and that would be so promisingly cultivated in the decade after 1925—would not last, in large part because writers such as Azorín had authorized the return of "unsubstantiated" critical exercises that scholars in the field thought to be a thing of the past in the late 1930s.

Demonstrating that the past is not free from the present (as I will explore more extensively in Chapter 4), in 1948, Azorín refuted all the accumulated charges against his style of subjective, traditional criticism. He started by describing two kinds of discourses available to the critic as equally acceptable and intellectually satisfying:

At this starting point two paths open: one leads to erudition, the other, to life. A Cervantist can follow one or the other [according to] his disposition and sense of responsibility, and nobody would be able to stop him. If the path to erudition is hard, the other one, to life, is equally severe. The erudite scholar is devoted to paper; the imaginative [critic] to sensation. We are attracted [as erudite Cervantists] to the manuscript, representative of time and action. The archive implies time and persistence. A present finding stimulates a future one. A fragmentary Cervantes awaits his totality .... [T]here is a pleasure, an intimate form of pleasure, in saying about Cervantes something that no other critic—past or present—has. But there is another pleasure [for the erudite critic] even more powerful than this, and more secret: knowing what those sensitive Cervantists don't. Could these erudite critics behave and hide their detachment and contempt for *psychological Cervantists*? Would they pronounce the terrible, irrefutable sentence of "lack of training"?

And what is going on, in the meantime, on the other path? *The path of the artist who can fall in love with Cervantes, who can aspire to understand him and mingle with him. Feeling* Cervantes is, more than anything, *actualizing* him. To feel Cervantes, we must strip him of any archaeology. *The artist is not afraid of any historical error,* because *with or without error, we can reach sensation*; it is the experiential sensation that leads him to Cervantes and this is [the discovery he] passes on to the reader. Should we *celebrate this deviation from erudition?* Do we voice, against the erudite scholar, the other terrifying accusation of "lack of sensibility"?[113]

One can easily see where Azorín is going. Although, at first glance, both critical options—an erudite (rational) criticism and an emotional (subjective) one—appear equally valid, by the beginning of the second paragraph it is clear that the second type is more advisable. The sensible, emotional critic—presumed to have the same intellectual and creative abilities as Cervantes—is the only one who can think like "an artist" and "aspire to understand and mingle with him," rather than simply "dissecting" the author. The work of acclaimed and erudite critics as Bataillon, while full of prestige, can therefore only be superficial and fragmentary compared to the deeper understanding of the sensitive, psychological commentator.[114] Thus, if the professional critic can accuse the subjective commentator of a lack of literary and historical accuracy or training, the latter can accuse the former of a "lack of sensibility" or of a basic understanding of the author.

Establishing a new incompatibility between scholarly rigor and emotional insight or sensibility, Azorín appears to defend critics' right to choose their own methodologies: "let each walk his path," he says, because "[i]f we cannot reach an agreement ... What can we do? Each [path] will have its followers."[115] Yet, he undermines this principle by dedicating considerable space to emphasizing the superiority of emotional discourse, by undermining, for example, the obligation of literary criticism to be factual or accurate: subjective critics are obliged only to make a "cordial attempt to be historical" (whatever "cordial" means), since such an attempt "is enough" to make it legitimate.[116]

By claiming an intellectual equivalency between cultivated, factually sound scholarship and free-writing commentary, Azorín undermined not only the value of erudition but also the professionalized stature that the field of Cervantism had acquired in the 1920s and 1930s. He thereby re-enacted the same "sentimental, patriotic, philosophical, and subjective" symbolic approach to literary criticism in general, and of Cervantism in particular, that had been dominant in the 1800s and among the Generation of '98.[117] The critical praxis that the Spaniard Jose María Pereda had described as the art of taking "to the most ridiculous extremes the most serious and respectable matters" would be dignified once again under the Francoist regime.[118]

The return to the essentialist arguments formulated about Cervantes by many Generation of '98 thinkers, which had been useful to proto-fascist writers such as Ledesma and Maeztu, would be welcomed again by fascist supporters and sympathizers in the 1940s.[119] By reinstating the kind of literary commentary practiced by imperialist thinkers in the late nineteenth century, and by elevating such commentary to the stature of intellectually sound critical approaches such as text-based scholarship, Azorín opened the door to the use of the Cervantine field to legitimate Francoist ideas of national destiny and dominion.[120]

We can see evidence of how easy it was in Azorín's mind to associate Cervantes and Franco when he compared them in his 1942 article "El Caudillo y Cervantes."[121] Here, contradicting the prevailing identification of Don Quixote with Spain's supposed decadence by the fascist front, Azorín argued that Cervantes does quite the opposite, since—like Franco— he dedicates the knight's heroic quest to the return of the country to its former glory. For Azorín, "Don Quixote might admit defeat, but his cause continues," and that cause seemed to be awaiting a new knight—in this case, Franco—to actualize it.[122] "Lying on his death bed, the dying knight remains in our sensibility surrounded by a bright, hopeful ideal. *For such ideals— hope, enthusiasm, generosity—our Caudillo has fought.*"[123] Azorín went on to reveal the attachment (still, in 1942) to the hope of the Generation of '98 of resurrecting the unified country of a victorious, Spanish past through the figure "and spirit" of Don Quixote. To Azorín, the knight's ultimate ideal was that of "our *Caudillo*," mainly "to see unite us, Spaniards."[124] Such identification was of obvious value to the Francoist program. Azorín takes the side of Francoist ideologues, declaring that the Spanish aspiration for glory only required the figure of a valiant warrior such as Franco to accomplish it.[125]

It is impossible to separate Azorín's vindication of amateur, subjective Cervantism from the blatantly politicized context in which he operated. Indeed, given the large number of Cervantine critics exiled, and the institutionalization of a literary censorship especially vigilant in matters relative to Cervantes, Azorín's defense of subjective criticism might have been the last blow to the revamped, professional Cervantism that had started flourishing only two decades earlier.

The Critical Aftermath: The Triumph of an Academic Anti-Cervantism

The consequences of criticism such as Azorín's coupled with fascist censorship were, unfortunately, easy to predict.[126] After a period in which amateur illiberal critics tore down and censored professional academic humanists, fascist "creative" critics stepped in and became the dominant professional model, establishing a new generation of conservative criticism with an official imprimatur. In 1949, a little-known critic, José María Fernández Menéndez, provided a telling evaluation of the state of the field from the academic pages of a University of Oviedo journal.[127] Despite an initial claim in favor of scientific analysis,[128] the author soon clarifies his position: "It is in this very moment ... after a cathartic war, that a book [i.e., *Don Quixote*] that became the intellectual indulgence of both camps gets a new interpretation, issued by a new generation, that of 1936, a group displaying the *distinct style and spirit of previous* critical generations."[129] Sheltered in this critical "Generation of 1936" platform are the anti-Cervantes views that Giménez Caballero had been voicing since 1932.[130] Demanding the liberation of Quixote from the erudite prison in which he had been contained, Fernández Menéndez claims that

> *Don Quixote* has been ridiculed by the erudite scholars, the superficial thinkers, and the idiots. Erudite scholars have been feverishly looking for first editions, grouping the great story of the Manchegan knight in five-line paragraphs; superficial thinkers by raising their voice or making up catchy sentences have become conceited stereotypes ... the idiots pay attention to everything that erudite scholars and superficial thinkers say.[131]

Once he has delegitimized all the basic elements of scholarly research and critical inquiry—erudition, textual and editorial analysis, and so on—Fernández Menéndez abandons all pretense of writing a serious academic study. He instead begins to issue categorical statements on critical questions that had been deeply debated in great nuance only a decade earlier, flatly and categorically denying Cervantes's humanism, for example.[132] "Progressive, Cervantes?" Fernández Menéndez asks rhetorically, only to bluntly assert: "Not at all. Clearly not that. Instead, he is a nostalgic knight of the best and most real knighthood."[133] Categorized as a fervent "defender of knighthood" (partidario de la caballería andante), Cervantes thus becomes quite the opposite of a humanist, since Fernández Menéndez considers him "a man of absolute positions, as is any Spaniard from any age."[134] He concludes by identifying in Cervantes "the embodiment of Spanish dogmatism ... the *dogmatism* that the *beneficial inquisition* brought us, that led us to our struggle against the Turk, and that shaped *Columbus's uncompromising* spirit when he was trying to discover America."[135] It is hard to imagine a better epitaph for the death of the field of Cervantism—the death announced by Giménez Caballero in the epigraph for this chapter—than this insistence that Cervantes is unnuanced and dogmatic, simply and transparently understood, nationalist and imperialist. In the place of historically and textually grounded humanist criticism, "another kind" of critical discourse duly took hold, one that used "resentment and sarcasm" to "corrode Spain's quixotic spirit" and to "murder [Cervantine] criticism," just as Giménez Caballero had wanted.[136]

When academic discourse in Spain began to voice claims such as Fernández Menéndez's, it illustrated Rosa Regàs's sad realization that education in Spain had lost not only the teachers and innovative methods of the suddenly distant Republican educational revolution, but also a basic understanding of the country's past, both recent and distant. Perhaps, then, it should not come as a surprise that when Close produced his *Romantic Approach* in the mid-1970s, he would end up grouping Romantic and Regenerationist critics and Francoist commentators in one block.[137] By merging the radically different methods, perspectives, and purposes of these groups—and everyone in between—Close inadvertently but categorically declared "accomplished" the mission announced by Giménez Caballero in 1932: to eradicate the progressive, sophisticated Cervantism that had emerged in the previous decade, by substituting one critical discourse for another.

Had Close been aware of the existence and fervency of this progressive criticism, and of the powerful critique of the Generation of '98 and the fascist thought that it conveyed, he might have produced a more nuanced assessment of the Romantic reach in Spanish letters. Instead, he concluded that Spanish Romantic critics engaged in overly subjective literary interpretation, choosing to ignore Cervantes's rich "artistic texture—probably because this is something difficult to analyze."[138] For Close, the "Romantic" excesses of Spanish Cervantism from the late 1940s until the 1960s were the result of a sterile critical tradition. His judgment, pronounced in the late 1970s, is a testament to the troubling success of Francoist censorship practices in suppressing or derailing progressive critical traditions, making them seem incompatible with Spanish "nature" or custom.

Close's arguments are more thoroughly examined in the next chapter, which shows the heated, though often forgotten debate between Romantic and conservative critics on one hand, and Republican-leaning thinkers and Cervantine enthusiasts on the other. The shifting paradigm that this debate implies provides an indispensable archive for understanding the fractured literary, political, and critical legacies of twentieth-century Spain, and for ultimately assessing the innovations and disruptions to its unsettled modernity.

3

A Generational Shift: Riding Away from the Empire

Most of the influential Cervantes criticism written in this century forms a fairly coherent tradition *stemming from Américo Castro's* El pensamiento de Cervantes *(1925). The tradition is idealist and humanist. By this I mean that it starts from something like Ortega y Gasset's position in his* Meditaciones del "Quijote" *(1914) ... and led by such figures as T.S. Eliot, Ernst Curtius, Leo Spitzer, and Eric Auerbach.*

ANTHONY CLOSE[1]

Cervantism was Cervantes's worst enemy.

GUILLERMO DÍAZ-PLAJA[2]

Vicente Gaos's claim that "no literary work, in the entire history of literature, has inspired more contradictory interpretations and plain lunacy than *Don Quixote*" was amply justified by the 1960s.[3] By then, the novel—and Cervantes's entire opus—had endured the bombastic, esoteric interpretations of the nineteenth century, the Romantic excesses of the turn of the century, and the politicized readings of the twentieth.[4] As Gaos lamented, "*Don Quixote* started to be very badly understood at the time when the novel was starting to attract the right kind of attention."[5] Just when those critical traditions that Américo Castro declared to be "profoundly dysfunctional" in 1925 were starting to disappear, displaced by a careful and text-centered form of analysis, the political winds of the 1930s revived the symbolic reflexes of the past, targeting Cervantes's work as an illustration of all the ills of the country's history.[6]

Gaos's passing in 1980 prevented him from witnessing the full effects of another contribution to this critical archive: Anthony Close's characterization of Spanish Cervantism as a stable Romantic continuum that stretched over almost two centuries (mid-1800s–1900s), a characterization that largely omitted the shifts, schools, and methods that emerged in five pivotal and defining decades (1900–50) of Spanish cultural history.

While the previous chapter examined the emergence of promising Cervantine cultures (popular and specialized) in the 1920s and 1930s, and their subsequent dismantling by the Francoist establishment in the late 1930s and 1940s, this chapter brings to the fore the critical developments unfolding on the progressive side, as writers associated with the Generation of '27 targeted the Romantic praxis of the '98 Generation (almost thirty years before Close published his seminal study) and the imperialistic interpretations of the novel that they had inspired.

The next three chapters, in fact, will explore the clash among these progressive and conservative (imperialistic) positions and discourses. This chapter specifically examines the heated debate between the Generations of '98 and '27, focusing in particular on how the '27 authors already in exile denounced the '98 hegemonic interpretations of *Don Quixote* that served as fodder for fascist interpretations of the country's destiny. Chapter 4 extends this exiled opposition to the pragmatic Francoist officials who, in the late 1940s, decided to drop their initial antagonism to Cervantes once they realized the striking propaganda opportunity that the three-hundredth anniversary of his birth provided the regime. Writers of the diaspora would then confront the mighty Francoist propaganda machine that—still following the '98 modes of reading Cervantes—attempted to turn the author into an illustration of the values of the dictatorship. Finally, Chapter 5 examines the ways in which Spanish exiles relied on Cervantine humanism after the Republican defeat in the Civil War in hopes of reconciling the history of colonization connecting their old and new homelands.

While Close (as in the first epigraph of this chapter) was right to see humanism and idealism at work in the Cervantes studies of the early twentieth century, it is only by excavating the interpretive battles that we yet have to recognize that we can understand the type of modern culture that this humanist turn was fighting to establish. In exploring these critical fractures, I am recovering the important work done by a wide range of anti-fascist critics, broadly associated with the Generation of 1927, who significantly expanded the critical perspective produced by the handful of scholars—Ortega y Gasset, Unamuno, Castro, Madariaga, and so on— whom Close's influential study taught us to rely on.[7]

Recovering a Critical '27 Legacy

One undeveloped subject in today's Spanish cultural historiography is an appreciation of the critical contributions made by many of the writers—not only poets—loosely associated with the Generation of 1927.[8] Only recently has it become clear, as Antonio Martín Ezpeleta writes, the extent to which "practically all" of the members associated with this generation cultivated the theoretical—critical—dimension in their work.[9] While some members, such as Max Aub and Pedro Salinas have received more attention than others in this regard, the caution that Enric Bou issued about the latter, Salinas— that considering him only as a poet, as extraordinary as he was in that register, was simply "a disservice" to his intellectual stature—could apply to almost all '27 authors.[10] Indeed, critical and creative writing regularly coexisted in the work of these thinkers, since as Cernuda acknowledged, "[e]very poet is, or should be, a critic, a silent and a creative one, not an unproductive chatterbox."[11] Creative, although not very silent, these authors became deeply involved in the exploration of pivotal questions of the day, whether strictly literary or not, considering among other topics the value of Cervantes's poetry and the role that classic works of fiction and art played— or should play—in societies of the day.[12]

Members of the Generation of '27 generally supported one another in this critical and interdisciplinary labor, sharing ideas about projects and commending one another for their work. They also repeatedly complained (especially once in exile) about the scant attention that international academic circles paid to their efforts. Recent studies on the female participants of these groups, such as the "hatless women" (*las sinsombrero*), have exposed the disadvantages that these women faced as poets, journalists, artists, and philosophers both inside and outside of Spain.[13] But even two poets as well recognized as Guillén and Salinas, who in exile were supposedly well situated in the North American universities, felt disregarded and blamed this critical indifference on the artificial constraints that American life and strict academic formats had placed on their work.[14]

Apart from the obvious impact of their exile, a major reason for the limited recognition of the footprint of such authors and creators is the fact that they had, prior to the Franco regime, seldom published in specialized literary magazines beyond the *Revista de Occidente* and *La Gaceta literaria*.[15] The bulk of their creative and critical activity in the 1920s and 1930s had appeared in experimental and regional poetic journals—*Mediodia* (Seville), *Carmen* (Santander), *Litoral* (Málaga), *El Gallo* (Orhiuela), and so on—rather than in official, national, and academic venues.[16] With good reason, Juan Manuel Rozas spoke of the '27 group as "the generation of literary magazines" (la generación de las revistas literarias).[17] As Juli Highfill argues, those smaller, well-crafted journals enabled the '27 group and other avant-garde practitioners to continue their artistic experiments and "richly productive inquiry."[18] Yet the regional and specialized scope of these publications also meant that, after the Civil War, "[t]he breath of this inquiry would be minimized, its heterogeneity suppressed, and its insights largely forgotten."[19] When the nature of these publications is considered in light of the limited sources in Close's study, it is clear why *The Romantic Approach to "Don Quixote"* was at that time unable to recognize the pivotal contributions of some of Spain's most significant thinkers both in Spain and in exile.

Literary historiography has often been guilty of such damaging omissions. While the cultural production of the Spanish diaspora is being fruitfully explored today, traditional literary histories—even those written after the end of the dictatorship—have seldom assigned exiled writers their rightful place in history.[20] Exile has been characterized as a "double symbol of the void, a hollow representation of Janus, a decentered and ghostly experience of the subject that never reconciles the lost ego with the lost id."[21] In the case of exiled writers, this ontological fracture is magnified by the loss, through censorship and exclusion, of their literary voice and self, since the literary tradition that once had created and nurtured these authors no longer recognizes them. Sometimes, the writer's acknowledgment of this dismissal happens in real time, as Aub publicly acknowledges, in the opening lines of his 1966 work, *Best Pages*: "Turns out, nobody knows me in Spain."[22] Other times, it is a much more intimate recognition; "In the midst of this total indifference," writers Guillén in a private letter in 1947, "this void is more painful every day, even though its presence has become by now part of my being."[23]

Through painful individual epiphanies and collective calls for action, the repressive workings of censorship and exile were clearly understood by the Spanish diaspora. Isidoro Enríquez Calleja, for example, complained about the invisibility of his progressive generation, expressing bafflement at the continued celebration of '98 authors in Spain in the 1940s,[24] pointing out that:

> In what we have seen of this century, Spanish life has unfolded full of twists and turns at an accelerated pace, especially after 1931 ... What took place in Spain should have filled the bookstores with suggestive and deep novels that defined our times in a different way. But what happened was quite the opposite. The writers who keep setting the tone ... are the writers of Generation '98.[25]

Indeed, after the Civil War ended in 1939, and the fascist regime tightened its grip in the subsequent decade, ignoring the critical contributions and protestations of a young and contestatory exiled group with limited means of publication became even easier. By uncovering these uncharted literary contributions and historical records, we can reconstruct the fascinating controversy that confronted twentieth-century critics both inside and outside the Peninsula. The rehabilitation of this contextualized legacy may not only permit a better appreciation of Cervantes and his age, but also facilitate a more accurate understanding of Spain's critical past, thereby broadening possibilities of more rewarding directions in its future.

The Generation of '27 versus the Generation of '98: A Critical Contrast

To obtain a deeper understanding of the conflicting legacies of the Generations of '27 and '98, we might start by assuming a healthy degree of independence between the two different groups. Much literary historiography has assumed that '98 writers had an enormous literary influence over their younger counterparts. Genara Pulido Tirado, for example, voices a general consensus when she claims that the '27 group "considered the Generation of '98 a milestone in the recuperation of a [national] consciousness," given that this earlier group had looked to the past in attempts to recover the essence of the people.[26] While valid, the general assumption that the Generation of '27 looked to the '98 group as a model, can gloss over the fact that various '27 writers actually expressed significant philosophical and critical differences from their predecessors, at least in the 1940s.[27]

With regard to Cervantes, while most members of both '98 and '27 generations considered him an exceptional representative of Spanish consciousness, each group interpreted the meaning of his work and this consciousness in strikingly different ways. The stated conservative outlook of '98 authors such as Azorín, Maeztu, and an early Unamuno was deeply influenced by the international collapse of the Spanish empire and by a nationalistic heroic idealism. They thus saw Don Quixote "as a sometimes stoic and mystical, sometimes redemptive and messianic hero who embodies the leadership ideals that these intellectuals believed could regenerate post-1898 Spain."[28] Through the chivalric nostalgia they projected onto Don Quixote, these writers don't only express a longing for a long-lost imperial glory, but also the belief that the Manchegan hero shows a path for its revival. Don Quixote here embodies "the Spanish national, essential heroic, empire-building characteristics" that could "regenerate" the country again, allowing it to regain its hegemonic place in the world.[29]

The '98 idea of regenerationism dramatically differed (at least in theory) from Joaquín Costa's (1846–1911) reformism, which was supposedly more interested in developing the country's agricultural productivity than in recovering its colonialist stature.[30] In 1898, Costa had famously asked his fellow representatives to "lock El Cid's sepulcher twice, so that he does not ride again," a metaphorical request that would become heavily despised by the most conservative forces of the moment and the new century.[31] Almost thirty years later, Ramiro de Maeztu used this reference of a "sepulcher" of Spanish chivalry, or heroism, as a justification for the radicalization of conservativism, arguing that

> When in 1898, Spain lost the few remaining vestiges of its colonial empire in the Americas, and the Far East, the figure of the Joaquín Costa arose exhorting us: Place a double lock on the sepulcher of El Cid so that he will never mount his horse again ... They [these renovators] beseeched us Spaniards to never be either Cids or Quixotes again, and it did not take long for those of us who, during those hours of humiliation and defeat, felt the need to rebuild the nation, to "regenerate" it ... to understand that this would not come about unless the regenerators adopted, at the very least, a bit of the forceful spirit of El Cid and the generous idealism of Don Quixote.[32]

Although expressed in different styles, a number of the members of the '98 group (including Maeztu, Azorín, and Angel Ganivet) agreed that Quixotism equated the "generous idealism" mentioned by Maeztu, what Azorín referred to as a "dormant" chivalric "fantasy," able to reawaken the "eternal [imperial] Spain," the country that according to them wanted to prove its greatness once again.[33] Ganivet, meanwhile, asserted that Cervantes (not only Don Quixote) was as much "a conquistador" as Cortés or Pizarro, since it was Cervantes's combative spirit that had enabled him to write *Don Quixote* and the reason why the book had become such a quintessentially Spanish masterpiece: "*Don Quixote* is not only our iconic Spanish novel because [Cervantes was] an independent writer, he was a *conquistador, and the greatest of all conquistadors because while others conquistadors* were busy conquering lands for Spain, he conquered Spain itself while being imprisoned in a jail."[34]

It is hard to overemphasize how useful this '98 call to revive the Golden Age of empire was to Francoism. As one fascist theorist, Antonio Tovar, argued in 1941:

> From 1898 to now, Spain has been feeling the loss of its empire, so this is where we come from, we the ones invested in [bringing back] all those ancient ideals ....We, who look not for the Spain of yesterday or the day before, but for an eternal Spain; the Spain that the Spanish people had defended with their blood, the Spain of the yoke and arrows, the Imperial Spain.[35]

That tribal fascist awareness of a collective "we" is here proudly tied to the catalyst events of 1898 and the literary generation associated with them. The Falangist Pedro Laín Entralgo underlines this political and literary association by declaring himself to be one of "the grandchildren of the '98 Generation" that had turned "literary criticism ... into national patriotism."[36] Christopher Britt-Arredondo has explored in detail the relationship between the '98 and ultra-conservative involvement and the historical responsibility borne by the '98 for the emergence and justification of the Francoist rebellion.[37]

What has been less examined is how the ultra-conservative legacy of the Generation of '98 was contested during these pivotal decades by the progressive thinkers of the moment. For most of the authors, theorists, and artists of a younger generation—whom I identify in a broader sense with the Generation of '27—the idea of another national crusade or imperial age was abhorrent and ridiculous. Progressive men and women growing up in the 1900s read *Don Quixote*'s chivalric follies as mocking rather than extolling the doomed ambitions of the empire, a political entity they considered morally reprehensible and politically unsustainable. In their view, the Spanish colonial past—and the mindset that defended it—had always stood in the way of true modernization of the country, a position that aligned them politically with a Republican ideology.[38] When the members of this younger generation turned to Cervantes, they found—despite the chronological distance—a familiar and accessible author, a man, as Castro would say, "who inspires you to treat him collegially" ([que] insta a que se le hable de tú), as well as a wise writer who had experienced an earlier version of the conflicts plaguing Spain and the rest of Europe from the 1920s through the 1940s.[39] For example, Aub, in his study of Cervantes's tragedy *Numancia*—which he had cast as a veiled reflection of European nationalism and imperialism—noted that

> [A]pparently, military fascists and conquistadors have always obeyed similar feelings, and exuded similar kind of behaviours. Nobody would notice the change if we took the words [that Cervantes gives to] Scipio and put them in Mussolini's mouth, just like nobody would see anything different if we assigned the words of the Numantines to the defenders of Madrid [against Francoist forces] ... Cervantes, as usual, voices popular expressions that are also eternal—being eternal precisely because they are deeply genuine. By sheer coincidence, a huge number of Cervantes's phrases acquire today, without changing a comma in them, statements of incredible relevance.[40]

The "eternal" values that Aub refers to here are not the values of a [fascist] "eternal Spain," but rather, the shared hunger for dominion among fascist, Nazi, and Roman empires that makes it almost impossible to distinguish one regime from the other. Rather than taking Quixote's chivalric and imperialistic delusions at face value, '27 authors such as Aub considered them a critical exposure of their baseness. Dissident and nonconformist thinkers of Aub's generation or sensibility became deeply interested in Cervantes's subtle but powerful commentary on authoritarianism. In their analysis of Cervantes's texts, these progressive authors would not be timid about expressing their strong critical disagreements with their predecessors.

The debate over Ortega y Gasset's famous view of *Don Quixote* as an unsolvable "colossal mystery" that "all the tirades of national eloquence have not been able to elucidate" offers a brief but telling example.[41] Believing that Cervantes's text was more accessible than the philosopher had characterized it to be, the usually measured Salinas—considering Ortega's categorical assertion a reflection of his scholarly vanity—quibbles: "Ortega's arrogance. What is that? There is really no Spaniard who has ever understood *Don Quixote*? So what? Isn't it true that millions of them have read it and cried or laughed with it? Or, did Cervantes write it so that it could be understood only by professors of metaphysics?"[42] Although the story we have inherited from Close holds that Ortega's voice defined Cervantine criticism and that subsequent critics followed in his footsteps, it is obvious here that Ortega did not always maintain a glowing influence over writers and critics like Salinas. His (Salinas's) generation would question, in fact, not only Ortega's metaphysical readings of Cervantes, but also some of his most famous assessments of the state of the nation. A 1946 editorial by Manuel Andújar and José Ramón Araña refuted the premise of Ortega's famous *Invertebrate Spain* (1921), rephrasing his title to claim that "Spain is not invertebrate, ... but intentionally disvertebrated, orthopedically disfigured and crippled."[43] Such criticism, voiced through the exile, adds an obvious political dimension to the literary.

Despite such literary and political rebukes, '27 writers recognized the beneficial impact of some of their predecessors' ideas. Cernuda, Salinas, and Aub, for example, commended Romantic critics for having brought "Cervantes back to the light."[44] They also gave credit to the Generation of '98 for having rescued the Golden Age author from "the contempt in which certain Spanish authors had placed him, (comically) believing themselves to be better than him."[45] Originally this judgment was directed toward early harsh critics of Cervantes such as Clemencín, who wrote in the early part of the nineteenth century, but many '27 voices also applied it as well to Unamuno, himself part of the Generation of '98.[46] Nobody was too iconic to be spared by the younger group of writers, who seemed to perfectly aware of the contributions and deficiencies of their country's critical past, especially given the monumental misunderstandings in the appreciation of Cervantes that had been left behind by Restoration and Romantic criticism.

As Cernuda's fine irony put it in 1940, a "mixture of decorative pomposity and intellectual emptiness ... finds its own tradition in Romanticism, which gave these attitudes social status."[47] And in a 1965 panoramic article that reflects on the state of the field of Cervantism, Gaos—ten plus years before Close—wonders almost in disbelief at the Romantic disregard for *Don Quixote*'s comic nature:

> How could they doubt that *Quixote* was a rewardingly comic work? It certainly is as humorous as it is a parody of books of chivalry. Perhaps these values are superficial (and I say "perhaps" because, after *Quixote*, we might have to consider putting humor in the highest place in the aesthetic hierarchy). But superficial or not, it is impossible to go into the depths of this or any other work without going through this first layer. "Esoteric" critics clearly skipped it altogether, as if humor and literary parody were incompatible with more profound and universal purposes.[48]

This lucid demolition of Romantic and esoteric interpretations of Cervantes had a long history in the 1960s, in great part thanks to Castro's early contestation of symbolic interpretations in the mid-1920s. It was in 1925 when, as a young historian, Castro declared that the amateur criticism of the "pseudo-traditional intellectuals" (*cobijo de los medios pseudotradicionalistas*) that had come before them had turned Cervantes "into a repository of foreign whims and a shelter for their dated Romanticism."[49] As seen, Castro and his generation dramatically attempted to change this critical panorama during the mid-1920s and 1930s, witnessing from exile the return of this despised symbolic tradition returned to Spanish letters after the Civil War ended. It was there, in exile, where authors such as Castro and Gaos painfully understood that in a Francoist Spain Cervantes would become not only an underappreciated author, but one tragically misinterpreted by the entire cultural and political establishment. Progressive authors then became fully aware of the colossal political implications of the Romantic approach to Cervantes and *Don Quixote*, which its originators seem to have overlooked.

Trying to come to terms with the political ramifications of the '98 critical ethos, Cernuda reflected in 1940 that "[f]or 1898 critics, … Don Quixote was a symbol, a mystic incarnation of Spain and its mysticism. But turning things into symbols is quite dangerous, and whoever does it must do so on his own without putting the destiny of somebody else's work at risk."[50] Employing considerably stronger terms, José Enrique Rebolledo concluded a few years later that the symbolic reading of the novel had

> disintegrated *Don Quixote* by mocking the hero and by dissociating him from us …. The Generation of '98 is a prime illustration of this practice. … By questioning Spain, they found in Quixote's tormented figure a faithful justification of their angst and pessimism. Their interpretation of Quixote is *a lyric and demonic tirade* stemming from their battered Spanish way of thinking.[51]

For his part, Salinas also censured the '98's misunderstanding of the specific material context that had forged Cervantes's literary experimentation. For Salinas, "the men of '98, like other Quixotic knights errant, set off to look for the ideal, Dulcinea-Spain, giving up on the other, more material Spain, Aldonza's."[52]

Taken together, these critiques of '98 critics' unchecked idealism contradict Close's thesis that studies of Cervantes had been homogeneous and consistently Romantic and '27 thinkers generally followed or idealized their predecessors. Sender went so far as to claim that "the young authors of my generation ['27] feel cheated and disappointed by the narcissist gang of '98."[53] Cernuda, building on a similar idea, stated in the 1950s that '98 writers needed to be historically accountable for their work, since

> We have not yet acquired a critical attitude with regard to the writers of [the '98] generation; we continue to show them a panegyric reverence despite the events of the last thirty years, which have commented on direly on the pages that they wrote with *strange irresponsibility*. They are still considered our contemporaries even though various new generations have displaced them, ... rendering their works obsolete.[54]

For Cernuda, this "irresponsible" attitude had to do not only with the '98 take on topics such as the empire, but with the "impressionistic" methods used to explore them. Cernuda highlights Azorín's role in promoting the "subjective," "impressionistic" approach to Cervantes explored in the last chapter. For Cernuda, Azorín's "psychological criticism" had improperly elevated Francoist political interests while invoking some form of professional, rather than arbitrary, criteria.[55]

Unamuno and the Return to Quixote's Sepulcher

Cernuda and other members of the Generation of '27 not only criticized the methods and quality of the earlier group's literary scholarship, but often objected to the "master," Unamuno, whose "influence," Close claimed, "[f]ew" in Spain had "fail[ed] to exhibit."[56] The impression we inherit from Close overstates Unamuno's legacy, at least during the 1930s and 1940s.[57] Aub, for example, characterized the Basque thinker as a "grumpy and bitter Quixote more driven by nationalism than truth"[58] and Domenchina and Sender would repeatedly criticize the "colossal, enormous, and ... atrocious *ego*"[59] that they believed had led Unamuno to famously disparage Cervantes as "that poor Cervantes, so inferior to Don Quixote."[60] Sender would not forgive Unamuno for claiming the knight "as more properly his own character

[Unamuno's] than Cervantes's," a vindication that for Sender constituted a "perplexingly flippant negation of Cervantes's literary consciousness of his own creation."[61] Speaking, in a sense, for his generation, Cernuda openly confronted Unamuno's personal antagonism toward Cervantes, claiming that "[i]f Cervantes bothers Unamuno so much, to the point that he leaves him to the side, *we* cannot be moved by the same motive, since *we feel only affection, admiration, and respect for him.*"[62]

It would also be Cernuda who addressed one of Unamuno's most troubling works, an essay titled the "Sepulcro del Quijote" later praised and adopted by fascist thinkers. Evoking a Regenerationist perspective, Unamuno's refuted Costa's famous exhortation to leave the chivalric past behind. Defiant, the philosopher conjured back once again the old heroic spirit through the more accessible figure of Don Quixote. While the move, not surprisingly would attract the praise and attention of the most militant and conservative thinkers of the day, it caused equal amounts of spurn among progressive, younger intellectuals.[63]

Unamuno had first published the essay separately in 1905, but he also included it in his 1908 edition of *Vida de Don Quijote y Sancho*.[64] Given the immediate applause that the tale received in ultra-conservative circles, Unamuno removed it from subsequent editions of the *Vida*.[65] But the damage was done: as Gallegos Rocaful sympathetically noted, "Unamuno's words were heard" but apparently "not as he had wanted."[66] Ultra-traditional, right-wing readers of the 1920s and 1930s appreciated Unamuno's invitation to embark on a new, holy, and dangerous crusade that would liberate Don Quixote (and Spain) from what Unamuno allusively calls "his old guardians"—that is, his enemies, or the obstacles in his journey. In tracing the return of the hero through a panorama strongly reminiscent of epic ballads of the Middle Ages, Unamuno had established an extra-textual but direct link between the Cervantine protagonist and the crusader's *ethos*:

> You will witness how, as soon as the sacred squadron gets on its way, a star appears in the sky, a star visible only to crusaders, a shiny and resounding star that will sing a new song in this night that enwraps us all. The star advances as soon as the crusaders advance, and once they win their fight, or once they all have died—which is the only way to win—the star will fall from the sky, indicating the place where the sepulcher is located. The sepulcher lies where the squad dies.[67]

It is almost impossible to miss the parallel between Quixote's sepulcher and Santiago's, the discovery of which re-energized the *Reconquista* between Christians and Muslims in Spain years after the fight had started.[68] This origin—and the disturbing parallel that Unamuno later establishes between Quixote and the best-known Spanish conquistadors—characterizes Quixote's heroism and pursuits as essentially imperialistic: "What led to the actions of Don Quixote, Columbus, Cortés, Pizarro, and Magellan, and all the other members of the lasting race of heroes? A generous and big dream: the dream of glory."[69] As he elaborates on this panegyric to heroism, Unamuno further associates *Don Quixote* with other conservative and jingoistic ideas, including the distrust of knowledge,[70] the blind exaltation of faith,[71] and the justification of a violent course of action:

> What are we going to do while we are on our way? Fight! Fight! And how? What if you encounter a lie on your way? Shout at the man on his face, "Lie!" and keep going! What if you find a man who steals? Shout, "Thief!" and keep going! What if you find one talking nonsense, who is listened to by a jaw-dropped crowd? Scream at all of them, "Stupid!" and keep going. Always, keep going![72]

Invocations such as these—which clearly detached the knight from Quixote's fictional framework and from Cervantes's humanist context—located character and author alike within the imperial dream.

The maneuver did not pass unnoticed by Francoist ideologues such as Ramiro de Ledesma and the ubiquitous Giménez Caballero. Indeed, in his *Conquista del estado*, Ledesma commends Unamuno's Cervantism for having given "the war tone" to young *falangistas*: "This man [Unamuno], who in 1908 imagined a crusade to rescue Don Quixote's grave, produced some of the most energetic pages that the universal [Spanish] spirit has seen lately, urging us to mobilize with our bayonets under the imperial cry to dominate." [73] Unamuno's image of the crusade provided a literary dimension to a recurring *topos* among fascist theorists and sympathizers. Jean Babelon, for example, would in 1948 publish an article in the *Revista de filología española* – titled "Cervantes y el ocaso de los conquistadores," – that picked up Unamuno's association of Don Quixote with the conquistadors and extended it to Cervantes himself: "If Don Quixote is the last of the knights errant, Cervantes can be considered the last of the conquistadors. One equals the other. Each one individually, and both of them together, embodies a dying ideal … in a life that has transfigured itself."[74] Assessments of this sort demonstrate the freedom with which ultra-conservative critics blurred literary and diegetical associations in the quest to attribute their own political convictions to the Golden Age writer and his most famous creation.

Yet, the subjective stream of consciousness (Azorín's "impressionistic" or "psychological") criticism of Ledesma's and Babelon's perspectives, repeated *ad nauseam* during the 1940s, in some ways misrepresents Unamuno's Cervantine thought and complex political views. Unamuno would, ironically, come to embody a brave opposition to fascism, epitomized in his famous (although perhaps not accurate) declaration "you will win, but you will not convince" (Venceréis pero no convenceréis) as he faced off with fascist generals.[75] Nevertheless, the fascist appropriation of his earlier pronouncements testifies to the ease with which Falangist and Francoist thinkers took advantage of the rich and suggestive imaginary left by him and other members of the '98 Generation.[76]

Demonstrating a strikingly different sensibility, Cernuda gave voice to his own literary group when he judged Unamuno's analogy to the crusaders to be a "strange confusion" (extraña confusión) and, at best, an "articulate rant" (elocuente tirada).[77] In this troubling pilgrimage, Cernuda argues that, Unamuno searches for Don Quixote's grave "as if finding that sepulcher would heal all the national evils and tragedies, although even Unamuno himself is not convinced that such a thing is possible."[78] By reminding his reader that "behind Quixote lies his author, Cervantes" (tras don Quijote está su autor),[79] Cernuda encouraged the more ideologically neutral reader to remember the eternity of Cervantes rather than the mortality of Don Quixote, thus deflecting Romantic—and Francoist—desires to both pin nationalist hopes on the image of the knight's tomb and embrace a vision of Don Quixote stripped of all critical, ironic, humorous, and amorous perspectives in favor of force.

For writers of the Generation of '27, Don Quixote, rather than providing Spain with a political or literary gospel, constituted a masterful tour de force that exposed the tragic and comical fractures of Cervantes's age and that still awaited serious literary and cultural examination. Thus, while Ledesma's imperialist understanding of Unamuno's metaphorical reading came to define the fascist approach to Cervantes and his protagonist in the late 1930s and beyond, Salinas, Cernuda, Rebolledo, and Aub provided readings of the novel that would characterize the corrective logic of this younger group. These '27 critics would strip away the facile political misconstructions that Generation of '98 critics and their later fascist highjackers had attributed to both the author and character and would embark on new and serious literary explorations of Cervantes's texts, focusing particularly on the least-examined dimensions of his opus.

Vindicating Cervantes's Corpus

While affection for Cervantes would remain consistent among liberal thinkers of the twentieth century, Francoist attitudes toward the author continued to evolve in the 1930s and 1940s. After all, the regime had exhibited a well-documented ideological pragmatism; without entering the Second World War officially, for example, the dictatorship was able to change sides. If, in 1939, it had shown every inclination to support the authoritarian Axis, once the allies' position had dramatically improved by 1943, the Francoist administration would recalibrate its message, presenting itself as a "unitary" state rather than a totalitarian one, and as a neutral bystander in the conflict rather than a Nazi collaborator.[80]

Such opportunistic ambivalence would apply to cultural assets such as Cervantes, albeit on a different scale. The initial disregard, even contempt, for the author would soften around 1947—given the major, worldwide commemoration of his birth—only to return to an institutionalized apathy in the 1950s. The regime had clearly preferred other Golden Age writers, such as the soldier-poet Garcilaso de la Vega, the "dogmatic" Calderón de la Barca, and father of "national" theater, Lope de Vega, writers all considered much more compatible with the regimen's values and messages.[81] The heroic poet Garcilaso de la Vega, for example, a soldier of Charles V killed in battle in 1536, provided a coincidence of dates that Francoist propagandists happily exploited as a poetic foreshadowing of the beginning of the Civil War four centuries later, in 1936.[82] In a warped and depleted cultural scene, a Renaissance poet who had never uttered a word about the morality of war would be reshaped into the embodiment of the Francoist crusade, as his work was used by the regime to offer an escapist vantage point from which to ignore the horrors of the war's aftermath.[83]

In theater, Francoist supporters would celebrate the work of Lope de Vega and Calderón de la Barca as faithful illustrations of the "eternal Spain" promoted by the regime.[84] Hegemony was, in fact, at the heart of the interest that ideologues such as Gimenez Caballero, José María Salaverria, and José María Pemán showed for Golden Age theater. Having taken good note of the success of Republican theater-based educational initiatives such as *La Barraca*, these fascist thinkers were eager to create their own versions of those programs, anxious to overturn what they considered Republican "desecrations" of classical texts. A series of national initiatives started to sharply reclaim the cultural capital of these Golden Age plays and literature, presenting them as inherently aligned with Francoist interests and agendas.[85]

While this fascist cultural reinscription is beyond the scope of this study, this general context provides an essential reference for understanding why so many exiled writers decided to continue exploring and invoking Cervantes both before and after the Civil War, and before and after the commemoration in 1947. Although they also explored the poetry of Garcilaso, among others, providing a counterpoint to the dictatorship's view of his verse, many of the poets and critics of the '27 group would continue to turn their attention to Cervantes focusing on little-known aspects of his opus.

The choice to focus on Cervantes seemed to have been, at times, a more or less conscious act of protest. "Since this year [1940] we are supposed to be celebrating some Lope commemoration," notes Cernuda, in an ironic allusion to a 1935 commemoration of Lope de Vega still invoked by the Francoist establishment five years later, "it seems to me that this is a ripe occasion to honor the subject of these pages"—that is, Cervantes's poetry.[86] Cernuda would not be alone in this attempt to reassess Cervantes's worth as a poet and a playwright, two literary dimensions traditionally considered weaker than his prose. Another lyricist Manuel Altolaguirre shared this aim, and tried to argue for Cervantes's poetic merit. Other exiles, including Aub and Alberti, directed a great deal of attention to Cervantes's undervalued theater plays, such as *La Numantia*. The body of work that the '27 group left behind reflects neither a homogeneous criticism nor a vision stuck in a Romantic past, offering instead a diverse testament of the disparate literary interests of their generation.

These critical sensibilities, furthermore, demonstrate the existence of an expansive perspective that surmounts Azorín's dualism of "professional" *Cervantistas* (archive-driven researchers) and "sensitive" impressionist critics (ruled by free thinking detached from the text and its historical circumstance). Most '27 figures operated in the healthy space between these poles, demonstrating how, in the heyday of New Criticism, sensitive readers—even without deep archival expeditions—were able to provide historically congruent and text-based literary commentary that also escaped the scientificism of structural approaches.

The '27 "Un-Romantic" Approach to *Don Quixote*

One of the literary themes that a good number of '27 authors would explore theoretically, sometimes simultaneously, was love. While this thematic epicenter had received substantial critical attention in Spain, in Cernuda's opinion the absence of a serious examination of the wide-ranging "mutations" of love in Spanish letters constituted an embarrassing oversight that he and some fellow exiles appeared determined to remedy.[87] Having treated the theme of *eros* superbly in their own work, a number of '27 poets and critics decided to tackle the question in Cervantes. While critical inquiries on the author had usually produced rich and intriguing results, the group soon realized that Cervantes' relationship with the emotion and its literary tradition was almost as awkward as Don Quixote's affair with his beloved.

For Aub, although Cervantes was obviously "deeply entrenched in the literary passions of his time," he did not seem interested in making Cervantes's love a central subject of his writing.[88] Gaos tentatively suggested that the cervantine resistance to the theme might have been caused by the "bleakness" (sequedad) and "intellectualism" (intelectualidad) with which Cervantes generally approaches the sentiment.[89] Samuel Gili Gaya concurred with Gaos, noting that such intellectualism was even obvious in the Cervantine incursions on the pastoral, the genre probably most prone to erotic and sentimental excess. There, Cervantes, a master of conceptual constructions, appears more interested in having shepherds such as Elicio "define [love] rather than sing of it."[90] This distant and measured treatment of love applies to almost all cervantine works, including *Don Quixote*, a novel so intimately steeped in chivalric fiction—probably the only other genre more open to sexual exploits than the pastoral. As many '27 writers noted, *Don Quixote* dramatically disrupts the traditional, fluid relationship of the heroic and the erotic of that genre when it presents a knight who, rather than enjoying the fruits of love with his lady, spends most of his time ruminating over her existence.

Only Salinas, by doubling down on the writer's cerebral approach to the sentiment would infer what most of his contemporaries could not: a detailed theory of Cervantes's view of love. Salinas, the so-called poet of love who masterfully reflected on that emotion in his own poetry, draws on his finest literary sensibility to show how a novel like *Don Quixote*, which so openly exposes the absence of a "real" beloved for the protagonist, is paradoxically able to produce "the most beautiful," if unusual, "love letter in Spanish literature."[91]

By focusing on a specific cluster of episodes (chapters 23–26) from Part I where Quixote composes an intimate love letter to Dulcinea that Sancho must impossibly "hand deliver," Salinas wittily identifies, through the many stages and accidents of this fictional composition, Cervantes's critique of the artificiality of Petrarchism and courtly paradigms of love, two literary models chiefly responsible for Quixote's misguided attempt to live as a knight errant.[92] After all, it is Quixote's devotion to Dulcinea— even though she does not exist—that allows him to justify his existence as a knight in accordance with his fictional models. Eros, in chivalric fiction, constitutes a "sort of professional obligation" that is supposed to determine all other heroic premises, and nobody better exemplifies that principle than the Manchegan knight, who illustrates the dependence of one concept— heroism—on the other—love.[93] As Quixote famously insists:

> There cannot be a knight errant without a lady, because it is as fitting and natural for them to be in love as for the sky to have stars, and, just as certainly, you have never seen a history in which you find a knight errant without love, for if he had none, he would not be deemed a legitimate knight, but a bastard who had entered the fortress of chivalry not through the door but over the walls, like a robber and a thief.[94]

And yet, the two parts of Don Quixote do nothing but bring this assumption into question. In fact, it was this inner contradiction (his inability to be a lover and knight) that gave the '98 critics license to complete Don Quixote's heroic profile without consideration of his amorous attachment to Dulcinea.

Arguing that a knight errant could exist without a lady, Unamuno, Azorín, Ortega, and Maeztu instead identified abstractions such as glory, beauty, and faith as substitutes for Quixote's beloved, Dulcinea. Unamuno specifically claimed that the knight would learn to love without the help or model of his lady, as it was ultimately his affection for Sancho that had taught him how to love humanity at large, "since it is in the face of your fellow companion that you love everyone else."[95] While Unamuno initially agreed that "all forms of heroism sprout out of a woman's love" and that "[t]he love of a woman has inspired the most profound ideals, the best philosophical formulations,"[96] he later warned that "caring for a woman ties up a hero's wings."[97] Ultimately, Unamuno had come to believe that Don Quixote avoided falling prey to such feminine "entrapments" (or "pregnancies" [embarazos]) precisely because he "wisely" pursued glory more than—or instead of—a beloved. At one point, Unamuno cannot avoid fusing both ideas, heroism and womanhood, into a unified abstraction, declaring that Quixote ultimately "loved the idea of Glory embodied in a woman."[98] In his Vida de Don Quijote y Sancho, then, Unamuno had cancelled out Quixote's intrinsic erotic drive replacing it with a purely chivalric inclination to be a "real" hero, the type who would allow Spain to recuperate its true dominating essence and past glory.

Salinas's view also implicitly acknowledges the absence of Dulcinea, but only to remind us how aptly Cervantes uses this void to play with and reflect on literary convention. Rather than using the lady's non-existence to elaborate on Quixote's heroic journey (as Romantic and symbolic critics had done) Salinas uses her absence to trace Cervantes's exploration of literary motifs such as Petrarchism or Neoplatonism in the "letter" episode. Following the text closely, this '27 critic allows us to discover a genealogy of this exceedingly "beautiful love letter in Spanish literature," formulating an analysis based on literary, rather than anachronistically philosophical, or nationalistic elements.

We—Salinas's readers—soon learn that the loveliness of this letter is not literal, and that it does not refer to the fictional Dulcinea or to Quixote's passionate intimations for her. Salinas pointedly notes that Quixote's amorous missive had not been inspired by Dulcinea's absence but by the arbitrary presence of another's man diary, a "libro de memorias," that the strange protagonist Cardenio had left behind. It is by reading the love poems and letters contained in this diary that Don Quixote first thinks of writing his own dispatch to Dulcinea.

After accidentally finding Cardenio's book, Quixote and Sancho glance over it trying at first to find an indication of the author's identity. What they find instead is a passionate plight that immediately stimulates Quixote's poetic and erotic imagination. As the knight glances over the pages of Cardenio's diary, he is increasingly inspired by its perfectly crafted poems, deeply imbued with courtly and Petrarchan conventions. Such conventions affect knight and squire quite differently.[99] As Don Quixote reads, and feels progressively enticed to produce a similar declaration of love, Sancho is increasingly annoyed by what (for him) seems to be nonsensical speech. Thus, after reading a sonnet cryptically dedicated to "Fili"—the generic name that many poets conventionally used to address the beloved— Sancho complains about the fact that "[f]rom this poem" they "can't learn anything" about its author or his lady.[100] Forced to agree with him, Quixote decides to look for hints about the author's persona in the more accessible prose of the love letters contained in the journal. But these accounts are not any clearer, and the knight has to reluctantly admit that from these epistles one can infer even "less ... than from the verses about the man who wrote it."[101] Everywhere Quixote and Sancho turn, they find—to Sancho's now full-fledged exasperation—the same customary "complaints, laments, suspicions, joys and sorrows."[102]

The episode cleverly identifies one of the greatest critiques against the alienating force of Petrarchism, a literary tradition that obviously dissolved the ontological specificity of its practitioners. Nobody better than Sancho to comically illustrate the extent to which this poetic paradigm had lost touch with the "real" subjects and stories it was supposed to portray than when in Chapter 25 he discovers the real identity of Dulcinea. When he understands that "Lorenzo Corchuelo's daughter, also known as Aldonza Lorenzo," is no other than "the lady of Dulcinea of Toboso," Sancho not only comprehends that this empress of la Mancha is in reality one of his own hair-on-her-chest fellow peasants but also finally grasps the extent of the delusional impasse between the idealized literary references of his master and the material realities they both have to contend with.[103]

Salinas emphasizes this impasse, calling attention to how Quixote's troubled letter brilliantly underscores the material divide of the knight's story; every corporeal detail of the knight's missive draws a starker contrast between the actual circumstances of the Manchegans and the insubstantiality of the amatory discourse that produced Dulcinea in the first place. It is by design, for example, that Quixote's love confession stand in "humiliating proximity" (proximidad humillante) to the "donkey's bond" (célula de pollinos) that the astute Sancho has forced his master to write as payment for his services. The comic textual juxtaposition cleverly advances the association between Dulcinea and the humble animal that will appear again during the "enchantment" that Sancho will cast on the lady in the second part of the novel.[104]

Through all these narrative shifts and turns, Cervantes epitomizes the clash of literary and experiential perspectives of the two main protagonists, who, as Salinas notes, are forced to engage in one of the most sincere, in-depth, and truly beautiful conversations about the use and sense of literary "[a]rtifice, verbal ostentation, and detachment from reality" in Spanish literature.[105] Sancho's "poetic" epiphany about Dulcinea's identity allows him to discern the absurdity of Quixote's quest and the impracticality of his plea for love, since there is no palace in El Toboso and no way, given

Aldonza's lack of education, that she could ever read a letter from a "knight" like Quixote—a man, in any case, whom she probably does not remember. With that discovery, the reader is invited to understand, like Sancho, that the fallacious amatory convention that Dulcinea represents fuels the delusion on which the entire edifice of chivalric heroism rests.[106] Moreover, this realization declares all heroic and erotic pursuits involved in Quixote's chivalric quest—so heavily dependent on courtly and Petrarchan ideals—to be ultimately thin as air.

Salinas brilliantly guides his readers to this grave conclusion, allowing them to recognize that, rather than the bold guidance toward individual and collective glory that the '98 critics had made it out to be, Quixote's journey constituted a deep and far-reaching critique of the "masterful" but "delusional logic" that ruled Golden Age literature. Quixote's lack of a real beloved in this absurd quest, far from indicating Cervantes's belief in the cosmic reach of love, conveyed a devastating critique of the empty amatory and heroic patterns that defined some of the most reputed literary developments of his time.

Whether conscious or not, Salinas's choice to write about this episode provides an indirect indictment of the Romantic critics and fascist writers who portrayed Quixote as a perfect chivalric hero. He demolished the idea that this literary exercise could be a glorification of any kind of imperial ambition. Salinas's Cervantine interpretation, like Aub's and Cernuda's, re-energized a particularly difficult moment of Spanish history—the 1930s and 1940s—with a refreshing dose of literary and critical apostasy. Their critiques, especially those written in the diaspora, managed to detach Cervantes from the symbolic excesses and political manipulation that had defined previous critical generations of the novel. In recovering the forgotten or overlooked dimensions of Cervantes's literary production, they ultimately sought to understand the literary prowess of the author, not the validity of their own pre-conceived opinions.

At the same time, their anti-imperial and anti-dictatorship investments guided this work, leading them to identify Cervantes's use of humor, satire, and irony in skewering the literary conventions and social imperatives that had governed his own era. Through their critical contributions, Cervantes was acknowledged as the most prominent representative of Spain's failed modernity, a modernity that countered the myth of imperial power and dominance eulogized by the Generation of '98 and refined by Francoist ideologues.

4

Anachronism as Weapon and Resistance (Quixotes Left and Right)

Every nation views its past through the prism of its present, and its present through the prism of the past.

JOHN ELLIOT[1]

In twentieth-century Spain, legislators, artists, writers, and theorists of every political inclination boldly cultivated the use of the past to define the goals of the present, apparently oblivious to the pitfalls of anachronism. At a time when thinkers and politicians including Luis Ariquistáin, Ramiro de Ledesma, Azorín, and Unamuno referenced the early modern age to justify their democratic, imperialistic, or chivalric aims, scholars such as Marcel Bataillon harshly censured this kind of widespread ahistorical extrapolation only to exhibit it in their own writing. Traditionally vilified, anachronism received such an unexpected revival in twentieth-century Spain that any study focusing on the perceptions of the Golden Age in that period must inevitably confront its ubiquitous and multi-layered presence.

While ahistorical thinking is generally considered an objectionable practice in historical inquiry, chronological congruence continues to be a delicate expectation in early modern studies. Serious scholarly pursuits in the field have often confronted the thorny question of whether the analysis of the past is determined "at least in part through the terms available by the present."[2] Indeed, much of Jacob Burckhardt's thinking on the Italian Renaissance reflects the unique circumstances of nineteenth-century Germany, where he received his academic training, just as influential views of Renaissance scholarship from the 1990s "can be made to speak of the concerns of late twentieth-century culture" given the "uncanny" similarities that some critics found between both periods.[3]

Parallels between the 1900s and the 1500s and 1600s continue to raise the question of whether it is useful or appropriate to identify such parallels at all. Such push-pull tension was particularly evident in the late 1920s and 1930s, as Bataillon was working on the composition and publication of his seminal *Erasme et l'Espagne* (1937).[4] In recognizing the continuing impact of Erasmus in the twentieth century, Bataillon became increasingly unsure of how to examine this continuity with scholarly rigor:

> *Perhaps we have the right to question* the principal reasons that urge us, Renaissance specialists, to approach Erasmus not only as the subject of careful study—still insufficiently studied—but as an author *very close to us, whose concerns are still ours* or *have become ours again*, and whose work, for all such reasons, we are moved to explore again being of *course very careful not to fall* into the sin of *anachronism.*[5]

Although Bataillon wonders if "we have the right" to read Erasmus as a modern author who shares the same concerns as Europeans of his day, the examination of this parallel would become a constant and painful preoccupation throughout his career. Aware of the impossibility of avoiding this anachronistic comparison altogether, Bataillon ended up hoping not to fall "too much" in taking this ahistorical license:

> Let's try, then, to approach Erasmus *without exaggerating* his proximity to us, remembering what makes him an exceptional representative of this sixteenth century *that we feel is so modern. If we feel close to him,* it is undoubtedly because this century left us with the problems that are relevant today, and because he faced them without being able to solve them, sometimes actually making them more acute than before.[6]

Despite his reluctance to embrace this anachronistic concern, Bataillon alludes here to emotional and empirical arguments to drop all objections—critics "feel" Erasmus's presence, and are "faced" with the same issues. Following this progression, it is hardly surprising that by the end of his career, when closing a reflection on the evolution of his approach to the subject (Erasmus) for forty years, Bataillon ends up wondering: "Wouldn't tomorrow enable us, better than today, to assess who Erasmus was, and his historical significance?"[7] Bataillon's hope that the future would find itself better equipped to understand the past encapsulates his lack of confidence in the twentieth century, which—just like Erasmus's own historical moment—seemed unable to process the enormous gifts of the humanist thinker, his defiance of authoritarian and monolithic thinking, his pleas for peace, tolerance, and the value of international cooperation, among others.[8]

Perhaps Bataillon's internal friction might have been at least partially alleviated had he been aware that other reputed French, British, American, and Spanish critics and historians were equally conflicted when grappling with the same issues of anachronism. For example, in reflecting on how the Spanish Baroque decadence that he was exploring in his books seemed to recall that of his own country at the time of writing, the British scholar John H. Elliot—someone certainly not associated with any anachronistic indulgence—noted in his compelling memoir, that "[i]t was *difficult not to see similarities between the situation of Spain in the 1620s and that of Britain in the 1950s*; an exhausted imperial power and a reforming government followed by disappointed expectations and at least the partial failure of reform. *Was my country going the way of Spain?*"[9]

A similar projection occurred on the other side of the Atlantic, as American writers and scholars, intrigued by the fourth centenary of Cervantes's birth, revisited the author's life and works, finding powerful parallels between his time and theirs. The connection seemed especially obvious in cases such as the Battle of Lepanto (1571), where the two greatest empires of the time, the Christian and Ottoman, clashed. Suggesting a strong correspondence between this scenario and the polarized landscape that had led to the Second World War, Charles B. Qualia argued in 1949 that "[Cervantes's] times bear close similarity to ours," and reflected on the early modern fight "for the freedom of Western Europe" through an obvious projection of his own time:[10] "Here's a powerful Oriental nation [the Ottoman Empire] sweeping westward, threatening Western civilization. Cervantes helped a *coalition of Western powers* to stop an Asiatic power from overrunning Western Europe."[11]

In Spain, the intimate overlap between the cultural and historical conditions of the 1500s and those in the 1900s was publicly and diversely manifested in the 1920s, 1930s, and 1940s: Republican intellectuals and politicians customarily addressed themselves as "the new Erasmists." Writers jokingly referred to each other as Golden Age characters—addressing Luis Cernuda, for example, as the antisocial glass graduate "licenciado vidriera" of Cervantes's tale, and critics regularly declared Baroque thinkers and writers such as Quevedo to be "men of their [present] time."[12] It might be little coincidence that, as Elliot reminds us, the term "early modern" was coined in the larger field during this transnational moment of anachronistic awareness, as historians of various traditions understood that, although "not medieval nor purely modern," the age of Cervantes, Shakespeare, and Erasmus "saw the coexistence of features regarded as characteristic of both epochs."[13] It seems to have taken us the rest of the twentieth century to at least begin to accept this coexistence.

By the late 1900s, the discipline of early modern studies was starting to acknowledge that anachronistic analogy had played a role in the foundations of the discipline, and that it continued to occur in its scholarship. The preoccupying question then became not only whether anachronism should be permitted, but, if it were, how to use it productively. In Golden Age studies, one of the most powerful voices addressing this difficult theoretical question was Carroll Johnson. Johnson argued that, since what attracted a good number of historians and literary critics to the early modern age was precisely the high level of historical or intellectual analogy it offered to their own time, specialists should be entitled to explore these parallels as long as they avoid doing so in a simplified or essentialized manner and instead show a clear understanding of the limits of such comparative analysis:

> *It is not only possible but quite reasonable* to characterize Cervantes as an ironic spokesman for the counterculture that was possible in his time and place. It is clear that we do violence to those specifically Hapsburg-era questions if we attempt to conflate them with the issues of here and now, and we similarly do violence to Cervantes if we ask him to address our specifically Reagan-Bush-Clinton-era problematics. Yet there is something in those Cervantine texts we keep returning to that engages us .... *What engages us are the multiple analogies between that society and its problems and ours.* Cervantes and I both live(d) in ethnically diverse societies where notions of purity and exclusivity clash with diversity and pluralism. We both inhabit societies characterized by an astounding unequal distribution of wealth and power. Our society is called upon to make choices similar to those faced by Cervantes's. *The trick with these social analogies*, I think, *is first to avoid the trap of mistaking them for identities.* (xix)

For Johnson, even strong analogies between two periods are ultimately forged in different historical conditions; thus, parallels do not imply an "identical" nature, nor do they simplistically justify essentialist claims to any kind of identity (racial, national, and so on). Similar literary trends, social processes, and political conflicts are distinctively articulated in each setting, and uniquely mediated—or interpellated, as Althusser defined that mediation process—by the different material and ontological conditions of each interpreter.[14]

Yet, by allowing historical contexts and their interpellations by present-day contexts to coexist, Johnson reconciles rigorous historicizing with ahistorical analogy.[15] And this careful, fluid historical approach may best fit the "age of transition" that the early modern period is supposed to be, an era that—as acknowledged in the 1930s by Bataillon—is characterized as a liminal space. Elliot defined this space as one where "the Medieval and the 'modern' interact in a fascinating combination,"[16] and the Cervantine critic Aubrey Bell, unusually aware of the possibilities and dangers of this polychronic combination, warned his fellow specialists not to fail to appreciate "the more generous outlook of those more spacious [and elastic] times" that for him constituted centuries such as the 1500s and the 1900s.[17]

Whereas early modern specialists today may wish to either refute or embrace such elastic chronological reasoning in their own approaches, any cultural or critical history of these decades of the twentieth-century must examine how often this spacious cultural reference of the "modern" appears to refer back to Cervantes's own.

This chapter uses the fruits of these debates on trans-chronological thinking to explore how Cervantes and the Golden Age became the targets of anachronistic cultural warfare in the 1940s. After the initial contempt that Francoist ideologues and ultra-conservative thinkers had shown for Cervantes in the 1930s, the writer's increasing repute and the 1947 celebration of the four-hundredth anniversary of his birth offered an international opportunity for national promotion that the pragmatic Francoist ideologues were unwilling to ignore. Thus, attempting to anachronistically turn Cervantes into an illustrious representative of the eternal Golden Age Spain that the Francoist regime claimed to have revived, the fascist government launched an unprecedented propagandistic campaign aimed at vindicating the author as the most celebrated representative of the inexhaustible Spanish imperialistic dream.

From abroad, progressive and left-wing exiles would forcefully oppose these fascist attempts despite the limited means at their disposal. The Cervantes that the diaspora would tirelessly work to celebrate was the humanistic author he had always been for liberal thinkers, a spokesman for the counter-hegemonic strain of Spanish thought who, like them, had been displaced from Spain starting in the sixteenth century. After 1939, and from their exiled locations, progressive thinkers identified with Cervantes perhaps more passionately than ever; their admiration translated in the creation of a wide range of new curricula, events, and special issues in honor of an ironic humanist rather than a heroic Cervantes, one that vividly undermined from within the imperial project vacuously celebrated by the Francoist "official culture."

While the progressive chorus was successful, and managed to prevent Cervantes from being tainted by a fascist patina, Spanish émigrés would once again win a major battle only to lose the bigger war. After 1948, no number of special events or publications from abroad would be enough to counterbalance the work of reputed scholars such as José Antonio Maravall, who, though reputed to be "neutral," would powerfully delegitimize the thriving humanist scholarship produced in the decade prior to 1936 and continued afterward in the diaspora. Liberal critical views that defended a dissenting, and secular, early modern past would thus be silenced by the very scholarly discourse and environment that was most clearly expected to protect these ideas. As one of the most respected figures of the academic establishment in Spain, Maravall would shape at least two enormously consequential redefinitions of the Golden Age: first, that Cervantes and his age were inherently traditional and imperial; and, second, that the academic discipline analyzing this period was as traditional and illiberal as its subjects of study. It has taken specialists from a variety of traditions several decades to contest the soundness of the research that helped to produce such a constrictive view of the period. While certain elements of Maravall's scholarship, such as his theory on Golden Age drama, have been long and thoroughly debunked, a full analysis of other distortions regarding Cervantes is still lacking. What follows, then, is an examination of the reach of Maravall's almost surgical excision of progressive thought from Cervantes's opus and criticism, aimed at exposing his impact in the dismantling of the vibrant critical legacy inherited from the 1930s.

A Contested Early Modern Paradigm: Quixotes of the Left and Right

Luis Cernuda superbly illustrated the extent to which, in the 1930s and 1940s, the understanding of the Golden Age as either an imperialistic or proto-democratic period depended on one's view of the country's present. He notes that "some want to erase any Spanish political past contrary to the Reformation, and others, with similar reasoning, want to wipe out our enlightened despotism; the former dream of a heterodox seventeenth century in our soil, and the latter of resurrecting the Inquisition in our day."[18] Here, Cernuda is perfectly aware that by identifying the Golden Age as a profoundly secular or essentially inquisitorial period, twentieth-century critics and historians aimed to build an anachronistic cultural genealogy— even a national identity—that justified their particular present-day agendas.

Perhaps this dynamic (reading the past to justify our present) is unavoidable, since, as Elliot asserts in this chapter's epigraph, every national history views its past through the prism of the present in one way or another, and vice-versa. Indeed, by identifying such projections, Elliot, like Bataillon and Cernuda before him, acknowledged the anachronistic realm of reference that had become an essential element of both an individual and national self-configuration in the 1930s and 1940s. At the same time, Elliot's formulation implicitly warns (as Johnson would later) that such anachronism provides a dangerous tool for essentializing discourses and practices.

While an anachronistic paradigm presents, as Matthew D. Stroud has noted, an "opportunity" and "obligation to review received texts in light of the shifting priorities of the contexts in which one reads them," in the 1940s context those shifting priorities had produced an abruptly altered reality.[19] After the civil war and the ensuing dictatorship, a drastic imbalance of power gave the victorious faction full dominance over the other, allowing it to carry out its commitment to erasing any dissenting views from present and past records.[20] The dangerous possibility of using anachronism to essentialize a specific identity—in the case, a national identity—became an official trademark of the Francoist government in its determination to establish specific coordinates that drastically reconfigured the country's present and past cultural histories.

Under a regime that had used the literary icon El Cid to ennoble its "courageous" and "knightly" (*valeroso* and *caballeresco*) dictator, and that had justified a military coup and civil war as "a crusade" against the inner foes of the estate, the forced assimilation of Cervantes with an imperialist agenda was anything but surprising.[21] The relatively sudden incorporation of the classic author into the Francoist orbit in the mid-1940s would be conscious, explicit, and pretty much determined by the upcoming international commemoration of his birth in 1947.[22] Wasting no time exploiting the author's heroic military past and war wounds, the first official announcement of the Organizing (Propaganda) Committee in charge of those festivities would characterize him as "*our first maimed hero*, the illustrious Cripple from Lepanto."[23] Presenting Cervantes as an illustrious representative of the "manifestly imperial" and "aristocratic" outlook characteristic of Francoist ideology, the note claimed:

> Reigning, like Cervantes, over a universal living reality means not only being a great author; it means being able to continue and maintain an Empire that not only was a simple political creation, but a work of the spirit, one that still allows us to participate in it through its immaterial existence. Cervantes is also our literary genius because he projected onto the world—better than any other writer—the Spanish nature, and its attitude towards life. Quixotism will always constitute an aristocratic contribution to the Spanish way of thinking and feeling.[24]

Cervantes's military past is here folded into an assumed intimate connection to the Spanish Empire, its "spiritual mission," and the "Spanish nature," elements that supposedly characterize the author and the "aristocratic contribution" he provided to Spanish cultural identity—to the "Spanish way of thinking and feeling."

Progressive thinkers who, from the 1920s, had been celebrating diametrically different dimensions of the Cervantine opus—modernity, humanism, and anti-imperialistic sensibility—would be quick to respond to this fascist maneuver, drawing on the author's multiple and critical commentaries on war, battle, and heroism. Thus, through the author's own words, exiled writers passionately countered the fascist co-optation of Cervantes's biography, eager to remind a transnational audience that Cervantes had gone to war because he was pressed by poverty rather than inspired by a hunger for glory. A couple of lines of casual verse from *Don Quixote* succinctly illustrates that perspective: (War calls me / and I have to go / If I had money / It wouldn't be so).[25] Thinkers like María Zambrano reminded her readership that Cervantes's biography demonstrates that the military heroism of an average citizen in the Golden Age rarely brought either honor or glory. In Cervantes's case, Zambrano writes, "his allegiance to the State translated first into the bloodshed of Lepanto, and later into the state tax that brought him jail and poverty."[26] Among the exiled community, the effort to emphasize Cervantes's criticism of warfare and detach him from the aristocratic and imperialistic mindset attributed to him by the official Francoist machinery—especially during the 1947 commemoration—became, in the words of writer and philosopher Julio Luelmo, "more important than any other accomplishment."[27]

Aiming to consolidate Cervantes's humanistic reputation, the diaspora produced new curricula at centers such as the Spanish Institute of London (1944),[28] and published a wide array of special issues of journals like *Las Españas* in Mexico (1947) (Figures 4.1 and 4.2), and the *Bulletin of Spanish Intellectuals* in Paris (1947). These efforts united an impressive group of contributors, including Benjamin Jarnés, Ernestina de Champourcin, Manuel Altolaguirre, Josep Renau, Antonio del Toro, Pedro Salinas, Concha Méndez, Sender, Pedro Bosch Campera, and Ramón Gaya, among others.

Because of the intellectual vacuum created by the exiles' absence and by the censorship of the regime, the homages of the highest quality around the quatercentenary were produced abroad, rather than on the Peninsula. Domestic volumes such as *La maiestas cesárea en el Quijote*, edited by Francisco Maldonado de Guevara in 1947, or the special issue on Cervantes published by the Royal Academy of Language (Real Academia de la Lengua Española, RAE), assembled by its president, the Falangist Jose María Pemán, and published in 1948, were coldly received abroad. As the Argentine journal *Realidad* noted with regard to the RAE's Cervantine tribute, "those who should have been first are last," as the RAE, despite being the most prestigious cultural academy in Spain, had been, in the journal's view, "outworked by everyone [else]."[29] Clearly absent from the RAE volume were "the new 'immortals'" (los nuevos "inmortales"), an ironic phrase that alluded to the international status of the critics and writers of the Generation of '27, now professors of literature abroad, who had not been invited to participate.[30]

Certainly not all commemorative events or volumes organized in Spain were as hollow as that Argentinian journal had deemed, nor as "rubbishly" mediocre as the exiled writer Juan José Domenchina characterized them.[31] As Genara Pulido Tirado reminds us, foreign critics and exiles often painted all these official events and publications with a harsh brush, criticizing them severely even before they occurred or were published.[32] In recognition of the anniversary, Spain produced an "important number of studies of widely varying character and merit,"[33] among them, a 1947 special issue of the journal *Insula,* dedicated to Cervantes, and various "novelized" editions of *Don Quixote*, such as the version written by Pemán, entitled *Don Quixote, a Compendium of Love Preceded by a Message from Dulcinea to All Other*

LAS ESPAÑAS

Revista Literaria

FIGURE 4.1 *Las Españas*. México (1946–56), Alicante: Biblioteca Virtual Miguel de Cervantes, 2001.

Women (Don Quijote, brevario de amor, precedido por un mensaje de Dulcinea del Toboso a las mujeres del mundo), published by the Falange. Yet, the majority of the events celebrated in Spain around Cervantes's four-hundredth birthday could too often fit the prediction made by José Ramón Araña and Manuel Andújar of "cycles of stuck-up lectures, organized by certain local authorities, in which lecturers would fly off on a tangent."[34]

It is fair to characterize the ceremonies organized by the Francoist Propaganda Committee as unique: The festivities were kicked off by a *Te Deum* service officiated by the Bishop Elijo Garay at the University of Alcalá on October 6, 1947, and included the visit to Don Juan's grave at El Escorial, a military exhibit on Lepanto at the National Maritime Museum, and a "most original" procession through Madrid's streets in

FIGURE 4.2 *Las Españas*. Detail. México (1946–56), Alicante: Biblioteca Virtual Miguel de Cervantes, 2001.

which ecclesiastical and military authorities, led by the *Caudillo* himself, commemorated the victory at Lepanto with a long cortege of Virgin icons, church choirs, military bands, and students.[35] When lectures were given, they highlighted Cervantes's language, and military and Christian sensibility, arguing that the "Quixotic spirit" of the author ideally "captured" the Spanish military ethos.[36] José Ibañez Martín—Minister of Education in 1947 and president of the Organizing Committee of the Cervantine anniversary—asserted in a twenty-five-page speech that did not include a single direct quote from Cervantes, the idea that the writer was a "prophet," an "austere, loyal, and unbending man," and "the ultimate representative of the universal Spaniard fired by the inextinguishable light of a faith," that in turn manifested "the militant Christian spirit of his soul."[37] The speech was pleasantly received by its audience composed by Franco himself and a select number of foreign scholars, prominent Falangists such as Pemán, government representatives, military officials, and ecclesiastic authorities— including a bishop from Argentina—who at times acted as *both* academic *and* religious representatives of various countries. To no one's surprise, there was no trace of the "new" or old "immortals"—that is, the most important Spanish intellectuals of the day.[38]

The official Francoist celebration of the Cervantine anniversary was, then, fitting for and consistent with a military dictatorship. Overall, it is hard to compare the quantity and quality of the commemorative efforts inside and outside Spain's borders. Despite the much more humble vehicles at its disposal (publications with limited funds, smaller research and cultural centers, less prestigious academic platforms), the diaspora managed to celebrate a humanistic view of Cervantes almost completely absent in Madrid, one that highlighted the author's critical reflections on knightly (military) ideals such as honor, duty, and self dignity. Rather than a glorification of violence and warfare, *Don Quixote* emerged in the diaspora as an illustration of the fallacy of these ideals. True honor and nobility stem from the novel's axiom that "each man is the son of his own deeds" rather than from the moral vacuum characteristic of the supposedly gallant aristocracy. Self-dignity appears to be associated with the humble but more sincere lower classes—an idea constantly celebrated by Republican thinkers—in figures such as Sancho or the goat-keepers.[39] Spanish exiles thus celebrated the social and political criticism implicit in Cervantes's works, which were for many the "deepest, and most comprehensive" of all Spanish literature.[40]

As the front cover of the special issue of *Las Españas* illustrates (Figures 4.1 and 4.2), in this anniversary year, Cervantes was also anachronistically commemorated abroad as an author who "[kept] standing up to the fight, charging against the Francoist system that [kept] vomiting its hatred" against him and all the values underlying his humanist vision.[41] Exiled scholars also merged author and character—Cervantes and Don Quixote—as they identified both with an explicit resistance to the Golden Age imperial orthodoxy that the Francoist regime was trying to reenact:

> Cervantes thought of his country, of Spain's decadence, of his duties as a writer. According to him, the duty of an intellectual—of one gifted with the ability to think critically and analyze the situation, one with the ability to write—must be to deconstruct all false ideas … Cervantes reminds us that all the wars fought in the 1600s that stem from the Middle Ages and were amplified in the Renaissance had been manufactured by European intelligentsia. They fed from [an imperial] past that had been glorious, but attempting to imitate such a past in the present only results in caricature. In religion, in arms and letters, Cervantes found a ridiculous parody of previous centuries. The time of crusades had passed; Castilian knights were living anachronisms.[42]

Anachronism, though an essential part of *Don Quixote*'s cultural critique, was read in the diaspora as a true caricature of the Holy Roman imperial past that had been already forcibly recuperated by Charles V, and that now—even more ridiculously—was being invoked again by the Francoist "crusade." While the conjuration of an "imperial" and proudly ahistorical "maiestas" (majesty) helped Franco develop a powerful persona on Spanish soil, exiles beyond Spanish borders characterized this anachronistic portrayal as little more than an "uncomfortable specter from the past."[43] Ironically, while literary critics of all eras have often agreed that *Don Quixote* conveys the message that "[a] life of anachronism is madness," the same ahistorical illusion, systematically incorporated into state ideology in the 1900s, translated into one of the longest dictatorships of the country's history.[44]

Thus, anachronism seemed as inescapable in mid-twentieth-century Spanish political affairs as it was in Cervantes's seventeenth-century novel. The international commemoration of the author's birth would unite the political and literary spheres of both centuries, as left- and right-wing thinkers, ideologues, and supporters invoked Cervantes and *Don Quixote* to cement or refute the political fabrications of the Francoist regime. The "constant exercise of re-reading and re-writing" (un ejercicio de relectura y reescritura constante) at the heart of *Don Quixote* would extend to its politicized readers and commentators of the novel in 1947, eager to strain their own ideological priorities through the porous fabric of Cervantes's fiction.[45]

Historicizing Anachronism: The Reinvention of a Cultural Tradition

The Cervantine anniversary exposed how differentiated, even antithetical, the regard for Cervantes was on both sides of the Atlantic. In 1947, Sender provided a reason for this difference, arguing that the values that the diaspora celebrated more enthusiastically in the author, modernity and humanism, could not be understood by fascist or Falangist theorists, who were largely ignorant about the cultural period that produced them:

> With Cervantes, Spanish fascists have shown that they need to negate the spirit of the Renaissance and go back to the Middle Ages to take shelter from the advances of a civilization that surpasses them in every way. These fascists believe that in negating *Quixote*, they can negate the entire Renaissance, but in going back to the Middle Ages they make a gross mistake, because it is in these fertile [medieval] liberties that Renaissance humanism was born and from which *Don Quixote* ultimately comes. In this, like in so many other things, fascists got it all wrong.[46]

Sender's compelling proposition was not completely true. Some deeply knowledgeable fascist critics, such as Giménez Caballero, did understand that *Don Quixote* entailed not only "an illustration of Spanish decadence" but also "a subtle yet *insidious* compilation of reformist religious ideas, relativist thought, and bourgeois logic that threatened a zealously Baroque Spain with European rationalism."[47] In the case of Giménez Caballero—as seen in previous chapters—it was precisely his understanding of Cervantes's opposition to orthodoxy that moved him to censure the writer and *Don Quixote* so harshly and irrevocably.

Some progressive thinkers lamented that there had not been enough of pushback against such fascist attacks on Cervantes in the 1930s and 1940s. Luelmo complained that it was "the lack of critical studies able to locate Cervantes in his historical context [that] allowed mechanisms very close to those used by the Counter-Reformation to produce another manipulated vision of our history."[48] After all, as other exiles also pointed out, "Giménez Caballero and Fascist 'intellectuals'" had gone where "the [Spanish] of the 1600s Inquisition had not" in their hatred of Cervantes: "They would burn him at the stake if they could for Erasmist and liberal," claimed an editorial in 1947, noting that "the only crime" of the writer "had been his profound humanity, a humanist sensibility that even preceded, and perhaps foresaw, Renaissance humanism."[49] The emotional charge of such anachronistic arguments is indicative of how significant Cervantes's humanism had become for both champions and critics of the writer.

It was within this highly confrontational critical context that Maravall, a rising star of Spanish historiography, published his famous *Humanismo de las armas en Don Quijote* in 1948. The stakes could not have been higher, since the antithetical, ideological understandings of Cervantes and the Spanish Golden Age—that ultra-conservative and progressive, the Christian and secular—sought more fervently than ever to undermine and invalidate one another. As a young but clearly promising historian, Maravall could have offered the contextualized political reading of Cervantes so emphatically demanded by many of his exiled counterparts. But instead of providing historically sound criticism, bringing to Spanish soil the humanist thesis born abroad, Maravall did quite the opposite. Ignoring the association of Cervantes with the modern and proto-democratic spirit of the *comuneros* (constantly invoked by progressive thinkers and critics), Maravall identified the writer, instead, with the most significant representative of the "victorious" Spanish empire, Charles V. Above all, his *Humanismo de las armas en Don Quijote* provided official Spain what it had been demanding since the days of Giménez Caballero anti-Cervantine invectives: a total refutation of Cervantes's Erasmism and humanism, the intellectual and cultural orientation so enthusiastically celebrated by liberal critics and thinkers since the mid-1920s.[50]

While, at first, Maravall declares his book a "*historical* interpretation" of Cervantes's "brilliant" novel, his study is far from even a minimally neutral or accurate historical contextualization of *Don Quixote*.[51] Maravall's monograph focuses on *one* major historical event supposedly pivotal for the understanding of Cervantes's life and literary production: the "arrival of the emperor Charles V" in Spain in 1516—an advent that he believed coincided with the "peak popularity of chivalric fiction among us [Spaniards]."[52] Maravall considers chivalric novels a straightforward manifestation of the "hard and brilliant heroism" that writers such as Cervantes supposedly "saw disappearing from their society."[53] For Maravall, rather than presenting an ironic rebuttal of a literary genre—chivalric fiction—*Don Quixote* reveals Cervantes's nostalgic "loud and bitter complaint" about the constraints on the heroic world in Spain during his time.[54]

This was not the first time that Maravall infused culture with political bias in his account of literary and historical developments. One of his most famous theories, the idea of a "cultura dirigida" ("guided culture," or propaganda model) considered Golden Age dramas as literal depictions—rather than mediations or contestations—of the will of the absolutist state. The thesis was soon widely censored by Golden Age scholars, precisely for assuming that *comedia* functioned as "little more than a well-oiled propaganda machine designed to produce and disseminate the ideology of the ruling elites," an assumption that of course ignores "the complicated functioning of the public *corral* and seriously understates the potential for multiple, even contestatory, responses to the performance text itself."[55] In Maravall's understanding of it, Golden Age theater was reduced to be a mere illustration or subservient tool of the political interests of a ruling oligarchy.

A similar objection could be raised about his reading of Cervantes's work, since his interpretation of *Don Quixote* as a nostalgic tribute to Charles V implies the author's (Cervantes's) straightforward support of Habsburg's imperial interests and values.[56] To Maravall, Quixote's continued allusions to the "emperor" are not to be understood ironically or critically, but as proof of Cervantes's sincere admiration for Charles V.[57] The historian claims that in contrast to Cervantes's view of Charles's son, Philip II (whom Maravall incorrectly declares that Cervantes mentions only once in his oeuvre), "Cervantes praises constantly the happiest eternal memory of the *invincible* Charles V."[58] This admiration is supposedly imprinted in Cervantes's configuration of Don Quixote, given the similarities that Maravall finds between Charles V and the Manchegan knight; they both "seek adventures," for example, in the hope of achieving a "glorious and lasting fame" (*busca la aventura "sólo por alcanzar la gloriosa fama y duradera*),[59] and fame in both figures does not equate vanity, but rather the "virtue and reputation" that result from the constant battle with inner and outer enemies.[60] By declaring the emperor and Manchegan knight as fighters of a higher cause, Maravall ends up characterizing them as late reconfigurations of the *Miles Christi* ideal. The move supposedly implies Cervantes's return to the archetypical, chivalric world of late medieval romance in order to embrace the Christian values that had inspired the emperor.[61]

This messianic view of Charles V underlies Maravall's understanding of empire, since, according to him, Charles V had not "imposed" but "inspired" (*hecho brotar*) his political ambitions onto his new subjects in Spain. Far from being met with the violent opposition of popular insurrections like the *comuneros* (which Maravall doesn't mention), Charles's imperial agenda had been "accepted" and even "embraced" with enthusiasm by Spanish citizens.[62] While the force and violence of empire were antithetical to humanism—as seen in Erasmus—Maravall claims that Charles's imperial aims were what characterized "the dream of humanists like Lope de Soria or Alonso Valdés. And this is, *in a way, in my view, Cervantes's own dream*."[63] An imperialistic and zealous worldview, in other words, was the aspiration—"the dream"—of the most prominent Erasmist humanists such as Alonso Valdés, and Cervantes himself. It was, then, Charles's will power what according to Maravall "Cervantes feels so close to."[64]

A "historical" interpretation of *Don Quixote* in which the "triumphant" figure of Charles V and the countless "moral victories" (*victorias morales*) of his rule are celebrated, aligns itself with the view of the early modern period fabricated by the fascist establishment: the idea that the Golden Age was an era of endless conquering campaigns in "service of Christianity." Maravall's definition of this Spanish Holy empire, in fact, could have been taken from a Francoist propaganda manual:

> The traditional institution of the [Holy Roman] Empire, which *carries a religious and moral mission* from its distant beginnings under Charlemagne, and is intimately connected to the church, has been charged by the *generations [of Spaniards] that fell under a Spanish government bearing the same title of Holy Empire to carry out the enhancement and purification of Christian life. [In Spain] the union with the [Holy Roman] Empire and, with it, the hope for a higher temporal jurisdiction of Christianity* ends soon; but it is not for that reason that the hope for or intimate belief in that extraordinary aim [of that empire] is uprooted [from Spanish soil]. In the midst of a social environment alien to it [i.e., the Holy Empire], Cervantes with *Don Quixote heroically fights for its survival or restoration*.[65]

The empire that Maravall describes here incorporates—and makes Cervantes and Don Quixote part of—some of the most unmistakable elements of the Francoist rhetoric and "mission": a "purification" of the country (that here can ambiguously echo inquisitorial policies and the Francoist campaigns of murder and retaliation that took place after the Civil War), the return to a "higher order of Christianity" (that in both cases justified such violence), and the forced "unification" of disparate territories (that here can allude to the assimilation of Hapsburg territories or to the Francoist suppression of all the diverse identities on Spanish soil) to name just a few.[66] In just one paragraph, Maravall groups some of the most central Francoist tenets affirming that the popular aspiration to become a "Holy Empire" again "was deeply rooted" in Spanish popular will, while ignoring explicit acts of resistance such as the Castilian *Comuneros*' revolt which had been endlessly celebrated by the Republic. By turning exclusively to Charles V, and by making him a glorious representative of the empire supposedly missed and nostalgically emulated by Cervantes and Don Quixote, Maravall turns both author and character into "heroic fighters" by which he means subservient defenders and sustainers of this authoritarian system.[67]

This simplistic and messianic portrayal of the emperor so artificially associated with Cervantes ignores almost every known historical and literary fact about the Habsburg's complicated relationship with the papacy, and the reception of chivalric ideals (and fiction) among Christian moralists.[68] Maravall's study obviously dismisses the overwhelming opposition that chivalric romance faced from Golden Age theorists such as Antonio de Guevara, Alonso de Fuentes, Menchor Cano, Juan Luis Vives, and Juan Valdés, among others, who considered it "indecorous, badly written, and full of lies."[69] Serious early modern historians despised chivalric fiction as well, fearing its corrupting effect on their discipline. In 1552, Diego Gracián complained that chivalric novels "discredited good, truthful historiographies" since they "undermined the credit of the real deeds told in those factual accounts."[70] None of these facts were of concern to a supposedly meticulous historian such as Maravall. To him, Cervantes simply "fell in love with this late [medieval] world," a world that in his view entailed a "heroic and Christian ideal ... that sustained the medieval idea of the empire whose last [historical] representative was Charles V."[71]

The Humanist Debacle

Maravall's sweeping reinscription of Cervantes as a pro-imperial and traditional writer offers a strong contrast to the Erasmist Cervantism that, as we have seen, had been widely disseminated two decades earlier by historians and critics such as Bataillon and Castro. Their research had established how, directly following Erasmus or not, Cervantes's combination of humor and criticism used the Erasmist weapons of irony and moral reproval to undermine, among other issues, the hegemonic and messianic programs of his day.[72]

Maravall's work helped dismantle the Erasmist critical culture built around Cervantes by not only providing the alternate reading of *Don Quixote* summarized above, but also calling into question the historical accuracy of Castro's and Bataillon's humanist approach. Claiming that this approach was based on a defective understanding of Erasmism, Maravall argues that "[e]ither in its Spanish version, or in its original source, Erasmus and that movement [Erasmism] requires today a sweeping re-evaluation and correction of the meaning that has been attributed to it."[73] The historian, furthermore, attributes "the source of this interpretative error" to an "insufficient understanding of the Renaissance" in Spain, a Renaissance that, according to him (Maravall), had actually maintained uninterrupted the conservative mindset of the Middle Ages.[74]

While progressive critics of the 1920s and early 1930s had considered "Cervantes's thought" a "precedent to the world of ideas of Galileo's physics," and thus representative of a modern, secular paradigm, Maravall insisted that this assumption was historically flawed.[75] To him, the Cervantine outlook was traditional and conservative: "The truth of the matter is that not only Cervantes, but the entire literature of the period—even those believed to have founded a new scientific method—have a traditional character."[76] Astoundingly, Maravall goes on to dismiss the entire Erasmist cultural and critical legacy in just a few pages, arguing that "Bataillon just thinks that everything is Erasmism," and that, in reality, what Bataillon refers to as "Erasmism" is nothing different from some form of traditional "reformism" that Maravall argued already defined Spain under Charles V.[77]

Ultimately, rather than considering the relevance of Erasmus's influence to Cervantes or his era per se, Maravall constantly downplays the transcendence of Erasmism altogether (especially in Spain) arguing that "[t]he Erasmist trend is not even worth noting in this context."[78] Other times, he blames the presumed importance of the reformist on Bataillon's obsession with the topic:

> Bataillon got carried away with the subject, *seeing Erasmism on everything he touched*, and that this is why the French critic interpreted the Manchegan knight as part of this trend, failing to note that [he, Don Quixote] is a supreme and definitive expression of *the moral humanistic* trend that had been rooted in Spain before Erasmus, and that *was completely different from any heterodox inclination,* as he [Bataillon] keeps on claiming, not always successfully.[79]

Maravall discredits Bataillon's thesis here without offering any proof against it other than his self-authorizing judgment. While claiming that what existed in Spain was a sort of moral "orthodox humanism" rather than Erasmism, he fails to define such humanism in its own terms or in relation to Erasmus. Similarly, he fails to provide the reasons why this orthodox humanism "had been rooted" in Spain "before Erasmus." Following these unsubstantiated and categorical arguments, Maravall simply moves on to his next item, Don Quixote's relationship with rural environments, considering the entire Erasmist question settled (he starts the next paragraph with a "Now, with regard to the vision of rural life").[80]

Whenever he can, Maravall dismisses the idea of Erasmism, substituting for it another form of Christian, "moral," and non-threatening humanism or reformism, which according to him was fully aligned with a Christian and imperial orthodoxy. With this view, he refutes not only Bataillon's thesis but also Castro's idea of humanism as predicated in *El pensamiento de Cervantes*. The latter obviously constitutes, in Maravall's opinion, another futile scholarly exercise that had also unsuccessfully tried to assert the presence of a secular humanism in Spain.

Maravall dismisses that groundbreaking study in another demolishing conclusion: "Castro tried to reconstruct Cervantes's thought. Cervantes and Erasmus appear in this interpretation aligned with the idea of the Renaissance sketched by Burckhardt. Anything that does not fit this [Burckhardt's description] and denotes an idea outside this pattern is considered [by Castro] a hypocritical concession."[81] Ironically, even the accomplishment that Giménez Caballero recognized in Castros's study—Castro's success in giving Cervantes a distinct intellectual perspective and worldview—is here questioned by Maravall.[82] The historian implacably concludes that Castro had "tried" to provide a humanist, intellectual portrait of Cervantes but had clearly failed to do so.

Once again, for being so categorically conclusive Maravall remains perplexingly diffuse in his arguments: What was exactly Burckhardt's idea of the Renaissance that Castro was supposed to have subscribed to? What are the elements that, according to Maravall, did not fit Burckhardt's paradigm? As Ruth MacKay has argued, Maravall not only "offers little historical and virtual no documentary evidence beyond the use of normative treatises, the occasional nuggets from Cortes minutes, and secondary sources," but also teaches his reader somehow, to accept "this incomplete linkage," and "to learn to live in the gap."[83] Is Castro's idea of Cervantine hypocrisy (soon amended by Castro himself) as simple and straightforward as Maravall asserts here? Of course not. As seen, Castro had indeed characterized Cervantes's subtle critique of dogmatism as an act of "hypocrisy" before he understood it as an existential necessity given Cervantes's precarious social status.[84]

A number of critics have reflected on the evolution of Castro's thought on this particular "hypocritical" question.[85] Specialists as disparate as EC Riley, Alban Forcione, Carlos Fuentes, Frederick de Armas, Adrienne Martin, and Stephen Boyd—to name just a few—agree that Castro's rethinking of his position, that is, hypocrisy, is not as relevant as his understanding of Cervantes's ambiguity.[86] Whatever Cervantes's intention behind it, what is most noteworthy about the ambiguity of his writing is that it allows him to detach this work from the religious and imperial expectations of the Habsburg rule.[87] Castro's criticism, remarks Fuentes, allows us to recover the opus

of a writer deeply enmeshed in an extraordinary cultural battlefield where he provides an unmatched critical vision intended to save the best of Spain from the worst of the country, by rescuing the liberating medieval past and the promise of the Renaissance from their common dangers. Cervantes's critical awareness is expressed through his fiction, as he structures criticism as a plurality of possible readings, not in the simplistic terms of naivete or hypocrisy; this is how Cervantes contests the monolithic, severed, self-contained, dogmatic Spain that results from the defeat of the *Comunero* rebellion, and from the Council of Trent.[88]

Fuentes, in other words, asserts a view of Cervantes and his age that is diametrically opposed to Maravall's and more firmly and historically contextualized in terms of the two major developments, the *Comuneros* revolt and Council of Trent, that defined the twentieth-century historiography of the Golden Age.

It is worth noting that Maravall even denied any kind of political awareness in Cervantes, an idea that of course neutralizes any counter-hegemonic intention of the author. However, Maravall contradicts his own energic assertion that "there is *absolutely no justification* for subjecting the beauty of a literary work *to the torture* of a *historical analysis* with only the purpose of extracting a *minuscule* political statement *of no value or relevance*"[89] only a few pages later, when he notes that "in a political sense, [*Don Quixote*] exhibits one contemporary position: a Spanish patriotism. He [Cervantes] has internalized this feeling deeply, especially as it pertains to the *unity* of Spain."[90] In this startlingly inconsistent approach, Maravall dismisses the value of applying a "historical approach" to the novel when that process can uncover counter-hegemonic positions, while giving free rein to ambiguous or anachronistic statements that can read "patriotism" into Cervantes through contemporary arguments such as the Francoist mandate for a "unified" Spain.

Maravall elaborates both ideas (Cervantes's "patriotic sensibility" and his support for Spain's "unity") through a no-less-troubling comparison with other Golden Age figures, such as Fray Luis de León, an author better regarded than Cervantes by Francoists's ideologues. Maravall argues:

> The homeland [patria] for Cervantes, just like for him [Fray Luis], will be a whole, unique Spain. Cervantes's characters, for example in *Persiles*, are Spaniards, *and their fervent desire*—like the captive in Don Quixote—*is to go back to Spain*. His praise for everything Spanish and his defense of a literary humanism in the Spanish language are well known. *He admires and is deeply proud of the power of Spanish kings and he loudly sings, exalts, and defends their undertakings.*[91]

Specialists and good readers of Cervantes know how mistaken the statement is; most of the protagonists of *Persiles* are "Barbarians," not Spaniards, inhabitants of a series of real or imagined Northern European islands; "their fervent desire" is reaching Italy (Rome), not Spain, and their journey toward the Mediterranean moreover suggests a careful inversion of the assumed attributions of these Barbarians—often modelled after Amerindians—who generally exhibit more morality, empathy, and civility than Italians and Spaniards.[92] Cervantists like Diana de Armas Wilson, Isabel Lozano-Renieblas, Michael Armstrong-Roche, Bill Childers, Rachel Schmidt, Mercedes Alcalá Galán, David Boruchoff, Marina Brownlee, and Christina Lee, among others, have generously explored the minor patriotic dynamics in the novel.[93]

After reading Maravall's study, it was easy to assume that in 1948, long gone were the days where critics such as Max Aub asserted that "criticism of any kind, moral, literary, or social, is the last thing to be absent in *Don Quixote*."[94] Yet Aub had published these words only one year earlier, in 1947. It was precisely Cervantes's critical awareness and his condemnation of orthodoxy and imperialism that would make him an appealing author beyond Spanish borders, as we will see in the next chapter.

In Spain, however, Maravall's disparaging and self-authorizing judgments about the "erroneous" understanding of Renaissance and Erasmism of progressive critics legitimized once again the most traditional interpretations of *Don Quixote*. The historian's heavy attacks on the historical accuracy of those humanistic theses rely, however, on a hazy logic and incomplete readings, given how carefully he picks over literary texts and chronicled records while ignoring events that could cloud his belief in the "deeply rooted [Spaniards'] desire" for a Holy empire.[95] Through this reformulation of Spain's entire historical and literary tradition, Maravall firmly aligns his conclusion that both Cervantes and his age were inherently traditional and imperial with the fabricated version of the period propagated by the Francoist ideologues who roamed freely in official Spain.

A Compromised Legacy

Maravall's oversimplified understanding of literature is usually attributed to deficient literary analysis, rather than to conscious ideological bias. However, as Aurora Hermida Ruiz has shown, it is hard to separate the two when the resulting distorted interpretations have the same, recurrent target—in this case, the vibrant humanist, Erasmist criticism forged in the 1920s and 1930s—and benefit only one side of the ideological spectrum— the (ultra)conservative.[96]

One of the reasons for Maravall's great impact on the field was the recognition that his work initially received abroad from American scholars that identified him as one of the most remarkable Spanish historians of his generation. A recurrent assumption was that "[i]n the decades immediately following the Spanish Civil War, the question of the Renaissance, *which had never attracted much scholarly attention even before the war*, almost completely disappeared from consideration in Spanish historical thought."[97] Hermida Ruiz has remarked on how much did this kind of view contribute to build the perception that Maravall's dedication to the Golden Age in the war's aftermath was deeply praiseworthy, especially "considering the isolation in which Spanish historians were working during the decades of the 1940s and 1950s."[98] The myth that there was very little scholarship on the early modern period before the war paved the way for Maravall to be seen as a lone, and therefore pivotal, voice in the field.

As shown in earlier chapters, the assumed Spanish disregard for the study of humanism, Erasmism, and Renaissance studies before and after the war is inaccurate. Scholars such as Hermida Ruiz and Mainer have reminded us of the immense labor of Castro and the *Centro de Estudios Históricos* in the years preceding the Civil War, and I have underscored the wealth and depth of the critical contributions that the rich Spanish culture of those decades produced, even outside of institutions such as the *Centro*. Neither Castro, Bataillon, nor all the other collaborators of the *Centro* (with their many contributions to the debate) operated in a vacuum; rather, they were surrounded by numerous philosophers, literary critics, artists, and politicians who worked both within and beyond official cultural channels and institutions.[99] The cultural panorama that emerged from this constellation of players contradicts assessments that have become traditional in the field—that is, that conservative scholarship on Cervantes such as Maravall's was accurate, significant, and abundant, while progressive scholarship, mainly limited to Castro, was plagued with errors and excessively ideological. Indeed, as Hermida Ruiz argues, scholars such as di Camillo were remarkably sensitive to only one ideological bias, the "obsessively counter-Francoist" mindset of critics such as Castro, "while remaining completely silent about Maravall's obvious sympathies with the dictatorial regime."[100]

As this chapter has shown, Maravall's bias is clear in his work, especially in early but crucial studies like the *Humanismo en las armas de* Don Quijote. His astounding audacity in neutralizing the differences between terms and ideas as incompatible as imperialism and Erasmism, in ignoring meaningful textual elements such as Cervantes's political awareness, or negating historical truths or events such as the *comunero*'s revolt, allowed him in short to repackage an entire school of literary criticism—Cervantism—molding it into the image of the dictatorship's agenda.

It is hardly surprising, then, that only at the end of the dictatorship, in the late 1970s, did Maravall express any interest in revising the conclusions of his 1948 study, in *Utopia and Counterutopia of "Don Quixote"* (1976). In that study, the historian claims that his interest in the topic—utopian nostalgia—was already present, although not fully developed, in the 1948 version: "I published *El humanisno en las armas en 'Don Quijote'* [*sic*] in 1948 as an effort to comprehend the novel by seeing in it a utopian construction which was a culmination of that aspect of sixteenth-century ideology."[101] Maravall's evolved views, though not as bluntly Catholic or imperial as those in his earlier analysis of the novel, still reduce Cervantes's political awareness to a mere "nostalgia" for what Maravall now frames as an ideologically neutral "utopia" rather than as an empire.

In the opinion of Hermida Ruiz, Maravall's *Utopia and Counterutopia* issued a "secret palinode," an understated political apology common among fascist supporters transitioning into Spanish democracy in the mid-1970s.[102] For her, Maravall attempted to correct in this book some of the most concerning conclusions from his 1948 tome, mainly the assumption that Don Quixote's embodiment of a traditionalist order, the empire, implied Cervantes's full support of that system. Cervantes's assumed resistance to modernity is, as Hermida Ruiz points out, presented by Maravall as a "proof of a very Spanish virtue."[103] In *Utopia and Counterutopia,* the utopic view of empire that supposedly nurtured the "destiny of the nation" is transformed into "an irrational, escapist, and archaic [vision], so absurd and demented that is unavoidably doomed."[104] Cervantes's novel constitutes a "counterutopia" precisely because it discredits these irrational, escapist, and archaic ambitions or delusions.

Agreeing with Hermida Ruiz, we can also point out a few key elements of Maravall's extreme ideological makeover. First, his astonishing retraction of his idea of the empire as a project or call for national destiny. If, in the *Humanismo,* Charles V had simply "inspired" the imperial ardor of the Spanish spirit "peacefully"—remaining silent about rebellions like the *comuneros*—in *Counterutopia,* the historian argues that "Charles V, *forcing* Castilians to employ all their energy as a secondary instrument in a policy *foreign* to their interests, *imposed* a change of direction in government *which paralyzed* the country and quickly provoked signs of economic and social crisis, thus *extinguishing those expansive* and reformist sentiments that had inspired *Renaissance Castille.*"[105] There is therefore now a Renaissance Castille and a proto-democratic Castilian government at odds with a foreign, imperial imposition. It is this Castilian repression that sets off the social and economic crises in Spain.

Rather than claiming that Cervantes *"admires and is deeply proud of the power of Spanish kings and he loudly sings, exalts, and defends their undertakings,"* Maravall now argues that "He admires and takes pride in the power of the kings of Spain, and there is no reason to doubt his sincerity when *on occasion* he celebrates and defends their enterprises."[106] The difference in tone and substance between these quotes reflects the care with which Maravall operates when updating his view of Cervantes and *Don Quixote* to the new realities of the 1970s.

Also relevant is his view of Bataillon. Rather than being brushed off as an irrelevant scholar simply obsessed with Erasmus, the French critic is cited throughout the book as "the authority" who confirmed Maravall's ideas on humanism. Bataillon is furthermore acknowledged in the *Prologue* as a "respected and most knowledgeable friend" whose main thesis—that is, Erasmism in Spain—Maravall had supported in his 1948 study: Bataillon's idea of "*Don Quixote* as a 'preacher of peace' ([is] *an idea to which I subscribe totally* and which is amply expanded in Chapter 5)."[107] Maravall is thus not fully retracting his 1948 views, but only "expanding" them.

Finally, there is now no doubt that *Don Quixote* had a political dimension. This time "the political world that Cervantes constructs" in the novel "does not represent the hope of a medieval restoration so much as a rejection of the modern state."[108] Maravall continues to identify modernity not as a force of progress but as the authoritarian drive that shapes the hegemonic, powerful state (an idea consistent with Michel Foucault's sweeping view of modernity).[109] "In the sixteenth century," the historian contends, modern ideas "were 'exactly the opposite' of innovation and equality, and that is why Cervantes symbolizes a current opinion resistant to such a *serious innovation,* and it is precisely the modern state that Don Quixote in effect rejects. He is totally opposed to new political forms that in his view have destroyed religion, peace, happiness, and justice among people" (Maravall, *Utopia and Counterutopia* 158).

At times, it seems that Maravall has been able to redefine all the elements of his analysis—modernity, state, empire, innovation, proto-democratic drive, humanism—in a way that convincingly aligns his study with the historical context of the late 1970s. But this is not always the case. His titanic effort to demonstrate that modernity equaled oppression, and the medieval, traditional spirit that he now lauds is not the imperial and dogmatic idea that he praised in 1948 often results in confusing and incoherent statements:

> What had been achieved in humanism, along the lines of restoration or restitution, however, was simply an adaption of beliefs that were really traditional in nature and were now articulated differently and supported by a new or partly new attitude. The end result was thus something that was not medieval, because it was combined with previously nonexistent ingredients that had nothing to do with the development of the modern spirit, either. It seems more an effort to force developments through a different channel, one closer to medieval ideas.[110]

What were the "traditional elements" that this humanism was articulating, and which "new or partially new attitudes" was it rejecting?[111] It seems that some of the rhetorical traits that Maravall had utilized so well before—his ability to audaciously merge contradictory elements through half-finished sentences, for example—now work against him.[112] It is fair to say that given all the omissions in his argument—the gaps Mackay had referred to— readers may never know what Maravall really thought about these issues. What it is clear, however, as Diana de Armas has brilliantly illustrated, is that

Maravall's view of the Cervantine utopia is troublingly "self-referential" and "peninsular," since it fails to consider any of the obvious cross-cultural and transatlantic utopic elements of the story characteristic of the American chronicles of conquest—*Crónicas de Indias*—that are irreverently parodied in the novel.[113] In her scrupulous study of the Ínsula episode, de Armas traces the cervantine colonial satire to the unglorious testimonies of those unhappy conquistadors-turned governors who, like Sancho, bitterly complained about hunger, insolvency, and the constant humiliation they received from their subjects.[114]

Maravall's *Utopia and Counterutopia* still denies, then—albeit in a sophisticated manner more in line with the new, democratic winds blowing at the time in the country—Cervantes's own critical awareness. To Maravall, the novel ultimately depicts a maladjusted protagonist who rejects the negative developments of the new age, the 1600s, being too attached to the old fantasies—utopias—of the past.[115] Lost again in this assessment are Cervantes's penetrating and parodic commentary and criticism of his age.[116]

Despite the care with which Maravall operates, the main thesis of his *Utopia and Counterutopia* continues to be intrinsically flawed, confusing, and unconvincing. As Myriam Yvonne Jehenson and Peter Dunn remind us, "[g]iven the authors's [Cervantes's] delicious irony, as well as the polyvalent voice of the text's [*Don Quixote*] utopian discourse, unequivocal answers of any kind," such as Maravall's, "are neither possible nor desirable."[117] By playing the utopian escapist card, Maravall delegitimizes not only Cervantes's irony, but also—once again—the many dissident, multidisciplinary, and attentively political readings of Cervantes by progressive critics, including those in the Spanish diaspora who continue to be largely ignored in his study.

Maravall's contribution to the eradication of the progressive, critical legacy of the 1930s and 1940s has had enormous consequences for perceptions of early modern Spain. In 2001, Hermida Ruiz rhetorically asked what would have happened to the Cervantine critical tradition "if" Cervantes, "instead of being a progressive and liberal spirit, were in reality a nostalgic supporter of Charles V's, the empire and his Christian crusade[?]"[118] Maravall, and the development of a critical life that continued to exclude the progressive perspective, clearly provided the answer. As progressive ideas about the Spanish Renaissance—just as the Regime intended—were muffled, the Golden Age came to be associated in Spanish, Anglo, and American academic spheres with orthodoxy and traditionalism.

Such labels could hardly apply to Golden Age studies, a discipline fully immersed in human ecologies, multicultural approaches, and intersectional frameworks. Blunt manipulations or simplifications such as Maravall's, on central questions such as ahistorical analogy and political thinking, are now either unthinkable or unlikely to result on a lasting influence. However, the reinvention of this field at both sides of the Atlantic over the last forty years, apart from Castro, has yet to reconnect with the earlier innovative explorations of Cervantes and the Golden Age examined in this monograph. Overlooking this critical legacy became almost automatic, thanks in great part to the erudite "corrections" of scholars like Maravall. Most progressive thinkers were well aware of this fact. While this sobering realization could have plunged them deeper into angst and despair, their defiant attachment to Cervantes's humanism would become one of their best coping strategies for riding out the unfavorable storms of exile.

5

Post Tenebras Spero Lucem: Attempts at Counter-Colonial Modernity in Exile

Out there, in that ungodly world, torn and bitter, wanders
a pilgrim Spain damned with all the curses of exile over its head.
God took the peace from those men, as he would from a cursed
caste, but not their intelligence, which they have kept awake
and honed by the pain.
GONZALO TORRENTE BALLESTER[1]

It was hardly divine intervention that took away the peace (and homeland) of the progressive Republican men and women who found themselves thrown into exile after 1939.[2] After the shock of defeat, and in their new destinies and destinations, Republicans émigrés gradually came to terms with the reality of their new condition. Vindicating an entire historical and cultural tradition that had been artificially severed from their country, writers such as Sender, Daniel Tapia, and Julio Luelmo declared in 1947 that, like them, *Don Quixote* had become "an exiled book," one whose "broad and diverse culture" was irreconcilable with "the empire of the fascist Spain" that had expelled them.[3] In a perverse parallel, the biblical axiom "Post tenebras spero lucem" (In darkness, I await the light) (*Job* 17:12), which appears in the *ex-libris* of *Don Quixote*'s title page (Figures 5.1 and 5.2), could be considered a fitting motto for the "dark days of waiting" that from 1939 defined the Spanish diaspora.[4]

Cervantes also places that axiom in Don Quixote's mouth as he airs his frustration with Sancho, after realizing the squire's unwillingness to undergo the penance necessary to save Dulcinea from her enchantment.[5] Anguished by the dim prospects for his lady, and frustrated by his forced return to the duke and duchess's court, the knight complains:

> O unfeeling soul! O pitiless squire! O undeserved bread and unthinking favors that I have given to you and that I intend to give to you in the future! Because of me you found yourself a governor, and because of me you have hopes of becoming a count or receiving another equivalent title, and the fulfilment of those hopes will take no longer than the time it takes for this year to pass, [for I] *Post tenebras spero lucem.*[6]

Three hundred years later, the exiled Manuel García Puertas alluded to the same adage in the title of an essay that described the slim hope for those who, like him, waited in America for the "disenchantment" of their homeland and its return to democratic governance.[7] Indeed, like the scant faith Don Quixote has in Sancho, the Republicans' trust that international intervention would free Spain from the Francoist regime progressively weakened, until the increasingly unlikely prospect completely vanished by the mid-1950s. By then, Franco's regime had officially been recognized by the United States (Pact of Madrid, 1953), the Vatican (Concordat, 1953), and the United Nations (1955).[8] Exiles would have to wait until the transition of the late 1970s to see a rekindling of Spanish democracy.

In the meantime, the trauma of civil war, the stark realities of the diaspora, and the Francoist disregard for secular culture turned Cervantes and Don Quixote into proxies for the exiled writers' own condition.[9] As García Puertas reflected, "Reading [Cervantes] continues to be the soothing tonic for those who, like us, continue to dream of a better future for the people of a nation so admirable and so unfairly treated."[10] Those who, like García Puertas, were lucky enough to escape prosecution, incarceration, or death would have to endure a wait for repatriation much longer than they had anticipated.

Given this long interim, Spanish emigrés were eventually moved to adapt to their new countries. Many assumed that this adaptation would be easier in Latin America than in the United States or Europe, given the region's linguistic similarities and presumed cultural affinity with Spain. But, in reality, those settling in states with former colonial ties to the Iberian Peninsula encountered additional challenges. As Mainer reminds us, in Latin American countries "the majority of exiled Spanish intellectuals faced the difficult task of reconciling the nationalistic views of their native and adoptive homelands, as they were compelled to approach the American, indigenous, and Hispanic perspectives."[11] Harmonizing Peninsular and anti-colonial nationalistic viewpoints would be particularly challenging in places where anti-Spanish sentiment had been brewing for decades.

Being generally unaware of the negative feelings that people in other Spanish-speaking countries had toward Spain as a colonizing nation,

EL INGENIOSO HIDALGO DON QVI-XOTE DE LA MANCHA.

Compueſto por Miguel de Ceruantes Saauedra.

DIRIGIDO AL DVQVE DE BEIAR, Marques de Gibraleon, Conde de Baracbana, y Baña-res, Vizconde de la Puebla de Alcozer, Señor de las villas de Capilla, Curiel, y Burgillos.

Año,   1605.

Con priuilegio de Caſtilla, Aragon, y Portugal.

EN MADRID, Por Iuan de la Cueſta.

Vendeſe en caſa de Franciſco de Robles, librero del Rey nſo ſeñor.

FIGURE 5.1 Miguel de Cervantes Saavedra. *El ingenioso hidalgo Don Quijote de la Mancha*. Title Page. Madrid: Juan de la Cuesta, 1608.

FIGURE 5.2 *El ingenioso hidalgo Don Quijote de la Mancha*. Title Page detail.

Republican exiles were ill equipped to confront the paradoxical situation that awaited them in their new lands.[12] In Mexico, for example, an exceptional first-hand witness like Max Aub observed that while Spanish exiles had been warmly received by the "revolutionary politicians in power, despite being by definition anti-Spanish ... those in the government's opposition, traditional and pro-Spanish [gachupines], welcomed them as Spaniards but disparaged them [us] as revolutionary. A mess."[13] Caught off-guard by the multiple and often contradictory ideological factions operating simultaneously in their new homelands, exiles came to realize the extent to which ideas about the Spanish "Golden" colonial past had determined personal and political perceptions of their country and themselves.

While, as preceding chapters have shown, Spanish thinkers were well acquainted with the potential implications of a particular view of the early modern past for the present, they were less cognizant of the implications of this chronological extrapolation outside of Spain. In addition, at least until the Civil War, Spanish citizens had the unspoken choice of interpreting the 1500s freely, whether as the age of the *comuneros* and the beginning of Spanish popular sovereignty, the "great" imperialist expansion of the Habsburgs, or anything in between. In Latin America, such options did not exist: As far as their past was concerned, Peninsular newcomers were more or less associated with the *conquistadores* who had arrived four hundred years earlier, and/or with the no less inglorious immigrants—the most recent "indianos" or "gachupines"— who emigrated in the early 1900s and expected to quickly return to their country with their "pockets bulging with money."[14] The lingering, negative stereotypes left behind in both cases obviously hampered the chances—or process—of adaptation for this third wave of Spanish travelers, which was dramatically different from the previous two.[15]

Republican exiles generally emphasized the warm and generous reception they were given in their memoirs and testimonies (especially in Mexico), even when they also acknowledged initial "resistance and opposition" by some factions of society, which at times was strong.[16] This impression is often confirmed by the recollections of local observers, who stated that such hostility eventually subsided, although they remained vague about timelines.[17] The Mexican ambassador to France Silvio Zavala acknowledged for example that while "[t]here were enormous divisions and struggles" in the Mexico that had opened its doors to the Republicans, "the weight and reality of [a positive] experience ended up easing them."[18] Another Mexican economist, Jesús Silva Herzog, concurred, pointing out that "if before the Republican immigration Mexicans used to call *all* Spaniards 'gachupines,' once they got to know them [these Republicans], they started addressing them simply as Spaniards," a small but apparently telling accomplishment.[19] Many of these testimonies emphasized that the Republican adaption to Latin America was accomplished faster and more easily in politically sympathetic countries such as Mexico, where there had been a strong "ideological affinity" between the government of the Second Republic and that of General Lázaro Cárdenas.[20]

Yet, recent studies on the Spanish Republican diaspora have started to provide a very different picture of their assimilation process, sometimes denying altogether that such assimilation occurred. In these critical accounts,

Spanish exiles, who are generally recognized as "lay, liberal, and Republican" thinkers who "envisioned a relationship with Latin America on a more egalitarian basis,"[21] are described as betraying soon after their arrival such egalitarian ideals and picking up "where their turn-of-the-century colleagues [i.e., Generation of '98 writers and imperialist theorists] had left off."[22] For these critics, Republican exiles as a whole ended up regarding themselves as "destined to carry Europe's, particularly Spain's, spiritual essence across the Atlantic toward the promised land of the future."[23] This portrayal is obviously at odds with the progressive behaviors and beliefs that have been explored in earlier chapters. As we saw in Chapter 1, progressive writers believed that the spirit of the *comunero* revolt represented the defining trait of the Spanish proto-democratic modernity of the early 1500s. Moreover, as later chapters demonstrated, these writers opposed both the Romantic myths about empire put forth by the Generation of '98 and the Fascist appropriation of that romanticized past. Taken as a whole, the progressive outlook and praxis were quite incompatible with the ultra-conservative stance of "turn-of-the-century colleagues" such as Maeztu and Ganivet.

In examining the counterhegemonic perspective of Republican thinkers in the diaspora, this chapter connects the anti-imperialistic views that they expressed in Spain prior to 1939 with those that they voiced afterward in exile. These pages do not only illustrate the Republican critique of Spanish imperialism in both settings, they also provide a larger ideological, literary, and historiographical context for the forging and maintenance of such anti-imperialist perspectives. Rather than denying or minimizing the harrowing nature of conquest during the early modern age, this chapter explores why most liberal exiles recognized the extreme consequences of the ruthless imperial continuum which for these thinkers, began to crystallize with Charles V's routing of the *comuneros* at Villalar in 1521.

In a way, and paraphrasing Luis Araquistáin, we could say that by having Latin America—especially Mexico—shelter Spanish refugees from Iberian authoritarianism more than four hundred years after the *comuneros* revolt, another historical circle had closed.[24] Claiming that the country had become a victim of its own despotism, José Gaos argues that "Spain had become its own last colony," and as such constituted "the only Latin American nation that remained subjected to that imperial past, unable to gain spiritual and political independence from it."[25] By neutralizing a traditional Peninsular/Latin American dyad, Gaos denounces the authoritarian forces that levelled the country's last democratic dream of 1931 just as it did in 1521, when the idea of *imperium* defeated that of a medieval popular sovereignty. Rather than considering Latin American independence movements a threat, Gaos regards them as an inspiration for progressive Spaniards still struggling against a Spanish state that had fallen victim to its own imperialist ideology.

Cervantes is once again of particular significance in these historical, counter-hegemonic formulations. As discussed earlier, it was in great part through him that progressives had not only denounced Spanish imperialism but also voiced their intention to transcend it through one of its most effective counterarguments—humanism. Although progressive Spanish exiles each had somewhat different ideas of what humanism meant, a good number of them would embrace this construct as one of their most cherished cultural values. The Spaniards who shared this awareness, moreover, considered Cervantes and *Don Quixote* as some of the clearest representatives of these values. Luis D'Olwer, a former Republican politician, stated for example in 1947 that "Cervantes's immortal work is a healthy lesson in humanism" given its "commitment to a generous understanding of the other, of mankind."[26] For D'Olwer, this dimension of the Cervantine legacy had become an essential reference for any society of the moment since "[w]ithout understanding, there is no tolerance, justice, or peace," and "mankind is degraded ... to an animalistic fight."[27]

This view of humanism as social and intellectual tool able to bring some form of peace and understanding to a world torn apart byconflict and war would be endlessly promoted not only by exiled Republicans but by the recently founded UNESCO of those years. An ambitious case study commissioned by this institution (UNESCO) in 1953 identified international conflicts as "problems" that essentially stemmed out of the "relations of cultures," and that could be solved by adopting a "*form of a new humanism*," here defined as "the recognition of *common values*," among disparate nations, societies, and cultures.[28] It is little surprising, then, that Spanish refugees continued to embrace so emphatically this humanistic formula, recognizing it as their best chance to minimize if not overcome their new intercultural struggles.

Among Spanish exiles, Cervantes had long been the principal patron of this humanist doctrine. If D'Olwer believed that Cervantes's humanism had taught societies "to practice the most formidable of qualities, a deep understanding," Salinas would add that, in his *magnus opus, Don Quixote,* "we all understand one another." Referring specifically to the American context, Salinas argues that Americans and Spaniards of all convictions and walks of life could find in the novel "a mutual understanding," adding that, while both viewpoints "might differ in many things," he suspected that such differences could be "transcended in this book [*Don Quixote*]."[29]

Exiles's hope that this kind of (Cervantine) humanism could provide a safe passage to cultural integration was particularly strong during the international commemoration of the author's birth in 1947. Authors such as Jorge Luis Borges and Julio Cortázar joined Spanish exiles in denouncing the co-optation and misrepresentation of Cervantes by official Spain that had made the author "the excuse for patriotic toasts, grammatical arrogance, and obscene luxurious editions."[30] After all, in Cervantes, most Latin American authors recognized the writer that their progressive Peninsular counterparts had long eulogized, "a man supremely aware of the [liberating] energy and deep contradictions of the Renaissance and of the inertia, the rigidity, and false assertiveness of the Counter-Reformation."[31]

Unfortunately, it was almost impossible to mobilize a community based on such literary and humanistic affinity. Progressive writers from both the Peninsula and certain Latin American countries tended to be in exile and dispersed across the globe during these years. From the 1940s, and over the next several decades, liberal writers from many regions would be forced to cross the ocean in both directions, seeking to escape censorship and oppression in their homelands. As a result, while a large Spanish Republican contingent settled in Latin America in the 1940s and 1950s, a number of important Latin American writers, fleeing dictatorships in their own countries, established themselves in Spain. The implications of such transnational displacement will be examined in the Epilogue.

Humanidad versus *Hispanidad*

An enormous challenge to the development of shared bonds between Spaniards and Latin Americans, and a source of deep mistrust, is the idea of *Hispanidad*. As a key hegemonic concept—revamped by proto-fascist writers like the prominent member of the Generation of 1898 Ramiro de Maeztu—*Hispanidad* presumes a romanticized unity between Spain and Latin America born out of colonization and maintained through the dominant—and dominating—structures of church and empire. At its core, the notion dismisses the sovereignty of Latin American democracies, and demands through official or unofficial channels the reinstating of the geopolitical order created by Iberian imperialism.[32]

Postcolonial criticism has rightly demanded a close examination of how Spanish writers in exile positioned themselves with regard to the colonial mindset and legacy underpinning this concept. Few inquiries have explored, however, the strong resistance to the notion of *Hispanidad* among a wide range of Spanish émigrés. For Francisco Piña, for example, the "ridiculous dream that Francoist ideologues pompously call *Hispanidad*" constituted nothing short of "a monstrous teleology of cadavers founded on the religion of death."[33] And, as Sender argued, the notion constituted another fascist historical fiction, a "badly chosen word loaded with falsehood" that "did not correspond to the truth," just like "historical facts don't materialize just because somebody makes them up."[34] Sender concluded that there never *was* a *Hispanidad* that assured racial and cultural uniformity on both sides of the Atlantic, because there was no *Hispanidad* even in Spain: There were "Castilian, Galician, Catalan, Asturian [identities] but not *Hispanidad*."[35] For Republican federalists such as Sender, "Maeztu's artificial creation" was not only "as absurd as the founding of a whole empire by decree" but also signified little more than a ridiculous "gesture, theater, arrogance ... and ruin."[36] In contrast, Sender, Piña, and a good number of their fellow Republican exiles would proudly hail Cervantes as the first and best heterodox "dissident" of this ruinous worldview.[37]

While Sender's critique of Maeztu's blunt imperialism might have been re-energized in exile, it was not a direct consequence of his relocation outside of Spain. Long before 1939, influential, progressive intellectuals and politicians had rejected these ideas and their various manifestations, whether originating from the Generation of '98, Regenerationists, or proto-fascists. The urgent need to oppose this outlook had been clear to young Manuel Azaña (1880–1940), one of the most highly reputed intellectuals of his day, even before he became the first and last president of the Republic. As early as 1923, Azaña had dedicated a whole lecture, "Defection from a '98 Man" (*La defección de un hombre del '98*), to dismantling the characterization of Spanish colonial wars as civilization campaigns, declaring them as mere byproducts of commercial "rapacity."[38] Azaña also pointed out that Spain could hardly be an "agent of colonial civilization"—a central argument invoked to maintain the Spain-led, geopolitical order—because the country had not yet mastered the main elements of civilization itself, such as "personal freedoms, and respect for the life and rights of men."[39] The Republican president equated the imperial ideal that Maeztu was trying to resurrect with the mechanical effort of trying to bring back the breath of a drowned man.[40] Maeztu's views on *Hispanidad* and colonialism constituted, for him (Azaña), a "national solution impossible ... to swallow," let alone to resurrect.[41]

Once on Latin American soil, Republican exiles such as José Moreno Villa, Pedro Bosch Gimpera, Azaña, and Sender, among many others, reaffirmed their rejection of this idea (*Hispanidad*), and worried that its new currency signaled an attempt to spread Francoist propaganda.[42] The opening in Mexico of the Council of Hispanidad (Consejo de la Hispanidad) in 1942, a Francoist "cultural" institution supposedly dedicated to the cultivation of Spanish–Latin American "unity" through the "loving presence" of a cultural delegation from the regime, set off alarms among these Spanish expatriates.[43] Spanish emigrés of different sensibilities denounced the council as a "fascist, Catholic, and imperialistic intrusion into American democracies."[44] In the pages of *Las Españas,* one of the most important publications of the diaspora, a former Republican congressman, Mariano Ruiz-Funes, warned that the council represented a fascist danger "that few were noticing in the Americas," a danger that, by invoking the old premise of *Hispanidad*, attempted to institute an "ideological colonization, the indispensable requirement for total colonization."[45] The loud and sustained outcry of the exile community was instrumental in the institute's closing only a couple of years later. The expats also maintained a continuing vigilance toward the expansionist aims of the Francoist government after it opened a much-more modest center in 1945, also in Mexico, the Hispanic Culture Institute (Instituto de Cultura Hispánica).[46] Spanish exiled groups continued to fight the spread of fascism in Latin America in ways that are only now starting to be systematically examined.[47]

One of the clearest Spanish contributions to this fight was the founding of the Spanish Athenaeum of Mexico in 1942. Hoping to build a solid wall around the Francoist colonialist incursions that institutions such as the Council of Hispanidad represented, exiles also aimed to counter the nostalgic, imperial fictions of '98 authors such as Maeztu who had first exhumed these ideas.[48] If the expatriates invoked links between Spain and Latin America, they would not do so through a messianic construct such as *Hispanidad*, but rather through the secular idea of humanism. For Spanish Republicans, humanism constituted the only viable cultural and political matrix able to build a lasting bond between their old and new homelands.

"Humanism" comprised a wide array of postulates and beliefs. As James Valender and Jaime Rojo note, while "[a]llusions to humanism as the foundation for a set of shared values" were "constantly" repeated by Spanish exiles, those values were not unanimously defined.[49] For some, humanism connoted a belief in rational thinking; for others, it referred to a capacity for tolerant and independent understanding; at times, this tolerant attitude was considered only in reference to Renaissance figures such as Cervantes and Erasmus, while at others, it is mentioned independently from them. Most frequently, humanism for Republican refugees involved an "ethical and moral reference" generally detached from any kind of religious dogma.[50] Their humanism was usually characterized by the qualities such as rationality, freedom, and tolerance, whose value stood in opposition to the authoritarianism, bigotry, and orthodoxy of dictatorships such as Franco's.

Such humanism, while valued in international organizations like the UNESCO, was starting to be contested in Spanish as well as Latin American academic circles.[51] Domestically, it was challenged by historians such as Maravall, who, as we saw in Chapter 4, managed to strip Cervantes and the Spanish Golden Age of their humanistic valence. In Latin America, meanwhile, emergent suspicions of the concept of "Hispanism" as an updated construct of the cultural channel of *Hispanidad* came to deprive pan-humanist arguments of much of their cultural weight.[52] Trapped once again in the middle of a cultural war whose scope and virulence all but overpowered them, Spanish exiles continued to affirm the Cervantist humanist legacy, which for them offered the only cultural bridge across the Atlantic.

The Humanist Fight against Eternal Spain: Charging against the Imperial Windmill

Exile to former colonies heightened Republicans' awareness of the profound damage caused by the Spanish imperial project. Earlier progressive attitudes toward Spain's colonial enterprise lay the groundwork for the attitudes of the Spanish diaspora, which continued to find in Cervantes inspiration for a counter-imperialistic sensibility. Throughout his intense political and intellectual life, Azaña had explicitly contradicted the traditionalist, bellicose understanding of Spanish history and identity by recourse to a convincingly humanistic argument.[53] Rejecting early on the imperial views articulated by "fascist prophets" such as Maeztu, the Republican president dared to refute, in 1932, the nationalist molds into which proto-fascist theorists were forcing Spanish history and identity. "Spaniards, by will or by nature," Azaña claimed, were actually "peaceful people, because it would be beyond suicidal to embark on military adventures."[54] Detaching Republican Spain's foreign policy from past militaristic ambitions, Azaña defended a political order both "inside and outside the country" (en el interior y en el exterior) based on this nonviolent stance, arguing that peace was essential for the prosperity and future of the country.[55] In a clear allusion to and celebration of a humanist past, Azaña echoed figures such as Erasmus, Andrés Laguna, and Thomas More in their rejection of the purported morality of war and their defense of an "ideal commonwealth" in which peace constituted the ultimate target. Azaña claimed that, at this point in history, "[i]f there is a nation that needs and wants peace, it is Spain."[56] He would repeat this call for nonviolence decrying Spanish imperialism in the numerous speeches he gave in the 1920s and 1930s.

Azaña's perspective on expansionism, peace, and war was consistent with an emerging progressive historiography. Manuel Ciges Aparicio (1873–1936), a rising star, captured a particular historical perspective of Spain's past and present in his influential *España bajo la dinastía de los Borbones 1701–1931* (1932), in which he traced the widening split between the will of the people and that of their monarchs. In Ciges Aparicio's study, "ignorance and hunger" appear as the two greatest legacies of the Spanish monarchy, both Habsburg and Bourbon.[57] His idea that flawed rulers had jeopardized the destiny of the Spanish people drew the attention of international critics. In 1933, in the pages of the American journal *Hispania*, historian Frances Douglas praised Ciges Aparicio's exploration of "Spanish decadence," which was clearly "attributed to the absolutist and centralizing power of the Austrian [i.e., Hapsburg] monarchs, the destruction of public liberties, humiliation of the nobility, and degradation of the people."[58] The unglamorous view of monarchy—obviously compatible with Republican ideals—emerging from such historical analyses extended to other progressive anthropologists and historians, including Bosch Gimpera, Anselmo Carretero Jiménez, and Francisco Puig-Espert, who propounded similar views about the calamitous effects of Spain's monarchic and imperial undertakings.

Puig-Espert, for example, a Valencian humanist, and General Inspector of Education in the Republican government in 1931–32, argued in 1947:

> Let's say it, without any further quibble or delay, that the greatness of Spain during the Golden Age was nothing but a deceiving mirage, fruit of an "elite" that never had behind it the support of the people, counting only with the support of those royal headmasters, those men guided by their own self-importance and uncontrolled greed, who wasted the energy and courage of a few, harming in the process a whole community that had been unable to revolt and gain independence from them.[59]

In dispelling the traditionalist associations linking wealth, imperial expansion, and Spanish will, Republican and other progressive thinkers provided an alternative approach to both Spanish history and the official discourse that had chronicled it. The official narrative that glorified colonialism had, in their view, artificially redacted the opposition to that enterprise, an opposition that for progressives dated back to the 1500s, to the age of Cervantes.

As Bosch Gimpera put it in 1948, "In that empire," plagued with "disenchantment over great and misguided military campaigns ... there was no room for Cervantes."[60] Bosch Gimpera reminds us that the grand idea of transatlantic imperialism whose impossible campaigns bankrupted the country was designed by distant kings who "buried in their mountains of files" easily forgot about fallen or captured soldiers such as Cervantes.[61] Firmly aligned with these impressions, Republican historians, ethnographers, and cultural critics rewrote the widely accepted story— asserted by conservative writers in the Generation of '98 and the fascist ideologues who followed—that the Spanish Golden Age represented an apogee of wealth and military might.

Azaña in particular would go so far as to assert that the Golden Age Spanish history had been maliciously distorted by an imperialistic, self-serving propaganda that had been promulgated for three centuries without being sufficiently problematized.[62] To him, one of the inherited historical responsibilities of the Second Republic was to dismantle the theocratic and symbolic frameworks built around the imperialistic ethos associated with the sixteenth century, since

> Spain ... is a victim of political propaganda originating in the sixteenth century. Its triumphal politics back then, dominant all over Europe, imposed its relatively Spanish and profoundly Catholic stamp with glimpses of universality ... This politics created its own propaganda and

doctrine. It wasn't a propaganda disseminated in papers, but through theologians, poets, painters, and all social and political means able to influence the consciousnesses within their reach. That political scheme ended .... Spanish imperialism passed ... but its propagandistic means continued; that doctrine has been perpetuated year after year ... *the men of my generation ... had to unroot the bedrock of such vicious propaganda, lethal given its anachronism, deceit, and inadequacy.* (Emphasis added)[63]

In tackling the task of dismantling this anachronistic propaganda, one of Azaña's priorities was to address the "brutish apathy ... of the Regenerationist officials" who in 1898 lacked the "civic courage" necessary to "allow the emancipation—instead of the sale or cession—of those [Latin American] countries" colonized by Spain.[64]

Azaña's demythologizing campaign had implicitly or explicitly recruited historians such as Palerm, Gallegos Rocafull, Bosch Gimpera, Carretero Jiménez, Puig-Espert, Eduardo Nicol, and Ciges Aparicio.[65] In the case of Ciges Aparicio, speaking from his powerful perspective as a chronicler as well as a veteran of the Spanish-American War, he would be able to document that "the majority of Spaniards [civilians *and* soldiers participating in the war] thought that Cuba should have been given its freedom."[66] The views of such prominent figures demonstrate not only an anti-imperialist strain in Spanish cultural and political life of the 1920s and 1930s, but also a firm opposition to the neo-colonial structures of control that followed the formal dissolution of colonial rule in 1898.

These intellectuals—Azaña, Ciges Aparicio, Palerm, Gallegos Rocafull, Bosch Gimpera, and so forth—would go as far to contend that what made the '98 crisis a catastrophe for Spanish modern history was the Spanish government's inability or unwillingness to replace a flawed colonial order with a more democratic one. For Azaña, a constellation of equal democracies was the only way forward. Under such a system, the president would argue, Spain could have found "the only true benefit it could aspire to have: the favorable regard of amicable or allied [independent] republics with which it could establish lawful treaties of literary [cultural] and commercial trade, justly arbitrated."[67] Predictably, a message aimed at the heart of *Hispanidad* was immediately deemed insulting by the conservative establishment, while it was favorably received by liberal supporters on both sides of the Atlantic.

In the 1920s, the Spanish-born international journalist Francisco Grandmontagne argued from Argentina that "[w]hat we need are solid trade treaties" rather than "patriotic toasts."[68] Urging his fellow Spaniards to drop the paternalist attitudes toward Latin America—"expressed in rhetorical nonsense"—Grandmontagne encouraged them to build, as "just and sensible" actors, a more solid, financial relationship with the region.[69] Progressive thinkers such as Azaña and Grandmontagne were clearly aware of the disastrous consequences that failing to pursue such a course of action and prolonging an unsustainable empire-driven political system would have for Spain's future development. In a resounding condemnation, Azaña concluded that the Spanish colonial past constituted the most powerful impediment ("la remora más poderosa") to the country's modernizing process.[70]

To Azaña and his fellow progressive cultural and political theorists, the full and unequivocal abandonment of the country's flawed imperial project was as essential for Spain's projection into the future as for an accurate accounting of its past. Refusing to accept the despotic legacy of the Spanish Empire as the political genealogy of their nation, a great number of Republican officials and supporters apparently did consider the Castilian proto-democracies abolished by Charles V as a much more accurate indication of the real political will of the country.[71] For these liberal advocates, if there was an event to be nostalgic for in the Spanish past, it should be the Castilian *Comunero* uprising against the emperor in an attempt to protect local liberties. It would be hard to overemphasize how loudly the echoes of imperial repression from this event resonated with Republican and left-wing sympathizers. "We, Republican Spaniards are the legitimate heirs of the popular troops, or *comuneros* of the sixteenth century," declared Carretero proudly in 1948.[72] He was only slightly exaggerating; under the Republic, even the national flag was altered to pay tribute to the revolt. One of the writers of the constitution, Araquistáin—a war veteran, from the Mexican revolution, where he fought on the revolutionary side—explained in 1932 that the distinct purple band added to the Spanish flag—which Franco would quickly remove—was a symbolic homage to "the Castilian [*comunero*] freedoms once erased by the Emperor" (*las libertades anuladas por el Emperador*) which the Republic was finally reinstating.[73]

Agreeing that the *Comuneros* Revolt in Villalar and Charles V's response to it constituted a foundational event for Spanish history, Bosch Gimpera used the rebellion as the organizing principle for an alternative historical timeline for the country. Tracing the ongoing popular repudiation of absolutism and imperialism through the ages, the historian stretches his timeline from the Roman to the Napoleonic invasions until it culminates in the constitution of the Second Republic:

> The new Spain that the Republic wanted to create had to be continuation of a political tradition calibrated by reason, not of the imperial country that does not in fact represent the true Spain. ... [T]hat real Spain has to be found under the superstructure of the Roman-Visigoth-Leones-Trastamaran-Habsburg-Bourbonic-Falangist empire, which is not Spain. And just as in that [imperial] system, peoples of different countries cannot establish any common parlance; true Spaniards cannot either.[74]

In Bosch Gimpera's overview of the tyrannical practices of Spanish absolutist governments—including the contemporary fascist dictatorship—

he established an equivalence between the subjugation of Castilians (and Spaniards) and that of Latin Americans: "Castille, like Spain, like America, had been the victims of the tyranny of its monarchs."[75] José Ramón Araña concurred, arguing in 1949 that Habsburg repression "through blood and fire" had been equally ruthless on both sides of the Atlantic, since by opening "Spain's veins through a series of catastrophic wars, it [the Habsburg dynasty] had also destroyed Latin America's colossal legacy."[76]

This equation between domestic and colonial tyranny, which was constantly repeated by Spanish exiles in the 1940s and early 1950s, appears to have been widely forgotten by later writers. A rare exception was Carlos Fuentes. Elaborating on the consequences that a failed, sixteenth century-Castilian uprising would have for the Latin American colonization and decolonization processes, he argues that[77]

> By defeating the democratic movement in 1521, Spain laid the groundwork for the defeat of its colonies as viable political entities. Hence, the terrible difficulty that Latin America would experience when seeking its independence: our struggle for decolonization had to fight, so to speak, a double colonization: we were, after all, the colonies of a colony. The colonizer had become the Indies of Europe.[78]

Fuentes noted that the same year that Habsburg forces in the Battle of Villalar smashed the *Comuneros*, Cortés conquered the great Aztec city of Tenochitlán.[79] The writer wonders what would have happened to Latin American lands if the vertical order of the Aztecs had been replaced by a more democratic approach of the *Comuneros,* if a popular form of sovereignty had finally dispelled from Spain the anachronistic "medieval imperium," and if a new geopolitical order, a commonwealth, had been instituted.[80]

It is clear that the Comunero uprising—the possibilities it raised, and the questions it posed— managed to produce a strikingly enduring cultural legacy despite its political failure. Some, like Fuentes, even argued that this legacy had been implicitly referenced by Cervantes, who had after all witnessed its events more closely. Examining the list of non-aristocratic participants of the rebellion (whose identity and profession had been, for punitive reasons, personally revealed by Charles V), Fuentes notes how the bakers, humanists, merchants, and barbers that appeared in the emperor's list almost "reads as the character's list of *Don Quixote*."[81] The parallel leads the critic to wonder if the protagonists of Cervantes's novel are not the same "that defied Habsburg absolutism and fought for the development of the civil rights of an entire population."[82] While aware that Cervantes's world was not the world of the *Comuneros,* of the "silent majority" defeated in 1521, Fuentes conjectures if "Cervantes voices what Castilian people could not express anymore" in the early 1600s, a strong collective spirit, a solitary trust in a higher moral order, and lingering counter-hegemonic spirit that rejects absolute or inquisitorial orthodoxy.[83]

After all, as the historian Carretero had reminded us, it was "only twenty-seven years" after the *Comunero's* foundational event, the *Junta de Avila*, "that Cervantes was born, and only fifty-eight years later that he published his first part of *Don Quixote*."[84] Some Cervantists, including Anthony Cascardi, have seen in treaties written under strong *comunero* influence, such as *Tractado de la república con otras hystorias y antigüedades* (1521), an understanding of the idea of public governance at play in Cervantes's novel.[85] This emerging connection between Cervantes and *comunero* values had then been long invoked and celebrated by Spanish progressives from the 1920s through the 1940s.[86] To them, a naïve liberator of the galley slaves like Don Quixote provided a strong echo of the credulous, freedom-seeking *comunero* spirit that demanded, with a confident and unilateral resolution, that *all slaves* in the Americas were liberated in 1520—an astounding mandate that was never close to being executed.[87] For Republican exiles, *Don Quixote* was consequently the product of that unextinguished *comunero* legacy that they proudly proclaimed as their own.

Personal Journeys, off the Imperial Path

Whether obliquely voicing the silenced *comuneros* or not, Cervantes's liberating and anti-imperialistic thrust had been widely recognized in Latin America even before Republican exiles praised this legacy in the 1930s.[88] Independentist heroes such as Simón Bolívar and José Martí had commended Cervantes as an author who, despite being born in the Habsburg Empire, "was never a spokesman for the glories of his king Philip."[89] For Martí, *Don Quixote* was a "the delight of literature," and Cervantes constituted "an impeccable study for the Cuban writer, an early friend of mankind who lived in a period irreconcilable with freedom and decency," and who "preferred life among the humble to that in the depravity of the court."[90] After 1898, the affectionate appreciation for Cervantes among Latin American authors was extended to little else coming from Spain.

The apathy was not lost to all Spaniards. In the early 1900s, perceptive thinkers such as Azaña were starting to realize that one of the unavoidable consequences of the colonial past was the exacerbation of a deep, persistent Latin American resentment toward Spain. Warning about the extent of this acrimony in the 1920s, Azaña would strikingly acknowledge in a review of the monograph *The Future of Spanish America* (*El porvenir de la América española*) by the Argentinian author Manuel Ugarte (1920) that Ugarte's stridently negative "feelings towards Spain and the Spanish legacy in [Latin] America" were "fair," adding that "any Spaniard with common sense will accept them."[91]

This sensible understanding of history was echoed in 1927 by Araquistáin, as he argued that in the long and troubled relationship between Spain and Latin American republics, "[e]motions had too often been abused."[92] For Araquistáin the re-establishment of an amicable "rapport among the Spanish-speaking nations" constituted the most important and "smartest, international Spanish policy" that could be adopted.[93] Rather than advocating for a policy of colonial unity, Araquistáin, emphasized the need for a critical and sensitive understanding of the different viewpoints held by each of the parties involved in such a relationship. National and nationalistic simplifications had, in his view, stood in the way of sincere and mutual international understanding.[94]

Rather than questioning or denying the independent existence of a Latin American identity or sovereignty—as Maeztu and his proto-fascist colleagues continued to do—Araquistáin underlined the need to recognize a plurality of voices, views, and identities involved in each of the Latin American republics, since understanding the diversity of participants was essential for establishing a new, more authentic relationship with them. If he speaks of a common bond between Latin America and Spain, he notes that such an association must "bring together those men that in Spain and in America aspire to a similar notion of freedom in all things of life."[95] Araquistáin writes of the institution of a new, global, and progressive order—a modern, and progressive commonwealth—founded on the preservation of freedom and the diversity of these multi-layered participants.[96]

Neither Azaña nor the Republic would have time to institutionalize the historical accountability that the president had advocated among "Spaniards of common sense." However, the cultural sensibility that he and Araquistáin spoke of was openly expressed by kindred Republican historians and cultural critics and continued to be loudly voiced from exile in the 1940s and 1950s. Among these thinkers were Francisco Giner de los Ríos (*Jornada hecha* [1935]), Juan Rejano (*La esfinje mestiza, Crónica Menor de México* [1945]), Díez Canedo (*Letras de América en las literaturas continentales* [1944]), Manuel Altolaguirre (*Las islas invitadas* [1944], *Nuevos poemas de las islas invitadas* [1946], *Presente de la lírica mexicana* [1946]), José Moreno Villa (*Cornucopia Mexicana* [1940]), and Luis Cernuda (*Variaciones sobre tema mexicano* [1952]). Their legacy—both during the Republic and in exile—contradicts the traditional critical assumption that Spaniards in the first half of the twentieth century advocated *only* for an "idealistic revitalization of Spain's imperial past and its civilizing mission."[97]

Some Spanish exiles, especially the historians and anthropologists among them—José Miranda, José Gallegos Rocafull, D'Olwer, Juan de la Encina, José María Ots Capdequí, and Angel Palerm Vich—would dedicate the rest of their careers to Mexican, Latin American, and Indigenous studies.[98] Their contributions to these fields can be extrapolated from a biographic note of Palerm Vich, which states that he[99] was "strongly informed by his drive to recover valuable traditions of knowledge and transmit them for use by future generations, *a drive undoubtedly enhanced by his awareness of the destruction of intellectual life in Spain and Europe during the 1930s and 1940s.*[100] The drama of fascism and its human and cultural destruction informed their research aims, enhanced by their awareness of the dangers faced by local cultures. A fellow Spaniard, Arturo Souto Alabarce would describe the clash of Latin American and Spanish perspectives as an event that caused most émigrés "to stop focusing on the particular problem of Spain, in order to contemplate a broader cultural landscape."[101] After all, the drama of exile "enriched" some thinkers, Souto noted, and "isolated" others, "radically changing" all.[102] A well-known example of how the expansion of cultural horizons was not always constructive was Américo Castro, whose remarks about Argentinian Spanish being somehow a defective linguistic variety of Castilian were notoriously rebuked by no less a giant than Borges.[103] Borges's depth, humor, and repute helped turn Castro's *faux pas* into a "*a supreme illustration* of the position that *Spaniards usually adopt,* when arriving into this land, whether they are philologists or not."[104] Ironically, it would have been hard to see "Segismundo-Américo"—as some Spaniards called him at that point—as the "supreme illustration" of the attitudes of Spaniards in America;[105] his correspondence from these years shows that rather than exemplifying the attitudes of his fellow exiles, he felt quite isolated from and misunderstood by them. Castro's linguistic snobbery, in other words, which was probably shared by other exiles, precipitated a level of generalizations on his contemporaries that sadly obscured the work and views of so many others that happened to passionately disagree with him.[106]

The anecdote exposed the wide range of difference of opinion that existed within the Republican contingent, a group that even in Spain had never been monolithic or consistent. At the opposite end of Castro's ethnocentric views, a good number of exiled painters, poets, and critics believed that their painful relocation after the war had bulldozed their nationalistic inclinations.[107] For Moreno Villa, for example, "Spain's sponge, full of blood, has cleaned all prejudice from my personal slate, washing away even the faith I ever had on my own perceptions."[108]

Some writers, such as Rafael Alberti, had reflected on the nature of these national prejudices even before their exile. Embarking on an exploratory journey throughout Latin America in 1935, Alberti warned his readers that he was "not a conquistador," but rather a Spaniard who "would soon be conquered" (*Yo no era un español de la conquista. Yo iba enseguida a ser un español conquistado*) by the pre-hispanic reality of the "New World" that Maeztu took such pains to minimize.[109] Alberti's expedition through Central America allowed him to confront head-on the drama of the Conquest through the perspective of one of its most reliable and critical chroniclers, Bernal Díaz del Castillo (1492–1581). "[S]ince for a Spaniard, especially if he is a poet, it is so hard to understand the complex Mexican reality," he explains, "I was lucky enough to find him [Bernal] and to explore these lands by his side."[110] Aware of the impact that an imperial past had on the present in Mexico, Alberti undertook a journey through both time and space, wondering:

> How much longer still would these wondrous lands ... inspire bitter poems ... and famous and anonymous voices and fists raised in protest? Dominated lands, dominated waters, dominated heavens. Just like before, booty for the most ruthless wars. North America 1808–1935. Spain, Spain ... a dark 1519 starts to emerge in the still wake left by my ship.[111]

Alberti's polychronic journey through the aftermath of the Spanish imperial undertaking is particularly insightful, although not unique.[112] Other Peninsular writers had embarked on similar journeys toward the past, even while still in Spain.

A case in point is María Zambrano as she reflected in Madrid on the fascination that the ultra-conservative ideology of her day (1937) felt for the absolutist displays of the period. Considering the Francoist reverence for Philip II—the controversial ruler that, as Azaña claimed, had "more supporters [from fascist opponents of the Republic] during the years of democratic government than when he ruled from El Escorial"[113]— Zambrano was quick to denounce the dangers of turning Philip II into a political model. Complaining against this reverence, she observes:

> They, the ones who call themselves "traditionalists," the ones who assumed the tragic and comic [imperialist] legacy of Spain in the world, claim to be the only ones who truly understood the meaning [of that legacy] ... And this is how they have created for the rest of us a nightmarish past, one that placed a weight on the shoulders of any given Spaniard so burdensome that at any point it may crush him, cancelling his agency, and forcing him to live in permanent terror. Very few Spaniards could keep from shaking with fear in front of Philip II, for example, feeling as if they had been "caught in the act" of who knows what terrible offense.[114]

Zambrano recognizes once again the deep wedge between rulers and citizens, underlining the suppression of individual agency for the average citizen that results from the institutionalization of an absolutist system. Her clear-eyed vision of the ways in which unchecked authority has through history wielded its power through fear, intimidation, and oppression served as a dire warning against the current totalitarian movement aimed at reviving that past.

By 1937, the Republicans' daring attempt to stand as a bulwark against imperialistic, messianic doctrine and propaganda had been eroded. It was obvious that the lifespan of Republican ideals and the reach of "common-sensical" Spaniards such as Azaña or Zambrano were already under existential threat. The somber tone of Zambrano's reflection above also suggests the possibility that the war against authoritarian impositions might have actually been "lost from its very beginning."[115]

A significant part of the work that thinkers such as García Puertas, Sender, and Zambrano produced in the diaspora would revolve around this "awareness of defeat." In the case of Zambrano, her mournful inquiries on the subject also found solace in Cervantes. *Don Quixote* often appears in her writing as an illustration of the tragic Spanish historical experience, although she reads the character in strictly literary terms as well. Considering the knight as the embodiment of a classical tragedy, she reminds that "victorious heroes do not belong in tragedy but epic," for "tragedy is populated by characters that prevail only once they've made it to the kingdom of Hades, once they've gone beyond life, or once they inhabit the memory of men …. Tragic heroes never win here and now, in front of everyone's eyes, in their own time. Their victory is transhistorical."[116] Zambrano's cathartic identification of Quixote with the essence of classical tragedy provides an alternative understanding of the calamity of the protagonist's story. In blending archetypes of victory, fate, memory, and redemption with the Cervantine idiom, the philosopher provides a new fictional and transhistorical reading of the novel and an alternative understanding for her own historical drama.

Cervantes and the Unlikely Modern Hero

This chapter has examined the cultural, political, and historiographic fabric that shaped the belief of Republicans and other progressives that a counter-imperial animus was fundamental to the genuine Spanish spirit. As I have argued throughout this book, unorthodox Spanish thinkers not only brought these beliefs to their readings of Cervantes, but used Cervantes's writing to formulate these counter-hegemonic beliefs. It is therefore not surprising that, given the humanistic and democratic values of these thinkers, they would increasingly pay substantial attention to the humble figure of Sancho, given the growth of his awareness and importance in the story.[117] The humble and illiterate squire that Quixote despises at the beginning of their shared journey transcends the limits of companionships to become not only a "brother"[118] to the knight, but also the guardian and architect of his story.

For Republican and other progressive exiles, one of the most powerful attractions of Sancho's quiet rise in the novel was his ability to outgrow his social and intellectual limitations while still being loyal to his "everyman" condition.[119] This "[r]ude Sancho," as Aub initially describes him, grows into a "Sancho full of good sense," a man who, as a "believer or skeptic," is able to "witness the crumbling world unaware that he has become a world anew, rather than the New World, that is about to replace it."[120] Few moments in the novel manifest more clearly the emergence of this new world order than when the peasant is granted the governorship of his *ínsula*. As has been widely recognized, the episode becomes a clear metaphor for and critique of Spanish colonialism, a textual indication that Cervantes was aware of the new and corrupting world set up by an ignoble Spanish aristocracy— epitomized in his novel by the duke and duchess—that controlled it.[121]

Literary studies (including and beyond Cervantes's) lacked the tools of postcolonial theory to justly evaluate powerful messages like that conveyed in this episode until a few decades into the twentieth century.[122] Obviously, the *ínsula* metaphor encapsulated a critique of imperialism that transcended the Spanish Caribbean. John Beverly fittingly adopts Walter Benjamin's concept of "illumination" to contend that Sancho's formidable governance, like a "sudden flash of lightning," announces the "possibility of another order of things [that] emerges before the reader, an order in which the subaltern not only speaks, but also actually governs, and governs well."[123] The core element of this powerful vindication—the possibility of governing well, and from below—illustrated one of the most straightforward beliefs behind the Republican idea of *pueblo*.[124] An unlikely rebel, Sancho embodies the *hombre de la tierra* (man of the soil) praised by Machado, which acquired such emblematic significance in the 1930s and 1940s—a man full of dignity and hungry for new rights and aspirations, who is seldom given equal opportunity or a fair share. Sancho, then, is praised by left-wing intellectuals for being the fair governor produced by that *pueblo*, one able to rule with justice and fairness to all.[125]

Equally significant from this progressive perspective is Sancho's decision to abandon his stewardship and governance. Jorge Guillén, for example, argued that if Cervantes had made history by allowing a humble peasant to become (and excel as) a governor, he had made an even more resounding statement by forcing him to resign from that honor to recover his human dignity. Presenting a world in which the power acquired by working for the imperial machine was inherently corrupting, Guillén's poem "Sancho's Resignation" (*La dimisión de Sancho*) freezes for the reader the quiet, epiphanic moment in which the squire, recognizing the vanity of earthly power, renounces his title of "victor of worldly ambition" (*Vencedor, hecho mundo*). Cervantes had enhanced this realization with poetic echoes that equate world power with "smoke" and "shadows" (*fue como en sombra y humo el gobierno de Sancho* [*IH* II: 53]), and Guillén zooms in on the figure of the squire to see him rise above them:

Amanece en silencio
El hombre
Se descubre a sí mismo
Despacio

Mientras, una vez más,
El sol consigue mundo.
Y Sancho se levanta y calla, calla.
Tal porte silencioso
Mueve el respeto, límites dibuja.
Expectación. Los burladores, mudos.
Dejan obrar a quien se impone, lento,
Sólo, desde el espíritu.[126]

[He rises in silence / The man / Discovering himself / Slowly / While, once again, / The sun prevails in the world. / And Sancho gets up, and remains silent, silent. / Such silent demeanor / imposes respect, draws limits. / Expectation. The tricksters, speechless. / They give the man space, as he moves around slowly, / alone, moving from a spiritual realm.]

A novel that is often considered a portrait of "the weakness and foibles of the man of his day" is evoked here for extolling the strength and wisdom of the everyman. The humble-but-dignified hero able to defeat the tricksters ("burladores") of Cervantes's novel, and perhaps those of Guillén's own time, provides a powerful retort to the dominant—and apparent victorious—forces of both historical moments.[127]

That dignified Sancho is the one who meets the exiled Ricote, and is able—after his own painful experience on the *ínsula*—to understand the scale of the Morisco's personal tragedy and the collective tragedy of his people.[128] The language used to describe this encounter underlines Ricote's emotional and epistemological standing. As Julia Domínguez points out, Ricote, the Morisco, gravely confides in Sancho, the squire, that "now I *know* and *feel* the truth of the saying that it is sweet the love of one's country."[129] This is an intimate revelation that only a defeated Sancho could understand, as the exiled Guillén noted. In his poem, Guillén filled the void left by Cervantes's description of how Sancho has expanded his emotional and cognitive ability to fully "*know* and *feel*" not only Ricote's truth but his own. While Ricote achieves this wisdom when forced to abandon the safety of his home and country, Sancho gains it by voluntarily relinquishing his dream of power. It is only at that significant moment, having reached a similar understanding—even if coming from opposite ends of the experiential and cognitive spectrum—that Cervantes makes these two characters cross paths and reflect on their respective journeys.

But it is Sancho, more than Ricote, who illustrates in this case Cervantes's striking assertion that the individual dignity of a man is solely the result "of his own deeds"—or, as Azaña put it, "of choosing virtuous hope instead of corrupting possession,"[130] an assumption that contradicts from its core the moral and societal hierarchies of imperial and fascist structures.[131] As a peaceful laborer, wise governor, and marginalized citizen, Sancho became, for exiled writer José Enrique Rebolledo, the epitome—or unlikely hero—of the "wholesome humanism" that progressive writers and critics like him were advocating for. Urging his fellow Spaniards to "reconstruct a new form of Spanish personhood" inspired by the squire, Rebolledo invites them:[132]

> Let's go back to Sancho, because through him we will conquer Don Quixote. Let's reintegrate the hero, broken by dukes and barbers, priests and bachelors. Let's build with Sancho and Don Quixote a wholesome heroism, a wholesome humanism, which is to say, let's create a Spanish humanism. Let's delve into our nature and, having once found it, let's rule it properly. "Ruling properly is preferable to expanding the empire."[133]

It is thus through a Cervantine character such as Sancho that the diaspora would perhaps most effectively express its commitment to the humanistic credo, a credo that would allow it to rebuild, on firm ground, a shattered individual and collective identity. It was, then, with and through Cervantes that Spanish exiles believed that such identity could be best reconciled with that of their host homelands. Salinas synthesized this ambitious aim as he voiced his desire to return to a free and dignified Spain, bringing with him "that *Quixote* that has been done here, in America, by the collaborative effort of Spaniards and Latin Americans."[134] This quixotic dream—of using Cervantes as a meeting space in which actors on both sides of the Atlantic could reaffirm and reconcile their very different histories and traditions, and "know" and "feel" their own truths—was not entirely fulfilled, despite considerable common ground. Like other grand aspirations of the moment, the humanistic dream of diasporic writers would need to wait for other disenchantments.

Epilogue: Humanism Suspended—The Reverberations of Silence

The significance of the cultural legacy recuperated by this study raises the question of how this buried strain of humanism and criticism, Cervantism, could have been evaded for so long. While this book has detailed the ultra-conservative and fascist efforts to undermine and obscure the work of counter-hegemonic thinkers well into the 1950s, it ends by asking: Why did the succeeding decades *sustain* this omission? An obvious element of the loss of control over the message (i.e., this legacy) is the disadvantaged position of the messengers. Given the stature of the thinkers and artists under discussion, the meager impact of their work illustrates the doubly marginalized status of the Spanish diaspora, both broadly—within the countries these thinkers inhabited as exiles—and narrowly—given the constraints of the academic and creative spaces in which they operated.

Although there was a significant influx of exiled Spanish intellectuals into the United States during and after the Civil War, the majority of these figures remained almost completely removed from positions of power within their academic institutions or communities.[1] Even famed poets like Cernuda, Salinas, and Guillén spent most of their careers as itinerant visiting professors, supporting themselves and their families on quite tight salaries. Only a minuscule group of fortunate scholars such as Américo Castro (Princeton University), Francisco Villanueva (Harvard University), and Joaquín Casalduero (University of California, San Diego) occupied influential and permanent positions. From Max Aub to María Zambrano, the majority of the exiled writers gathered in iconic volumes like the one that *Las Españas* dedicated to Cervantes in 1947 occupied less visible appointments, remaining largely unfamiliar to specialists like Anthony

Close, who were left to assess the field of Spanish criticism in the twentieth century based on a partial record.

Almost as debilitating for the voice and reach of those Spanish émigrés was their necessary "adaptation" to the publication requirements of the Anglo-American academic world. As Joan Ramon Resina and Sebastiaan Faber have shown, the decision of leading journals in the field, such as *Hispania*, to "completely exclude the subject of [the Civil] War," and the willingness of others, such as *Revista Hispánica Moderna*, to "only timidly" mention that conflict in the "literary news" section, severely limited the expression of these Spaniards.[2] Restricting to private settings the political and social perspectives they had so freely poured into their publications before emphasized their sense of cultural, political, and institutional isolation. "I cannot speak to anybody, absolutely anybody," complained Salinas; "[a]mong other things, I would not know with whom I could discuss these issues of international affairs or war; bringing them up means seeing your interlocutor's facial expression freeze, shutting them down."[3] Writers like him only had to add the limitations of language to this ongoing frustration to reduce even further the dissemination and reach of their ideas.

These structural constraints worked both ways, however. The Anglo-American scholarly platforms unwilling to give free rein to these authors for the sake of a neutral, textually bound kind of analysis locked Cold War Hispanists into "historicist and philological traditions" that caused the discipline to sidestep more innovative approaches and themes, such as historical materialism, ethnic studies, and feminism.[4] Despite the groundbreaking development of frameworks such as postcolonialism, Spanish studies continued to be concerned with narrowly defined literary subjects into the 1970s, maintaining traditional national boundaries and disciplinary divides. The contours of the discipline in the American division provide a stark contrast to the politically invested and culturally inclusive literary criticism that had flourished forty years earlier in Spain, during the late 1920s and 1930s.

Furthermore, while progressive exiles were mandated to strip their historical and social perspectives from their literary analyses, historians such as Antonio Maravall received overwhelming international recognition for infusing their work with a conservative bias. Many of his distorted views on the period, and even on authors like Cervantes, would become the default setting of the field for decades. As a result, cultural and political developments in Spain increasingly reinforced the burgeoning idea that Spanish studies had always entailed a conservative approach to literary— especially Golden Age—texts.

Equally important to the consolidation of that perception is the fact that after the not-overtly successful Cervantine commemoration of 1947, the pragmatic Francoist regime adopted another effective strategy to distract attention from the authors and critics who were absent or who had stood in critical resistance to their government. In the 1960s, a focus on the profitability of Spanish Peninsular publishing houses coincided with the commercial rise of a new generation of young Latin American fiction writers who, fleeing dictatorships in their own countries, had been allowed to relocate to Spain and publish their works. The surprising role that the Peninsular editorial establishment played in the dissemination of the "Latin American Boom" throughout the Spanish-speaking world reflects, in part, the financial success of these authors, which ironically led to "the relaxation of restrictions on the publication and distribution of works that would have previously been considered subversive in Spain."[5] The new fascination with this Latin American literary revolution also managed to further displace the works, experiences, and views of Spain's own exiles.

By the late 1960s, Spain had turned the page on Cervantes and closed the book on its humanist past. Even the transition to democracy in the late 1970s did not immediately resuscitate the progressive critical voices that had preceded and punctuated the Civil War and the long years of the dictatorship. Spanish cultural and academic institutions were slow to reconstruct the traces of a struggling and fragmented literary generation whose work had been wiped away almost forty years prior. Much effort to recover this legacy has been undertaken from the explosive 1980s onward, and I happily leave to others the closer examination of this body of work. But with regard to the humanistic and humanizing Cervantine splendor that started in the 1920s and was so regretfully disrupted in the Civil War, much work lies ahead. The progressive strain of Cervantism I recuperate in this volume acquired a new physical address in the diaspora but was unable to find a new intellectual home.

Perhaps the best way to honor and restore this important chapter of Spanish critical history is by considering it not as a static moment or particular site in the country's cultural heritage, but as a bridge to the multiple discourses that it advanced. The themes and values of the criticism I have highlighted in this book—humanism, erasmism, modernity, and so forth—remain critically relevant to Spain and other Spanish-speaking countries, including the United States, where the question of how to form a modern state and what to take or re-enact from the past still carries enormous weight.

It is my hope that with books like this, Golden Age studies can strip away the distorted patina imposed by its long years under the Francoist regime and be fully recognized as the rich, liberating educational field that it was at its inception a century ago, and continues to be today at both sides of the Atlantic. Illuminating its progressive legacy only confirms the indispensable place and purpose of a discipline that has quite a bit to say about how delusions of greatness can disrupt social norms and political spheres. For Spain in particular, deepening our understanding of the cultural struggles and democratic ambitions of this field might allow us to assimilate a bit better the complexity of our past and the possibilities of our future. At the very least, awareness of these critical, antifascist chapters may remind us that even if modernity does not seem to ever fully arrive, our Golden, humanistic reference is guaranteed to never leave.

NOTES

Preface

1   The Golden and Silver Ages of Spanish culture correspond roughly to the 1500s and 1600s and the years between 1898 and 1936, respectively. The designation of both periods is under constant redefinition; the Golden Age "refers now by common consent to the literature of both the sixteenth and seventeenth centuries," as argued by Jeremy Robbins ("Renaissance and Baroque, Continuity and Transformation in Early Modern Spain," in *The Cambridge History of Spanish Literature*, edited by David T. Gies [Cambridge University Press, 2004], 134–48, 134). I will be addressing this period and cultural production as Golden Age and early modern age indistinctively, following the well-established, New-Historicist and Cultural Studies turn in the discipline. As Margaret Greer reminds us, "whether we chose the Golden Age or early modern, our view should include both the Renaissance incorporation of Italian Literary models and the baroque development of a uniquely Spanish response." "Thine and Mine: 'The Spanish Golden Age' and Early Modern Studies" (*PMLA*, 126 no. 1 [2011]: 217–24, 221).

    Hilaire Kalledorf's important volume (*A Companion to the Spanish Renaissance* [Brill, 2019]) has opted for the encompassing term of "Renaissance" as an appellation for this historical moment and its culture. In doing so, she adopts the cultural designation that Jacob Burckhardt had emphatically denied to Spain and that "Hispanists have yet to embrace" (13). Given its complicated, critical history, some specialists had warned about the implications of such attribution—see Alison Weber's caution about it ("Golden Age, or Early Modern: What's in a Name?" *PMLA* 126, no. 1 [2011]: 225–32). *Cervantes, the Golden Age, and the Battle for Cultural Identity* supports both of these views, embracing this Renaissance appellation, and providing a generous context for the critical and methodological struggle behind it.

    With regard to the *Edad de Plata*, there is greater consensus for the term. As an established but inclusive parameter, the idea of "edad de plata" refers now to a fertile and open cultural movement taking place from the end of the 1800s into the first decades of the 1900s. There are slight disagreements about its beginning (1898, 1902, or 1913), and a common understanding that it ends either with the start of Second Republic (in 1931), or at the beginning of the Civil War (in 1936). Although José Carlos Mainer did not invent the phrase "Silver Age," he certainly popularized it (*La edad de plata, 1902–1931* [Asenet, 1975]). Other studies that preceded or consolidated the concept were Pedro

Cerezo Galán, José María Jover Zamora, Pedro Laín Entralgo et al., *La edad de plata de la cultura española, 1898–1936* (Espasa Calpe, 1993), and Luis de Llera Esteban, Ortega y *la Edad de Plata de la Literatura Española 1914–1936* (Bulzoni, 1991). The idea of "edad de plata" now encompasses other authors and subjects traditionally not recognized as part of this cultural revival—female contributors, visual artists, musicians, essayists, theorists, and so on. Examples include Murga Castro, Idoia, *Escenografía de la danza en la Edad de Plata (1916–1936)* (Consejo Superior de Investigaciones Científicas, 2009); Antonio Fernández Torres, *Ignacio Sánchez Mejías, el hombre de la edad de plata* (Almuzara, 2010); and Emilia Cortés Ibáñez, *Zenobia Camprubí y la Edad de Plata de la cultura española* (Universidad Internacional de Andalucía, 2010).

2　Robbins understands the Golden Age as a moment in which "the literary models of the Italian Renaissance were adopted," which leads him to understand the literature of the moment to be "consciously imitative" of the Italian "preexisting cultural model whose literary style was largely alien to its native traditions and practices"; the difference between this kind of "Renaissance" literature and the "Baroque" is that "[i]n sharp contrast… the Spanish baroque drew upon European trends in thought, it was a direct response to the major epistemological developments that led elsewhere to the new philosophy and sciences, there were no preexisting models to emulate in assimilating and responding to these" (138).

3　Geraldine Heng, *The Invention of Race in the European Middle Ages* (Cambridge University Press, 2018), 22. Early modern specialists continue to produce enlightening explorations of modernity in the period; I have benefited immensely from the work of David R. Castillo, William Egginton Enrique García Santo Tomás, Rachel Schmidt, William Childers, and Eric Clifford Graf, among others. Castillo and Egginton, in *Medialogies: Reading Reality in the Age of Inflationary Media* (Bloomsbury, 2017) offer one of the most provocative accounts of the relevance of the 1600s literary and epistemological structures in the virtual age of the twenty-first century; Schmidt's *Forms of Modernity: Don Quixote and Modern Theories of the Novel* (University of Toronto Press, 2011) opens new interpretative paths for the novel by providing a sophisticated, theoretical understanding of Cervantes's use of genre; Hanno Ehrilicher and Stephen Schereckenberg's collection *El Siglo de Oro en la España contemporánea* (Ibericana, 2011) introduces some of the early modern age critical and historical topics reinterpreted during the twentieth century, such as the shifting readings of Don Juan's myth, or the cinematographic adaptations of icons like Santa Teresa; Enrique García Santo Tomás, in his *Modernidad bajo sospecha: Salas Barbadillo y la cultura material del siglo XVII* (Anejos de Revista de Literatura, 2008), illustrates how the material conditions and social changes of the 1600s propelled the development of an extraordinary literary culture in Spain; Graf's *Cervantes and Modernity* (Bucknell University Press, 2007) supplies an analysis of how Cervantes's prose and age discursive and material configurations advance our own; William Childers's *Transnational Cervantes* (University of Toronto Press, 2006) shows how to push through scholarly boundaries, examining the thread of Cervantine narratives and influences through disparate chronologies and national traditions.

4   The binary opposition that I allude to here, traditional versus liberal, (ultra) conservative versus reformist or progressive, necessarily simplifies the convoluted net of cultural and ideological affiliations of each side. While the right was overall able to unify its major ideological strands—Falangists, Carlists, Monarchists, and Catholic conservatives—into the "National Movement" first, and the Francoist dictates later, the left was not able to fully integrate all liberal factions—federalists, anarchists, communists, reformists, and so on. Furthermore, beyond the right and left split, each of these spectrums was heavily punctuated by sectarian differences, "pitting periphery against the centre, the revolution against modernization, and militias against the army." Mark Lawrence, *The Spanish Civil Wars: A Comparative History of the First Carlist War and the Conflict of the 1930s* (Bloomsbury Publishing, 2017), 14. See also Stanley Payne and Javier Tusell, *La guerra civil: una nueva visión del conflicto que dividió España* (Temas de hoy, 1996); Helen Graham, *The Spanish Republic at War* (Cambridge University Press, 2002); and Chris Ealham and Michael Richards, *The Splintering of Spain: Cultural History and the Spanish Civil War, 1936–1939* (Cambridge University Press, 2005).

Introduction

1   "En abril de 1521, el absolutismo austríaco, instaurado en España, aniquiló en Villalar a los comuneros, representantes de las democracias municipales. En 1931, los Ayuntamientos españoles derrotan, jurídicamente, a la Monarquía absolutista y restauran la República. Se cierra un gran ciclo histórico. Se consuma, pacíficamente, una honda revolución que, en su sentido etimológico quiere decir volver al punto de partida. Volvemos a 1521, a la suprema soberanía popular. Son cuatro siglos y diez años. Muchos siglos y muchos años .... España, paciente pero no muerta, como muchos otros creían, ha dado un magnífico ejemplo de dignidad histórica." Luis Araquistáin, "Un gran ciclo histórico 1521–1931," *El Sol*, April 15, 1931. Emphasis added. All translations, unless otherwise noted, are my own.

2   Clearly, however, Spanish modernity did not die with the *Comunero* revolt, in and beyond the early modern period and literature, as seen, for example, in the innovation of Spanish arts and letters developed throughout the 1600s.

3   Richard L. Kagan, *Spain in America: The Origins of Hispanism in the United States* (University of Illinois Press, 2002), 8.

4   The whole quote in Spanish reads: "*[E]n el siglo XVI, en la España del imperio y la contrarreforma, el cenit de su historia .... [L]os fascistas tendieron a reinventar un siglo XVI español cuyo catolicismo imperial se pobló de valores fascistas, totalitarios ... heroicos, guerreros, y agresivos en su defensa, imperiales en su proyección, a tono con los tiempos en su moment.*" Ismael Saz, *España contra España: los nacionalismos franquistas* (Marcial Pons, 2003), 406. See also Alex Bueno, *Memory and Cultural History of the Spanish Civil War: Realms of Oblivion*, edited by Aurora Morcillo (Brill, 2014), 93.

5   Filipe Ribeiro de Meneses, *Franco and the Spanish War* (Taylor and Francis, 2003), 99.

6 Duncan Wheeler, *Golden Age Drama in Contemporary Spain: The Comedia on Page, Stage, and Screen* (Wales University Press, 2012), 17.

7 See in this regard Jacques Lezra, *Contra todos los fueros de la muerte: El suceso cervantino* (La Cebra, 2016).

8 Many of the most foundational texts on this idea of the neobaroque appear in Parkinson Zamora and Monika Kaup, eds., *Baroque New Worlds: Representation, Transculturation, Counterconquest* (Duke University Press, 2010). Essential texts included here are, for example, José Lezama Lima, "Baroque Curiosity" (1952), 212–40; Alejor Carpentier's "Questions Concerning Latin American Novel" (excerpt, 1964), 259–64; Haroldo de Campos, "The Rule of Anthropophagy: Europe under the Sign of Devoration" (1972), 319–40; Severo Sarduy, "The Baroque and the Neobaroque" (1972), 270–91; Gonzalo Celorio, "From the Baroque to the Neobaroque" (Del barroco al neobarroco) (1988), 487–507. Some of the essential critical reflections on the subject include works by John Beverly: "Barroco de estado: Góngora y el gongorinsmo," in *Del Lazarillo al sandisnimo: Estudios sobre la función ideológica de la literatura española e hispanoamericana* (Prisma, 1987), 77–97; "Going Baroque," *Boundary* 215, no. 3 (1988), 27–39; and *Una modernidad obsoleta: Estudios sobre el barroco* (Fondo editorial, 1997). In addition, the following: Omar Calabrese, *Neo-Baroque: A Sign of the Times*, translated by Charles Lambert (Princeton University Press, 1992); Gregg Lambert, *The Return of the Baroque in Modern Culture* (Continuum, 2004); William Egginton, "The Baroque as a Problem of Thought," *PMLA* 121, no. 1 (2009), 143–9; William Egginton, "Reasons, Baroque's House (Cervantes, Master Architect)," in *Reason and Its Others: Italy, Spain, and the New World*, edited by David Castillo and Massimo Lollini (Vanderbilt University Press, 2006), 186–203; and William Childers, "Baroque Quixote: New World Writing and the Collapse of the Heroic Ideal," in Zamora and Kaup, *Baroque New Worlds* (Duke University Press), 415–49.

9 Celorio, "From the Baroque to the Neobaroque," 497.

10 de Campos, "The Rule of Anthropophagy," 328.

11 Ibid., 328.

12 Ibid., 327.

13 Antonio Maravall. *Culture of the Baroque: Analysis of a Historical Structure*, translated by Terry Cochran (University of Manchester Press, 1986), 90.

14 James M. Boyden. "Antonio Maravall," in *Encyclopedia of Historians and Historical Writing*, Vol. 1 (Fitzroy Dearborn, 1999), 761–2. Maravall is still described as the ultimate authority of Spanish Baroque in John D. Lyons, *The Oxford Handbook of the Baroque* (Oxford University Press, 2019), 550–1.

15 Specialists of the field consider Maravall's view of literature in general, and of Baroque theater in particular, to be deeply flawed. See the detailed critiques collected in Laura Bass's enlightening volume *The Comedia and Cultural Control: The Legacy of José Antonio Maravall*, special issue of *Bulletin of the Comediantes* 65, no. 1 (2013). Bass opens this special issue reminding us that "Maravall did not invent socio-historical approaches to the genre [*comedia*] any more than Lope de Vega fathered the 'arte nuevo,'" the historian's great accomplishment (like Lope's) was that "he brought them into the mainstream" (Laura Bass, Introduction. *The Comedia and Cultural Control*, 1–13, 1). Maravall's analysis has been considered as a "simplistic paradigm" (Jonathan

Thacker, *Role-play and the World as Stage in the Comedia* [Liverpool University Press, 2002], 5) that often incurred in a "sociohistorical parochialism" (Duncan, Wheeler, "Contextualising and Contesting José Antonio Maravall's Theories of Baroque Culture from the Perspective of Modern-Day Performance," in *The Comedia and Cultural Control, Bulletin of the Comediantes* 65, no. 1 (2013), 15–43, 24), and cannot be considered either historical nor social in nature (Ruth MacKay, "The Maravall Problem: A Historical Inquiry," in *The Comedia and Cultural Control*, Vol. 1 (2013), 45–56, 45). For MacKay, Maravall's most essential problem was not to consider "the possibility that institutions and individuals (monarchy, nobility, culture, secularization, protest, and so on.) develop in contradictory fashion; that we are not all the same; and that repression and culture and power are never monolithic or static" (49). Carlos Gutiérrez believes that Maravall's framework is not as rigid or unuseful as some of his critics have described it, being ultimately right in its fundamental thesis: the existence of complicated seigneurial network of interests and values defended by implicit and explicit mechanisms created for this very purpose. For Gutiérrez, where Maravall went wrong was in his excessive usage of literary examples and in assuming the straightforward political applicability of those texts (Carlos Gutiérrez, *La espada, el rayo, y la pluma: Quevedo y los campos literario y de poder* [Purdue University Press, 2005] 206). Golden Age specialists have understood the historian's narrow focus on the period, believing it to be a projection of his "own historical moment—namely … Franco's decades-long dictatorship in Spain" (Hillaire Kalleadorf, *Sins of the Fathers: Moral Economies in Early Modern Spain* [Toronto University Press, 2013] 210).

16 As late as 2015, in a volume published by the MLA, Jonathan Tacker considers Anthony Close's approach responsible for the defining critical shift that stirred away from Romantic interpretations, rehabilitating instead "the comic dimension of the novel" in *Don Quixote* in English Translation," 39–55. *Approaches to Teaching Cervantes's Don Quixote,* edited by James Parr and Lisa Vollendorf (MLA, 2015), 41. Close's critique of Cervantes and Cervantism has been widely used to divide the critics working in the field as harsh (not sympathetic to Cervantes's protagonists) or "soft" (viewing the novel *Don Quixote* as a humorous literary exercise). While the extent and comic interpretation of Close's reading have often been questioned, by José Montero Reguera (*Quijote y la crítica contemporánea* [Centro de Estudios cervantinos, 1997], 108–9) and (Adrienne Martin, "Humor and Violence in Cervantes," in *The Cambridge Companion to Cervantes*, edited by Anthony Cascardi [Cambridge University Press, 2002], 160–85, 176–7), for example, the main tenets of Close's Romantic critique have been largely unquestioned.

17 Anthony Close, *The Romantic Approach to "Don Quixote"* (Cambridge University Press, 1978), 28.

18 Ibid., 90.

19 For fluid approaches to the group Generation of 1898 (from now on, Generation of '98, or '98 group), see José Carlos Mainer, *Modernismo y 98* (Barcelona: Crítica, 1994); Roberta Johnson, "From the Generation of 1898 to the Vanguard," in *The Cambridge Companion to the Spanish Novel from 1600 to the Present*, edited by Harriet Turner (Cambridge University Press, 2003), 155–71, 156; and Joan Ramon Resina, "A Spectre Is Haunting Spain: The Spirit of the Land in the Wake of the Disaster," *Journal of Spanish*

Cultural Studies, 2, no. 2 (2001), 169–86. For an extra-academic assessment of the group, see Sender, *Los Noventayochos* (Las Américas, 1961).

20 Close, *Romantic Approach*, 136.

21 Ibid., 256. Although Close's study has not been truly refuted, some Cervantists such as Ruth El Saffar noted that *Don Quixote* always gets "the last laugh," being often able to transcend the literal, symbolic, or historic awareness—and limitations—of its readers and critics. In her Review of *The Romantic Approach to "Don Quixote,"* she suggested that the real task of criticism might be reconciliation of a contextualized interpretation of a text with its literal meaning, but *without* having one reading disparage the other. (*MLN* 94, no. 2 [1979], 399–404, 404).

22 Close, *Romantic Approach*, 257.

23 Anthony Close, "Theory versus the Humanist Tradition Stemming from Américo Castro," in *Cervantes and His Postmodern Constituencies*, edited by Anne Cruz and Carroll B. Johnson (Garland, 1999), 1–21, 1.

24 There are numerous and valid objections against a generational historiographic model for the study of Spanish literature and culture. It is easy to see such structure perpetuated, as Christopher Soufas argues, by a "misguided sense of devotion to the 'national critical tradition' or from a lingering sense of comfort" (*The Subject in Question: Early Contemporary Spanish Literature and Modernism* [Catholic University of America Press, 2007], 4). The artificial division of an entire literary production into generations, has, in fact, "effectively shut off Spain's modern literature from the rest of Europe. Instead of having a modernist period and an avant-garde, Spanish literature was conceptualized as consisting of the so-called Generation of 1898, a Generation of 1914, a Generation of 1927, and so forth" (Juan Herrero-Senés and Eduardo Gregori, *Avant-Garde Cultural Practices in Spain (1914–1936): The Challenge of Modernity* [Brill, 2016], 2). The generational perspective furthermore assumes some form of artificial uniformity among the members of each group, tending to mythologize the relationships between their members and all other factions; it also uses a set of fixed templates—generic and artistic boundaries, chronologies, and geographies—that consider them "unique," which underlines the idea of a Spanish exceptionalism, halting any "attempts to situate early contemporary Peninsular literature in a transnational context" (Soufas, *The Subject*, 4).

Mainer confessed in 2019 to having engaged in two "onomastic battles" against the use of the terms such as "Generation of 1927 and Generation of 1898," which he lost ("Of periodizations and polemics" in "Repositioning Modernity, Modernism, and the Avant-Garde in Spain: A Transatlantic Debate at the Residencia de Estudiantes," *Romance Quarterly* 66, no. [2019] 159–72, 168). For Mainer, it is clear that despite constant opposition, both appellations continue to enjoy good health in 2019. In the case of the '27 designation, Mainer blames the continuing acceptance of the name

> [O]n a myth, on an emotional yearning (confirmed again in the centenaries of 1992–1993) and perhaps—as Bergamín pointed out—on the interests of its beneficiaries. The myth of 1927 was born early on because since 1925 the word "generation" circulates widely as a slogan of self-recognition.
> ("Of periodizations" 168)

Despite these justified reservations, critics generally concur with Jeremy Robbins that the benefits of using labels of this kind—being able to speak of these complex, intertwined cultural processes—outweigh "the problems inherent in their usage" ("Renaissance" 137), at least as long as these terms are used in hybrid and inclusive manners.

It is with that open understanding that I will be speaking of the Generation of 1927 as Generation of '27 or '27 group. By this designation, I refer to a group of writers and artists that includes, among others, Rafael Alberti (1902–99), Manuel Altolaguirre (1905–59), José Ramón Araña (1905–73), Max Aub (1903–72), Francisco Ayala (1906–2009), Luis Cernuda (1902–63), José Gaos (1900–69), Federico García Lorca (1898–1936), Pedro Salinas (1891–1951), Sender (1901–82), José María Luelmo (1904–91), Manuel Andújar (1913–94), José Bergamín (1895–1983), and María Zambrano (1904–91), as well as painters José Caballero (1915–91), Eugenio Granell (1912–2001), Alfonso Ponce de León (1906–36), Maruja Mayo (1902–95), and Gregorio Prieto (1924–96). I follow the general understanding of Mainer's *Edad de plata*, Anthony L. Geist, *La poética de la generación del 27 y las revistas literarias* (Guadarrama, 1980); Francisco Javier Díez de Revenga, *Panorama crítico de la generación del 27* (Castalia, 1987); Antonio Martín Ezpeleta, *Las historias literarias de los escritores de la generación del 27* (Arco, 2008); and Janet Pérez and Maureen Ilhrie, *The Feminist Encyclopedia of Spanish Literature* (Greenwood Press, 2002).

25 Aubrey Bell 1934, "Cervantes and the Renaissance," *Hispanic Review* 2, no. 2 (1934), 89–101, 93.

26 Juan Goytisolo, *Forbidden Territory and Realms of Strife: The Memoirs of Juan Goytisolo* (Verso, 2003), 105.

27 Manuel Vázquez Montalbán, *La Aznaridad. Por el imperio hacia Dios o por Dios hacia el imperio* (Modadori, 2003).

28 "El libro más antinacional, peligroso, inmoral y trágico de España." Ernesto Giménez Caballero, "Un peligro nacional. La vuelta de *Don Quijote*" (*La Gaceta Literaria* 122 [1932], 3).

29 "El peor veneno para España." Ibid., 3.

30 Luis Cernuda, *Estudios sobre poesía española contemporánea* (Guadarrama, 1957), 64.

31 I am concerned here with this specific moment in history (1920–40). For the monumentalization of Cervantes as a national icon prior to the twentieth century, see Jesús Pérez Magallón, *Cervantes, monumento de la nación: problemas de identidad y cultura* (Cátedra, 2015).

32 Pedro Salinas, Quijote *y lectura: defensas y fragmentos*, edited by Enric Bou (ELR Ediciones, 2005), 67.

Chapter 1

1 Dagmar Vandebosch traces how a nostalgic, imperial quixotism was constructed by the Generation of '98 and honored by later thinkers such as Ortega; "Quixotism as a Poetic and National Project in the Early Twentieth-

Century Spanish Essay," in *International* Don Quixote, edited by Theo D'haen and Reindert Dhondt (Brill, 2009), 14–32.

2   See the data in Stanley G. Payne, *The Collapse of the Second Republic, 1933–36: Origins of the Civil War* (Yale University Press, 2006), 8–9; also, Payne, *A History of Spain and Portugal*, Vol. 2 (University of Wisconsin Press, 1973), 578–632; Nicholás Sánchez Albornoz, *The Economic Modernization of Spain, 1830–1930* (New York University Press, 1987); José Luis Malo de Molina and P. Martín-Aceña, eds., *The Spanish Financial System: Growth and Development since 1900* (Palgrave Macmillan, 2011); and Javier Moreno Luzón, *Modernizing the Nation: Spain during the Reign of Alfonso XIII, 1902–31* (Sussex University Press, 2012), 1–47.

3   The rise in income took place in only six years, between 1914 and 1920, Joseph Harrison, *An Economic History of Modern Spain* (Manchester University Press, 1978), 129–30. Mark Lawrence claims that the population of most Spanish cities actually doubled between 1900 and 1930. See *The Spanish Civil Wars. A Comparative History* (Bloomsbury, 2017), 17. Gabriel Tortell, "Demographic Modernization," in *The Development of Modern Spain: An Economic History of the Nineteenth and Twentieth Century* (Harvard University Press, 2000), 241–66. Some historians consider that the average life expectancy was even shorter (thirty-five years) in early 1900; see, for example, David Sven Reher's *Perspectives on the Family in Spain, Past and Present* (Clarendon Press, 1997), 251.

4   For literacy rates in particular, see Luzón, *Modernizing the Nation*, 23.

5   Harrison, *An Economic History*; Payne, *A History*, 578–632.

6   See Moreno Luzón's "Social Transitions" and "Cracks in the Turno" in *Modernizing the Nation*, 72–86.

7   For the Morocco crisis, see Susana Sueiro Seoane, "Spanish Colonialism during Primo de Rivera's Dictatorship," in *Spain and the Mediterranean since 1898*, edited by Raanan Rein (Routledge, 1999), 48–65, especially 55.

8   Javier Moreno Luzón, "The Restoration 1874–1914," in *The History of Modern Spain: Chronologies, Themes, Individuals*, edited by José Alvarez Junco, and Adrian Shubert (Bloomsbury, 2018), 46–63, 47.

9   Juli Highfill, *Modernism and Its Merchandise: The Spanish Avant Garde and Material Culture* (Pennsylvania State University, 2014), 5. To gain a deeper understanding—from a strikingly different perspective—of the issues left unsolved by Primo de Rivera's regime, like the pending agrarian reform later inherited by the Republic and then badly addressed in Franco's policies, see Bibiana Duarte Abadía, "Colonizing Rural Waters: The Politics of Hydro-territorial Transformation in Guadlhorce Valley, Malaga, Spain," *Water International* 44, no. 2 (2019), 148–68.

10 This flexible outlook allows us to escape the trappings of the Romantic exceptionalism that has long considered Spain a backward country that, in the words of Prescot, had collapsed under the weight of its religious bigotry and monarchic absolutism. Richard Kagan refers to this idea as the "Prescott paradigm," underlining the ways in which the American historian constructed Spain's history as an antithesis of that of the United States. "America was the future—republican, enterprising, rational; while Spain—monarchical, indolent, fanatic—represented the past." Kagan, *Spain in America*, 9–10; for Spanish

exceptionalism, see 22–3 and 263–4. Pere Gifra-Adroher also covers the *Romantic, Exceptionalist Perception of the Country in between History and Romance: Travel Writing on Spain in the Early Nineteenth-Century United States* (Fairleigh Dickinson University Press, 2000), 33.

11   "[E]n la Restauración nada falta. Hay allí grandes estadistas, grandes pensadores, grandes generales, grandes partidos, grandes aprestos, grandes luchas: nuestro ejército en Tetuán combate con los moros lo mismo que en tiempo de Gonzalo de Córdoba; en busca del Norte enemigo hienden la espalda del mar nuestras cadenas, como en tiempos de Felipe II; Pereda es Hurtado de Mendoza y en Echegaray retoña Calderón. Pero todo esto acontece dentro de la órbita de un sueño; es la imagen de una vida donde solo hay de real el acto que la imagina. La Restauración, señores, fue un panorama de fantasmas, y [Antonio] Cánovas [del Castillo] el gran empresario de la fantasmagoría." José Ortega y Gasset, *Las meditaciones del Quijote* (Espasa Calpe, 1943), 96.

       Antonio Cánovas del Castillo (1828–97) served six terms as Spain's prime minister and was an essential player in the Restoration of the Bourbon dynasty in Spain. He was also one of the architects of the system of government that saw the two parties holding power on an alternating basis. See José Alvarez Junco, "History, Politics, and Culture 1875–1936," in *The Cambridge Companion to Modern Spanish Culture*, edited by David T. Gies (Cambridge, 1999), 67–85.

12   Ortega y Gasset's devastating account of the late 1800s blames the absence of any major political or literary "accomplishments" in this era on the lack of "complexity, reflection, [and] intelligence" (complejidad, reflexión, plenitud de intelecto) of its protagonists (*Meditaciones*, 96). Even a well-established genre such as "the nineteenth century-novel" was, for him, doomed: In contrast to a classic like Don Quixote, he wrote, the Spanish realist novel "would very soon be unreadable" (*será ilegible muy pronto*) (*Meditaciones*, 81).

13   Renato Poggioli, *The Theory of the Avant Garde* (Harvard University Press, 1968), 55.

14   The German art historian Carl Einstein (1885–1940) theorized a foundational view of primitive art that explicitly rejected the aesthetic and capitalist values of the European tradition (*Mythology of Forms*, translated by Charles W. Haxthausen [University of Chicago Press, 2019], 124). For how this aesthetic manifesto applies to other artistic languages, see Ben Etherington, *Literary Primitivism* (Stanford University Press, 2018), 33–4.

15   Poggioli, *The Theory*, 55. Beyond the iconic example of Picasso's reconciliation with primitive, futuristic, and traditional (Golden Age) elements, Thea Portman explains how the Mexican painter Fernando Botero, for example, blended all such pictorial references in his vaguardist and personal symbiosis. Lisa Shaw and Stephanie Denninson's *Pop Culture Latin America! Media, Arts, and Lifestyle* (CLIO, 2005), 329–31.

16   Qtd. in Poggioli, *The Theory*, 55.

17   The tercentenary of Góngora's death made 1927 a year of conferences, homages, and special issues dedicated to the poet. One of the most consequential occasions was the celebration of a collective homage in Córdoba, in June; this would come to be considered the foundational act

of the Generation of '27, exemplifying its literary and poetic idiosyncrasy. In truth, the homage was far from a foundational ceremony; rather than reflecting the collective will of the group, it mostly illustrated the preferences of the organizer, Gerardo Diego (helped by Dámaso Alonso). See, "Gerardo Diego to Manuel de Falla," Letter, May 3, 1927. Gabriele Morelli, ed., *Gerardo Diego y el III Centenario de Góngora* (Pre-textos, 2001), 151. See also María Isabel Navas Ocaña's assessment of differences among the group of 27 in *España y las vanguardias* (Almería: Servicio Publicaciones Universidad de Almería, 1997), 32.

18 Wendy Steiner, *Pictures of Romance: Form against Context in Painting and Literature* (University of Chicago, 1988), 121; and Margaret H. Persin, *Getting the Picture* (Bucknell University Press, 1997), 54.

19 Pablo Picasso, *Góngora*, translated by Alan S. Trueblood. Introduction by John Russell (Braziller, 1985), 5.

20 *The Entierro del Conde de Orgaz* (Barcelona: Gustavo Gili and Ediciones Cometa, 1969); *Vingt poèmes de Góngora* (Lacourière, 1948). See Claustre Rafart Planas, *Picasso's Las Meninas* (Meteora, 2001).

21 See, for example, González's sculpture of *Don Quixote* (ca. 1929–30), Jackson Pollock's *Don Quixote* (1944, Peggy Guggenheim Collection), Dalí's illustrated version of *Don Quixote* (Random House, 1946), Charles Pollock, *Don Quixote* (ca. 1950, Smithsonian American Art Museum), Hofmann's rendition *Don Quixote* (1963, Berkeley Art Museum & Pacific Film Archive). Dore Ashton, Giménez, Carmen, and Francisco Serraller provide in *Picasso and the Age of Iron* (Abrams, 1995) an enlightening exploration of this artistic attention.

22 Peter Read, *Picasso and Apollinaire: The Persistence of Memory* (University of California Press, 2008), 42–43, and Rafael Inglada. "Pablo Picasso: *La Numancia* de Guernica," http://museupicassobcn.org/congresinternacional/inglada/, Accessed on January 5, 2021.

23 Qtd. in Edward Hirch, *A Poet's Glossary* (Harcourt, 2014), 266. To understand the obsessive regard for Góngora, see Enrique Selva, *Ernesto Giménez Caballero entre la vanguardia y el fascismo* (Pre-Textos, 2000), 86.

24 Quote by Salinas, "Góngora, a Difficult Poet," in *Obras completas*, Vol. II. edited by Enric Bou (Madrid: Cátedra, 2007), 256–60, 257.

25 "La suma gongorina que como todas, debiera contener sólo a sus sumandos, por definición a los clásicos, los rebasa y resulta desconocida, moderna" (*Gaceta literaria* 11 [1927], 2).

26 As Pedro Salinas wrote, most poets sought "to provide simple descriptions of the world, just as it is, but luckily for us—and for him—Góngora is far from that." Salinas, "Góngora," 259.

27 "Todos los andaluces somos un poco surrealistas … como Don Luis de Góngora y Argote." Roberto Otero, *Lejos de España: encuentros y conversaciones con Picasso* (Dopesa, 1975), 86.

28 Edward Hirch, *A Poet's Glossary* (Houghton Mifflin Harcourt, 2014), 266.

29 *Don Quixote* II, translated by Edith Grossman (HarperCollins, 2003), 71: 923; "el pintor y el escritor son todo uno," *El ingenioso hidalgo Don Quijote de la Mancha*, edited by Luis Murillo (Castalia, 1978), 2.71: 574. From now on, all quotes from the novel either in English or Spanish would

be of these two editions referred to as *DQ* and *IH*. Cervantes argues, for example, that "history, poetry, and painting resemble one another and indeed are so much alike that when you write history you're painting, and when you paint, you're composing poetry" (*The Trials of Persiles and Sigismunda*, translated by Celia Richmond Weller and Clark A. Colahan [Hackett, 1989], 3.14: 272) ("la historia, la poesía, y la pintura simbolizan entre sí, y se parecen tanto, que cuando escribes historia pintas, y cuando pintas, compones") (*Persiles*, edited by Juan Bautista Avalle Arce [Madrid: Castalia, 1986] III.14: 371).

30 Juan Cano Ballesta, *La poesía española entre pureza y revolución (1930–1936)* (Gredos, 1972), 121 n.47.

31 "[U]n silencio verde ... La guitarra es un pozo/con viento en vez de agua." "La guitarra" en *Obras Completas*, Vol. 1, edited by Francisco Javier Díez de Revenga (Alfaguara, 1996), 157.

32 The musical quality of Lorca's own poetry would not only respond to an unusual understanding of poetic form, but to a deeper artistic intention, at the heart of the avant-garde primitivism: the attempt to capture through a multidimensional verse the unfiltered essence of a cultural identity, in this case Andalusian. The aim was shared by the Lorca's common collaborator and personal friend, Manuel de Falla (1876–1946). While Timothy Mitchell is critical of what he sees as Lorca's orientalism in this avant-garde poetry ("Flamenco Deep Song" [Yale University Press, 1994], 38–50), Alice J. Poust considers this "primitive" drive a constructive alternative to modernity ("Federico García Lorca's Andalusia in Light of Oswald Spengler's Theory of Magian Culture," in *Lorca, Buñuel, Dalí: Art and Theory,* edited by Manuel Delgado Morales and Alice J. Poust [Bucknell University Press, 2001], 175–90). Federico Bonaddio, *Federico García Lorca* (Tamesis, 2010), provides a larger context for this controversy (46).

33 As the first lines of a poem like the one dedicated to that instrument show, "The guitar's lament/is starting up./Goblets of dawn/break apart" (*Empieza el llanto/de la guitarra./Se rompen las copas/de la madrugada*), quoted by Nelson R. Orringer, *Lorca in Tune with Falla: Literary and Musical Interludes* (University of Toronto Press, 2016), 67. The poem in question is also dedicated to the guitar, and goes much deeper than Diego into musical allusion. Orringer shows how Lorca renounces metric regularity, using specific phonic combinations (liquid consonants and doubly trills, such ll-, l-, rr-, r-, and -r-) to imitate "the lambent strumming" of the instrument (67). This is why Lorca is so often described as "Prosa cantada," as Luis García Montero explains in his contextual introduction (*Rafael Alberti's Lorca, poeta y amigo* [Andaluzas Unidas, 1984], 30–6, 36). Orrigner agrees, 236.

34 "Hoy, en España se hace la más hermosa poesía de Europa." Letter to Miguel Hernández, 1933, in *Federico García Lorca, obras completas,* edited by Arturo Hoyo (Madrid: Aguilar, 1964), 1681–2.

35 Buñuel's artistic identity was enormously fluid. In the *Last Sigh* (Vintage, 1983), the refers to the "infamous Generation of 1927" as "my" generation (70). As it is well known, Buñuel had lived at the Residencia de Estudiantes (1917–25), interacted throughout his life with the '27 group, and lived in exile, Mexico, with the progressive Spanish diaspora. Aesthetically, he identified as a surrealist (71).

36 Wallace Stevens, "Relations between Poetry and Painting," a 1951 lecture included in *The Necessary Angel: Essays on Reality and the Imagination* (Random House, 1951), 157–78, 171.

37 Carol Hess, *Sacred Passions* (Oxford University Press, 2005), 90. The educational ideal behind the Residencia was described in detail by J. B. Trend in *A Modern Spain* (Constable, 1921), 33–44; see the description of visitors such as Einstein in Alberto Jiménez Fraud, *La Residencia de Estudiantes* (Ariel, 1972), 36–7. For an insider's account *in Alfonso Reyes La Residencia de Estudiantes* (Residencia de estudiantes, 1926), and for a perceptive analysis of such perception, "'Telling it like it was?' The 'Residencia de estudiantes' and its 'image,'" in Alison Sinclair and Richard Cleminson, eds., *Alternative Discourses in Early Twentieth-century Spain: Intellectuals, Dissent and Subcultures of Mind and Body*, special issue of *Bulletin of Spanish Studies* 81, no. 6 (2004), 687–95.

38 Álvaro Ribagorda, *Caminos de la modernidad: espacios e instituciones culturales de la Edad de Plata (1898–1936)* (Biblioteca Nueva, 2009). Some of the most interdisciplinary analysis of the last two decades can be found in Alison Sinclair, *Trafficking Knowledge in Early Twentieth-Century Spain: Centres of Exchange and Cultural Imaginaries* (Tamesis, 2009), Juan José Lahuerta, *Dalí, Lorca y la Residencia de Estudiantes* (Sociedad Estatal de Conmemoraciones Culturales, 2010).

39 Mainer, *Historia de la literatura española: Modernidad y nacionalismo: 1900–1939* (Barcelona: Crítica, 2010).

40 Helen Graham, *The Spanish Republic at War 1936–39* (Cambridge University Press, 2019), 181.

41 "Toda la literatura actual, joven (y aún la vieja que se renueva) está teñida de inevitable gongorismo. La técnica desarticulada (articulada de otro modo) y malabarista domina." "Pespuntes históricos sobre un núcleo gongorino actual," *Gaceta Literaria* 11 (1927), 7.

42 "[E]liminar los ingredientes 'humanos, demasiado humanos' y retomar sólo la materia púramente artística" Ortega y Gasset, 1925 (*Revista de Occidente*, 1976), 56. In contrast, Juan Ramón Jiménez (1916–56), the future Nobel laureate, defended this artistic principle and practice, dubbing it a search for "pure, intellectual poetry." At least until 1928–29, Juan Ramón won the argument. Urging artists and writers to recover these qualities, by 1928 the novelist José González Fernández attempted to change that poetic state of affairs by inviting his contemporaries to challenge those conventions in a defining article to "Let's go back to being human" ("Volvamos a lo humano," *Posguerra* 10 [1928], 17–18); his defense of the human dimension of art, as an ethical enterprise compatible with a profound aesthetic renovation was taken up a couple of years later by José Díaz Fernández, who elaborated that claim, explaining why the modernization of an aesthetic was not incompatible with human-related subjects. See his "New Romanticism" in *Prosas* (Obra fundamental Santander-Hispano, 2006), 339–449. There, Díaz Fernández claims that "the true avant garde is that [artistic expression] able to adjust its new forms to the new intellectual concerns of the day" (*La verdadera vanguardia será aquella que ajuste sus formas nuevas de expresión a las nuevas inquietudes del pensamiento* [357]). Even at the height of the

formal experimentation of the 1920s, personal, subjective reflection on social and political issues was far from absent in the Spanish literary scene. It had sporadically resurfaced—more insistently after 1928—as a sign of the emerging social consciousness and artistic dissatisfaction that would come to dominate the 1930s. As a subjective discourse emerged in the late 1920s, divergent ideological strains became more apparent. For further information on José Díaz Fernández, see José López de Abiada, *El nuevo romanticismo: polémica de arte, política y literatura* (J Esteban, 1985).

43   *La Gaceta* 8 (1927), 1. See "'El meridiano intelectual de Hispanoamérica:' polémica suscitada en 1927 por 'La Gaceta Literaria,'" José Carlos González Boixo, *Cuadernos Hispanoamericanos* 459 (1988), 166–71.

44   "[Ese asco ex profesional, apolítico] ha hecho que la literatura gongorina se desarrolle a gusto bajo los regímenes de dictadura. Los dictadores respetan la literatura pura." "Pespuntes históricos sobre un núcleo gongorino actual," *La Gaceta* 11 (1927), 6–7.

45   Giménez Caballero writes that Góngora's verse "Vuelta poemática a la décima, el soneto, y la silva ….es un regreso al antiguo nacionalismo. ... [E]s lo que Mussolini ha logrado en Italia ….la revolución desde arriba." "Visitas literarias. Gerardo Diego, poeta fascista" *El Sol,* 26 (1927), 327–31.

46   Gerardo Diego (emphasis added, *Lola* 2 [1927], 5).

47   The survey posed four main questions: (1) Does the avant-garde still exist/has it ever existed in Spain? (2) How would you define it? (3) What are the literary principles of this movement? (4) How do you think it relates to the politics of the day? The answers were included in issues 83–87 and 94 of the *Gaceta Literaria*, all of them published in 1930. John Buckley and Ramón Crispin, *Los vanguardistas españoles 1925–1933* (Alianza, 1977), reproduce the survey in Appendix 1, 391–414.

48   Buckley and Crispin, *Los vanguardistas españoles*, 402–3, 402.

49   "Me parecen legítimos y son para mí formas válidas, siempre que en ellas el intelectual mantenga su supremacía, sin tolerar vejaciones a la inteligencia" (Ibid., 413).

50   The accuracy of Astray's and Unamuno's famous words has been recently questioned by Severiano Delgado Cruz's *Arqueología de un mito: El acto del 12 de octubre de 1936* (Silex, 2019). For the destruction of educational institutions, see, for example, Gonzalo Pasamar Alzurria, *Historiografía e ideología en la posguerra Española: la ruptura de la tradición liberal* (Prensas Universitarias de Zaragoza, 1991).

51   As stated by one of the fascist presidents of the "Political Responsibilities Tribunal" (*Tribunal de responsabilidades políticas*), Enrique Suñer Ordoñez. The larger quote in Spanish reads: "Para nosotros no cabe la duda: los principales responsables de esta inacabada serie de espeluznantes dramas son los que, desde hace años, se llaman a sí mismos, pedantescamente, «intelectuales». Estos, los intelectuales y pseudo-intelectuales interiores y extranjeros, son los que, tenaz y contumazmente, año tras año, han preparado una campaña de corrupción de los más puros valores éticos, para concluir en el apocalíptico desenlace a que asistimos, como negro epílogo de una infernal labor antipatriótica que, por serlo, pretendía desarraigar del alma española la fe de Cristo y el amor a nuestras legítimas glorias nacionales." Enrique Suñer Ordoñez, *Los intelectuales y la tragedia española* (Española, 1938), 6.

Suñer Ordoñez, for example, characterizes the Giner de los Ríos educational revolution and funding of the *Institución de Libre Enseñanza* as a "fatal" development of Spanish history, since this "sect" had removed the sense of Christian morality from the child; "Por desdicha, los resultados de su labor fueron fatales para España, y esto por dos motivos: el primero, porque al arrancar del alma del niño la creencia en Dios, destruyó el principio de toda moralidad, en la vida práctica, de muchos de los que siguieron más tarde las enseñanzas institucionistas; el segundo, porque fundó una secta que, simplemente por serlo, ha dañado inmensamente a la Patria" (emphasis added, 13–14).

52 María Zambrano, "hay un funcionamiento fascista de la inteligencia: una utilización del poder de la inteligencia y sobre todo el poder de enmascararse, de falsificar, que tiene la inteligencia … el fascismo lo utiliza y enmascara … [para mostrar] el mismo desprecio del orden de las cosas y de las cosas mismas. Y esto es lo que hace no ya que el fascismo cometa crímenes, sino que él mismo sea un crimen" (*Los intelectuales en el drama de España. La tumba de Antígona* [Anthropos, 1986], 36–7).

53 Some essential references for the emerging, fascist ideology include Juan Vázquez de Mella, *El ideal de España, Tres dogmas nacionales* (1915), Victor Pradera, *El estado nuevo* (Española, 1937), Vicente Marrero, *La guerra española y el trust de cerebros* (Madrid, 1961), Constancio Eguía Ruiz, *Los causantes de la tragedia hispana. Un gran crimen de los intelectuales españoles* (Difusión, 1938), Pedro Laín Entralgo *Descargo de conciencia (1930–1960),* José Pemartín, *Qué es lo nuevo, Consideraciones sobre el momento español presente* (Cultura española, 1938), and of course, Giménez Caballero whose *Genio de España. Exaltaciones a una resurrección nacional y del mundo* (Jerarquía, 1939) was a book "widely read by the [conservative] youth that went to war" (Aznar Soler, *Pensamiento*, 89). Here, Giménez Caballero defines intellectuals as "people with opinions, reactionary and twisted. We the mystics, theologians, preachers, and priests of godlike causes, are always positioned against them. We, who do not live in our heads or walk on our heads. We are those who our Saint John of the Cross had described as not guided by any other light or fire than that burning in our hearts" (*Gentes de opinar contrario y al revés, Enrevesados. Frente a ellos estuvimos siempre los "místicos," los "teólogos," los "predicadores," los sacerdotes de causas divinas. Los "curas" de almas. Los que no andamos con la cabeza ni de cabeza. Aquellos que definió nuestro San Juan de la Cruz: 'sin otra luz ni guía / sino la que en el corazón ardía*) (quoted by Aznar Soler *Pensamiento*, 90 n.106).

To trace the configuration of a falangist and fascist theory, see Paul Preston's "War of Words: the Spanish Civil War and the Historians" in *Revolution and War in Spain 1931–1939* (Routledge, 1984), and Herbert Southworth *El mito de la cruzada de Franco* (Ruedo Ibérico, 1963). For an updated and contextualized assessment, see Preston's *The Politics of Revenge: Fascism and the Military in 20th Century Spain* (Routledge, 1995), 29–45. For a general assessment of the dissemination of fascist ideas during the Republic, Eduardo González Calleja "La prensa carlista y falangista durante la Segunda República y la Guerra Civil (1931–1937)," *El argonauta español* 9 (2012), https://journals.openedition.org/argonauta/819#citedby

54   Emphasis added, Buckley and Crispin, *Los vanguardistas españoles*, 403–4.
55   Along the same lines, Espinosa, who identified himself in the survey as a
     "Catholic, apostolic, anti-constitutional monarchist," declared himself to be
     awaiting "the militant hour that sets off a crusade against an atheist, liberal
     Europe" (Buckley and Crispin 1977, 406). The loaded labels chosen in his
     answer—Catholic, militant, crusader, atheist—carry echoes of a hegemonic
     Renaissance, an imperial Golden Age, that he would more explicitly posit in
     other works. In his "Literatura and semáforo" (Literature and a Traffic Light)
     essay, for example, he advocated for a return to a key Golden Age author
     who, for him, embodied this rigid, "renaissance" orthodoxy, qtd. in Mainer
     (1981), 251.
56   Luis Buñuel, *My Last Sigh:* 67.
57   Salinas's letter to Jorge Guillén, March 19, 1931, *Obras completas,* Vol. 3,
     494–6, 495.
58   "Republicano sin fe, antimonárquico convencido," that was Pedro Salinas's
     political self-definition to his friend Jorge Guillén on April 2, 1931. *Pedro
     Salinas/Jorge Guillén. Correspondencia 1923–1951,* edited by Andrés Soria
     Olmedo (Tusquets, 1992), 134–6, 135.
59   "Días de lucha, menuda y continua" (ibid., 136).
60   Stanley Payne, *Fascism in Spain, 1923–1977* (University of Wisconsin Press,
     1999), 54.
61   I am referring here to the theory of Spanish Decline as a product of Spanish
     inner corruption, an unavoidable result of the flawed Spanish character. For
     classic summaries of this theory, see John Elliot, "The Decline of Spain," *Past
     and Present* 20 (1961), 52–75, and Henry Kamen, "The Decline of Spain: A
     Historical Myth?" *Past and Present* 81 (1978), 24–50. For a very good, recent
     update, go to Aurelio Espinos, *The Empire of the Cities. Emperor Charles V,
     the Comunero Revolt, and the Transformation of the Spanish System* (Brill,
     2014), 1–34. Espinosa and Carla Rahn, "Time and Duration: A Model for
     the Economy of Early Modern Spain," *American Historical Review* 92, no. 3
     (1987), 3–4, provide solid alternatives to this Decline's model.
62   "El fascismo necesitaba un aparato mitológico de gran envergadura, y
     Giménez Caballero era el más cualificado productor de essa mitología del
     imperio para el fascismo español." Aznar Soler, *República literaria y revolución
     1920–39,* Vol. 1 (Sevilla: Renacimiento, 2010), 242–3.
63   The Treaty of Westphalia was not one, but a series signed in Osnabrük and
     Münster, that have been traditionally considered as the beginning of a new
     international order, an order that relegated Spain from its international
     preeminence. See, for example, Derek Croxton, *Westphalia, the Last Christian
     Peace* (Palgrave, 2013), MC. Fernández Nadal, *La política exterior de la
     monarquía de Carlos II, El Consejo de Estado y la embajada de Londres
     (1665–1700)* (Gijón: Ateneo Jovellanos, 2009), B. J. García García and A.
     Alvarez-Ossorio Alvariño, *Vísperas de Sucesión. Europa y monarquía de
     Carlos II* (Fundación Carlos de Amberes, 2015).
64   David Onnekink, *War and Religion after Westphalia, 1648–1713* (Taylor
     and Francis, 2016), 26. Onnekink has exposed the long-lasting myths about
     Spain and its decline that were forged in these treaties, and that have affected

the way historians approach the country and the period, what Henry Kamen coined as the "dark ages of Spanish modern history" in *The War of the Succession in Spain 1700–15* (1969) (Onnekink n.8, 26). An exception to that rule, other than Onnekink's is C. Storrs *The Resilience of the Spanish Monarchy 1665–1700* (Oxford University Press, 2006).

65 Ramiro de Maeztu claims that "[A]unque el *Quijote* sea un libro de decadencia, el mejor libro de decadencia que haya producido la literatura española," *Don Quijote, Don Juan, y La Celestina. Ensayos en simpatía* 1926 (Espasa Calpe, 1939), 68–9. Maeztu had famously asserted that "A partir del siglo XVII, perdió España la iniciativa histórica," ibid., 74–5. For more on this view of the Golden Age, see Gonzalo Pasamar, *Apologia and Criticism: Historians and the History of Spain, 1500–2000* (Peter Lang, 2010), 196.

66 Giménez Caballero, "Vuelta," *La Gaceta Literaria* 122 (1932), 3.

67 Ibid.

68 "[L]o específicamente cristiano—el sentido fraterno del amor ... encontrará un eco profundo en el alma española, *no en la calderoniana*, barroca y eclesiástica, *sino en la cervantina*, la de nuestro generoso hidalgo Don Quijote, que es a mi juicio, la genuinamente popular, nada católica en el sentido sectario de la palabra, sino humana y universalmente cristiana." Antonio Machado, "Carta a David Vigodsky," *Hora de España* Abril (1937), 5–10, 7.

69 Both labels—"nacionalizador de vanguardia" (xv) and the man responsible for the "pérdida de la inocencia de los escritores españoles de su tiempo" (xvi)—are given by Mainer in *"Ernesto Gimenez Caballero o la inoportunidad,"* in *Ernesto Gimenez Caballero: Casticismo, Nacionalismo, y Vanguardia,* edited by Mainer (*Obra fundamental*, 2005), ix–lxviii, xv–xvi.

70 Salinas, letter to Gerardo Diego. Madrid. February 2, 1932. *Obras completas,* Vol. 3, 276.

71 Gerardo Diego reached this decision two weeks before the publication of Caballero's "Visitas literarias. Gerardo Diego, poeta fascista." In the original: "[c]reo que llegado el caso de romper seriamente con él y con su *Gaceta*, retirerle públicamente de toda colaboración y de publicar nosotros una *Gaceta* antiliteraria" (Gerardo Diego, letter to Dámaso Alonso, June 9, 1927. Morelli, ed., *Gerardo Diego y el III Centenario de Góngora,* 61–2).

72 "A usted, Giménez Caballero, hay que dejarle ya solo." Giménez Caballero, *Memorias,* 36. Quoted by Selva, 195.

73 *El Robison literario* was published in 1931–32, as the last issues of *La Gaceta Literaria.* Mainer's "Ernesto Giménez Caballero o la inoportunidad," lv.

74 Pasamar, *Apologia and Criticism,* 196.

75 "Yo soy español integral, y me sería imposible vivir fuera de mis límites geográficos; pero odio al que es español por ser español nada más. Yo soy hermano de todos y execro al hombre que se sacrifica por una idea nacionalista abstracta por el solo hecho de que ama a su patria." Lorca, *Obras completas,* edited by Arturo del Hoyo (Aguilar, 1964), 1814–17, 1817.

76 Salinas's letter to Jorge Guillén, January 11, 1931. OC, Vol. 3, 494–6, 495.

77 Schammah Gesser, *Madrid´s Forgotten Avant-Garde. Between Essentialism and Modernity* (Sussex Academic Press, 2015), 22–3.

78 Ibid.

Chapter 2

1 "¡Hay que ir al Antiquijote en España! … ¡Hay que utilizar la crítica, la ironía, el rancor, y el sarcasmo, para volver marcha atrás, para corroer el espíritu quijotesco de España! … ¡Asesinar nuestro criticismo a fuerza de criticismo!" Giménez Caballero, "Un peligro nacional," 3–6.

2 "La guerra [civil española] dejó sin futuro a los que perdieron … pero a los que ganaron los dejó sin pasado, y no saben nada y siguen educando sin pasado." Rosa Regàs, "Creo que hemos tenido una educación siniestra" Juan Cruz, *El País,* May 14, 2013, https://elpais.com/elpais/2013/05/13/eps/1368455992_855263.html Accessed February 15, 2020.

3 Miguel Angel Hernando, *Prosa vanguardista en la generación del 27: Gecé y La Gaceta literaria* (Prensa Española, 1975), 106. He was the author of an essential reference for Francoist education, *España nuestra. El libro de las juventudes españolas* (Vicesecretaría de Educación Popular, 1943).

4 For this negative view of Cervantes, see Ferran Gallego, "El fascismo español y el mito de don Quijote. Una revisión," *eHumanista/Cervantes* 3 (2014), 396–41. The reverberations of this animosity for Cervantes were multifaceted. Pedro Laín Entralgo puts Cervantes in jail in a poem "Spaniards in Jail" ("Españoles en chirona. Décima arromanzada," in *Dionisio Ridruejo. Memorias de una imaginación.* Collected unedited papers [CCS, 1993], 227), which summarizes the anti-intellectual bias of many ultra-conservative theorists of the 1930s and 1940s:

> *Cervantes, por infeliz,*
> *Juan de la Cruz, por celeste,*
> *Por deslenguado, Quevedo,*
> *Jovellanos, por decente,*
> *por aguileño, Unamuno*

> Cervantes is in jail for unhappiness, Juan de la Cruz for [being too] heavenly, Quevedo, for speaking [too loosely], Jovellanos, for decency, Unamuno, for sharpness.

Rafael Calvo Serer rejected any Cervantine deviation from the Counter-Reformation alluding to "the mistaken nature of recent approaches to Cervantes, Erasmo, and Valdés," the latter, the other great Erasmist writer of the Golden Age (*los recientes estudios sobre Cervantes, Erasmo, y Valdés son ejemplos paladinos*) *Teoría de la Restauración* [Rialp 1952], 175). Castro's view of a Humanist Cervantes for Calvo Serer clearly reflected the desire "of imposing our own conviction to the past. Thus, Castro's thesis is merely a reflection of a more-or-less conscious desire to transform the spirit of Spanish history according to a specific ideology," qtd. in David K. Herzberger, *Narrating the Past: Fiction and Historiography in Postwar Spain* (Duke University Press, 1995), 30.

5 Ismael Saz Campos, "Entre el fascismo y la tradición. La percepción franquista del Siglo de Oro," in *Tradicionalismo y fascismo europeo,* edited by María Victoria Grillo (Eudeba, 1999), 35–53.

6   In the last thirty years, the modernization paradigm that considers modern societies literate, and that links the acquisition of literacy to "improved socioeconomic standing through entry into or mobility within the industrial work force" has come under justified scrutiny. See Shirley Brice Heath, "Critical Factors in Literacy Development," in *Literacy, Society, and Schooling, A Reader*, edited by Suzanne De Castell, Allan Luke, Kieran Egan (Cambridge University Press, 1985), 209–29, 209. Harvey J. Graff was one of the first to call attention to the contradictory relationships among key factors and consequences of industrial development, since the European industrial revolution, for example, did not produce a more literate society right away, nor was it built by literate workers. The technological advancement of a society does not necessarily imply an increase in literacy levels, at least in the short run. See his "The Legacies of Literacy: Continuities and Contradictions in Western Societies and Cultures" in *Literacy, Society, and Schooling, A Reader,* 61–86, and "The Literacy Myth at Thirty," *Journal of Social History* 43, no. 3 (2010), 635–61, where Graff confirms his views from *The Literacy Myth: Literacy and Social Structure in Nineteenth-Century City* (New York: Academic Press Inc, 1979).

     In the Spanish context, Antonio Viñao Frago reminds us that when assessing the real impact and level of literacy in a population as diverse as that of the 1930s, it is necessary to consider the geographical and class-based dissemination of literacy given the persistence or coexistence with other forms of reading (oral cultures), and the access of the newly literate to print culture. "The History of Literacy in Spain: Evolution, Traits, and Questions," *History of Education Quarterly* 30, no. 4 (1990), 573–99, 591.

7   In 1932, the European "Association of Revolutionary Artists and Writers" was founded, creating a year letter its own journal. One year later, a group of Revolutionary Spanish writers, artists, and intellectuals was also founded. Manuel Aznar Soler, *República literaria y revolución*, Vol. 1 (1920–39) (Sevilla, 2010), 235.

8   "A National Danger: The Return to *Don Quixote*," 1932, 3.

9   The first national mandate to require the reading of the novel in a school curriculum dated back to 1856, and was continued by the educational decrees of 1906, 1912, and especially 1920. The last had most directly reinforced the need to use and discuss Cervantes's texts (not only *Don Quixote*), and not only for grammatical purposes.

10   Such editions would slowly begin to include specific pedagogical resources for teachers at a time when pedagogy was starting to materialize as a field in school and university settings. The transformative pedagogical methods applied in curricula were inspired by the prestigious Free Educational Institute (Institución Libre de Enseñanza) founded by "the first modern Spaniard," Francisco Giner de los Ríos, who, from the late nineteenth century, helped reform Spanish education. The Institute, which existed from 1876 to 1936, integrated diverse subjects (the humanities, sciences, music, foreign languages) in a dynamic educational environment that sought the development of the creative, ethical, and moral—not just cognitive—skills of its students, on the principle that the holistic education of the individual would be transformative for society. Fernando Millán Torres, *La revolución laica: del Instituto libre de enseñanza a la escuela de la República* (Ciencias Sociales, 1983), 190–3.

11 Of those 400 new editions worldwide, Suñé Benages notes that 148 were published in Madrid, 101 in Barcelona, and a few more throughout the Peninsular geography, which accounts for 296 new Spanish editions between 1917 and 1937. Juan Suñé Benages, *A Critical Bibliography of the Editions of Don Quijote* (Harvard University Press, 1939), xv–xvi.

12 Francisco Aguilar Piñal "El Anti-Quijote (1805)," in *Desviaciones lúdicas en la crítica cervantina,* edited by Antonio Bernat Vistarini and José M. Casasayas (Universidad de Salamanca, 2000), 125–38, 131.

13 Miguel Herrero, Introduction. *El ingenioso Hidalgo don Quixote de la Mancha* (Hispánica, 1939), 7–8.

14 The critical attention to these itinerant companies continues to be productive. For a basic reference, see Javier Huerta Calvo, *Cervantes y Lorca: La Barraca* (Ministerio de educación, 2014); Sandie Eleanor Holguin, *Creating Spaniards, Culture and National Identity in Republican Spain* (Wisconsin University Press, 2002); Jordana Meldenson, *Documenting Spain: Artists, Exhibition Culture and Modern Nation 1929–1939* (Pennsylvania State University Press, 2005); Duncan Wheeler, *Golden Age Drama in Contemporary Spain: The Comedia on Page, Stage, and Screen* (Wales University Press, 2012).

15 The reinvention of autos is particularly significant from a wide variety of ideological perspectives; see Carey Kasten's *The Cultural Politics of Twentieth-Century Spanish Theater: Representing the Auto Sacramental* (Bucknell University Press, 2012), especially 25–44.

16 Quoted Huerta Calvo *Cervantes y Lorca,* 4.

17 However, Wheeler has shown how despite his supposed refusal to adapt these classics, Lorca's abridged version of *Fuenteovejuna* did entail quite a personal view of the play *Golden Age Drama,* 79–81.

18 "En el mismo Congreso se votaba una ley favorable a la mujer: el divorcio. En las Misiones Pedagógicas se representaba 'El juez de los divorcios, de Cervantes,' donde el problema se soluciona a la manera vieja, según la antigua ley de desconsideraciones masculinas. Por los pueblos se debió representar un nuevo entremés de los divorcios, donde la ley votada por la República se popularizase y fuese enseñada a usar en justicia." (León, "El teatro internacional. Teatro de masas," in *El Heraldo de Madrid* [July 7, 1933], 5).

19 Lorca, 1934, OC 1749. "Which government," asks Lorca, "whatever its political orientation, would not consider the Augustan greatness of the Spanish classical theater ... and would not use it as the safest vehicle for the cultural improvement of the villages and inhabitants of this country?" (*¿qué Gobierno, cualquiera que sea su orientación política, va a desconocer la grandeza augusto del teatro clásico español ... y no va a comprender que es el más seguro vehículo de la elevación cultural de todos los pueblos y todos los habitantes de España?*) ("Theater for the People" [Teatro para el pueblo] 1934, OC 1747).

20 Dionisio Pérez, "Resurrección de Cervantes en el Mundo" (*ABC*, December 16, 1931), 4. The topic seems in line with the social humanism later developed by thinkers such as Fernando de los Ríos, an intellectual trend that encouraged the "return to the inner self" as the solution to the dehumanizing conflicts of the twentieth century. For this trend, see de Hoyos Puente, ¡*Viva la inteligencia! El legado de la cultura institucionalista en el exilio republicano de 1939* (Madrid: Biblioteca Nueva, 2016), 173–7.

21 "[A] medida que la humanidad se siente más cercada, cohibida y oprimida por las complejidades de la realidad social que ella misma crea, aparece la novela de Cervantes más vivificada" (Pérez 4). Pérez provides a link between the French Romantic view of Victor Hugo, Chateaubriand and so on that first inspired the article and the very material modern sensibility. Thus, he concludes the quote above as follows: "the novel of Cervantes appears revitalized through those symbols that *reveal the more defining than ever ideas and sensibilities of the modern man's state of mind" (aparece la novela de Cervantes más vivificada de símbolos que revelan ideas y pensamientos acordes y más expresivos y más definidores del estado de la conciencia actual del hombre)* (Pérez, "Resurrección," 4; emphasis added).

22 "[E]n un mundo conturbado de inquietudes novísimas, resucita el soldado de Lepanto, gran vencido de la vida española, trayendo al siglo el consuelo de su humorismo de filósofo, que parece tristeza gemidora a Byron y Chateaubriand, pero que goza el pueblo como si fueran carcajadas de buzón" (Pérez 4).

23 Emilia Pardo Bazán, "Los pedágogos del Renacimiento: Erasmo, Rabelais y Montaigne," *Boletín de la Institución libre de enseñanza* 13 (1917), 129–32, 132. Being from a previous generation, Pardo Bazán had passed away in 1922.

24 "Hace poco más de un mes, señalaba en un diario madrileño [ABC 16 de diciembre] el escritor Dionisio Pérez la 'Resurrección de Cervantes en el mundo.' Citando algunas breves notas bibliograficas que vale la pena de completarlas ahora mismo" (Giménez Caballero, "La vuelta" 3).

25 Giménez Caballero, ibid., 3.

26 "Más de uno ha llegado a calificar ese Cervantes de Castro como el primer fundador de la Institución Libre de Enseñanza, como un ilustre antecessor de Francisco Giner, como la incorporación al liberalismo español (al reformismo hispánico) de la figura más preclara y nacional de nuestra literatura. Un servicio a la causa democrática de España, que la República compensaría justamente. Yo soy de los que creen eso" (Giménez Caballero 1932, 4).

27 "Castro se quedó corto al modernizar a Cervantes ... [y] al prever el peligro nacional que comportaba para España el que su máximo ingenio— Cervantes—escribiese" (Giménez Caballero, ibid., 4).

28 "[L]a cura del quijotismo; señalar esa plaga secular de nuestro espíritu como el médico diagnostica una tara indecible y hereditaria .... Me pertenece esta hora crítica de España, en que Don Quijote, el Condenable, y Condenado Don Quijote ... está levantando sus armas de cartón y haciendo una nueva salida y poniéndose nuevamente a la moda española" (Emphasis added. Giménez Caballero 1932, 3).

29 "The plebeians' background from where Quixote's figure emerges" (los fondos plebeyos donde erguiría *Don Quijote* su figura) (Giménez Caballero 1932, 4).

30 Ibid.

31 Castro (1925, 9).

32 See pages 9–10 of this book.

33 Close, 102.

34 Close examined a wide range of abstract interpretations of the novel, distinguishing, for example, "Esoteric critics" who believed that there were hidden meanings in Cervantes's texts, from "Romantic" (those that followed the lead of Georg Friedrich Hegel, Karl Friedrich Schlegel, and Arthur

Schopenhauer), and "Regenerationist" (those that read the novel with a reformist outlook, and considered it as an allegory "of the problem(s) of Spain") (109). The Hispanist privileged the Romantic influence since he believed that the German preoccupations of nineteenth-century German Romantics had most deeply affected the critical outlook of the most prominent Spanish thinkers; to him, those associated with the Generation of 1998, and their "relentless quest for a national or existential philosophy of the novel" (93). It should also be noted that Close presupposes that a study of the symbolism (of any form, such allegory, myth, etc.) of the novel is almost incompatible with a careful examination of its text. The work of a long list of Cervantine scholars, such as Ruth El Saffar, Diana de Armas, Alban Forcione, Aurora Egido, Frederick de Armas, Mary Gaylord, Edward Friedman, Ann Cruz, Mercedes Alcalá Galán, Marina Brownlee, Susan Byrne, Rachel Schmidt, Maria Antonia Garcés, Wiliam Childers, Michael Armstrong-Roche, David Boruchoff, among others, proves this assumption wrong.

35   In Spain, Close recognizes two exceptions: Mayans y Siscar and Vicente de los Ríos. "Both refer frequently and specifically to Cervantes's text; and the former's prologue is seminal," notes Close, adding that the "Análisis del Quijote" by de los Ríos "sets out to demonstrate 'analytically' Cervantes's right to be regarded as a classic author" (14). De los Ríos' exploration, however, suffers in Close's opinion from "the typical limitations of neo-classicism and is likely to prove off-putting to a modern reader" (15).

36   "[L]o que hoy se llama interpretación simbólica del Quijote" constituted a "un cervantismo nimio y mezquino que por largo tiempo ha permanecido entre nosotros," "A la interpretación simbólica del Quijote," *Obras Completas de Manuel de la Revilla*. Prologue by Antonio Cánovas del Castillo. Edited by Urbano González Serrano (Ateneo de Madrid, 1883), 365–75, 371. For *de la Revilla*, this symbolic form of criticism is ultimately "vain and careless" (vano y temerario [*OC* 395]).

37   "Buscando la piedra filosofal, se halló la química, tratando de descifrar el supuesto simbolismo del *Quijote,* acaso se reconstruya la oscura y mal conocida biografía de Cervantes" (*OC*, 395). This is a point and image (alchemy as the mother of chemistry) that would be repeated by Menéndez Pelayo a few years later in an almost identical manner, declaring his hope that the amateur symbolic criticism of *Don Quixote* would constitute only an awkward and transient phase leading to the development of a "scientific and empiric [discipline] focused on the understanding and interpretation of Cervantes." The whole quote in Spanish reads, "Quién sabe si el cervantismo simbólico será una especial de alquimia que prepare y anuncie el advenimiento de la verdadera química; es decir, de la era científica y positiva en el conocimiento e interpretación de la obra de Cervantes," qtd. in Gutiérrez 119.

38   "Estudiése la crítica literaria de la época, léase con antención a Menéndez Pelayo y a Valera, y se advertirá esta falta de perspectiva. De buena fe aquellos hombres aplaudían la mediocridad porque no tuvieron la experiencia de lo profundo ... En estas circunstancias, ¿cómo esperar que se pusiera a Cervantes en su lugar?" (*Meditaciones del Quijote* [1914], 87). Gasset

imagines Cervantes patiently awaiting more capable readers and critics, "sitting down in those Elysium prairies for more than three hundred years, looking melancholically around, until a worthy grandson is born, one able to fully understand him" (se halla sentado en los elíseos prados hace tres siglos, y aguarda, repartiendo en derredor melancólicas miradas, a que le nazca un nieto capaz de entenderle!). While Castro would not be the only Cervantine grandson—a good number of poets, critics, and essay writers, many associated with the '27 group, would try to be that from the late 1920s on—he would certainly provide new approaches that improve this critical understanding.

39 José Carlos Mainer, *Edad de Plata*, 265, Aurora Hermida Ruiz, "Secreta palinodia: La Contrautopía de José Antonio Maravall como descargo de conciencia," *BHS* 78 (2001), 503–16, Javier Varela Tortajada, "La tragedia de los intelectuales y la historiografía de Américo Castro," *Insula* 563 (1993), 20–2. For a general overview of the role and productivity of the Centro, see Francisco Abad Nebot, "El Centro de Estudios Históricos de la Junta de Ampliación de Estudios (1907–1938)" *Cauce* 30 (2007), 7–39, https://cvc.cervantes.es/literatura/cauce/pdf/cauce30/cauce30_02.pdf. Accessed on March 1, 2020.

40 This institutional response, for Mainer, owes its strength to the studies like the ones published by Federico de Onís (on Spanish culture), Castro (on Cervantes), and José Fernández Montesinos (on Lope and the Erasmist Alfonso de Valdés). The whole quote in Spanish reads: "La defensa e ilustración del Renacimiento español debió mucho al esfuerzo de Federico de Onís, al libro de Castro sobre Cervantes, a los trabajos de Montesinos sobre Valdés, y acabó siendo una apasionada respuesta española a las acusaciones de los eruditos protestantes alemanes que habian negado su exitencia en la Península," José Carlos Mainer, *Edad de Plata*, 265.

41 While Victor Klemperer asks if Spain had a Renaissance in "Gibt es eine spanische Renaissance?" *Logos. International Zeitschrift für Philosophie der Kultur* 16 (1927), 129–61, re-elaborating an old view by Jacob Burckhardt, his contemporary, Hans Wantoch, elaborates a negative response infused with prejudice in *Spanien, das Land ohne Renaissance* (Munich, 1927).

42 "Esos tres fantasmas que cercaban la personalidad ideal de Cervantes sin dejarla definirse: a) Que Cervantes era un ingenio lego … —b) Que Cervantes era un contrarreformista, [or] un reaccionario … y —c) Que Cervantes fue un humanista y un liberal" (Giménez Caballero 1932, 3. Emphasis is the author's).

43 Giménez Caballero 1932, 3. *The Bulletin of the Cervantes Society of America* (Spring 2019) dedicated the issue to the idea of *Ingenio Lego*. As the editor of the volume, Rachel Schmidt explains, today "Scholars take as a given that Cervantes was an author engaged with his society, knowledgeable of major discourses and problematics, and in control of his art. Far from appearing as the rustic genius who wrote a masterpiece in spite of himself seen in some nineteenth-century criticism, the vanishing author of high modernism and new criticism, or the 'dead' author of post-modernism, here the author Cervantes emerges as a necessary presence whose knowledge of extratextual codes of conduct or knowledge systems serves as the key for interpreting the text" (Introduction, 18). What is at stake now is exploring why Cervantes choses

to give that impression of an *ingenio lego*, what were the reasons or gains for producing such a literary and poetic persona (ibid.).

44   Cesare de Lollis, *Cervantes reazionario* (Fratelli Treves, 1924).

45   Helmut A. Hatzfeld, "Thirty Years of Criticism," *Hispania* 30, no. 3 (1947), 321–8, 321. See also Maria Caterina Ruta, *Memoria del Quijote* (Centro de Estudios Cervantinos, 2008), 22–3.

46   Hatzfeld points out how other contemporary critics, such as Karl Vossler (who would become much more conservative over the years), were "moved to remark at the time [1924] that Cervantes's great novel unfortunately was an event which is in conflict with de Lollis's [orthodoxical] thesis" (1947, 321). Hatzfeld extends this judgment to Cervantes's most allegorical work, *Persiles,* concluding that even in this work, "De Lollis's interpretation ... proved a failure" (ibid.). Marina Brownlee notes how De Lollis's allegorical reading has been "followed by other prominent scholars in privileging," often much more successfully, "allegory as the meaning of the work as whole," and cites as prominent examples of that direction accomplished specialists including Ruth El Saffar, Alban Forcione, Aurora Egido, and Diana de Armas Wilson among others, "Introduction," 16, 4.

47   "Castro papeleteóse todo Cervantes, y su resultado fué [*sic*] que Cervantes ni fué un ingenio lego ni un reaccionario, ni liberal, sino un espíritu máximo de su época: un genial hipócrita, a la manera de sus correlaíores Descartes, Galileo, Erasmo y todas aquellas magnas figuras que practicaron eso que llamó Ortega y Gasset, con frase fundamental para Castro, 'la heroica hipocresía de los hombres del XVII.' Un espíritu entre dos vertientes. Eso que yo he denominado—me parece que con término exacto—aplicándoselo a Goya (Goya, un Cervantes retrasado de la plástica): un vértice" (Giménez Caballero 1932, 4).

48   In this work, Giménez Caballero compares Cervantes to Goya, believing that both of them are "[figuras] divisorias de dos mundos: el que muere y el que nace. El mundo del dogma y el del individuo. El del absolutismo y el de la libertad. El mediévico y el renacentista. El católico y el nacionalista emphasis added" (Giménez Caballero 1932, 4).

49   "Todo el resto de su vida ... tenderá ... según Castro ....hacia la vertiente secular, ya que llegó a morir Cervantes como un sabio [humanista] y no como un místico o devoto [Cristiano]" (Giménez Caballero 1932, 4).

50   "El hallazgo de Castro respecto a Cervantes consistió en encontrarle lo que consistentemente se le había negado; un pensamiento, una Weltanschauung, un mundo cervantino" (Giménez Caballero 1932, 3).

51   "Habría que proceder de dentro a fuera, y no al revés. La cultura de Cervantes es elemento funcional y constituyente dentro de su obra; para este hombre, tildado de espíritu mediocre y vulgar, tachado de poseer naturaleza análoga a los que le circundaban, no hay aspecto y detalle que no hayan sido esencialmente pensados .... [E]l poco cuidado con que entre nosotros seguimos nuestra historia intelectual (a veces sobrepreciada, a veces negada) ha hecho que se soslayen los problemas de esta índole que ofrece Cervantes" (Castro, *El pensamiento de Cervantes* [Hernando, 1925], 18–19).

52   "[L]e llaman ingenio lego, lo que en el lenguaje de la época quería decir que, aquel a quien así se calificaba, no había pasado las losas de la universidad; sin embargo, es presumir que en dicha culta ciudad, comunicó sobre asuntos literarios con personas entendidas, y nutrió su espíritu por medio de la lectura, el estudio, y la reflexión." Brief school edition in sixteen pages of Cervantes's biography. *El Príncipe de los ingenios* (1936), 5 (National Library of Spain CERV.SEDÓC/12/9).

53   This critical popularity of Cervantes might have been the reason for the panegyrical criticism that flourished in the first four decades of the twentieth century, as noted by James Fitzmaurice-Kelly (1921, 229). Close would later characterize this panegyric revival as an offshoot of Romantic criticism.

54   Fitzmaurice-Kelly was the author of the most respected Cervantes biography at the time. His research—dedicated mostly to the study of the Cervantine opus—earned him the official title of first chair for Spanish studies at a British university (Liverpool) and unofficial recognition as the founder of the "British school of Cervantes scholarship" J.A.G. Ardila, "The Influence and Reception of Cervantes in Britain, 1607–2005," in *The Cervantean Heritage: Reception and Influence of Cervantes in Britain*, edited by J. A. G. Ardila, 2–32, 23. Several Spanish editors referred to his analyses in 1920s and 1930s editions of Cervantes, alluding also to his earlier biography of the author (*Life of Miguel de Cervantes* [1892]), considered "the most accomplished biography of Cervantes at the time of its publication until the second half of the twentieth century," Ibid. Fitzmaurice-Kelly's *History of Spanish Literature* (New York and London: D. Appleton, 1921) dedicated several sections to Cervantes and was equally influential in Spain and England.

55   Giménez Caballero does not directly provide the publication references for the authors and works he discredits. We can identify most of these references as being from Hämel Adalbert's edition of *Don Quijote de la Mancha* (Halle, 1925) and James Fitzmaurice-Kelly's *History of Spanish Literature* (New York and London: D. Appleton, 1921). Other critical texts that Giménez Caballero mentions in the article include Rodríguez Marín's edition of *Don Quixote* (1927), which, although inaccurate, was profusely annotated, and G. K. Chesterton's *The Return of Don Quixote* (1905), a novel set in England, inspired by the Cervantine hero. Only in passing does Giménez Caballero refer to Marcel Bataillon's elogious review of Castro's book, "Cervantes penseur, d'apres le livre d'A. Castro," published in the *Revue de Littérature Comparée* 8 (1928), 318–38. However, at this time, Bataillon was collaborating with the *Centro de Estudios Históricos*, writing the prologue for an edition of Erasmus's works that the *Centro* was preparing. The book—and, especially Bataillon's prologue—would not be published in 1928, as censorship under the regime of Primo de Rivera considered it "anticlerical" (Esiseo Serrano, ed., *Erasmo y España. 75 años de la obra de Marcel Bataillon* [Zaragoza: Letras 2015], 25).

Giménez Caballero also briefly notes studies on the reception of Cervantes in Italy (R. Flaccomio, *La fortuna del Don Quijote in Italia nei secoli XVII e XVIII* [Palermo 1928]) and France (Maurice Bardon's *Don Quichotte en France au XVIIe et XVIII siècles* [Paris: Champion, 1931] and the early edition of the novel, the *Critique du Livre Dom Quichotte de la Manche* commented by Pierre Perrault in 1679 and published by Maurice Bardon in 1930 [Paris, Les Presses Modernes]). With regard to the United States, Giménez Caballero briefly mentions Esther Crooks, *The Influence of Cervantes in France* (Baltimore, MD: Johns Hopkins University Press, 1931). Certainly, by 1932, Cervantes criticism was thriving, and Spanish critics, even those without the best intentions, such as Giménez Caballero, were clearly informed of these international trends.

56 For Hatzfeld, this variety was, however, a very good thing: "It is a gratifying fact," he happily remarks, "that Cervantes, four hundred years after his birth, has not diminished but increased in general interest and admiration" ("Thirty Years of Cervantes Criticism, 1917–1947" *Hispania* 30 [1947], 321–8, 321). Francisco Aguilera would provide "Further Additions to the Cervantes Collection" (*Hispania,* 30 [1947], 85–8) and three years later, Victor Oelschläger would considerably broaden the bibliographical perspective ("More Cervantine Bibliography," *Hispania* 33 [1950], 144–50). These bibliographical efforts seemed to have been started "tentatively" in the 1930s with *Cervantes: A Tentative Bibliography of His Works and of the Biographical and Critical Material Concerning Him,* edited by Jeremiah D. M. Ford and Ruth Lansing (Harvard University Press, 1931). Today, we count on the impressive *Bibliografía del Quijote por unidades narrativas y materiales de la novela: Títulos completos,* edited by Jaime Fernández, Jaime Antonio Fernández (Centro de Estudios Cervantinos, 2008), available online through the Proyecto Cervantes of the Texas AM University and the Universidad de Castilla La Mancha. http://cervantes.tamu.edu/V2/Bibliografias/biblquijot/A. htm.

57 It seems that prior to Franco's ascent to power in 1939, the different languages and the diversity of publishing venues were not an obstacle to the discussion and exchange of ideas. See Klemperer and Castro's opposing views of the impact of Renaissance in Spain, for example, in Gilman, 249–53.

58 Castro contextualized Cervantes's works and worldview within the major European trends and references of his time, associating Cervantes's poetic distortions with Tasso's, his skepticism about science and dogmatism with Montaigne's (1925, 115), and his use of popular idioms (refranes) with Erasmus's *Adagios* (1925, 191). Such contextualization was an essential element of the Cervantine rebirth, one that obviously was of concern to proto-fascist theorists such as Giménez Caballero.

59 "Cervantes es un racionalista que nos da los limites de lo racionalmente estructurable" (1925, 61).

60 Castro, 62–3.

61 Azaña, "Sin quitar ni poner coma en su obra, Cervantes pudo igualmente ser generoso o envidioso, avaro o esparcido, conversable o taciturno, manueto o camorrista" (*Cervantes y la invención del Quijote* [1930. Espasa Calpe, 1934] 49).

62 In 1925, Castro blamed Cervantes himself for this ambivalence or hypocrisy (*El pensamiento* 249–50); when, revising the book in the late 1930s, however, Castro corrects his label, declaring Cervantes's approach a necessary survival skill in the rigid social and literary environment subject to inquisitorial constrains.

63 Although the book was first published in 1937, it had been presented in formal and informal events in Spain already in the late 1920s. Castro refers to it in an article on Erasmus and Spain of 1931.

64 Even Giménez Caballero quotes this statement in his article "The Return" (4), aware of its significance. Castro, indeed, elucidated how much of Cervantes's worldview drew on Erasmus. The most significant element of this influence is the way the unstability of reality affects individual and collective perception: "Everything in life is so dark, unstable, contradictory," Erasmus had written, "that we cannot be certain of any truth" (*todo en la vida es tan oscuro, tan diverso, tan opuesto, que no podemos asegurarnos de ninguna verdad* [qtd. in Castro 86]). Castro believed that, like Erasmus, Cervantes "applies to the church [and faith] this critique of appearances" (*Erasmo aplica a lo religioso este método de superación de las apariencias* [85]) in order to declare the church's—and individuals'—inability to make moral judgments over others. "Cervantes censures behavior in a formulaic manner," Castro admitted, but "he never punishes [his characters]"; therefore, Castro concludes, "[u]nder the discreet pretense demanded by the Counter-Reformation, his new and revolutionary morality can be seen quite clearly" (*Cervantes censura por formula, pero ... no castiga .... [b]ajo toda aquella discrección a la que obligaba la Contrarreforma, se descubre bien clara una moral nueva y revolucionaria en su tiempo* [358]). Cervantes, understood in this way, could hardly be the counter-Reformationist writer he had traditionally been thought to be.

65 "[L]a idea de codear a Cervantes con los grandes ingenios del Renacimiento constituyó un liberador rayo de luz y la evidencia, para muchos escandalosa, de su familiaridad creadora con Erasmo vino a mostrarse como vertebral de la nueva visión crítica" ("Erasmo y Cervantes una vez más," *Bulletin of the Cervantes Society of America* 4 no. 2 [1984)] 123–37, 123).

66 Erasmus had been able to temporarily escape the growing calls among the orthodox to declare him heretical, thanks to the protection of Charles V, the Cardinal Cisneros, and the inquisitor general Alonso Manrique and the admiration of the Spanish intellectual elite, including Alonso de Virués, Juan de Valdés, Alfonso de Valdés, and the archbishop of Toledo, Alfonso de Sonseca Bartolomé Carranza, but that protection eventually wore off. Erasmus's position in Spain became heavily compromised with the inquisitor Manrique's fall to disgrace in 1529, along with the deaths of Luis Vives (1540) and Juan de Valdés (1541). The death of Charles V in 1556 would be the final blow for such protection.

67 "Nosotros nos preparamos a aniquilar toda Asia y Africa con la espada" (qtd. in Bataillon 69).

68 "Menos mal—seguía diciendo—es ser francamente turco o judío que fingido cristiano" (ibid.).

69 The Erasmism of de los Ríos was widely recognized by his contemporaries— Federico García Lorca dedicated a few lines to "Fernando, the Erasmist." See Carlos García De Andoin. "El erasmismo de Fernando de los Ríos," *Bulletin d'Histoire Contemporaigne de l'Espagne* 51 (2017), 173–95.

70 Fernando de los Ríos was only tangently related to Francisco Giner de los Ríos; they shared the same last name by pure chance (more or less, Fernando

changed his original last name, "Río" for "de los Ríos") and because Fernando married a niece of Francisco Giner. Yet, as a minister of Education in the Republic, Fernando became one of the greatest defenders of Giner de los Ríos's Institución de libre enseñaza, supporting the creation of García Lorca's *La Barraca,* the International University of Santandar, the Centre of Arabic Studies of Madrid. Fernando was also one of the best representatives of the Krausean movement in Spain. Krauseanism in this context was an intellectual and reformist current deeply "connected the heterodox, liberal thinking of Erasmus" and "to the enlightenment," since both forms moral/civic reform encouraged and depended on "intellectual freedom" (El krausismo conectó con esa corriente subterránea heterodoxa y libertaria que venía desde Erasmo hasta la Ilustración y que representaba la línea de renovación y de libertad de conciencia), Manuel A. Suances, *Marcos Historia de la filosofía española contemporánea* (Síntesis, 2006), 69.

Other significant Krausean intellectuals were Francisco de Paula Canalejas, Federico de Castro y Bravo, and Urbano González Serrano. Adolfo Posada in his *Breve historia del Krausismo español* identifies Antonio Machado and Américo Castro as Krausean practitioners (Universidad de Oviedo, 1981), 87. See Juan López Morillas, *El krausismo. Perfil de una ventura intelectúal* (Mexico: Fondo de Cultura Económica, 1956) and *The Krausist Movement and Ideological Change in Spain, 1854–1874* (Cambridge University Press, 1981). Also useful is Juan José Cremades Gil's *El reformismo español. Krausismo, escuela histórica, Neotomismo* (Ariel, 1969).

71   "[N]osotros, los heterodoxos españoles, que somos los hijos de los Erasmistas .... somos los hijos espirituales de aquellos cuya conciencia disidente individual fue estrangulada durante siglos." *Fernando de Los Ríos, Discursos parlamentarios,* edited by Gregorio Cámara Villar (Congreso de los Diputados, 1999), 316.

72   Progressive thinkers of the early twentieth century, including Fernando de los Ríos, lamented the significance of the Royal Edict signed by Philip II in June of 1564, in which he announced the enforcement of all the Tridentine prerogatives in his kingdoms, and with it, the prosecution of "all minorities and all forms of dissidence," which of course included reformists and heterodox thinkers such as Erasmus. Henry Kamen, *Inquisition and Society in Spain in the Sixteenth and Seventeenth Centuries* (Indiana University Press, 1985), 79.

73   De los Ríos OC (2: 407), qtd. in Carlos García De Andoin, "El erasmismo de Fernado de los Ríos," *Bulletin d'Histoire Contemporaine de L'Espagne* 51 (2017), 173–95, 181.

74   Martin Austin Nesvig, *Ideology and Inquisition: The World of the Censors in Early Mexico* (Yale University Press, 2009), 7–11.

75   "[T]odavía colea el erasmismo." Aub, *Manual de literatura Española,* 260.

76   In the review of the book that appeared in *Hispanic Review* in 1935. Quoted by Agustín Redondo "La recepción del [sic] Erasmo y España de Bataillon (1937–1950)," in *Erasmo y España. 75 años de la obra de Marcel Bataillon (1937–2012),* edited by Eliseo Serrano (De Letras, 2015), 17–52, 24, n. 23.

77   Hatzfeld, 325.

78   *Cervantes and the Humanist Vision: A Study of Four Exemplary Novels* 1982 (Princeton University Press, 2017), 18.

79   Ibid.

80   Ibid., 20.
81   "Erasmo es aquí un escritor cristiano y edificante, como sin duda lo era para
      no pocos y para el mismo Cervantes, pero no para la España oficial de su
      tiempo" ("Erasmo y Cervantes," 124).
82   En este libro la Inquisición y su espíritu sencillamente no existen, y todo él
      transcurre dentro y al abrigo de una *España sin problema.* Nada, pues, de
      compromiso, *de inhibición ni de autocensuras creadoras.* Dada la *inquietud,*
      más o menos abierta con que buena parte de la crítica ha venido considerando
      la cuestión del erasmismo en Cervantes, el libro de F. vendrá a ejercer
      sobre ella un efecto *liberador o catártico. La oportunidad de reducir a una*
      dimensión técnica lo que antes era el caso de conciencia de un Cervantes más
      o menos disidente o "del otro lado," se halla sin duda destinada a caer como
      un bálsamo sobre ciertos sectores de opinión (ibid., 124, emphasis added).
83   Menéndez Pelayo censures even rationalists operating within the church,
      such as Erasmus, but is especially vehement in his condemnation of secular
      rationalists such as the Kraussists. For him, "[t]he Krausean intellectuals"
      (*los pedantes krausistas*), "extremists" (*fanáticos*), ultimately "believe in
      a heretical metaphysics that in essence conveys a pantheist belief-system"
      (*viene a reducirse la metafísica de todo este grupo de sistemas y herejías,*
      en su esencia panteísticos) (*Historia de los heterodoxos españoles* [Librería
      Católica, 1881], 936).
84   Paul Preston explains that the agrarian oligarchy—in an unequal partnership
      with the industrial and financial bourgeoisie—is the traditional dominant
      force of Spanish capitalism. They had partnered in the wake of the prosperity
      experienced by the country during its neutrality in the First World War,
      consolidating the country's monopoly of power. The dominance of this
      monopoly became challenged during the three Bolshevik years (1917–20),
      when laborers throughout the Spanish geography demanded better conditions
      (in rural areas, mostly in the south, and in industrial sectors, especially
      Catalonia, Basque Country, and Asturias). After suffering postwar recessions
      with heavy layoffs and wage-cuts, worker demands produced "a spiral of
      provocations and reprisals" that were violently suppressed by the army,
      obviously in service of the financial elites. *The Spanish Holocaust: Inquisition*
      and Extermination in Twentieth-Century Spain (W. W. Norton, 2013), 18–20.
          Madrid had seen the formation of its first National Anti-Masonic
      and Anti-Semitic League in 1912, which had received explicit and strong
      ecclesiastical support from more than twenty bishops. One of them, the
      bishop of Almería, would already speak of the country being "ready for
      the decisive battle that must be unleashed between the children of the light
      and the children of darkness, between Catholicism and Judaism, between
      Christ and the devil." It was not only one bishop; to see the extent to which
      the Spanish Catholic establishment (the "episcopado") legitimized and
      disseminated these theories, see Herbert R. Southworth, *Conspiracy and the*
      Spanish Civil War: The Brainwashing of Francisco Franco (Taylor & Francis,
      2002), 1–127.
85   Ribeiro de Meneses, *Franco,*105.
86   It helped that the primate of Spain, Cardinal Isidro Gomá, authorized on
      July 1, 1937, a collective letter from all Spanish bishops to the world, in

which they warned about the dangers of the Marxist revolution in Spain. See William Viestenz *By the Grace of God: Francoist Spain and the Sacred Roots of Political Imagination* (University of Toronto Press, 2014), 5. As Ribeiro de Meneses has explained, "It is impossible to overestimate the importance of the Church's role in providing legitimacy and in securing the domestic and foreign support he [Franco] needed" (*Franco and the Spanish War*, 104). He continues: "Franco never spoke of a civil war: what was taking place in Spain was a crusade against a foreign enemy [Republican forces aided by international volunteers], a spiritual conflict both to rid Spain of foreigners and their corrupting ideas and to uphold the primacy of the Catholic Church ... Just as medieval popes had issued bulls for the prosecution of holy wars against Islam, so too did the Spanish Church weigh in behind the Nationalists, recognizing the principles of the crusade, and participating willingly in the search for empire" (ibid.).

87   Stanley G. Payne contextualizes "Por el imperio hacia Dios" outcry in *Franco and Hitler. Spain, Germany, and World War II* (Yale University Press, 2008), 69. Manuel Vázquez Montalbán had extrapolated and deconstructed such dictum in his *Aznaridad: Por el imperio hacia Dios, o Por Dios hacia el imperio* (Grijalbo, 2003). Viestenz (*By the Grace of God*) has exposed in detail all the religious, cultural, and military implications of this ideological construct.

88   Any element that did not fully support the messianic program of this crusade would be considered an affront and danger to the country, an enemy of the state. After all, any political theory that defines the national identity through the consecration of one particular community in sacred terms validates its righteousness at the expense of others (Viesteinz 8). Formulating the political stakes in this way, fascists left no room for dissent, and they characterized those who resisted the Francoist crusade as representing not simply a dissenting political faction but the "anti-Spain"—a danger to the fascist nationalist agenda. Jorge Hoyos Puente explains the workings of this dynamic, noting that Francoists justified their coup against the Republican government with "a discourse that merged a wide variety of references to define a perverse enemy" (*un discurso justificador que mezclaba todos los elementos para definir un enemigo perverso*) (¡*Viva la inteligencia!* 40).

89   "Todos representaban lo mismo a ojos de los sublevados ... todos ... eran caricaturizados y minimizados de forma sistemática como entes perniciosos y extranjerizantes que no habían fomentado más que la erradicación de las tradiciones hispanas" (ibid.).

90   Viestenz, *By the Grace*, 64.

91   Giménez Caballero 1932, 4.

92   Cervantes *DQ*, I.13: 90 (*IH*, I.13: 175). All quotes from *El Ingenioso Hidalgo* are from Murillo's edition, and all translations from Edith Grossman's *Don Quixote*.

93   It is still difficult to assess the reach of this campaign and the harm it caused. See Justo Cuño Bonito, "Reform and Counter-Reform in the Primary School Teaching during the Second Republic and the Rise of Fascism" (1932–43), *Revista Historia de la Educación Latinoamericana* 15, no. 21 (2013),

89–106; Elena Sánchez Madariaga, ed., *Las maestras de la República* (Catarata, 2012); José Pedro Marín García de Robles and Alvaro Moreno Egido, "Los expedients de revision de depuración del Magisterio español en el Archivo Central de Educación" (ACME), http://www.mecd.gob.es/servicios-al-ciudadano-mecd/dms/mecd/servicios-al-ciudadano-mecd/archivo-central/educar-archivos/comision-depuracion/Revision-depuracion.pdf. Accessed on November 27, 2019; Beatriz Peyrot Marcos, "Female Republican Teachers" (Maestras Republicanas), http://maestrasrepublicanas.blogspot.com.es/2013_03_07_archive.html. Accessed on November 27, 2017; Francisco Morente Valero, *La escuela y el estado nuevo: La depuración Del Magisterio Nacional, 1936–1943* (Ámbito, 1997).

94   To learn more about this censorship and its consequences, see María Josefa Villanueva Toledo, *Los tres centenarios de Cervantes en el siglo XX: Fuentes documentales en el Archivo General de la Administración* (Madrid: Ministerio de Cultura, Secretaría General Técnica, 2005), 53. A series of censoring decrees were executed by and entrusted to different agencies. The first major fascist censorship operations, which occurred during the Civil War, were carried out by the army and dependent on the "Commission for Culture and Learning"—later more accurately titled the "State Delegation for Press and Propaganda." The ban of April 29, 1938, had already been conceived and put into operation by this propaganda ministry (Villanueva Toledo 53). Manuel Abellán reminds us that the first censorship mandates applied to literary works published in Spain and abroad, and that the scope of these directives was subsequently broadened— after the decree of July 15, 1939—to theater, cinema, and the visual arts (Manuel Abellán, *Censura y literaturas peninsulares* [Rodopi, 1987], 28–9).

95   Goytisolo, *Forbidden Territory,* 105.

96   Poch Noguer, ed., *Don Miguel de Cervantes Saavedra* (Dalmau Charles, 1936), Proemio.

97   "[E]l exacto cumplimiento del deber y cuánto de más noble y elevado nos ofrecen los gigantescos caracteres de caudillos insignes" Federico Torres, *Miguel de Cervantes* (Sánchez Rodrigo, 1936), ix. Not surprisingly, this biography would be reissued in 1947 and 1956.

98   Paloma Alfaro Torres and Sandra Sancha García, "La lectura obligatoria del Quijote en las escuelas," in *Don Quijote en la percepción del análisis Don Quijote en el aula: la aventura pedagógica,* edited by Juan José Pastor Comín and Angel Gregorio Cano Vela (Ediciones de Castilla la Mancha, 2006), 17–26.

99   Francisca Montilla, *Selección de libros escolares de lectura* (CSIC, 1954). *See* Nieves Martín Rogero, "El uso del *Quijote* en el aula. Revisión histórica de ediciones escolares y paratextos didácticos," *OCNOS* no. 3 (2007), 77–90.

100 Josefa Villanueva Toledo, *Los tres centenarios de Cervantes,* 53.

101 "Dada la nefasta personalidad del autor de este trabajo, que por otra parte no tiene ningún valor literario, no debe permitirse la circulación de esta obra." Quoted in Villanueva Toledo 2005, 50.

102 José Montero Reguera, *Cervantismos de ayer y hoy. Capítulos de historia cultural hispánica* (Publicaciones de la Universidad de Alicante, 2011), 133.

103 Ibid., 133.

104 Ibid., 133–4.

105 "Los que traicionaron a la democracia española no podían ser leales a su cultura y si desde el empíreo donde descansa pudiera hablarles Cervantes, les diría sin duda palabras de comprensivo sabio desdén mezcladas quizá con aquel 'Tate, tate folloncicos … ' de la última página del Quijote. Ellos lo saben y lo odian. Lo odian hoy como entonces," Sender, "Hace cuatro siglos," *LE* 4 (1947), 3.

106 (*DQ* 2: 74, 939) (escribir con pluma de avestruz grosera y mal deliñada las hazañas de mi valeroso caballero [*IH* II: 74, 939]).

107 Esther Almarcha Núñez-Herrador and Isidro Sánchez Sánchez have explored in detail the implications of Azorín's complicity with the Francoist government in "La Mancha y basta" in *La ruta del Quijote* (Ediciones de la Universidad de Castilla La Mancha, 2005), 9–30, especially 15–19.

108 The quote from Almarcha Núñez-Herrador and Sánchez Sánchez 12. In 2004, Rafael Conte, reviewing a new edition of "Con permiso de los cervantistas," also calls Azorín the "maestro" (November 6, 2004). https://elpais.com/diario/2004/11/06/babelia/1099701555_850215.html. Accessed July 26, 2018). In 2014, in the prologue to Francisco Fuster García's edition of Azorín's works, Andrés Trapiello declares that "there hasn't been in the entire twentieth century a critic as observant as him, if by critic we understand he who instils in his readers curiosity and enthusiasm" (No ha habido en todo el siglo XX un crítico tan fino como él, si entendemos por crítico aquel que va prendiendo en sus lectores la curiosidad y el entusiasmo) "Leer, vivir?" *Libros, Buquinistas y Bibliotecas. Crónicas de un transeúnte Madrid-París,* edited by Francisco Fuster García, Prólogo *"Azorín"* (Fórcola, 2014), 5, http://www.elboomeran.com/upload/ficheros/obras/02_azorn_adelanto.pdf. Accessed on March 1, 2020.

109 "[P]or su parte nota Azorín: 'El mayor daño que se puede hacer al Quijote es seguir laborando sobre ese misticismo cervantista, etc'" (Castro 1925, 15).

110 The whole quote in Spanish (summarized in the text) reads: "aunque ello sea paradójico, esta penuria de trabajo científico en torno a Cervantes, procede del ambiente fetichista que se ha ido formando alrededor de aquel" (Ibid., 9).

111 Ibid., 13, 10, 12.

112 "¿No sería hora de intentar un estudio concordado de las obras de Cervantes, serenamente, sin prejuicios, con propósito muy circunscrito?" (Ibid., 17). Castro considered earlier twentieth-century criticism to be based on "ideas prompted by sheer laziness, or by the vague, inspiring echoes of the aesthetic, foreign recognition of the novel [Don Quixote] that particularly pleased a supposedly ingenious [Spanish] commentator" (ideas que buenamente desprendía el ocio o de los ecos que llegan de tal página que a un hombre de genio inspiró el goce estético de la internacional novela) (Ibid., 10).

113 José Martínez Ruiz, *Con permiso de los cervantistas* (Madrid: Biblioteca Nueva, 1948), emphasis added. In the original:

> En este punto de partida se dividen dos caminos: uno es el de la erudición; otro, el de la vida. El cervantista puede seguir uno u otro, a su talante, con su responsabilidad, sin que le ataje nadie. El camino de la erudición es áspero; el de vida, acerbo. El erudito se consagra al papel; el imaginativo se dedica a la sensación. Nos atrae el documento, representativo del tiempo y de acción. El archivo es silencio y perseverancia. El hallazgo de

ahora, estimula para el conocimiento de mañana. Cervantes, fragmentario, espera su totalidad. Podremos o no lograr esa totalidad en el conocimiento de su vida; pero lo procuraremos con ahínco. Y luego—confesémoslo— hay un placer, un íntimo placer, en decir de Cervantes lo que los demás, antes y ahora, no han dicho. Y hay otro placer; todavía más hondo, todavía más secreto: el de saber lo que los cervantistas imaginativos, sensitivos, no saben. ¿Nos reportaremos o no? ¿Podemos ocultar o no nuestro despego por los cervantistas psicólogos? ¿Llegaremos a pronunciar la frase terrible, inapelable de "falta de preparación"?

  ¿Y qué pasa en el otro camino? Por el otro camino va el artista que puede enamorarse de Cervantes; que puede aspirar a sentir, a comprender, a compenetrarse con Cervantes. Sentir a Cervantes es, ante todo, actualizar a Cervantes. Para sentir a Cervantes es preciso, antes que nada, despojarle de todo arqueología. No tiene miedo el artista al error histórico; con error, como sin error, se llega a la sensación; la sensación de la vida—en un determinado momento—que ha experimentado Cervantes y que nosotros tratamos de que experimente el lector. ¿Nos ufanaremos de nuestro desvío hacia la erudición? ¿Se establece la compensación, respecto del erudito, y si él ha pensado—no pronunciado—la frase vitanda, podríamos pronunciar nosotros otra frase aterradora: falta de sensibilidad? (5–6; emphasis added).

114 Like Castro, Bataillon was generally admired and respected in the 1920s and 1930s for his erudition. He supports his claims through "long stays in archives and libraries" "erudición que se apoya en largas búsquedas en archivos y bibliotecas" (Redondo 27).

115 Martínez Ruiz, *Con permiso*, 6.

116 Ibid.

117 Close, *Romantic Approach*, 2.

118 In the original, "[esta crítica] lleva … hasta el ridículo las cosas más serias y respetables" (Quoted in Mainer, *Moradores* 27).

119 Christopher Britt Arredondo, *Quixotism: The Imaginative Denial of Spain's Loss of Empire* (Albany, NY: Suny University Press, 2004), 8, 13, 69, 142, 173.

120 Quixote became an "abstract" but heavily militarized "ideal that rises above time and space to touch the heart of those men who have set their goals higher than they have means to reach" (*abstracto, idealizado, elevándose por encima del tiempo y del espacio hasta tocar el corazón de los de cuantos hombres han puesto sus sueños más arriba que sus medios para ralizarlos*) (Maeztu 44). The knight is thus a "true and superior hero" (Ledesma 61) whose failure could only anticipate new triumphs and ideals (Ledesma 127).

121 Azorín. "El Caudillo y Cervantes." *ABC*, November 6, 1942, http://www.cervantesvirtual.com/obra-visor/articulos-de-azorin-publicados-en-el-abc-seleccion–0/html/00237ff6-82b2-11df-acc7-002185ce6064_2.html#I_27_].

122 "Don Quijote se declara vencido y la causa por la que él ha luchador permanence" (ibid.).

123 "Tendido en su lecho y expiante el caballero, queda en nuestra sensibilidad, luminosamente, el ideal alentador. Por ese ideal—esperanzas, entusiasmos, generosidad—ha luchodo nuestro Caudillo." Ibid.

124 "que nuestro Caudillo anhela que nos una fraternalmente a españoles"
(ibid.). It's worth noting that the full quote does not say "anhela que nos
una fraternalmente a españoles" but "anhela que nos una fraternalmente
a españoles y americanos," which alludes to the Conquistador attributions
of Don Quixote/Franco. The imperialist dimension of this discourse will be
studied in Chapter 5.

125 Britt Arredondo, *Quixotism*, 13.

126 While in 1971, Vicente Gaos could freely claim that "Azorín's judgements
... should not be taken too seriously" (De cualquier modo, de los juicios de
Azorín ... hay que hacer poco caso), few could have voiced a similar critique
in the 1940s. Gaos, "Cronología y mérito del Pesiles," in *Claves de literatura
española* (Madrid: Guadarrama, 1971), 227–68, n.15, 263.

127 While the author of the article "La generación del 36 ante El Quijote" signs as
Jose Maria Fernandez Menendez [*sic*], he appears to be José María Fernández-
Ladreda y Menéndez-Valdés, a nobleman who had been a military strongman
in the Rivera's dictatorship and served under Franco as Minister of Public
Affairs from 1945 to 1951. His article is considered here since it was not
published by a state or military bulletin, but by the *Revista de la Universidad
de Oviedo. Facultal de Filosofía y Letras* 59 (1949), 85–106. I will be referring
to him as the author of the essay and as Fernández Menéndez.

128 Fernández Menéndez starts by saying that:

> [I]n our day, the sciences continue to divide and subdivide their
> disciplines, subjecting their objects of analysis to a scrupulous analysis
> and diagnosis; commentaries on specific words, phrases, sentences,
> turns, themes, and details are forged; it is the moment of erudition and
> dissection. There is an ambitious attempt to reconstruct an ideology
> that strives—like the Erasmism that attracts Americo [*sic*] Castro—to be
> political, or—in the work of other researchers—to be esoteric.
>
> [E]n días cercanos a nosotros, las ciencias se dividien y subdividen
> es especialidades y todo se somete a un análisis y balance minucioso;
> y surgen los comentarios de palabra por palabra, y el espigar frases,
> refranes, giros, temas, y detalles; es la época de la erudición y de la
> disección. A todo más, se intenta la reconstrucción de una ideología que
> va, lo mismo de erasmiana que atriye [*sic*] Americo [*sic*] Castro, a la
> política, o a la exotérica de algún otro investigador.

129 Emphasis added. In the original: "Y en este momento ... tras una guerra
catártica, en la que bien pudo ser el libro un recreo intelectual entre dos
ataques, una nueva generación, la del 36, emite su nuevo juicio, y evidencia
un estilo y conformidad spiritual a la manera de otras generafiones que le han
precedido en la misma tarea crítica" (87).

130 For the author, this critical generation included names (explicitly cited) such
as José Luis Colina, A. Abad Ojuel, Jesús Revuelta, Rafael García Serrano,
Jesús Revuelta, Rafael García Serrano, Manuel Suarez Caso, and, of course,
Ernesto Giménez Caballero (88).

131 A Don Quijote "lo han escarnecido los eruditos, los superficiales y los idiotas.
Los eruditos buscando afanosamente ediciones Príncipe y numerando de

cinco en cinco los renglones que contienen la gran historia del hidalgo manchego; los superficiales hinchando la voz o inventando frases redondas, que en el andar de los tiempos se conviertieron en tópicos … los idiotas haciendo caso a los eruditos y los superficiales" (Fernández Menéndez 88–9). One can see the effects of the purification of the Spanish educational system, including in higher education. See also L. Pérez Moral, "Entre la politización y la instrucción. El giennense Don Ángel Cruz Rueda, 1930–1942" *Boletín del Instituto de Estudios Giennenses* 192 (2005), 213–24. Jordi Gracia, *El atroz desmoche la destrucción de la universidad española por el franquismo, 1936–1945* (Crítica, 2006).

132 The article names Giménez Caballero's "La vuelta del Quijote" as a reference. It also refers to an article about Giménez Caballero: Eugenio Fruto's "Ettore Zuani ataca a Giménez Caballero y difama a España" (*El Español* 232 [1947], n.p.), and an article by Rafael Sánchez Mazas "A don Angelito, sobre la compasión a Don Quijote" (*El Español* 232 [1947], n.p.).

133 "¿Cervantes liberal? De ningún modo. Bien claro está que no. Caballero nostálgico de una ceballería [*sic*] de la mejor y más real caballería andante" (Fernández Menéndez's 95).

134 Ibid., 94; "hombre de posturas absolutas, como lo fué [*sic*] y lo es siempre el español" (99).

135 My emphasis. In Spanish "la exteriorización de la intransigencia … la intransigencia *que nos trajo el beneficio de la inquisición, de las luchas contra el turco, de Colón—intransigente y sin admitir distingos*—cuando intentaba descubrir un nuevo mundo" (Enfásis añadido, Fernández Menéndez 99).

136 See this chapter's epigraph.

137 Close, *The Romantic Approach*, 257.

138 Ibid., 28.

Chapter 3

1 Emphasis added. Close, "Theory versus the Humanist Tradition Stemming from Américo Castro," 1–21, 1.

2 Don Quixote, *en el país de de Martín Fierro* (Hispánica, 1952), 10.

3 "Ninguna otra obra de la literatura universal ha suscitado no ya tantas opiniones contrarias, sino pura y simplemente, tantos dislates." "Sobre historia de la crítica cervantina" [1962]. *Claves de literatura española* (Madrid: Guadarrama, 1971), 207–17, 209.

4 See Castro's assessment of the Cervantes's critical tradition he had inherited in 1925, 10–17 and 386–7. For other reviews on the field, check Dominick Finello "Notes on Nineteenth-Century *Quijote* Scholarship," *Cervantes: Bulletin of the Cervantes Society of America* 7, no. 1 (1987), 59–69, and Yolanda Vallejo Márquez, "Aproximación al cervantismo decimonónico" *Draco: Revista de literatura española* (1993–34), 243–65, Anthony Close's "Sobre delirios filosóficos y aproximaciones ortodoxas," *Desviaciones lúdicas en la crítica cervantina: Primer Convivio internacional de Locos Amenos,*

edited by Antonio Bernat Vistarini y José María Casasayas (University of
Salamanca, 2000), 53–70, and Steven Hutchinson "Perlas críticas surgidas
a la luz del patrioterismo aplicado al *Quijote*," 281–90 also in *Desviaciones
lúdicas,* Jorge Enrique Rojas Otálora, "El cervantismo," *Literatura, teoría,
historia, y crítica* 7 (2005), 293–302, Perdomo Batista "Orígenes del
cervantismo: el descubrimiento de la «patria» de Cervantes y las polémicas
lingüístico-literarias de la época," *Anales Cervantinos* 51 (2019), http://
analescervantinos.revistas.csic.es/index.php/analescervantinos/article/view/455.
Accessed on February 1, 2020. Carlos Gutiérrez provides a useful resource in
his "Bibliografía del cervantismo finisecular (1880–1910)," in *Cuatro estudios
de literatura,* edited by Pedro Ojeda Escudero, Teresa Gómez Trueba, Juan José
Sendín Vinagre, and Carlos Gutiérrez Gómez (Grammalea, 1995), 97–149.

5   "El Quijote empieza a entenderse mal en el preciso momento que empieza a
entenderse bien" Gaos "Sobre historia de la crítica cervantina" (*Gaos* "Sobre
historia de la crítica cervantina," 212).

6   Américo Castro describes this critical legacy as "disfunctional" when he
claims that "If the development of our Cervantes's criticism had been normal,
all of this [esoteric commentaries by Benjumea] would have vanished when
it became clear that Cervantes was issuing deep, artistic, and philosophical
formulations" (*Si el desarrollo de nuestra crítica literaria hubiera sido nomal,
todo esto [lucubraciones esotéricas] se habría desvanecido al averguarse que,
en efecto, Cervantes formulaba graves problemas, artística y filosóficamente*)
(*El Pensamiento de Cervantes,* 9 my emphasis). Castro also identifies
Cervantes as a "verdadero 'capus emissarius' de nuestras desventuras" (384).

7   The limited scope of Close's study led him, in fact, not only to miss the
intellectual stature of many formidable critics who wrote in the 1920s,
1930s, and 1940s but to also skip over their regular channels of expression—
magazines, special issues, and so on—overlooking with it the expansion
and incipient professionalization of Cervantes studies, documented in the
bibliographical articles published by A. del Río, "Quijotismo y cervantismo:
El devenir de un símbolo," *Revista de Estudios Hispánicos de Puerto Rico* 1,
no. 3 (1928), 241–67, Helmut Hatzfeld, "Thirty Years of Cervantes Criticism,"
Hispania, 30 (1947), 321–8, Gaos "Sobre historia." Close concentrated instead
on critical volumes such as *Cervantes across the Centuries* (Dryden, 1947)—a
volume that, published abroad, included only a few prominent Spanish figures,
such as Menéndez Pidal, Joaquín Casalduero, and Américo Castro. Note
that, of these three authors, two, Menéndez Pidal and Casalduero, hold quite
traditional views, and Castro carried his own set of controversies.

8   The fact that I speak of a generation or group does not mean that this was
a cohesive monolithic group. There was obviously competition and friction
among some members. While some of the members continued their solid
friendship even in exile, the case of Salinas y Guillén in the United States with
Dámaso Alonso, there were also some loud disagreements from the inception
of the group. The case of Miguel Hernández and Federico García Lorca, for
example, has been well-documented; see Juan Cano Ballesta, "Peripecias de
una amistad: Lorca y Miguél Hernández," *Cuadernos Hispanoamericanos*
433–4 (1986), 211–20, also "Miguel y Federico: la Amistad que no creció,"
Información 5.3 (1992), and José Carlos Rovira "Lorca-Hernández: crónica

de un desencuentro" (Federico García Lorca e il suo tempo, edited by Laura *Dolfi* [Bulzoni, 1999], 137–50). In exile, one of the clearest feuds was that between Juan Ramón Jiménez and poets including Salinas and Guillén, Javier Rodriguéz Marcos delineates such conflicted relationship in "Amor y odio en la Generación del 27" (*El País,* April 22, 2012). The fictions with Francisco Ayala have been explored by Miguel Ángel García "Confrontaciones: Ayala y los poetas del 27" (*Mélanges de la Casa de Velázquez* 49, no. 1 [2019]: 245–67).

9 Antonio Martín Ezpeleta explores the critical contributions of "practically all the participants of the so-called Generation of '27 (born around 1891 and 1905)" that in one moment or another "engaged in literary criticism" (prácticamente todos los integrantes de la denominada generación del 27 [nacidos en torno a1891 y 1905] ... en un momento u otro cultivaron la crítica literaria). *Las historias literarias de los escritores de la Generación del 27* (Madrid: Arco, 2008), 81.

10 Enric Bou, "Afterword," in *Love Poems by Pedro Salinas,* edited by Enric Bou (University of Chicago Press, 2009), 199.

11 "Todo poeta es, o debe ser, un crítico; un crítico silencioso y creador, no un charlatán estéril." In "El crítico, el amigo, y el poeta. Diálogo ejemplar" (1948) in *Poesía y literatura,* Vol. 1 (Barcelona: Seix Barral, 1960), 205–29, 227.

12 See, for examples, Pedro Salinas (1945) "Don Quijote en presente," in *Ensayos completos,* Vol. 3, edited by Solita Salinas de Marichal (Taurus, 1983), 71–82; and "Lo que debemos a Don Quijote" (1947), in ibid., 51–65.

13 The rediscovery of these female participants, widely popularized by the *Sinsombrero* project (http://www.rtve.es/lassinsombrero/en/webdoc/participa/ tania-ballo) would not have been possible without the work of Shirley Mangini, *Las modernas de Madrid: Las grandes intelectuales españolas de la vanguardia* (Península, 2001), Susan Kirkpatrick, *Mujer, modernismo y vanguardia en España (1898–1931)* (Cátedra, 2003), and the work of Janet Pérez among others.

14 See, for example, Aub in *De Max Aub a Cervantes* (Segorbe, 1999), 67n.7 and 68n.8. On the other hand, some critics like Bou, felt that some of Salinas's own lectures and commentaries could not be considered scholarly, rigorous pieces of criticism, but regarded as texts closer to a divertimento than to critical exercises (*Pedro Salinas Quijote y lecturas,* edited by Enric Bou [ELR, 2005], 21–2).

15 It is apparently because of this lack of "scholarly" publications that Guillén, for example, could not get a position at Yale University. In December of 1946, he confides to Salina: "Yale wants a 'scholar' and I am not one of them [lacking] Publications!" (*Yale quiere un "scholar" y yo no lo soy, [por falta de] ¡Las publicaciones!*). Guillén was a reputed poet and intellectual at the time, widely published too, although not in academic platforms. His frustration obviously refers to academic, or scholarly publications, or their lack of thereof. *Pedro Salinas/Jorge Guillén. Correspondencia 1923–1951,* edited by Andrés Soria Olmedo (Tusquets, 1992), 406–8, 407.

16 Mainer argued that even in the 1920s and early 1930s, the quality and quantity of the critical reflections by the writers of the Generation of '27 made them "avant garde scholars," approaching with a defiant, playful, and insightful attitude a wide range of literary topics. See *La Edad de Plata (1902–1939)*

(Cátedra, 1981), 210–30. For a more specific study on the subject, see Anthony Leo Geist, *La poética de la generación del 27 y las revistas literarias: de la vanguardia al compromiso* (Guadarrama, 1980), Manuel José Ramos Ortega, *Las revistas literarias en España entre la edad de plata y el medio siglo: una aproximación histórica* (Ediciones de la Torre, 2001), and the three-volume study compiled by the latter, Ramos Ortega, *Revistas literarias españolas del siglo XX (1919–1975)* (Ollero y Ramos, 2005).

17 Juan Manuel Rozas, *El 27 como generación* (Sur, 1978), 117–26, Ramos Ortega pays homage to this critic's vision (*Las revistas literarias*, 9).

18 Highfill, *Modernism and Its Merchandise*, 6.

19 Ibid.

20 The ways in which this literature and culture are to be approached continue to be under heated debate. José María Naharro Calderón, Antonio Muñoz Molina, and Miguel García Posada believe in examining the cultural production of the diaspora "within a wider spectrum frame" that also analyzes "discourses within territorial Spain—the cultural spaces of what we call interexiles (where texts from inside and outside of Spain confront, reflect, and refract each other" ("Twentieth-century literature in exile" in *The Cambridge History of Spanish Literature,* edited by David T. Gies [Cambridge University Press, 2009], 620–7, 620). Manuel Aznar Soler, however believes that such contextualization of discourses runs the risk of forcing the erasure or normalization of the specifically challenging conditions of exile, a fact that ultimately benefits the producer of that displacement and violence, in this case, the Francoist establishment. See "Franquismo e historia literaria: Sobre la reedición en el año 2000 de Mis páginas mejores (1966) de Max Aub," in *Los Laberintos del exilio: diecisiete estudios sobre la obra literaria de Max Aub* (Renacimiento, 2003), 129–43. A number of approaches to the topic examine the issue of exile as a more or less autonomous category. See Francisco Cadet, *Hipótesis sobre el exilio republicano 1939* (Fundación Universitaria Española, 1997), Jose Luis Abellán, *El exilio como constante y como categoría* (Biblioteca Nueva, 2001), AAVV, *El exilio literario de 1939,* edición de Maria Teresa González de Garay Fernández y Juan Aguilera Sastre (Universidad de la Rioja, 2001), 197–348, Henry Kamen, *The Disinherited. Exile and the Making of Spanish Culture, 1492–1975* (HarperCollins, 2008). Sebastiaan Faber, *Exile and Cultural Hegemony: Spanish Intellectuals in Mexico 1939–1975* (Vanderbilt University Press, 2002). While "[p]olitical exile," claimed a collected volume published in 2012, "is still an under-researched topic" ("Introduction," *Exile and the Politics of Exclusion in the Americas*, edited by Lluis Roniger, James Naylor Green, and Pablo Yankelevich [Sussex University Press, 2012], 4).

The Spanish Republican exile has built a solid bibliography. Of special interest is Jorge de Hoyos Puente's recent assessment on the matter in "Los estudios del exilio republicano de 1939: Una mirada personal" *Dictatorship and Democracies* (2017), https://www.researchgate.net/publication/328978212_Los_estudios_del_exilio_republicano_de_1939_a_revision_una_mirada_personal

21 Jose María Naharro Calderón, "Twentieth-century Literature in Exile," in *The Cambridge History of Spanish Literature,* 620–7, 621.

22 "De hecho, soy un escritor desconocido en España." *Mis páginas mejores* (Gredos, 1966), 1.

23 Jorge Guillén's letter of December 23, 1947 reads in Spanish: "En medio de la indiferencia del mundo ....cada día me duele más este vacío, este vacío cuya compañía forma ya parte de mi ser," *Pedro Salinas/Jorge Guillén. Correspondencia 1923–1951,* 429–30, 430.

24 Cernuda explicitly states that the Romantic "attitude, that in its day had beneficial consequences, with regard to the knowledge and estimation of our literature … [is] today sustained and exaggerated to incredible extremes by the most reputed intellectuals on our soil, turning into something [i.e., a critical outlook] that is not only false but absurd" (*esta actitud, que en su día tuvo sin duda consecuencias beneficiosas respecto al conocimiento y estimación de nuestra literatura sostenida anacrónicamente y exagerada hasta un extremo increíble para los eruditos más reuputados de nuestra tierra, se ha convertido en algo no sólo ya falso, sino absurdo) (Estudios sobre poesía española contemporánea,* 25).

25 In Spanish: "En todo lo que va de siglo, la vida española se ha desenvuelto a un ritmo acelerado de visicitud, y en los últimos años–de 1931 a la era del refugiado político—han pasado cosas como para abarrotar las librerías de novelas sugestivas y profundas que hubiesen definido nuestro tiempo de modo definitivo. Pues no; continúan partiendo el bacalao … los novelistas de la Generación del 98." Isidoro Enríquez Calleja, "Emilia Pardo Bazán," *LE* 2 (1946), 9 and 12, 9.

26 "[C]onsideraban a la Generación del 98 un hito en la recuperación de esta conciencia por dirigir su mirada hacia atrás y buscar su pueblo" (Genara Pulido Tirado, "El Quijote de Pedro Salinas en su contexto," *eHumanista Cervantes* 3 [2014]: 1–19, 3). Anthony Close had similarly remarked that "As the generation of '98 had done, Castro looked at Spain's past through the windows of the present, and sought compensation for its inadequacies in *Don Quixote,* which allowed a glimpse of a Utopian future" (*Romantic Approach* 233).

27 Most writers, like Salinas, Aub, Guillén, would progressively soften their explicit criticism of other Spanish authors in the next decade when teaching in foreign universities. A good number of the members of the Generation of '27 were professors of literature before the war, and continued that work in exile. This was the case with Salinas (Sevilla, Johns Hopkins, Wesley), Cernuda (Glasgow, Cambridge, Mount Holyoke), Amado Alonso (Centro de Estudios Históricos, Instituto de Filología in Buenos Aires, Harvard), and Francisco Ayala (Princeton, Rutgers, New York University, among others). The fact that they were hired to teach Spanish literature seems to have compelled them to defend the literary legacy of their '98 predecessors, at least officially. For more specific information about these teaching appointments see Jose María Naharro, "Calderón Twentieth-century Literature in Exile," in *The Cambridge History of Spanish Literature,* edited by David Gies (Cambridge, UK: Cambridge University Press, 2009), 620–7. For more on the exile of these writers, see José Luis Abellán, *El exilio español de 1939* (Madrid: Fundación universitaria, 1997); Estaban Luis de Llera, *El último exilio español en América, grandeza y miseria de una formidable aventura* (Madrid: Mafre,

1996); José María Balcells and José Antonio Pérez Bowie, *El exilio cultural de la Guerra Civil (1936–1939)* (Salamanca: Ediciones Universidad, 2001); Francisco J. Caudet, *Hipótesis sobre el exilio republicano de 1939* (Madrid: Fundación universitaria española, 1997); and Michael Ugarte, *Shifting Ground: Spanish Civil War Exile Literature* (Durham: Duke University Press, 1989).

28 Britt Arredondo, *Quixotism*, 13.

29 Ibid., 13. After the loss of the last overseas colonies, Puerto Rico, Cuba, and Philippines in 1898, one of the most coherent intellectual discourses trying to move from this crisis into a brighter, Spanish future was Regenerationism. The move to infuse a new national identity and sense of destiny into a demoralized country was not only conservative, however. Regenerationism offered a variety of proposals for reforming Spain from a plurality of political viewpoints; progressive, conservative, centralist, and regionalist. Javier Krauel, *Imperial Emotions: Cultural Responses to Myths of Empire in Fin-de-Siècle Spain* (Liverpool University Press, 2013), 135 and Carolyn Boyd, *Historia Patria: Politics, History, and National Identity in Spain, 1875–1975* (Princeton University Press, 1997), 124–30, 128.

30 According to Stanley Payne, Costa's Regenerationism consisted in his demand for a "developmental policy based on education, irrigation, and agrarian improvement. Together with an emphasis on technology." Payne also remembers that Costa had been the first to coin the phrase "revolution from above," and the metaphor of an "iron surgeon" (*The Franco regime, 1936–1975* [University of Wisconsin Press, 1987]), 10. Brit Arredondo adds that it is with ideas like that of the iron surgeon that "Costa began to reveal a darker side" to his regenerationism: "that surgical policy," affirmed Costa, "has to be entrusted to an iron surgeon who is capable of governing the nation's anatomy," an idea that according to Arrendondo placed Spanish sovereignty in the hands of a "regenerating dictator" (*Quixotism* 43). Arredondo defends his dictatorial reading of Costa with a reminder that when Primo de Rivera assumed power in 1923, he "justified his *golpe de estado*, in part, by evoking Joaquin Costa's call for a curative iron surgeon" (ibid.). The fact that Costa was an ambivalent figure who justified these two competing readings (liberal and/or dictatorial) of his regenerationist theory is supported by the perceptive contemporary analysis of Dionisio Pérez. In his *El enigma de Joaquín Costa, ¿revolucionario? ¿oligarquista?* (Iberoamericana, 1930), Pérez seemed unable to choose one over the other, noting that Costa's ideas about reform were brief, ambiguous, and sparse. Yet they remained so compelling that "after 1900, there was no political party or leader that failed to invoke Costa's ideology, the medicinal prescription with which he wanted to restore Spanish greatness" (14).

31 Costa, *Reconstitución y europeización de España* (1900), 20. Costa's message is not as anti-imperialistic as this quote may suggest, since in his *Crisis Política de España* (Biblioteca Costa, 1914), he revisited the statement—of "locking up El Cid and Don Quixote's sepulcher"—and denied trying to erase "from the heart and memory of Spaniards the figures of El Cid and Don Quixote." He reminded his reader that years prior, he had "promoted the celebration of a Colonial Geography Symposium ... and the creation of a Geographic Society" that precisely intended to "acquire wide extensions of territory in the African

continent that would extend the empire of El Cid and Don Quixote" (borrar del corazón y la memoria de los españoles las figuras del [Campeador y Don Quijote] .....me lo decían a mí, que ... había promovido la celebración de un Congreso de Geografía colonial, y la fundación de una Sociedad Geográfica precisamente para eso, para adquirir vastas extensions de territorio en el continente africano, que ensancharan el imperio del Cid y de Don Quijote en lo futuro!(Costa, *Reconstitución* 21). See P. Tedde de Lorca, "De la primera a la segunda Restauración" *Ayer* (1996), 15–49. Javier Varela, "El mito de Castilla en la Generación del 98." *Claves de la razón práctica* 70 (1997), 10–16, Britt-Arredondo, *Quixotism*, 79.

32 "Al consumarse en 1898 la pérdida de los restos del imperio colonial español en América y el Extremo Oriente, se irguió la figura de Don Joaquín Costa para decirnos 'Doble llave' al sepulcro del Cid para que no vuelva a cabalgar. ....Don Miguel de Unamuno formuló también su sentencia: Robinsón ha vencido a Don Quijote .... Se pedía a los españoles que no volviesen a ser ni Cides ni Quijotes, y los que en aquellas horas de humillación y de derrota sentíamos la necesidad de rehacer la patria, de 'regenerarla' ... no tardamos en ver que no se lograría sin que los regeneradores se infundiesen un poco, cuando menos, del espíritu esforzado del Cid y del idealismo generoso de Don Quijote" Ramiro de Maeztu, *Don Quijote, Don Juan, y la Celestina*. 1926. (Madrid: Espasa Calpe, 1981), 64, in a paragraph quoted and well-explained by Christopher Britt-Arrendondo, 148–9.

33 "Y un día de pronto ... *todas las fantasías, hasta allí en reposo*, vibran enloquecidas y se lanzan al ensueño. ¿No es esta la patria del gran ensoñador don Alonso Quijano? ¿No está en este pueblo compendiada la *historia eterna* de la tierra española?" Azorín. *La ruta del Quijote*, edited by H. Ramsden (University of Manchester Press, 1966), 68.

34 My emphasis: "*El Quijote*, no ha sido sólo creado a la manera española, sino que es nuestra obra típica, 'la obra' por antonomasia porque Cervantes no se contenta con ser un 'independiente:' fue un *conquistador, fue el más grande de los conquistadores*, porque mientras *los demás conquistadores conquistaban* países para España, *el conquistó a España misma*, encerrado en una prisión." *Idearium español* (Madrid, 1905), emphasis added, 79.

35 "De la España del 98 acá, de la España que ha sentido la pérdida de su Imperio, venimos nosotros, lo que nos queremos arraigados en todo lo antiguo y ... los que buscamos no la España de ayer, ni tampoco la de anteayer, sino la España eterna; la que en la sangre del pueblo español nunca ha renunciado al yugo y las flechas de su Imperio" *Imperio* (Afrodisio Aguado, 1941), 75.

36 "[E]l patriotismo nuestro ... ha llegado por el camino de la crítica" Pedro Laín Entralgo. *España como problema. Desde la "generación del 98" hasta 1936.* 1949 (Aguilar, 1956), 13. Even their literary style is supposed to be indebted to their '98 grandparents, as Laín Entralgo points out in his dedicatory preface to the falangista Dionisio Ridruejo (co-founder of the journal Escorial): "We are perfectly certain that without them [the members of the Generation of 1898] our language would not be what it is. Our literary style ... denotes the great stylistic deed achieved by our granparents, and as such, rests in our granparents's legacy" (*Sabemos con plena certidumbre que sin ellos no sería nuestro lenguaje el que efectivamente es. Nuestro estilo literario ....supone*

la ingente obra estilística cumplida por nuestros abuelos y se apoya en ella).
Emphasis added, ibid.).

37 Britt Arredondo, *Quixotism,* see especially 8, 69, 142, 173.

38 A good number of Generation of '27 intellectuals occupied prominent
positions in the Republican government: José Bergamín was a Director
General of Social Action, Juan José Domenchina, headed the Spanish
Information Service; and María Zambrano and Luis Cernuda participated
in the *Pedagogical Missions.* Under the Republic, Zambrano would later
lead the Propaganda Department, while Salinas would be appointed
as a researcher at the Centro de Estudios Históricos. Many others,
including Rafael Alberti, Manuel Altolaguirre, and León Felipe, would
be even more militant in their defense of the Republican government:
Felipe and Altolaguirre enlisted and fought in the Republican army, and
Alberti became the poetic voice of the Republican resistance in Madrid.
For a detailed retrospective on the subject, see D. Moss's first chapter,
"Intellectuals and the Second Republic," *in Political Poetry in the Wake
of the Second Spanish Republic* (London: Lexington, 2018), 1–32. For
more on the political inclinations of the '27, see Juan Cano Ballesta, *Voces
airadas* (Madrid: Cátedra, 2013) and Manuel Aznar Soler, *República
literaria y revolución (1920–1939)* (Madrid: Renacimiento, 2010).

39 Castro, *El pensamiento,* 386.

40 "Por lo visto, los generales y los conquistadores han obedecido siempre a
sentimientos muy parecidos, o mejor dicho, cortados por el mismo patrón.
Nadie desdecería las palabras de Escipión en boca de Mussolini, como nadie
hallaría diferencia entre las palabras de los numantinos y las de los defensores
de Madrid ... Cervantes, como siempre, halla las expresiones populares—
eternas por populares, populares por eternas—y por carambola histórica,
multitud de sus frases cobran hoy, sin cambiar un tilde, una curiosísima
actualidad." "Actualidad de Cervantes" in *Max Aub y la vanguardia
teatral (Escritos sobre el teatro 1928–1938),* edited by Manuel Aznar Soler
(Universidad de Valencia, 1993), 159.

41 Ortega's whole quote reads: "Let's be clear: Quixote is a misleading text. All
the efforts of national eloquence to clarify it were useless. None of the erudite
approaches to Cervantes's life have shed any light on this colossal riddle either.
Is Cervantes mocking somebody? Who? From afar, Quixote's silhouette bends
on itself like an exclamation mark, as if he were protecting a Spanish secret,
the secret of our Spanish, cultural troubles" ("Seamos sinceros: el Quijote es
un equívoco. Todos los ditirambos de la elocuencia nacional no han servido
de nada. Todas las rebuscas eruditas en torno a la vida de Cervantes no han
aclarado ni un rincón del colosal equívoco. ¿Se burla Cervantes? ¿Y de qué
se burla? De lejos, sólo en la abierta llanada manchega la larga figura de Don
Quijote se encorva como un signo de interrogación: y es como un guardián
del secreto español, del equívoco de la cultura española") *Meditaciones del
Quijote* [Publicaciones Residencia de Estudiantes, 1914], 127.

42 "La petulancia de Ortega. ¿Qué es eso? ¿No hay español [que] haya entendido
el Q[uijote]? ¿Y qué? No hay millones que lo han leído y llorado con él?
¿Es que Cer[vantes] lo escribió para que lo entendieran los profesores de
metafísica?" "La última palabra de Don Quijote." *Pedro Salinas. Quijote y
Lectura. Defensas y fragmentos,* edited by Enric Bou (*ELR,* 2005), 128–30, 129.

Salinas is not the only one complaining about Ortega y Gasset. Isidoro Enríquez Calleja laments that Ortega's flowery rhetorical style "worked well for him, [but] prevented his contemporaries from advancing into more significant narrative experiments." Calleja argues that "[m]ore than one of his students in la *Revista de Occidente* complained, behind closed doors, that 'this damn José had taught me to say' byzantine 'nonsense' about the novel 'rather than helping me find a straight way to write one'" (*A Ortega y Gasset le arroba lo narciso, le encanta lo abstracto, aquello que habla sin contenido sólido, que se traduce, a fin de cuentas, en espirales de humo y bonitos vuelos de mariposa. Y naturalmente, que se salva él, por ensayista magnífico, pero hace la santísima a los demás ... A más de un discípulo de la Revista de Occidente hemos oído por detrás del muro, esta lamentación: "Maldito don José que me enseñó a decir tonterías bizantinas" "en torno a la novela" en lugar de señalarme el camino recto de hacerla*). Both of Enríquez Calleja's quotes are from "Emilia Pardo Bazán," *LE* 2 (1946), 9. Another exile, Juan Marinello, includes Ortega among the "traitors" who accepted the protection of the Francoist regime, and that being part of the Spanish intellectual elite once (*tuvieron obra y garbo*), they were only "a sad choir of ghosts in service toda, to an anti-cultural and anti-intellectual government" (*integran hoy un triste coro de fantasmas. Servidores de un gobierno anticultural y antinteligente*) ("Franco y la Cultura," *LE* 7 [1947], 29).

43 "España no es invertebrada, sino desvertebrada intencionalmente, desfigurada y torcida a fuerza de ortopedias." Manuel Andújar and José Ramón Araña Editorial (*LE* 2 [1946], 2).

44 "Sacar Cervantes a la luz," Aub (1956) *"La Numancia de Cervantes"* Reprinted in Aznar Soler, *De Max Aub a Cervantes* (Segobrbe, 1999), 19–70, 55.

45 Aub (1955), "Algunos Quijotes," *Reprinted*. Ibid., 41–7, 42.

46 Diego de Clemencín. *Comentarios a Don Quijote*. 1833 and 1839. Sender explicitly argues that the real reason his former teacher, Unamuno, disregarded Cervantes was nothing but a "deplorable and comical" envy of his ability to write a novel like Don Quixote (*Examen de ingenios: Los Noventayochos. Ensayos críticos* (Las Americas, 1961), 21. This attitude, for Sender, extended to other members of the '98 group: "muchos partidarios entre aquellos universitarios de la generación pasada [generation of 98] que [le] consideraban inferior a su obra. Como si Cervantes no hubiera sabido lo que hacía cuando la escribió" ([Cervantes] did not have many defenders among the graduates of a previous generation ['98], who considered him inferior to his oeuvre, as if he had no idea what he was doing it when he wrote it) (Sender, *Examen de Ingenios*, 22). Vicente Gaos does not name names when he critically wonders why a past generation of Cervantists "who were constantly finding errors in Quixote and correcting the great author were the same Cervantists who later spoke of him with ecstatic rapture" (*los que han solido poner esas tachas al Quijote han sido los cervantistas que, al mismo tiempo que enmiendan al gran autor, hablan de él en actitud de ecstático arrobo*) (*Cervantes, Novelista, Dramaturgo, Poeta* 1971 [Planeta, 1977], 11). Gaos attributes to Unamuno, however, a great mistake forged in this critical attitude, claiming that "to Unamuno ... we owe the dissemination of a most unfortunate judgment about Cervantes: that he is inferior to his work and to his protagonist [Quixote]" (*A*

Unamuno ... hay que imputar la propagación de un desafortunadísimo juicio:
la de que Cervantes es inferior a su obra y al protagonista [Quijote] de ella)
(*Claves de literatura* 80).

47   "[L]a mezcla de pomposidad decorativa y vaciedad intelectual ... tiene
también su tradición, porque fue el romanticismo quien le dio estado social."
Luis Cernuda, "Poesía popular" (1941). *Poesía y literatura*, Vol. 1 (Seix Barral,
1960), 13–34, 31.

48   "¿Cómo puede dudarse de que el Quijote es una obra cómica regocijante? Lo
es, como es una parodia de los libros de caballerías. Son sus valores acaso más
superficiales (y digo 'acaso' porque, después del Quijote, no sé si habrá que
pensar que lo cómico es la máxima jerarquía estética). Pero superficiales o no,
es imposible llegar a ningún fondo sin pasar por la superficie. Y los críticos
esotéricos se la saltaron, como si la comicidad y la parodia caballeresca fueran
incompatables con propósitos más profundos y universales." Vicente Gaos
"Sobre la historia de la crítica cervantina" (1965) in *Claves de literatura*
207–16, 213.

49   "[H]ace de los españoles [para bien o para mal] un reposadero para
las veleidades de los extraños y un refugio para cualquier trasnochado
romanticism." Castro's "Reseña de la obra de Ludwig Pfandl *Historia de la
literatura nacional Española en la Edad de Siglo de Oro.*" *Revista de filología
española* 12 (1934). In *De la España que aún no conocía*, Vol. 3 (México:
Finisterre, 1972), 127–45, 129.

50   "Para la gente de 1898 ... Don Quijote es un símbolo: encarnación mítica
y mística de lo español. Pero convertir las cosas en símbolos es un tanto
peligroso y quien tal haga, hágalo a su cuenta y razón, pero no debe arriesgar
el destino de la obra ajena" (*Poesía y literatura*, Vol. 2 [Seix Barral, 1960], 16).

51   "[D]esintegrado a Don Quijote porque hemos burlado y disociado al héroe
... ahí está la Generación del 98 como testimonio fiel .... Pregúntandose por
España, encontraban en la atormentada figura de Don Quijote verónica fiel
para su desazón y pesimismo. Su interpretación del Quijote es una escapada
delírica y luciferina del abatido pensamiento español." My emphasis. José
Enrique Rebolledo, "Sobre el quijotismo de Sancho Panza," *LE* 5 (1947), 8.
Rebolledo acknowledges Eugenio Imaz for his understanding of the '98 legacy,
but does not provide a specific reference for this quote. Pedro Salinas alludes
tangentially to '98 literary criticism for its tendency to dissociate Don Quixote
(as a character and text) from its context. This interpretative praxis "easily
forgets, from atop the stilts of critical arrogance, that a poem has been written
to be read and lived by the reader. The critic's only role is bringing the poet
closer to the reader, not using him as a bell to announce his own glory" (olvida
muy fácilmente desde los zancos de la pedantería profesorial que el poema
has sido escrito para ser leído y vivido por el lector ... la función del crítico es
aproximar el poeta al lector y no encaramarse sobre ellos y que les sirvan de
escabel para su gloria) Pedro Salinas, *Quijote y lectura. Defensas y fragmentos*
(Madrid: ELR Ediciones, 2005), 20.

52   "Los hombres del '98 parten como tantos otros caballeros andantes
aquijoteados en busca de España-Dulcinea, la ideal, desdeñosos de España-
Aldonza, la material" (Salinas 1961, 279). Salinas demonstrates to be aware
of how this critical reference influenced other specialists that being part of the

98 generation were maintaining their interpretative praxis. In 1945, writing about Cervantes's posthumous novel *Persiles*, and the analysis of a fellow critic, Casalduero, Salinas gives Guillén a succinct summary of the study, and establishes clear differences between a still symbolic method like that Casalduero's and his own. Although Salinas admits Casalduero's study had helped him understand Cervantes's novel better, he points out:

> I could not always accept Casalduero's arguments. As I have told him [Casalduero], the *problem arises from forcing this symbolism, turning it [the novel] into an allegory, creating a tight correspondence* [between both text and allegory]. What *I am* really passionate about is the fact that *Persiles* is an exact contemporaneous work to the second *Quixote*. That relationship [between both novels] and the man that sustains them fascinates *me*, but of course Casalduero does not consider the issue. Emphasis added.
>
> [Casalduero] me ha ayudado a entender el libro [*Persiles*] aunque no pueda aceptar siempre sus interpretaciones. Como le he dicho a Casalduero, *el peligro está en forzar el símbolo, convirtiéndole en alegoría, es decir, en equivalencia demasiado rigurosa*. Por otra parte, *me apasiona* pensar en el *Persiles* como obra exactamente coetánea del segundo *Quijote*. Esa relación, y el hombre que la sostiene, *me fascina*. Claro que Casalduero no toca ese problema.
>
> (Emphasis added. November 13, 1945, *Correspondencia*, 362–4, 262)

53 "[L]os jóvenes de mi época se sienten engañados y decepcionados por la cuadrilla de narcisistas del 98." "Santyana, español del 98," *LE* 23–4 (1950), 4.

54 "Aún no se han tomado, respecto a los escritores de esta generación una actitud crítica, sino que subsiste la panegírica, y eso que los acontecimientos de los últimos años ha puesto un comentario terrible a muchas de las páginas que escribieron con responsabilidad extraña. Se les sigue considerando como contemporáneos nuestros cuando varias generaciones nuevas los han desplazado, y ... sus obras [son] ya caducas" (*Estudios sobre poesía española contemporánea*, 64, emphasis added).

55 According to Cernuda, Azorín improperly characterized this kind of criticism as "psychological" (lo llamó sin razón "crítica psicológica" [*Estudios poesía* 65]).

56 Close, *The Romantic Approach,* 157.

57 Some authors seem to have softened their opinions of the philosopher in the 1950s, especially when writing literary histories. See Salinas, Aub, and Cernuda, for example, in a lecture by Salinas "What we owe to Don Quixote," he speaks of Unamuno with deference, acknowledging valuable insights in his reading of Cervantes "Unamuno, en una de sus grandes genialidades dijo que ... " (Salinas, *Quijote y Lectura*, 61). In his *Literary History,* Aub gently speaks of the evolution of the philosopher's thinking from a humanist mindset to an "religious and mystic irrationality" (471). Finally, Aub concludes that Unamuno's influence "did only grow with time, becoming the most important Spanish writer of the twentieth century" (474).

58 "[U]n Quijote malhumorado y agrio llevado más por el nacionalismo que la verdad" (Max Aub in *Pruebas,* an anthology collected and published decades later [Ciencia Nueva, 1967]).

59 "descomunal, ingente ... atroz ego" Domenchina (*Poesías escogidas. Ciclo de mocedad, 1916–1921* [Madrid, Ediciones Mateu, 1922], 11–14.

60 "Ese pobre Cervantes, tan inferior a Don Quijote." Sender, "Hace cuatro siglos de Cervantes," *LE* 4 (1947), 3.

61 "[considerar] que don Quijote era más suyo, más de Unamuno, que de Cervantes mismo .... Es sorprendente la ligereza de Unamuno negando a Cervantes la conciencia de su creación." Ibid.

62 "Y si a Unamuno le molesta Cervantes, y pretende dejarle a un lado, no pueden movernos las mismas razones a quienes sólo afecto, admiración y respeto sentimos hacia él." Cernuda, *OC* 672, emphasis added.

63 See, for example, Jose M. Gallegos Rocafull, who opens his "Aún hay sol en las bardas" wondering why Unamuno used such an image—a pilgrimage to Don Quixote's sepulcher. "Did Don Miguel believe that Don Quixote was really dead? Did the '98 anti-Spanish pessimism sentence him [Don Quixote] to death?" (¿Creería de verdad Don Miguel que había muerto Don Quijote? ¿Le condenaría el aburdo pesimismo antiespañol del '98?) "El mensaje de esperanza de Cervantes. Aún hay sol en las bardas," *LE* 5 (1947), 11.

64 See Pulido Tirado's exploration of Unamuno's Vida as a Christ-like characterization of Don Quixote. *El Quijote y el pensamiento teórico-literario,* 461.

65 All quotes of this work are from the Austral edition of 1908.

66 "No cayeron en el vacío las palabras de Unamuno .... no como el soñara." Gallegos Rocafull, "El mensaje de esperanza," 11.

67 "Verás cómo así que el sagrado escuadrón se ponga en marcha aparecerá en el cielo una estrella nueva, sólo visible para los cruzados, una estrella refulgente y sonora, que cantará un canto nuevo en esta larga noche que nos envuelve, y la estrella se pondrá en marcha en cuanto se ponga en marcha el escuadrón de los cruzados, y cuando hayan vencido en su cruzada, o cuando hayan sucumbido todos—que es acaso la manera única de vencer de veras—la estrella caerá del cielo, y en el sitio en donde caiga allí está el sepulcro. El sepulcro está donde muera el escuadrón." (Unamuno, *Vida* [Austral, 1908], 27)

68 Britt-Arredondo, *Quixotism,* 13.

69 Unamuno, *Obras completas,* Vol. 3 (Madrid: Escelicier), 957.

70 ("[D]esconfía del arte, desconfía de la ciencia, por lo menos de eso que llaman arte y ciencia y no son sino mezquinos remedos del arte y de la ciencia verdaderos" (distrust art, distrust knowledge, because that which they are calling art and science are only miserable traces of the true art and science) (Unamuno, *Vida* [1908], 23).

71 "Que te baste tu fe. Tu fe será tu arte, tu fe será tu ciencia" (your faith should be enough. Your faith will be your science). Ibid., 24.

72 Qué vamos a hacer en el camino mientras marchamos? ¿Qué? ¡Luchar! ¡Luchar!, y ¿cómo? ¿Cómo? ¿Tropezáis con uno que miente?, gritarle a la cara: ¡mentira!, y ¡adelante! ¿Tropezáis con uno que roba?, gritarle: ¡ladrón!, y ¡adelante! ¿Tropezáis con uno que dice tonterías, a quien oye toda una muchedumbre con la boca abierta?, gritarles: ¡estúpidos!, y ¡adelante! ¡Adelante siempre!. (ibid., 19).

73   "Este hombre [Unamuno], que imaginó una cruzada para rescatar el sepulcro de Don Quijote, lanzó a los aires hacia 1908 las páginas más vigorosas de que el espíritu universal de estos años últimos –movilizado con bayonetas al grito imperial de predominio." Ramiro de Ledesma, "Grandezas de Unamuno," *La conquista del estado* n. 2 (marzo, 1931), 1, http://filosofia.org/hem/193/lce/lce021a.htm. Accessed June 1, 2016.

74   "Si Don Quijote es el último de los caballeros andantes, Cervantes puede considerarse como el último de los conquistadores. Tanto vale uno como el otro. Cada uno de por sí, y juntos entreambos, encarnan el ideal que agoniza ... dentro de una vida transfigurada." Jean Babelon. "Cervantes y el ocaso de los conquistadores," *Revista de filología española* 32 (1948), 206–12, 206.

75   Kevin M. Cahill, *To Bear Witness: A Journey of Healing and Solidarity* (Oxford, UK: Oxford University Press, 2013), describes the famous scene when Salamanca had fallen to Franco's forces and Unamuno, as the provost of the university, defied the Falangist general, who entered the academic space crying "Muerte a la inteligencia" (Death to intellectuals). Unamuno, as Cahill describes, "waited in vain for quiet and then slowly responded, 'you will win, but you will not convince'" (Venceréis pero no convenceréis), "You will win because you possess more than enough brute force, but you will not convince since to convince means to persuade. And in order to persuade you would need what you lack, reason, and right in the struggle. I consider it futile to exhort you to think of Spain. I have finished" (92). The anecdote has been questioned by Delgado Cruz (*Arqueología de un mito* [Sílex, 2019]). Although the general agreement is that the clash between Unamuno and Astray was that tense and antagonistic, "We know the events but not the literal words," reminds Andrés Trapiello. https://www.vozpopuli.com/altavoz/cultura/acerca-palabras-Unamuno-generanhistoriadores_0_1134188112.html

76   One of the ultimate, and most extreme, examples would come from Giménez Caballero, who equated Nationalist forces with Cervantes's hero, claiming that "[c]uando nuestras juventudes triunfaron de todos los fracasos de tres siglos españoles y salieron un día de su maravillosa Cueva de Montesinos—victoria del 1 de abril de 1939—se sintieron como Don Quijote, digno de codearse con héroes fabulosos y contar a todas las gentes su grandeza" (when, after three centuries of failures, our young ones finally triumphed, and emerged from the Cueva de Montesinos—with the victory of April 1, 1939—they felt like Don Quixote, worthy of rubbing shoulders with the most mythical heroes, and to announce to people this greatness). *Don Quijote ante el mundo (y ante mí)* (Inter American University Press, 1979), 250.

77   Cernuda, *Obra Completa (OC)*, Vol. 2, edited by Derek Harris and Luis Maristany (Siruela, 2002), 673.

78   "[C]omo si al encontrar al fin aquel tan deseado sepulcro, aunque Unamuno mismo no está convencido de que tal cosa sea posible, todos los males y desgracias nacionales se curarían casi por ensalmo." Ibid., 673.

79   Ibid.

80   As it had done before with the description of the Civil War, after the D-Day, the editorials of the Francoist regime denounced the "'fascist/antifascist' terms of the Combat as 'anachronistic polemic' Suggesting instead the real struggle was between 'culture and barbarism,' with the Soviet Union presenting

barbarism and the West, culture." Wayne H. Bowen, *Spain during World War II* (Missouri, 2006), 90. Franco had been able to avoid entering the Second World War due to factions and hesitation rather than skill (Bowen, 16); the dictator was particularly indebted to Nazi support of the Nationalist cause, which he had personally sought through special emissaries in 1935. Robert H. Whealey, *Hitler and Spain, The Nazi Role in the Spanish Civil War, 1936–1939* (University of Kentucky Press, 2015), 6. After the war, Francoist pragmatists reinforced messages of international neutrality, and (through cosmetic reforms), touted an emerging liberalism for the government, claiming to constitute, by the late 1940s, a Catholic organic "democracy." Stanley Payne, *Franco and Hitler, Spain, Germany, and World War II* (Yale University Press, 2008), 253.

81 This vision of a "dogmatic" and uniquely Spanish Calderón de la Barca is widely refuted today. See, for example, Evangelina Rodríguez-Cuadros, *Calderón de la Barca*, Los cabellos de Absalón (Espasa Calpe, 1989); Susan Fisher, "This Thing of Darkness I/acknowledge mine: Segismundo, Próspero, and Shadow," in *The Prince and the Tower. Perceptions of* La vida es sueño, edited by Frederick de Armas. (Associated Presses, 1993), 147–64. Also by Fischer, "Calderón and the Ideology of Egalitarism, 'Más bien al dado:' El alcalde de Zalamea," in *Reading Performance, Spanish Golden Age Theater and Shakespeare on the Modern Stage,* edited by Susan L. Fischer (Boydell and Brewer [Tamesis], 2009), 59–76, "Beyond the Black Legend of Calderón's Wife Murder Plays: Amourous Strife, Violence, and the Comedia" in *On Wolves and Sheep: Exploring the Expression of Political Thought in Golden Age Spain,* edited by Aaron M. Kahn (Cambridge Scholars Press, 2011), 113–46; Ana Laguna, "*Life Is a Dream* and the Fractures of Reason," *MLN* 129, no. 2 (2014), 238–54.

82 Celebrated by the Francoist establishment, Garcilaso was turned into "the kind of [heroic] profile that the Regime was interested in exploiting in those initial years." Under the auspices of the Falange, one of the most important literary magazines in postwar Spain, *Garcilaso,* would be named after him (it would run uninterrupted from 1943 through 1946), Trevor J. Dadson, *Breve splendor de mal distinta lumber: Estudios sobre poesía Española* (Renacimiento 2005), see specifically 235–60. The conservative critic Victor García de la Concha observed that the honor was well deserved: many ultra-conservative thinkers were "moved by [Garcilaso's] military and Renaissance literary stature" and treated his figure and works as both a contemporary and a classic references. "[W]e elevate his name," García de la Concha continued, "as an invocation and the flag of our Enterprise" (Nosotros, convencidos por su paso militar y renaciente, actual y clásico, levantamos su nombre como una invocación y una bandera a la cabeza de nuestra empresa). Cited in Dadson 236.

83 As José Agustín Goytisolo notes ironically in his *Psalms to the Wind* (Salmos al viento) (1958), "to sing the affairs/wonderfully meaningless, is to say/it is time to forget everything that happened/in order to compose verses empty, perhaps, but resounding" (cantar los asuntos/maravillosamente insustanciales, es decir/el momento de olvidarnos de todo lo ocurrido/y componer hermosos versos vacíos sí pero sonoros). Ibid., 238.

84 Calderón embodied a "[m]odelo indiscutible de la dramaturgia hispana, el creador del Teatro Nacional," according to Joaquín Entrambasguas, who defines this national genre in racial terms, arguing, that "[f]or us, our Spanish

condition has a defining role in our culture, 'national drama,' then is the theater that provides a dramatic manifestation of that racial spirit, regardless of its technique or achievement, as defined by other contexts." So strongly was Lope embraced by Francoists, that Giménez Caballero would consider it "literary heresy" for the playwright's work to be produced by Lorca's *La Barraca* theater company during the Republic. See Marta Castillo, "Las herejías literarias de García Lorca desde la estética franquista." *Lancha Boletín de Arte* 30–1 (2009–10), 301–25, 311.

Duncan Wheeler study *Golden Age Drama in Contemporary* Spain is a formidable reference. See also Sultana Wahnón "Estética y Teoría del Arte en Arte y Estado, de Giménez Caballero," in *Estética y Crítica Literarias en España (1940–1950)* (Universidad de Granada, 1988), 23–110, Susan Byrd, *La Fuente Ovejuna de Federico García Lorca* (Pliegos, 1984), and David Rodríguez-Solas, "La Barraca, 1933: *El giro lopiano de García Lorca.*" Faculty Publication Series, https://scholarworks.umass.edu/spanport_faculty_pubs/?utm_source=scholarworks.umass.edu%2Fspanport_faculty_pubs%2F1&utm_medium=PDF&utm_campaign=PDFCoverPages.

85 Francoist theorists were well aware of the need for the ideological reshaping of this classic theater, especially after the popularity and significance of dramas such as *Fuenteovejuna* as directed by Lorca and adapted by Alberti. As José María Pemán proudly observed, "[r]epresentar *Fuenteovejuna* es un poco como ganarle una posición al enemigo" (performing *The Sheep Well* is a bit "like winning a position from the enemy") (Quoted in Wheeler, 82). As Wheeler has shown, the overreaching propaganda program that followed the Francoist victory in 1939 would in fact win not only that position, but the entire cultural war fought by that program (82). An exiled Salinas would describe the fascist theater endorsed by Eduardo Marquina and Pemán as the opposite to "the authentic and poetic theater—seen in Lorca's plays and interludes" (El teatro o es auténtico y profundamente poético—en los dramas y farsas de Lorca—o finge serlo ... en la escuela de Marquina y Pemán) Salinas *Ensayos de literatura hispánica* (Aguilar, 1960) 288. Marquina and Pemán are considered today the main responsible of the national-historical plays of the period. See Julio Rodríguez Puertolas, *Historia de la literatura fascista española*, Vol. 2 (Akal, 2008), 803–4.

86 "Pues que en este año se cumple no sé qué centenario de Lope de Vega, se me ocurre que tal vez la efemérides sea la adecuada para dedicarla al tema indicado como título de estas páginas" ("Cervantes, poeta" [1940] OC 692–701, 692. According to these, the first lines of a brilliant essay on Cervantes's poetry—a dimension of Cervantes's opus, traditionally despised by criticism—Cernuda appears to rebuke to the Francoist preference for Lope de Vega.

87 Luis Cernuda, *Estudios sobre la poesía Española contemporánea* (Madrid: Guadarrama, 1957), 77–8.

88 "[M]etido hasta el cogollo en las pasiones literarias de su época." Max Aub, *Manual*, 303.

89 Vicente Gaos, *Cervantes Novelista, dramaturgo, poeta* [*sic*] (Barcelona: Planeta, 1979), 184.

90 "[S]us pastores, y singularmente Elicio, definen más que cantan [el amor]."
    Samuel Gili Gaya, *Galatea o el perfecto y verdadero amor* (Madrid: [s.n.],
    1948), 3.

91 Pedro Salinas, "La mejor carta de amores de la literatura española" [1952],
    16 *Anthropos* (1989), 118–24. Also reprinted in *La generación del 27 visita a
    Don Quijote* (Madrid: Visor, 2005), 39–55.

92 As inspired by the poetry of Francis Petrarch (1300–74), and the idea of love
    generally extracted from that poetry, that "turns the figure of an unattainable
    beloved into the ubiquitous source of poetic inspiration" (Aileen A. Feng,
    Writing Beloveds. Humanist Petrarchism and the Politics of Gender [Toronto
    University Press, 2017]), 4.

    The Spain of the 1600s experiences Petrarchan convention intertwined
    with a Neoplatonic inspiration, in a way that rather than "appeasing
    Petrarchan woes," resulted in the weakening of a Neoplatonic doctrine.
    Incapable of producing a well-defined ideology of love, Neoplatonism in the
    Iberian Peninsula translated into a series of stereotyped and disconnected
    topos that identified love with "the motor for the world, spiritual elevation,
    the absent lover, images engraved on the soul, the light of eyes, and other
    similar themes" (Alfonso Reyes, quoted by Ana Laguna and John Beusterien,
    "Introduction," in *Goodbye Eros*, edited by Ana Laguna and John Beusterien
    [Toronto University Press, 2020], 152).

93 The quote is by Close, from a separate study on love: "Don Quixote's Love for
    Dulcinea," 246.

94 ([N]o puede ser que haya caballero andante sin dama, porque tan propio y
    tan natural le es a los tales ser enamorados como al cielo tener estrellas, y a
    buen seguro que no se haya visto historia donde se halle caballero andante sin
    amores … sin ellos, no sería tenido por legítimo caballero, sino por bastardo, y
    que entró en la fortaleza por la caballería dicha, no por la puerta, sino por las
    bardas, como salteador y ladrón.) Cervantes, *El Ingenioso higalgo*, I.13: 175;
    Don Quixote, I.13: 90.

95 "[P]ues [es] en cabeza de un prójimo y en la comunidad donde se ama a todos
    los demás." Unamuno, 74.

96 "[D]el amor a mujer brota todo heroísmo. Del amor a mujer han brotado los
    profundos ideales, del amor a mujer las más soberbias fábricas filosóficas."
    Unamuno, *Vida*, 104.

97 ([E]l cuidado a la mujer ata las alas a otros heroes), adding, to reinforce
    the domestic connotations of the warning, that "women hinder [heroes]
    tremendously!" (¡cómo embaraza la mujer!), ibid., 105.

98 "[A]mó a la Gloria encarnada en mujer." Ibid., 109.

99 The allusion to Fili reads:

> If I say you, Phyllis, then I am wrong,
> for evil has no place in so much good
> nor does my woe rain down on me from heav'n.
> Soon I must die, of that I can be sure;
> when the cause of the sickness is unknown
> only a miracle can find the cure. (*DQ* 1.23: 175–6)

Si digo que sois vos, Fili, no acierto,
que tanto mal en tanto bien no cabe,
ni me viene del cielo esta rüina.
Presto sabré de morir, que es lo más cierto;
que al mal de quien la causa no se sabe
milagro es acertar la medicina. (*IH* I.23: 282)

100 (DQ 1.23: 176) "Por esa trova ... no se puede saber nada" (*IH* I.23: 282).
101 (*DQ* 1.23: 177) "Menos por ésta que por los versos se puede sacar más de que quien [*sic*] la escribió" (*IH* I.23: 283).
102 Ibid.
103 (*DQ* 1.25: 199), "[¿Qué] la hija de Lorenzo Corhuelo es la señora Dulcinea del Toboso llamada por otro nombre Aldonza Lorenzo [?]" (*IH* I.25: 311).
104 Salinas, "La mejor carta," 114–15. For more on the donkey-Dulcinea dyad, see Laguna, "Eroticism in Unexpected Places: Equine Love in Don Quixote," in *Sex and Gender in Cervantes/Sexo y género en Cervantes. Ensayos en honor de Adrienne Laskier Martin*, edited by Esther Fernández Rodríguez and Mercedes Alcalá Galán (Kassel: Reichenberger, 2019), 113–32.
105 "artificio, encumbramiento verbal, su apartamiento de toda naturalidad" Salinas ("La mejor carta," 117).
106 Ibid., 117.

Chapter 4

1 Elliot, *History in the Making*, 44.
2 Jean Howard, "The New Historicism in Renaissance Studies," in *Renaissance Historicism: Selections from English Literary Renaissance*, edited by Arthur F. Kinney and Dan S. Collins (University of Massachusetts Press, 1987), 3–33, 7.
3 "Northrop Frye 1912–1991," in *Twentieth-Century Literature Criticism: Excerpts from Criticism of the Works of Novelists, Poets, Playwrights, Short Story Writers & Other Creative Writers Who Died between 1900 & 1999*, edited by Thomas J. Schoenberg and Lawrence J. Trudeau (Cengage Gale, 2005), 138–264, 180.
4 Bataillon published in an article titled "Erasmo, ayer y hoy" (1973) a written exchange with Américo Castro in 1928, in which they discussed the censorship that Bataillon would face if he decided to publish the "Prologue" for Erasmus's *Enchiridion* as he had written it—during Primo de Rivera's censorship. Castro cannot contain his frustration as he explains this editorial limitation:

You know the situation in which we [researchers] live, battled, slandered, in terms quite similar to what Erasmus's friends experienced four hundred years ago ....I don't need to tell you how burdensome it is for me to realize that we have changed so little in the four hundred years that have passed since that trial was celebrated in Valladolid.

> Usted conoce la situación en que vivimos, combatidos, calumniados, en suma en una situación algo parecida a la que se encontraban los amigos de Erasmo hace cuatrocientos años .... No necesito decirle cuán fastidioso es para mí el ver que se haya adelantado tan poco a los cuatro cientos años de haberse celebrado la junta de Valladolid. "Erasmo, ayer y hoy," republished in *Erasmo y el Erasmismo edited by Francisco Rico.*
>
> (Crítica, 1977), 360–71, 362–3

Unexpected delays in the publication of the *Enchiridion* allowed it to be released in 1932 (*Revista de Filología Española* 16 [1932] 5–84), exactly as Bataillon had written it, since it was published during the Second Republic. But Bataillon's main opus, his seminal *Erasmus and Spain* (1937), would again face unsurmountable challenges. The first edition appeared in France, *Erasmus et l'Espagne. Recherches sur l'histoire spirituelle du XVI siècle* (Droz, 1937), becoming immediately and severely censored in Spain. A translation into Spanish was delayed thirteen years until it eventually appeared in Mexico, under the title of *Erasmo y España* (Fondo de Cultura Económica, 1950 and 1965). Francisco Rico edited the last version, *Erasmo y el Erasmismo,* translated by Carlos Pujol (Crítica, 1977). All my quotes are from this last, expanded version.

5   "*[Q]uizá tengamos derecho a interrogarnos* sobre las principales razones que nos impulsan a nosotros, especialistas del Renacimiento, a dedicarnos a Erasmo, no sólo como un objeto de estudio cuidadoso, todavía incompletamente explorado, sino incluso como *un autor muy próximo a nosotros, cuyas preocupaciones son aún en parte las nuestras (o han vuelto a convertirse en las nuestras)*, y de quien, tal vez por esta causa, nos sentimos movidos a explorar mejor ciertos aspectos, *guardándonos bien,* desde luego, *de caer en el pecado del anacronismo.*" "Actualidad de Erasmo" in *Erasmo y el Erasmismo,* emphasis added, 13–30, 15.

6   Emphasis added. In Spanish "Tratemos pues, sin aproximarlo abusivamente a nosotros, de discerner a Erasmo lo que hace de él un representante excepcional de este siglo XVI *que sentimos moderno.* Si nos *sentimos cercanos a él* es sin duda porque este siglo legó a los siguientes problemas que están en candente actualidad, porque se enfrentó a ellos sin resolverlos y a veces agravando sus dificultades" (ibid., 16; emphasis added).

7   "¿No es mañana, mejor que hoy, cuando vemos quién fue Erasmo en su vitalidad histórica?" (ibid., 371).

8   The striking inconsistency of such a conclusion is easy to understand in the ahistorical crescendo of his study's last chapter, "Erasmus, Yesterday and Today" (Erasmo, ayer y hoy), in *Erasmo y el Erasmismo,* 360–71.

9   Elliot *History,* 12. Emphasis added.

10   Charles B. Qualia, "Soldier and Humanist," *The South Central Bulletin* 4, no. 1 (1949), 1–11, 10.

11   Ibid., emphasis added.

12   Salinas calls Cernuda "the most degreed Glass of all" (*el más licenciado Vidriera de todos*), as if there were more than one, "the one that repels people that most" (*el que más aparta la gente de sí*) (Salinas, *OC* 355), Jorge Guillén calls Castro "Don Américo-Segismundo," implying that what is a bit lost

"is his Hispanic-Arabic labyrinth" (February 16, 1946, *Pedro Salinas/Jorge Guillén Correspondencia (1923–1951)*, 373–83, 375). Critics who declared Baroque poets such as Quevedo to be "men of their time" included Benjamín Jarnés, "Quevedo, figura actual," *LE* 1 (1946), 1, 8; and Luelmo, who notes that ultimately "We cannot go back to the classics. We are with them or they are with us. Without that spirit they ... would not be classics" (No se puede Volver a los clásicos. Se está con ellos, o ellos están con nosotros. Sin ese espíritu no ... serían clásicos) "El teatro" *Romance* 15 January (1941), 16.

13 Elliot, *History*, 58.
14 "Interpellation" is usually defined in the Althussian sense as "the constitutive process where individuals acknowledge and respond to ideologies, thereby recognizing themselves as subjects." *The Chicago School of Media Theory*, https://lucian.uchicago.edu/blogs/mediatheory/keywords/interpellation/.
15 As Johnson elegantly puts it, "the diachronic relativism signaled by the presence of analogies rather than by identities is overlain and further complicated by the synchronic relation of a multitude of different interpreters using a multitude of interpretive codes" ("Introduction," in *Cervantes and His Postmodern Constituencies*, edited with Anne Cruz [Routledge, 2000], ix–xxi, xix).
16 Elliot, *History*, 60.
17 Bell, "Cervantes and the Renaissance," 89–101, 93.
18 [A]sí unos quieren borrar la política española contraria a la Reforma y otros, con reacción equivalente, quieren borrar nuestro despotismo ilustrado; los primeros sueñan con un heterodoxo del siglo XVII en nuestra tierra, y los segundos con resucitar en tiempos modernos la Inquisición. (Cernuda, *OC*, Vol. 2, 672–3).
19 Matthew D. Stroud, "Infallible Texts and Righteous Interpretations: Don Quijote and Religious Fundamentalism," in *Cervantes y su mundo III*, edited by A. Robert and Kurt Reichenberger (Reichenberger, 2005), 543–58, 544.
20 See Chapter 2, on fascist's views of dissidence and enmity.
21 Paul Preston, *Franco: A Biography* (HarperCollins, 1995), 321. Dacia Viejo-Rose, *Reconstructing Spain: Cultural Heritage and Memory after Civil War* (Sussex University Press, 2011), 68–78. For a deep analysis of how the fascist evocation of the Golden Age was used culturally and politically, see also Duncan Wheeler, *Golden Age Drama in Contemporary Spain*.
22 The Comité de Propaganda (in charge of the commemoration of the anniversary), first announced a Cervantine exhibit at the Biblioteca Nacional on these terms. Quoted by Vicente Sánchez Moltó, "Una celebración marcada por las postguerras: el IV centenario del nacimiento de Cervantes," *eHumanista Cervantes* 3 (2014), 465–556, 466.
23 "El primero de nuestros Mutilados, el insigne Manco de Lepanto" (Moltó, "Una celebración" 466).
24 Printed with the title of "Decreto del 17 de enero de 1947 por el que se crean las comisiones que han de preparar los actos conmemorativos del centenario de Cervantes" in the *Revista Nacional de Educación* 69 (1947):

Imperar, como Cervantes, sobre tan universal realidad viva, es algo más que un gran escritor: es ser subsistencia y perduración de un Imperio, que

porque no fue una simple creación política, sino también obra del espíritu,
participa de algún modo de su inmaterial supervivencia. Príncipe de
nuestros ingenios es también Cervantes, porque proyectó sobre el mundo,
como ningún otro escritor, el modo de ser español y su mejor actitud ante
la vida. [...] El "quijotismo" será eternamente una aristocrática aportación
española al repertorio de lujo de los modos humanos de pensar y de sentir.
(104–5)

25   The translation is not by Edith Grossman this time, but Paul Archer, http://
     www.paularcher.net/translations/miguel_de_cervantes/war_calls_me.htm.l In
     Spanish: "A la guerra me lleva/mi necesidad;/si tuviera dineros,/no fuera, en
     verdad" (*IH* II.24: 226). See Nicolau d'Olwer's, for example, reference to this
     quote. *LE* 5 (1947), 3.

26   "[E]l Estado, que es para Cervantes, tras la sangre derramada en Lepanto,
     unas alcabalas que le traen cárcel y miseria" María Zambrano, "La reforma
     del entendimiento español" *Hora de España* 19 (1937), reprinted in *Los
     intelectuales y el drama de España* (Madrid: Hispamarca, 1977), 100–16,
     115.

27   Julio Luelmo, "Los valores renacentistas en la obra de Cervantes" *LE* 5
     (1947), 8. As Bou has argued, "[t]he republicanos, exiles from democratic
     Spain like Salinas, had the singular duty of recreating their oevre and their
     lives while keeping alive a Spain that was missing in reality, and that was
     now being transformed into the vengeful fascist regime of the Generalissimo
     Francisco Franco, Cacique of Spain, by the grace of god." This mission was
     even more pressing and significant with regard to Cervantes. (Afterword.
     Pedro Salinas between the Old and the New. Love Poems by Pedro Salinas
     [Chicago: University of Chicago Press, 2010], 197).

28   See Instituto Español (London): *A prospectus, Londres* (Instituto Español,
     1944). Luis Monferrer Catalán, *Odisea en Albión: los republicanos españoles
     exiliados en Gran Bretaña, 1936–1977* (de la Torre, 2007).

29   "[Q]uienes primero deberían haberse hecho presentes, llegan los últimos ...
     [r]ebasada por todos," Francisco Romero, *Realidad, Revista de Ideas* (Buenos
     Aires 13–15, 1947), 250.

30   Ibid. The special volume of *Revista de filología española* collected studies
     on topics clearly unrelated to the relevant historical or social issues at
     hand—for example, "Shepherds in Cervantes" ("Los pastores en Cervantes")
     by J. A. Tamayo, "Cervantes's Narrative Technique" (La técnica narrativa
     de Cervantes) by Diaz Plaja, or "Cervantes's Doctrinal Significance" (La
     significación doctrinal de Cervantes) by L. E. Palacio. More worthy of
     attention were Allison Peers's "Contributions of Foreign Hispanists to the
     Study of Don Quixote" (Aportaciones de los hispanistas extranjeros al
     estudio del Quixote), and Gerardo Diego's two contributions to this volume,
     "Cervantes and Troubador Love" (Cervantes y el amor trovadoresco), and
     "Cervantes and J. Filgueira's Poetry" (Cervantes y la poesía de J. Filgueira),
     which nonetheless carefully avoid any mention of historical context.

31   Juan José Domenchina, "la cosecha de pampiroladas, badajadas, laboriosas
     improvisaciones ... y demás—completamente de más ... con que se festeje el
     norte y naciencia del manco ... de Alcalá de Henares va a ser opima" (the rich

harvest of nonsense, rubbish, and laborious improvisations, and such—that goes without saying, should be left unsaid) "Apostillas," *LE* 5 (1947), 5.

32 Genara Pulido Tirado, *El Quijote y el pensamiento teórico-literario*, 453.

33 "[E]xiste una cantidad importante de estudios de carácter y valor desiguales" (ibid).

34 "Un ciclo de estiradas conferencias que fragua un municipio y en la que los conferenciantes se irán por los cerros de Úbeda," Editorial *LE* 5 (1947), 1.

35 Joaquín Arrarás, from the supposedly academic platform of the *Revista de filología española* 32 (1948), 537–92), chronicled all the Cervantine celebrations that had taken place around the world the year before. See 554–5.

36 Arrarás quotes the closing remarks of José Ibañez Martín after the Cervantine week of Alcalá de Henares, where "[a]ll" scholars had lauded "unanimously, the Christian root of Spanish culture and history" (549). The quote, about Cervantes's ability to capture "the military spirit and ethics," is by the director of the Naval Museum, D. Julio Guillén (552). Arrarás copies the official announcement from the State Bulletin and repeats over the first two pages the idea that "Cervantes es algo más que un escritor; es ser substancia y perduración de un imperio" (Cervantes is something more than a writer; he is the substance and realization of an empire) (538).

37 Cervantes is a "profeta" (Ibañez Martín, *Símbolos hispánicos del Quijote* [Madrid, 1947], 12), "austero, leal, y recto" (ibid., 14), "el prototipo español de todos los tiempos" que "lleva, dentro de sí, como una antorcha inextinguible, un rico caudal de fe ... en cuya alma milita el espíritu Cristiano" (ibid., 12–13). Ibañez Martín abundantly quotes commentators such as Ortega y Gasset, Ángel Ganivet, and Pemán at the expense of citing Cervantes himself.

38 Monseñor Franceschi, see Joaquín Arrarás, "Crónica del IV Aniversario de Cervantes," *Revista de filología Española* 32 (1948), 537–92.

39 Julio Luelmo, "La estirpe caballeresca que destruyó Alonso Quijano El Bueno," *Nuestro Tiempo* 5 (1952), 57–68.

40 "Editorial," *LE* 5 (1947), 2.

41 "[Implica] un eterno lanzazo a esas sombras de odio y muerte que flotan sobre España. Cervantes sigue en pie de lucha, sigue atacando, y el fascismo vomita su odio [contra él]" (ibid.).

42 In Spanish: "Cervantes pensaba en su país, en la decadencia de España, y en el deber del escritor. Según él, la tarea intelectual de aquellos que tiene el don de pensar y escribir es la desbaratar las ideas falsas .... [E]stablece que todas las guerras del 1600 provienen de la Edad Media, complicadas por el Renacimiento y elaboradas por la inteligencia contemporánea. El pasado había sido grande .... pero querer en el presente imitar al pasado es hacer una caricatura. En la fe, en las letras, en las armas, Cervantes encontraba una parodia ridícula de los siglos pasados. El tiempo de las cruzadas no existía más; los caballeros castellanos eran anacronismos vivientes" (Manuel García Puertas, *Cervantes y la crisis del Renacimiento español* [Universidad de Montevideo, 1962], 110).

43 Enrique Moradiellos, *Anatomy of a Dictator* (London and New York: I.B. Tauris, 2018).

44 Jeremy Tambling, *On Anachronism* (Manchester, UK: Manchester University Press, 2013).

45 Bou (Pedro Salinas. Quijote y lectura), 14.

46 In the original: "Ante Cervantes los fascistas españoles han mostrado que necesitan negar el espíritu del Renacimiento y retroceder hasta la Edad Media para refugiarse en ella contra los riesgos de una civilización que por todas partes les rebasa y les excede … El Quijote … lo fascistas lo niegan creyendo negar el Renacimiento entero. pero refugiarse en la Edad Media es un error porque del fermento de sus libertades sale el humanismo renacentista, y de éste, Don Quijote. En eso, como en tantas cosas, los fascistas andan mal de información," Sender, "Hace cuatro siglos que nació Cervantes," *LE* 4 (1947), 3.

47 "[E]l Quijote no sólo era un libro de decadencia sino un sutil e insidioso corifeo de aquellas ideas reformistas en religión, relativistas en gnoseología y burguesas en cuanto imagen de la vida, que asediaban desde la Europa racionalista a la España enfervorizada del Barroco," Mainer, "Cervantes (y sus personajes), vistos desde el exilio," in *Cervantes y la narrativa moderna*, edited by László Scholz and László Vasas (Debrecen, 2001), 104–22, emphasis added, 105.

48 "[L]a falta de una actividad crítica que situara a Cervantes en su contexto histórico y cultural … la responsable de una tergiversación más de nuestra historia, determinada ésta por mecanismos parecidos a los que se usaron en la contrarreforma," Luelmo "Valores renacentistas" 1 and 8.

49 "Giménez Caballero y la 'intelectualidad' franquista, han llegado donde no llegó la Inquisición del siglo XVII. Si pudieran quemarlo lo llevarían a la hoguera acusándole de Erasmista y liberal, pero efectivamente, por un solo delito: su españolidad profunda, es decir sus sentido humano de la vida, anterior al humanismo renacentista y acaso antecedente suyo" "Cuarto Centenario de Don Miguel de Cervantes," Editorial. *LE* 5, Special issue (1947), 1.

50 After the publication of Américo Castro's *Hacia Cervantes* (1925). See Chapter 2.

51 Maravall at first vows to provide "[la] interpretación *histórica* que nos muestre … las geniales páginas [de Cervantes]" *Humanismo de las Armas* (Instituto de Estudios Políticos, 1948), emphasis added, 6. All quotes are from this edition.

52 Maravall claims that Pascual de Gayangos's monumental study on chivalric fiction *Libros de caballerías* (Madrid: Rivadeneyra, 1857), "rightly pointed out how the arrival of Charles V in Spain coincided with the greatest success of chivalric novels among us" (Acertadamente Gayangos unió la venida a España de Carlos V con el auge de los libros de caballerías entre nosotros) (11–12). Maravall does not offer any specific reference for the idea he attributes to Gayango—who appears to pay very little, if any, attention to the emperor (see his reference in passing in Discurso Preliminar LIX, for example). What the historian (Maravall) seems to take from Gayangos, however, is the idea that chivalric novels, while extraordinarily hyperbolic and colorful in their narratives, offer "despite their absurd elements, useful [moral] lessons, and indicate in a clear and distinct way how civilization advances, in terms of its changes in norms and customs" (Prologue) (*en medio de sus absurdos, estos libros contienen lecciones muy provechosas, señalan de una manera clara y distinta la marcha de la civilización y el cambio de ideas y costumbres*) (i).

53 I am paraphrasing Maravall, as he claims that "Alguien llegó a pensar que la marcha de la sociedad de aquel tiempo llevaría a dejar el duro y brillante camino de heroísmo, y ello hizo nacer en su alma una melancolía invencible" (10).

54 I am summarizing Maravall's quote, which reads: "De ese modo nace el Quijote rompiendo las arcaicas marcas de los libros de caballerías ... Acaba en amarga y sonora queja de una época que amenaza en negar al héroe su puesto en ella" (10).

55 George Mariscal, *Contradictory Subjects: Quevedo, Cervantes, and Seventeenth-Century Spanish Culture* (Cornell University Press, 1991), 21.

56 Such is the ultimate view of literature in the "guided culture" idea, the understanding that "literature [is] at bottom committed to upholding order and authority" *Culture of the Baroque*, 58.

57 For Maravall, "[e]s sintomático que, como en varios pasajes del Quijote, pueda comprobarse para él la palabra 'emperador'" (228). Ricote's ironic justification of the ruthless repression against moriscos must also be understood as a literal illustration of Cervantes's support for the royal expulsion of 1609, since according to Maravall, Cervantes supports "the king's just intention to watch out for Christian purity," a mission ultimately performed and conceived as a national enterprise (*Humanismo*, 230).

58 Cervantes "exalta la 'felicísima' memoria del '*invictísimo* Carlos V' que es y será eterna (IV-22), sólo tiene una breve referencia a través de su obra, una líneas antes de la que acabamos de citar, a uno de los reyes de quienes fue contemporáneo, Felipe II, al que tan sólo llama 'nuestro buen rey Don Felipe,' a pesar de recordarle con ocasión de Lepanto" (Emphasis added, ibid., 231).

59 According to Maravall, Don Quixote achieves such fame through the "imperial command that he has over his will" (Muchas veces tal es el imperio con que domina en la voluntad-busca la aventura "sólo por alcanzar la gloriosa fama y duradera" (ibid., 97–8).

60 "What really matters to Don Quixote [is] ... that his untainted virtue and reputation are maintained in their public manifestation as a moral victory" (Lo que de verdad importa a Don Quijote [es] ... que se mantenga sin mancha su virtud y la honra, que es su pública manifestación: su victoria moral) (ibid., 133).

61 Ibid.

62 According to Maravall, the only thing that differentiated the Middle Ages from the early modern age was that the emperor in the 1500s was Spanish rather than German. "[E]n la fecha en la que Cervantes vivió, Carlos I trajo a España, o mejor, hizo brotar en España otros ideales. No eran exactamente estos los de la Edad Media, porque el titular del Imperio Cristiano medieval era el Emperador germánico ... y en el siglo XVI, español" (ibid., 229). It is worth noting that the historian, aware of his Comunero's gap would publish his unclear interpretation on the matter a few years later (*Comunidades castellanas: una primera revolución moderna* [Madrid: Revista de Occidente, 1963]).

63 Tal es el *sueño de humanista*s como Lope de Soria, o como Alfonso de Valdés. Y tal, en cierta forma, *a mi parecer, el sueño de Cervantes*" (ibid., emphasis added, 229).

64 Ibid., 231.

65 "La institución tradicional del Imperio que lleva consigo una misión religiosa y moral, desde sus lejanos orígenes carolingios, en conexión con la Iglesia, es aprovechada por las generaciones que caen bajo el gobierno de España

del mismo titular del Sacro Imperio, para una tarea de perfeccionamiento y depuración de la vida de los cristianos. La unión con el Imperio y con ello la esperanza de una dirección Española de las más alta jurisdicción temporal de la Cristiandad, acaba pronto; pero no por ello quedan desarraigadas las íntimas creencias que aquella extraordinaria pretensión apoyaba. En medio de un ambiente social ajeno, Cervantes, con Don Quijote, lucha heroicamente por su mantenimiento, o, ya, su restauración" (ibid., emphasis added, 13–14).

66   Maravall's projections and patriotic elocutions allow him to constantly bridge this construed past with a Francoist present, justifying the latter with former. He draws on values supposedly exemplified in Cervantes, positing, for example, that "it is in that long heroic tradition, so lasting among us [Spaniards] that Cervantes shaped his modern activism, propelling him to launch his hero to fight for his ideal" ([l]a vieja tradición heroica, tan longeva entre nosotros [españoles] se une en Cervantes en su activismo moderno y lanza a su héroe a pelear por su ideal) (ibid., 167).

67   Ibid.

68   This is messianic view of Charles V would be revisited in "Las etapas del pensamiento de Carlos V" ("The Stages of Charles V's Political Thought," *Revista de estudios políticos* 100 (1958), 95–146). Here, Maravall still describes Charles as a "great humanist" (*Las etapas*, 95), deeply invested in all the crusades of Christendom during his rule (*Las etapas*, 94–6). For Maravall, the emperor is still driven by a "late medieval, chivalric spirit," and an imperial desire to maintain the unity of the Christian faith (*Las etapas*, 110). This perspective on the emperor is confirmed in another study, *Carlos V y el pensamiento político del renacimiento* (Instituto Político, 1960), where the historian elaborates on his hyperbolic view of the ruler as man of a "royal personality ....able to plot and achieve a well-conceived plan if it were virtuous enough, given his unified sense of virtue, that is, the solid virtue of this whole, well-rounded man" (*ese ideal configuró en parte la real personalidad del Emperador—el hombre capaz de una acción meditada, en la que se implicara la virtud, en su sentido unitario, esto es, la virtud de un hombre entero*) (*Carlos V*, 53).

69   In Spanish, "además de ser mentirosissimos, son tan mal compuestos, assi por dezir las mentiras muy desvergonzadas, como per tener el estilo desbaratado," in *Diálogo de la lengua*, edited by Juan de Valdés (Società tipografica, 1957), 170. The English scholar Henry Thomas had published in 1920 a formidable study on chivalric fiction, *Spanish and Portuguese Romances of Chivalry in the Spanish Peninsula, and Its Extensions and Influence Abroad* (Cambridge University Press, 1920), translated into Spanish with the title *Despertar de la novela caballeresca en la Península Ibérica y expansión e influencia en el extranjero*, 1920, translated by Esteban Pujais (CSIC, 1952), which puts chivalric action at odds with moral ideals. In Maravall's Humanism, such opposition is mentioned only in passing, as on page 11.

70   Quoted in *Cervantes and the Pictorial Imagination* (Bucknell University Press, 2009), 107. See the discussion of Charles V's relationship to chivalric fiction, historiography, and Cervantes's satire of Charles V's propagandistic obsessions and historical ambition (95–121).

71 "Cervantes [era] ya tardío enamorado de ese mundo" (*Humanismo,* 285),
    "se mantiene un ideal heroico y Cristiano ... según el cual se concibió la idea
    imperial de la Edad Media y cuyo último representante fue Carlos V" (ibid.,
    284).

72 As noted by Stroud 545. For a sample of this form of reading besides
    Maravall, Castro, and Bataillon, see Boruchoff, "Cervantes y las leyes
    de reprensión cristiana," *Hispanic Review* 63, no. 1 (1995), 39–55, and
    Armstrong-Roche, Michael. *Cervantes' Epic Novel: Empire, Religion, and the
    Dream Life of Heroes in Persiles* (Toronto University Press, 2009).

73 Tanto en su version española como en su original fuente, en el propio Erasmo,
    ese movimiento exige hoy una profunda revision del significado que se la ha
    venido atribuyendo (*Humanismo,* 14).

74 Ibid., 14–15.

75 "[E]l pensamiento de Cervantes ... se juzga ... como una anticipación del
    mundo de las ideas de Galileo." Ibid.

76 "[L]o cierto es que esos conceptos, no sólo en Cervantes, sino en toda la
    literatura de la época, incluso en los que se consideran fundadores de un
    nuevo método científico, tienen una significación tradicional" (ibid.).

77 "A Bataillon todo se le vuelve erasmismo .... Pero en este caso, baste con
    referirse al reformismo que se da en la época de Carlos IV" (ibid., 16–17, n.2).

78 "De la corriente erasmiana no es necesario ni detenerse a señalar el fenómeno"
    (ibid., 86).

79 "Bataillon que, arrastrado por su tema, *cuanto toca se le convierte en
    Erasmismo,* interpreta en este sentido la figura admirable del hidalgo
    manchego, sin advertir que [*Don Quijote*] es la suprema y definitiva expresión
    de la corriente moral del humanismo español, dibujada mucho antes de la
    penetración de Erasmo y ajena a la dirección heterodoxa, según la cual insiste
    siempre, y no siempre con acierto, en exponerla dicho autor" (ibid., emphasis
    added, 212–13).

80 "Pues bien, a la visión de la vida humana y ... " (ibid., 213).

81 "Castro trató de reconstruir la línea del pensamiento de Cervantes. Cervantes
    y Erasmo aparecen interpretados unívocamente sobre la imagen del
    Renacimiento que dibujó Burckhardt. Todo lo que no coincide con esto y es
    conservación de un ideal anterior se estima como una concesión hipócrita"
    (ibid., 15). As Hermida Ruiz points out, Maravall's early works were not
    so much the product of original research as they were attempts to debunk
    the Erasmist and Renaissance theories developed by Castro (Hermida Ruiz,
    "Secreta palinodia," 506).

82 See Chapter 2, especially 50–7.

83 Mackay, "The Maravall Problem," 46.

84 Castro's formulation of hypocrisy in *El pensamiento de Cervantes,* 244–50.
    Ortega y Gasset had qualified as "heroic." Ortega's quote is from *Meditaciones
    del Quijote,* 184.

85 Forcione had commented on the evolution of Castro's thesis, in which he turns
    a rebellious Erasmist and secular Cervantes of *El Pensamiento* into moralists
    who simply wish "to 'pontificate in that society in which he believed himself to
    be duly established'" (Forcione, *Cervantes and the Humanist Vision,* 13).

86 EC Riley, "Cervantes and the Cynics," *Bulletin of Hispanic Studies* 53, no. 3 (1976), 189–99, 199; Adrienne Martin, *Cervantes and the Burlesque* (University of California Press, 1991), 3; Frederick de Armas, "Cervantes and the Italian Renaissance," in *Cambridge Companion to Cervantes* (Cambridge University Press, 2005), 32–57, 35; Eric Ziolkowski, *The Sanctification of Don Quixote: From Hidalgo to Priest* (Pennsylvania State University Press, 2008), 24–6; Stephen Boyd, *A Companion to Cervantes's* Novelas Ejemplares (Tamesis, 2005), 135. In a way, William Childers agreed with Castro's idea of a built-in hypocrisy in the Christian daily performance of the practice. See *Transnational Cervantes* (Toronto University Press, 2006), 119.

87 Furthermore, as Carlos Fuentes puts it, "just by reading his text, it is impossible to decide if Cervantes, being too naïve, did not know what he was saying, or if, as a hypocrite, he did know more than he claimed" (Si nos atenemos al texto del Quijote, es imposible decir que Cervantes el ingenuo no sabía lo que hacía o que Cervantes el hipócrita sabía más de lo que decía) (*La crítica de la lectura*, 35).

88 In the original, "[La obra] de un escritor inmerso en un extraordinario combate cultural, en una operación crítica sin paralelo para salvar lo mejor de España de lo peor de España, los rasgos vivos del orden medieval de sus rasgos muertos, las promesas del Renacimiento de sus peligros. Es al nivel de la crítica de la creación dentro de la creación y de la estructuración de la crítica como una pluralidad de lecturas posibles, y no en la parquedad de la ingenuidad o de la hipocresía, como Cervantes da respuesta al monolitismo de la España mutilada, encerrada, vertical y dogmática que sucede a la derrota de la rebelión comunera y al Concilio de Trento" (Fuentes, *Crítica* 35).

89 "*[N]o tiene en absoluto justificación* someter la tersa belleza literaria de unas obras *a la tortura de extraer de ellas alguna minúscula idea política, sin valor ni transcendencia*" (Maravall, *Humanismo*, Emphasis added 19).

90 "[E]n el aspecto político una posición moderna concretamente en esto: su patriotismo español. Posee [Cervantes], por de pronto, medularmente enraizado, el sentimiento de la unidad de España" (ibid., 228; emphasis added).

91 La patria, para él [Fray Luis] se llamará única, totalmente, España, lo mismo que para Cervantes. Los personajes de éste, por ejemplo, en el *Persiles dicen que son españoles, y su ferviente deseo,* como el del cautivo en el Quijote, *es volver a España.* Su elogio de lo español y su defensa de un humanismo literario en lengua española son bien conocidos. *Admira y siente el orgullo del poder de los reyes hispanos y con exaltación canta y defiende su empresa* (ibid., 228–9; emphasis added).

92 Diana de Armas Wilson's *Cervantes and the New World* (Oxford University Press, 2000) consolidated this emerging realm of cultural and transnational attribution. See also Bill Childers's *Transnational Cervantes,* 83–161. Four foundamental resources to understand *Persiles* today are *the* monographs by Isabel Lozano-Renieblas, *Cervantes y el mundo del Persiles* (Centro de Estudios Cervantinos, 1998) and *Trabajos de Persiles y Sigismunda,* introductory study by Isabel Lozano-Renieblas (Real Academia Española, 2018), and Armstrong-Roche *Cervantes' Epic Novel.* Also essential are the recent volumes by Alcalá Galán, "'Si ya por atrevido no sale con las manos en la cabeza': el legado poético del «Persiles» cuatrocientos años después." Special issue, *eHumanista/Cervantes* 5

(2016) and Brownlee's *Persiles and the Travails of Romance* (University of Toronto Press, 2019).

93   It is Christians rather than Barbarians, in other words, who often exhibit irrational or depraved behaviors. As Armstrong-Roche argues, "Greed for the fat reward in gold ore and pearls has led many non-Barbarians—including the Christian Prince Arnaldo" (*Cervantes' Epic Novel*, 147).

94   For Aub, "no son páginas de crítica, y desde todos los aspectos, las que faltan en *El Quijote*: moral, literaria, social" (*Max Aub a Cervantes* [Segorbe, 1999], 105–6).

95   Maravall would eventually acknowledge the significance of the *comunero* episode in his study of the Comunero revolt, considering it however the imperial victory as beneficial for the personal freedoms of the country. For him, the defeat of the Comuneros provided a step forward in the achievement of political freedom, of the modern state (la derrota de las Comunidades significó el triunfo del Estado moderno) (*Las comunidades*, 33).

96   Aurora Hermida Ruiz, "Secreta palinodia."

97   Quoted in Hermida Ruiz 503, emphasis added.

98   Hermida Ruiz, 504.

99   The impact of this kind of publication has been widely assessed by Ortega, *Las revistas literarias en España entre la edad de plata y el medio siglo*, and Manuel Aznar Soler, *Escritores, editoriales y revistas del exilio republicano de 1939* (Renacimiento, 2006).

100   Hermida Ruiz, 503–4.

101   *Utopia and Counterutopia*, 30. I am and will be quoting directly from the English edition.

102   Like the notorious Pedro Laín Entralgo's *Descargo de conciencia* (1976). The genre would be satirized by Joan Marsé *Muchacha de las bragas de oro* (1978). Angel L. Prieto and Mar Langa Pizarro, *Manual de literatura Española* (Castalia, 2011), 1988.

103   The whole quote in Spanish goes "Y es que Maravall ... estima la inadaptación política y de Cervantes a ala sociedad moderna como prueba de una virtud muy española" (Hermida Ruiz, 509).

104   "Maravall le da pues completamente la vuelta a su obra de 1948, y se propone demostrar que la utopía quijotesca es arcaica, espacapista, irracional, y en último termino, tan absurda y dsparatada como digna de ser condenada al fracaso" (Hermida Ruiz, 511).

105   *Utopia and Counterutopia*, 31.

106   Ibid., 159, compare to *Humanismo*, 228–9, emphasis added in both quotes.

107   *Utopia and Counterutopia* 19, emphasis added.

108   Ibid., 158.

109   Maravall's view of modernity and power is as somber as that of Foucault, whose work emerged in the late 1960s. The seminal *Discipline and Punishment. The Birth of the Prison* was published in 1977. Both scholars articulate their critique of the power structure in divergent ways, however. As MacKay reminds us, "Unlike Foucault, who understood the multiplicity and ubiquity of power, Maravall reduces its boundaries and assigns it one singular place" ("The Maravall Problem," 49).

110   Ibid.

111 Many more questions are prompted by that statement; in what sense is the end result medieval? What kind of "modern spirit" was so different or distant from *that* humanism?

112 Consider for example, the promising but inconclusive assertion: "Our view is that reality is present in utopias because of their ties (not always acknowledged) with history. But we shall not get into polemics on this point" (ibid., 181). The intention "not to get into polemics" might be why Maravall hints constantly at ideas without ever fully fleshing them out.

113 Diana de Armas Wilson "Rethinking Cervantine Utopias: Some No (Good) Places in Renaissance England and Spain," in *Echoes and Inscriptions. Comparative Approaches to Early Modern Spanish Literatures*, edited by Barbara Simerka and Christopher B. Weimer (Bucknell University Press, 2000), 191–209, 200.

114 Ibid., 202.

115 Maravall summarizes the thesis of the book with the argument that "Cervantes constructs that brilliant combination of a chivalric pastoral novel first, on the negative side, to highlight the resounding 'no' [rejection] that the type of character he portrays [Maravall has switched now from Cervantes to Quixote] says to 'this hateful age of ours,' and second, as in a positive vein, to set forth the values of the Golden Age. Maladjustment and negation of the present are evident both in the negative and positive aspect" (ibid., 184).

116 A similar view can be found in Beatriz Pantin, "El historiador y el exorcista. El *Quijote* entre utopía y contrautopía según José Antonio Maravall," in *Lectores del Quijote 1605–2005*, edited by Sarah de Mojica and Carlos Rincón (Pontificia Javeriana, 2004), 223–56.

117 Myriam Yvonne Jehenson and Peter Dunn, *The Utopian Nexus in Don Quixote* (Vanderbilt University Press, 2006), 26. While this study on utopia in Cervantes is not the only rebuttal to Maravall's approach to the subject, it is one of the best-documented ones.

118 Hermida Ruiz, 506.

Chapter 5

1 "Por esos mundos de Dios, desgarrada y amarga, anda la España peregrina, con todas las maldiciones del destierro sobre su cabeza. Dios les quitó a los hombres el sosiego, como a casta maldita, pero no la inteligencia, que conservan más despierta y sensible por el dolor" (Gonzalo Torrente Ballester, "Presencia en América de la España fugitiva," *Tajo*, August 3, 1940). As a writer and academic passing judgment on the diaspora, he would not be too well received. "Mr. Torrente Ballester," wrote Pedro Salinas, "seems to me more foolish than arrogant ... a half-ludicrous, brainless professor" (*El señor Torrente Ballester ... me parece más fatuo que insolente ... majadero a medias, majadero professor*). (*Pedro Salinas/Jorge Guillén, Correspondencia*, edited by Andrés Soria Olmedo [Tusquets, 1992], 533).

2 Essential reference works include Abellán, *El exilio español de 1939* ; *El exilio español en México, 1939–1982*; Yankelevich, *México país refugio*; Patricia

W. Fagen, *Exiles and Citizens, Spanish Republicans in Mexico* (University of Texas at Austin Press, 1973), and Clara Lida, *La Casa de España en Mexico*, Jornadas, Vol. 113 (El Colegio de Mexico, 1975), and Rosa Lida's *Los españoles en el México independiente: 1821–1950. Un estado de la cuestión. Historia Mexicana* 56, no. 2 (2006), 613–50. Tomás Pérez Vejo, "España en el imaginario mexicano. El choque del exilio," in *El exilio español y su impacto sobre el pesamiento, la ciencia, y el sistema educativo mexicano*, edited by Agustín Sánchez Andrés y Silvia Figueroa Zamudio, De Madrid a México (Comunidad de Madrid-Universidad Michoacana, 2001), 23–93.

3   "El Quijote es un libro exiliado" since "la cultura de la que procede y sobre la que proyecta su grandeza [está] proscrita del imperio de la España Fascista." Sender, "Hace cuatro siglos que nació Cervantes," *LE* 4 (1947), 3. See also Daniel Tapia, "Don Quixote desterrado," *LE* 5 (1947), 5, and Julio Luelmo, "Los valores renacentistas en la obra de Cervantes," *LE* 5 (1947), 8.

4   "Estos negros días de espera." J. Giner Pantoja, "Los amigos del Museo del Prado," *Bulletin de la Unión de Intelectuales Españoles* 4.28–29 (1947), 1.

5   The removal of Dulcinea's enchantment requires Sancho to endure a heavy physical penance, which he is not willing to accept (II: 68).

6   (*DQ* 2.68: 903). ¡Oh alma endurecida! ¡Oh escudero sin piedad! ¡Oh pan mal empleado y mercedes mal consideradas las que te he hecho y pienso de hacerte! Por mí te has visto gobernador y por mí te ves con esperanzas propincuas de ser conde o tener otro título equivalente, y no tardará el cumplimiento de ellas más de cuanto tarde en pasar este año; que yo "post tenebras spero lucem" (*IH* II. 68: 552–3).

7   García Puertas, "Post tenebras spero lucem," in *Cervantes y la crisis del Renacimiento español* (Madrid: Uruguaya, 1962), 109.

8   There are ample sources on the subject. Some of the essential references are Chapter 18 of Stanley G. Payne's *Fascism in Spain, 1923–1977* (Madison: University of Wisconsin Press, 1999), 401–30, and *The Franco Regime, 1936–1975* (Madison: University of Wisconsin Press, 1987), 413–59. For more specific or recent studies on 1950s pacts with the dictatorship, see Ángel Viñas, *Los pactos secretos de Franco con Estados Unidos: Bases, ayuda económica, recortes de soberanía* (Madrid: Grijalbo, 1981), "Congress and Franco's Spain: The Pact of Madrid, 1953," in Philip Briggs, *Making American Foreign Policy: President-Congress Relations from the Second* (Lanham: Rowman and Littlefield, 1994), 47–68, and "Reluctant Allies, 1951–53," in *Truman, Franco's Spain, and the Cold War*, edited by Wayne H. Bowen's (Columbia: Missouri University Press, 2017), 127–52.

9   "Don Quixote misses everything," claims Tapia, "even the enchanters that had made him go mad, and get all righteous" ([Don Quijote] lo añora todo, hasta los libros que le volvieron el seso, que le hicieron liberal). Tapia, "Don Quixote desterrado," *LE* 5 (1947), 5 and 14.

10   José María Gallego would agree, noting that although Spanish literature offers, for the most part, "an anthology of hope," Cervantes constantly renews this trust for a better future, turning "ruined expectations into a hope, more solid than ever" (de las ruinas de estas esperanzas surgen más firme que nunca su esperanza) *LE* 5 (1947), 11.

11   "Al vincularse la mayoría de los intelectuales españoles a los países de América Latina, la consideración del exilio les obligó a afrontar la convivencia, a

menudo difícil, del nacionalismo de los países receptores y el nacionalismo español de los recién llegados, así como el acercamiento de los intelectuales españoles a lo americano, indígena, o hispánico" (Mainer *Moradores de Sansueña. Lecturas cervantinas de los exiliados republicanos de 1939* [Universidad de Valladolid, Servicio de Publicaciones e Intercambio Editorial, 2006], 13).

12   Between 1939 and 1948, the Servicio de Evacuación de Republicanos Españoles (the Republican, Evacuation Service, or SERE) estimated that 21,750 refugees arrived in Mexico, mainly from France, where more than 280,000 exiles awaited some kind of international rescue. Only three Latin American countries—Mexico, the Dominican Republic, and Chile—"admitted Republican refugees on a collective, not an individual basis" (Nicolás Sánchez-Albornoz, "El exilio español en Mexico en perspectiva comparada," in *Mexico: País refugio. La experiencia de los exilios en el siglo XX*, edited by Pablo Yankelevich [Plaza y Valdes, 2002], 197–204, 202).

13   "Los revolucionarios [mexicanos] en el poder, antithispanistas por definición, los acogían con simpatía política, los opositores—carcas y gachupines—los vieron con buenos ojos por españoles, repudiándolos por revolucionarios Un lío." Max Aub, *La verdadera historia de la muerte de Francisco Franco* (Mexico, 1960), 16. Aub here captures the deep political divide in Mexico and its powerful projection into Spanish politics. As Friedrich E. Schuler points out, "the front line in the struggle between Mexican conservatives and liberals had been relocated to the battle fields of the Spanish Civil War," in *Hitler and Roosevelt: Mexican Foreign Relations in the Age of Lázaro Cárdenas, 1934–1940* (Albuquerque: University of New Mexico Press, 1998), 57. The fear of Cárdenas and the revolutionary faction of Mexico was that the defeat of the Spanish Republic would encourage the spread of fascism in Latin America (Sebastiaan Faber, *Exile and Cultural Hegemony* [Vanderbilt University Press, 2002], 12).

14   Michael Kenny, "Spanish Expatriates in Mexico," *Anthropological Quarterly* 35, no. 4 (1962), 169–80, 177. In the early 1900s, a large number of the Spanish immigrants to Mexico were from the country's northern provinces (Galicia, Asturias, Basque Country, Catalonia) and were fleeing extremely adverse circumstances. They were, thus, "landless, penniless, illiterate, and unskilled. They came to the strange land of Mexico knowing that only after many years of hard work among suspicious people could they ever return to Spain even for a visit" (ibid., 171). Some of these penniless immigrants would go on to become powerful allies of Porfirio Diaz's oligarchy; Mario Cerutti has illustrated the self-enrichment process of this minority in a specific area, "La Laguna," a "region of lagoons" in northern Mexico that spreads through the states of Durango and Coahuila. See "Propietarios y empresarios españoles en La Laguna (1870–1910)" *Historia Mexicana*, 48, no. 4, *España y México: relaciones diplomáticas, negocios y finanzas en el porfiriato* (April–June 1999), 825–70. Ana Lía Herera-Lasso illustrates how this Spanish minority was able to consolidate its influence in the Mexican elite ("Una élite dentro de la élite: el Casino Español de México entre el Porfiriato y la Revolución (1875–1915)," *Secuencia* 42 [1998], 177–205). The success of this group made them doubly unpopular among the Mexican population at large, and particularly among the progressive minority that fought the Mexican Revolution (1910–20) and

held power through the Party of the Mexican Revolution (1938–46) under President Lázaro Cárdenas from 1934 to 1940. For a major overview of the period, see Engelbert Schuler, *Mexico between Hitler and Roosevelt: Mexican Foreign Relations in the Age of Lázaro Cárdenas, 1934–1940* (University of New Mexico Press, 1999), 50–6.

It was because of Cárdenas's support of the Second Republic that Spanish exiles of the second wave (after 1939) were allowed to settle in Mexico, a move that "proved to be as great a stimulus to the Mexican economy as it was to the arts and sciences at a time, when Mexico itself was fast developing. Mature, skilled, and highly adaptable, with a desperate desire to make good that lent them boundless energy, they appeared to have met a number of obstacles, not least of which was longstanding opposition from Group A [conservative Spaniards who had arrived in a previous migratory wave] and from certain Mexican [conservative] groups." Unlike the Spaniards of that previous generation, they were largely intellectuals and while prominent "with few exceptions" in their fields and professions, they did not amass the "immense fortunes" that many of their older compatriots had (Kenny, "Spanish expatriates" 176). However, Patricia Fagen notes that the Spaniards of this post-1939 migratory wave showed a "remarkable skill for working their way from poverty to financial success, often in fields in which they had no previous experience," which generated some uneasiness among locals. *Exiles and Citizens*, 76, n. 45. See also Pilar Pérez Fuentes, "La es-valledelhenares.centros.castillalamancha.es/sites/ies-valledelhenares.centros. castillalamancha.es/files/descargas/emigracion_espanola_a_america_0.pdf. Accessed on March 1, 2020.

15 Works of essential reference are Abellán, *El exilio español de 1939*: *El exilio español en México, 1939–1982*; Pablo Yankelevich, *México país refugio: la experiencia de los exilios en el siglo XX* (Plaza y Valdés, 2002); Fagen, *Exiles and Citizens, Spanish Republicans in Mexico*; Lida, *La Casa de España en Mexico;* Jornadas and Rosa, *"Los españoles en el México independiente,"* 613–50. Vejo, "España en el imaginario mexicano. El choque del exilio," 23–93.

16 The ships of Spanish refugees were often greeted with cries of that asked them "to go back to their country," addressing them as "communists, anti-Christs, and 'gachupines'" ("Cuando llegaban los barcos a Veracruz, mucha gente iba a gritarles: 'Váyanse a su tierra, comunistas, anticristos, gachupines'"), "Entrevista con Juan Ramón y Federico Arana," in *Las Españas, Historia de una Revista del Exilio (1946–1963)*, edited by James Valender and Gabriel Rojo Leyva (Colegio de Mexico, 1999), 322–59, 342.

17 In the majority of interviews and testimonies by Mexicans and exiles in *El exilio español en México, 1939–1982* (Salvat, Fondo de Cultura Económica, 1982) and Valender and Rojo Leyva (*Las Españas, Historia de una revista del exilio*) note that this initial resistance was brief (296–360).

18 The entire quote in Spanish reads, "Desde el punto de vista de las ideas políticas, de los sentimientos de las gentes, hay *enormes divisiones y luchas*, en consecuencia la emigración era un fenómeno que estaba ligado a esos sentimientos y fue muy combatida por ciertos sectores y por cierta prensa y

sólo el peso y la realidad de la vida y de su presencia acabó por amortiguar esas tensiones," Silvio Zavala, "Entrevista" *El exilio español*, 901–09, 908.

19   "[A] todos los españoles les decían gachupines y después de la emigración hasta la gente del pueblo se acostumbró a decir españoles," Jesús Silva Herzog, "Entrevista" *El exilio español en México* (Fondo de Cultura, 1982). 886–90, 888. Marco Antonio Landavazo defines "gachupín" as the Spaniard or colonial "respect for monarchy, defense of [Catholic] religion, and Spanish nation" (*respeto al dominio monárquico, la defensa de la religion, y de la patria*) "Para una historia social de la violencia insurgente: el odio al gachupín," *Historia Mexicana 59*, no. 1 (July–September 2009), 195–225, 195. See also Leticia Gamboa Ojeda, "De 'indios' y 'gachupines'; Las fobias en las fábricas textiles de Puebla," *Tiempos de América: revista de historia, cultura y territorio* 1999, no. 3, 85–98, https://www.raco.cat/index.php/ TiemposAmerica/article/view/105047. Accessed March 1, 2020.

20   "[L]os exiliados españoles ... alcanzaron un valor político especial por la semejanza de la ideología del gobierno mexicano y de la segunda República Española [sic]," notes the Argentinian Antonio Martín Baez "Entrevista" *El exilio español*, 896–900, 896. Nicolás Sánchez-Albornoz believes that the real reason for the acceptance of Spanish refugees in some countries and not others was financial rather than ideological, and that the Argentinian refusal to accept more Spanish exiles was ultimately an attempt to protect domestic workers during a moment of profound international contraction (*The Economic Modernization of Spain, 1830–1930* [New York: New York University Press, 1987] 198–200).

21   Sebastiaan Faber, *Exile and Cultural Hegemony: Spanish Intellectuals in Mexico, 1939–1975* (Vanderbilt University Press, 2002), 136.

22   Faber, *Exile and Cultural Hegemony* 43. José Luis Venegas argues that "in promoting Spanish hegemonic ambitions through culture," the Civil War exiles "embraced and reformulated the intellectual legacy of thinkers such as Maeztu, Unamuno, Ganivet, and Ortega y Gasset" with regard to "the challenges that Hispanic civilization was facing in the 1930s and 40s." *Transatlantic Correspondence: Modernity, Epistolarity, and Literature in Spain and Spanish America, 1898–1992* (Ohio State University Press, 2016), 78–9. Emphasis added. Faber evaluates the ideological tendencies of the Spanish Republican exiles through Antonio Grasmci's theories, which Faber claims to have inspired the Republican Spaniards (*Culture and Hegemony* 28). Gramsci's ideas, for Faber, are essential for understanding the "role of intellectuals in maintaining and or modifying the political status quo" and regarded culture and ideology serving "both to legitimize exploitative political structures and revolutionary struggles aimed at overthrowing those structures" (*Culture and Hegemony*, 29). Faber does use a current, theoretical model to evaluate the exiles' ideological template, which is articulated in his view by fairly conservative ideas about nation, culture, and nostalgia, which end up forming shaping not "forward-looking .... modernity" (29). It is through Gramsci's influence that Faber applies a strict idea of "cultural hegemony" to the marginalized group of exiles in Mexico, characterizing their impact as a form of "Conquest" (35). If Republicans never managed to triumph politically

in Spain and oust Franco, their "struggle for cultural hegemony" in Gramscian sense was, however, "more successful" (37). See also Faber, 45.

23   Faber, *Exile and Cultural Hegemony*,131. The idea suggests the understanding that "For *most Spanish intellectuals of the 1930s* and 1940s, the key to solving the contradictions of modernity is not to be found in the sort of scientific and technological development dominant in materialistic Europe and North America, but in the *idealistic revitalization of Spain's imperial past and its civilizing mission*" (Venegas, *Transatlantic*, 82). Certainly, Salinas's work and personal correspondence expose a clear fear of modernity. Such anxiety, rather than being based on a rejection of the "scientific and technological development dominant in materialistic Europe and North America," as noted above, appears to be rooted in apprehension of the "great atomic war," which at the time of his death in 1951, seemed to be looming. In a private letter to the Chilean poet Gabriela Mistral, for example, Salinas confesses this apprehension through a reference to a poem, "Zero" (Cero), that he had written in 1944, but fears has become even more relevant in 1948 (the date of his letter). Salinas states that

all these [worldwide] politicians and military men suffer, among other diseases, from a limited and short-sighted imagination. Because a war that can use this arsenal of atomic, biological bombs and all the rest, presents itself—to those of us who do have imagination and use it—as something so horrific and terrible that one would be moved to avoid it at all cost.

todos estos políticos y militares, padecen entre otros males, el de la parvedad o inopia imaginativa. Porque una guerra con todo el acopio de bombas atomicas [*sic*] y no atómicas, de gérmenes, y compañía, se presenta a la imaginación—del que la tenga y la use—como algo tan tremebundo y espantable que empuja a impedirla por todos los medios. Salinas's letter to Gabriela Mistral, February 1, 1948. National Libray of Chile. http://www.bibliotecanacionaldigital.gob.cl/bnd/635/w3-article-149155.html. Accessed on January 25, 2020.

Written as a protest against the Second World War, "Zero" had indeed offered an "uncanny prophecy" of the overwhelming destruction caused by atomic weapons (*Columbia Dictionary of Modern European Literature,* edited by Jean Albert Bédé and William Benbow Edgerton [Columbia University Press, 1980], 711). The continued anxiety that Salinas speaks of usually reflects his concern that the escalating tensions of the Cold War would precipitate an even more catastrophic and global atomic disaster.

24   Araquistáin, a Republican who had participated in the Mexican revolution on the revolutionary side, reflected on the cause and movement in his book *La revolución mejicana: sus orígenes, sus hombres, su obra* (1929. Renacimiento, 2006 [Reprint]).

25   "España es la última colonia de sí misma, al única nación hispanoamericana que del común pasado imperial queda por hacerse independiente, no sólo espiritual sino también políticamente," José Gaos, *Pensamiento de lengua española* (Stylo, 1945), 28.

26 "Cervantes nos impulse a la práctica de la más destacada de las cualidades cervantinas: la comprensión" ("Cervantes o la comprensión," *LE* 5 [1947], 3).

27 "Comprensión sin la cual no existe la tolerancia, ni justicia, ni paz—sin la cual la humanidad desciende … al estadio de la lucha zoológica." Ibid.

28 "If nations achieve mutual understanding, confidence may replace fear and tension." *Interrelations of Cultures: Their Contributions to International Understanding* (Paris: UNESCO, 1953), 381.

29 The whole, uninterrupted quote in Spanish reads "Al *Quijote* debemos los colombianos, los americanos y los españoles, un entendimiento común. En el *Quijote* nos entendemos todos. Diferiremos en muchas cosas, pero sospecho que nos encontramos acordes en este libro," Pedro Salinas. *Quijote y lectura: defensas y fragmentos*, edited by Enric Bou (ELR Ediciones, 2005), 67.

30 "[O]casión de brindis patrióticos, de soberbia grammatical, de obscenas ediciones de lujo," in *Jorge Luis Borges. Obras Completas 1923–1972*, edited by Carlos Frías [Emecé, 1974], 450).

31 "[E]ra un hombre supremamente consciente tanto de la energía, el flujo y las contradicciones del Renacimiento, como de la inercia, la rigidez, y la falsa seguridad de la Contrarreforma" (Carlos Fuentes, *Cervantes o la crítica de la lectura* (Centro de estudios cervantinos, 1994), 1).

32 David Jiménez Torres, *Ramiro de Maeztu and England: Imagines, Realities, and Repercussions* (Boydell and Brewer, 2016), 149.

33 "[S]ueños ridículos que constituyen lo que la parva mentalidad franquista llama pomposamente Hispanidad," Francisco Piña, "El hambre de Camillo Camilo J. Cela," *LE* 13 (1949), 11–12.

In a 1949 editorial of *Las Españas* "Hispanidad," the board argues:

> *Hispanidad* … is a monstruous teleology of cadavers founded on the religion of death. It cannot capture any of Spain's living past, echoing only distant voices and death. It's another Escorial full of laconic shadows and rotten Charles-es and Philipos [sic]. In its name, people are erased and killed. Cervantes was dubbed "incompatible with Hispanidad," by those that call the [true] voice of Spain's history and pulse of its people the "anti-Spain."
>
> La hispanidad [sic] es como una monstruosa teología de cadáveres en la que se asientara la religión de la muerte. Del pasado vivo de España no quedan ahí en ella, sino ecos y cenizas. Es otro Escorial lleno de sombras taciturnas, podrido de Carlos y Felipes. En su nombre se excomulga y mata. A Cervantes se le llama heterodoxo de la Hispanidad: se llama la anti-España a quienes oyen la voz de su historia y sienten el pulso de su pueblo (*LE* 6 [1947], 9).

34 "[U]na palabrita mal elegida y troquelada, cargada de sentido falso [que] no respondía a la verdad … porque esas cosas [hechos históricos] nunca surgen del capricho de un señor," Sender, *Examen de los ingenios. Los Noventayochos* (Las Américas, 1961), 247.

35 "Había entonces castellanidad, galicidad, catalanidad, asturianidad, pero no Hispanidad" (ibid., 262).

36 "La creación artificial de Maeztu era tan absurda como la creación de un imperio por decreto. Gesto, escenario ... y ruina. Con el ridículo implicito" (ibid., 242).

37 Ibid., 242.

38 Manuel Azaña, *Obras Completas*, Vol. 2, edited by Juliá Santos (Taurus, 2008), 172.

39 Ibid.

40 "[C]rear un ideal, suscitar mecanicamente—como quien provoca la respiración artificial de un ahogado" (*OC*, Vol. 2, 171).

41 "[L]os remedios del señor Maeztu se nos atragantan" (ibid.).

42 Speaking of Puerto Rico, and a group of unnamed Spaniards, Salinas complains that "they have behaved quite *politically*, issuing propaganda that was not openly Francoist but in support of *Hispanidad*. Another tainted word!" (han estado bastante *politicos*, propaganda no franquista declarada, pero sí de *Hispanidad*. ¡Otra palabra mancillada!). Italics are the author's. Pedro Salinas, January 12, 1949. *Correspondencia*, 517–19, 519. Salinas claims that his book on Rubén Darío had been harshly criticized by the Francoist Antonio Tovar. "Splendid!" Salinas boasts, "My book will not contribute to their murky Hispanidad propaganda" (¡Espléndido! ... no les sirve para su turbia propaganda de Hispanidad) (March 9, 1950, *Correspondencia*, 525–6).

43 Valender and Leyva, *Las Españas*, 147–9; see also David Marcilhacy, "La Hispanidad bajo el franquismo. El americanismo al servicio de un proyecto nacionalista," in *Imaginarios y representaciones de España durante el Franquismo*, edited by Xosé M. Núñez Seixas and Stéphane Michonneau (Casa de Velázquez, 2014), 73–102. In Spain, fascist forces had founded in 1938 a similar establishment with the name of "Spanish Institute." This Institute was born to absorb all the Royal Academies of Spain—History, Language, Science, Fine Arts, etc.—so that they could be aligned, ideologically, with the regime. Salinas jokes with Guillén about the "Oath of Office" that was required to work in that Institute in Madrid, "a hilarious formula" that invoked God "and the Guardian Angels" in the mandatory commitment to serve, "perpetually," the "*redeemer* of our people [Franco]." Salinas observes, "[l]a fórmula del Instituto de España, no menos hilarante. Nunca pudo pensar que Valle Inclán que España se iba a convertir en esperpento con tanta fidelidad" (February 3, 1940, Pedro Salinas/Jorge Guillén, *Correspondencia*, edited by Andrés Soria Olmedo [Tusquets, 1992], 218–19).

The formula of the oath that Salinas refers to is: "Do you swear by God and the Guardian Angels to serve Spain's tradition and Catholicism, as embodied in Rome's Pontiff, and represented in its continuity by the redeeming caudillo of our people, perpetually and loyally?" (¿Juráis a Dios y a los Ángeles Custodios, servir perpetua y lealmente a España en su tradición viva, en su catolicidad que encarna el Pontífice de Roma, en su continuidad hoy representada por el Caudillo salvador de nuestro pueblo?) *Revista Hispánica Moderna* 4 (1938), 227, qtd. by Andrés Soria Olmedo, Pedro Salinas/Jorge Guillén, *Correspondencia* [Tusquets, 1992], note D, 218).

44 "[U]na penetración falangista, católica, imperialista en las democracias americanas," *Las Españas* 10 (1948), 12. The anti-Francoist protests by exiled Spanish intellectuals in places like Mexico are well-known even outside of Mexico thanks to those magazines. From the United States, Salinas writes for example: "I read in *Las Españas* that an Institute of Culture Hispano-Mexican has just opened to channel Francoist propaganda. Republican Spaniards would take a belligerent position against such institute .... Always that damned propaganda, poisoning everything we want clean it from [literature]" (*leo en Las Españas que acaba de instalarse allí un Instituto de Cultura Hispano Mexicana, un organismo de propaganda franquista. Los españoles republicanos toman una actitud beligerante contra él ....Siempre la maldita propaganda, el envenenamiento deliberado de lo que se quiere limpio*) (October 24, 1948, Pedro Salinas/Jorge Guillén, *Correspondencia*, edited by Andrés Soria Olmedo [Tusquets, 1992], 462).

45 "Colonizaje ideológico, premisa indispensable al colonizaje total." The quote is from an unsigned article titled *"Un Instituto Hispánico A.M.D.G.,"* (*Las Españas* 10 [1948], 12), that follows Mariano Ruiz Funes's "Encuesta sobre la penetración franquista en América," published on the same page, *Las Españas* 10 (1948), 12. I am assigning both essays to Ruiz Funes, but the first one could be an editorial note usually written by the entire editorial board.

46 See Españas, *Historia de una revista de exilio (1946–1963)*, 137–60.

47 Many of the émigrés who, unlike Salinas, resided in Latin America, are being increasingly recognized for their role in providing "a counterpoint to the work of their Francoist rivals in the region" to prevent the fascist destabilization of left-wing, revolutionary governments like that of Mexico. "While the prospect of a Falangist attempt to set up a puppet state in Mexico or an outright protectorate may now seem grossly exaggerated or even preposterous, it was a serious concern of both the Mexican government and U.S. intelligence" in the 1930s and 1940s. See Mario Ojeda Revah, *Mexico and the Spanish Civil War: Political Repercussions for the Republican Cause* (Sussex Academic Press, 2016); Aaron Navarro, *Political Intelligence and the Creation of Modern Mexico, 1938–1954* (Pennsylvania State University Press, 2010), 122–3; David Brydan's study, *Franco's Internationalists: Social Experts and Spain's Search for Legitimacy* (Oxford University Press, 2019), 117.

48 On the rejection of the Generation of '98 literary and political ideas, see Chapter 3. The most obvious exception is the ambiguous figure of Unamuno. In the small Spanish microcosm in Mexico captured in a magazine like *Las Españas*, there is a gradual softening of the harsh criticism against him that had appeared in the first issues. Unamuno had always been a controversial figure, having been an explicit supporter of fascism before the 1936 coup and a heroic critic of fascism afterward. His political ambivalence was not helped by a questionable critical interpretation of Cervantes not shared by most Generation of '27 authors.

49 Valender and Rojo Leyva, Las Españas, *una revista*, 280–1.

50 Ibid., 281.

51 The pattern was unfortunately repeated in 2010, when the UNESCO identified again a "New Humanism" as the fundamental value for the twenty-first century, and the proclamation unfortunately had little impact in humanities

departments. http://www.unesco.org/new/en/media-services/single-view/
news/a_new_humanism_for_the_21st_century/.

52 An examination, even an understanding, of the complex history of Hispanism
    falls outside of the limits of this study, but a brief contextualization of the
    long controversy prompted by the term is needed. Defined quite neutrally,
    Hispanism connotes "the study of the language, literature, and history of
    Spain and Latin America," Richard Kagan, *Spain in America: The Origins
    of Hispanism in the United States* (University of Illinois Press, 2002), 2.
    Frederick B. Pike, focusing on a period like period, 1898–1936, equates the
    idea of Hispanism with that of "Hispanidad," since "Hispanism rests ...
    on the assumption that Spaniards, in discovering and colonizing America,
    transplanted their lifestyle, culture, characteristic, traditions, and values to the
    New World" (*Hispanismo, 1898–1936: Spanish Conservatives and Liberals in
    the Relations with Spanish America* [University of Notre Dame Press, 1971],
    1). In his view, this colonial understanding of Hispanism shapes right and left
    inflections of Spanish politics, eliding any real differences between conservative
    and liberal followers. To Pike, all Spaniards "whether conservative or liberals"
    are ultimately concerned with "the preservation of a hierarchical, stratified
    society threatened, so they believed, by the leveling forces of inorganic
    democracies and communism" (330).

    Maribel Moraña then argues that Hispanism as a discipline "constitutes
    an institutionalizing and legitimizing space for a nationalist appropriation of
    pre-Columbian history" (*Ideologies of Hispanism* [Vanderbilt University Press,
    2005], xii). She adds that "[a]s an ideologically charged cultural practice,
    Hispanism produced different results and managed to define very diverse
    political agendas, depending on the project in which it was instantiated, the
    international conjuncture in which it was immersed, and the goals pursued
    by intellectual sectors connected to its diverse field" (ibid., xii). Carlos Botti
    offers a powerful reminder that "even in a global world, we can continue to
    have historiographical cultural boundaries that too often entail rigid national
    borders" ([e]n el mundo global siguen existiendo culturas historiographicas
    nacionales que a menudo represtan unas fronteras rígidas) ("Qué es y dónde
    va el hispanismo historiográfico," *Memoria del hispanismo: miradas sobre la
    cultura española*, 149–56, 156), he declares the Hispanist a "historiographic
    intermediary" (intermediario historiográfico) among such scholarly and
    national boundaries, one who employs this powerful and symbiotic
    perspective to crystalize misconceptions and stereotypes in the collective
    imagination (155).

    David T. Gies reminded fellow "Hispanists" that there should be
    and always have been multiple worlds of "Hispanism[s]," since multiple
    intellectual sectors and discursive practices inform the understanding and
    examination of Hispanic cultural practice (*Aspectos actuales del hispanismo
    mundial: Literatura —Cultura—Lengua*, edited by Christopher Strosetzki [De
    Gruyter, 2018]). Román de la Campa also offers a pluralistic understanding of
    the discipline:

    A post-national understanding of Hispanism could perhaps begin by
    tracing the following contours: a) the large-scale migration from half the

Latin American nations to the United States and Europe; b) the onset of
Hispanic enclaves—a majority in some instances—in the major urban
centers of the United States; and c) *the growing sense of cultural, if not
national pluralism within Spain during the post-Franco era.* Together
these elements *signal a shift within the nation-state equation,* albeit in
widely different forms that, while specific to each country, evidence certain
patterns. *It is not an end of the nation, as many have augured, but rather
a symptom of its cultural dissemination,* if not dispersal, that deserves
special attention by those who study culture and literature. *It also implies
opportunities for shaping the links between new transatlantic Hispanic
constellations and American Studies, without abandoning discourses
pertaining to Peninsular and Latin American traditions.* Indeed, one
might even suggest that a new *comparativism within the post-national
sphere could renew our understanding of the Humanist past,* as evidenced
in Derrida's suggestive re-reading of Marx and Shakespeare, as well as
Negri's and Hardt's poignant re-articulation of Renaissance thought in
"Doing and Undoing Hispanism."

(*Debating Hispanic Studies: Reflections on Our Disciplines,*
edited by Francisco Ocampo and Nicholas Spadaccini, *Hispanic
Issues* 1, no. 1 [2006], 23–9), https://conservancy.umn.edu/bitstream/
handle/11299/182511/hiol_01_02_delacampa_doing_and_undoing_
hispanism_today.pdf?sequence=1&isAllowed=y. Accessed on March 1,
2020).

This impressively open formula, forged in an anti-hegemonic perspective,
could acquire a different weight or traction had it taken into consideration
the anti-imperialistic reference voiced by Spanish Republicans or left-wing
oppositors to Francoist and imperialistic schemes.

Joan Ramon Resina ("Cold War Hispanism and the New Deal of Cultural
Studies," in *Spain beyond Spain: Modernity, Literary History, and National
Identity,* edited by Brad Epps and Luis Fernández Cifuentes [Bucknell
University Press, 2005], 70–108), and Sebastiaan Faber (*Anglo-American
Hispanists and the Spanish Civil War* [Palgrave Macmillan, 2008]), have
identified the roots of the American disregard for this counterhegemonic
perspective. Both studies have exposed the clash between Peninsular and
North American perspectives and material conditions in American academia
that lead to the general disregard of a Spanish, anti-imperial political
perspective and critical innovation.

53 War, in Azaña's view, "only weakens the invading party, ... threatening the
stability of its institutions, impoverishing the country, driving it into madness,
and putting it at the mercy of the bellicose resentment of the invaded people[;
it] is a fatal error, in which a country can destroy itself for the sake of the
assumed task of spreading civilization, [an even more delusional aim] given
how little of that—civilization—we have here" (pone en peligro la resistencia
del Estado que la emprende ... amenaza la establidad de las instituciones, ...
empobrece al país, que lo eloquece, y lo pone a merced del humor belicoso del
pueblo invadido, es un trance mortal, donde puede perderse, por el supuesto
encargo de esparcir la civilización, la poca que a nosotros nos queda) *Obras*

*Completas (OC),*Vol. 2 (Centro de Estudios Políticos y Constitucionales, 2007), 172.

54 "Los españoles, por instinto natural, por deshábito, son absolutamente pacíficos, y además [sería] ... suicida entrar en aventuras bélicas" (ibid., Vol. 4, 64–5).

55 Azaña emphatically insists on the need for peace and order both within and beyond Spain: "Yes, domestically and internationally! Domestically to be free, and internationally to do the same. Also internationally!" (*Sí, en el interior y el exterior! En el interior, para ser libres, y en el exterior, también. ¡En el exterior también!*) (ibid., Vol. 4, 65).

56 "Si un pueblo necesita y quiere la paz, es España." (ibid.).

57 Ciges Aparicio was acclaimed within and beyond Spain as "the new Tacitus." See, for example, Frances Douglas's assessment in his view of "Contemporary Spanish Literature," in 1933 (*Hispania* 16, no. 4 [1933], 447–54, 448–51).

58 Ibid., 449. Douglas notes how the "story" told by Ciges "of intrigue and corruption, or heroism and sacrifice" was "amazing," as it provided a fresh alternative to the traditional national historiography through comprehensive, solid data.

59 "[D]igamos sin ambajes ni rodeos que la grandeza de España en el siglo de oro no fue más que un espejismo engañoso fruto solamente de una 'élite' que no tuvo nunca detrás de ella a un pueblo que la mantuviese y si delante de ella, como rectores, a unos hombres-reyes que aleccionados por su amor propio y desmesurada avaricia malgastaron las energías y valor de unos cuantos en perjucio de la comunidad impotente para elevarse y manumitirse," Francisco Puig-Espert, "Grandeza y misericordia de un pueblo (Contribución a la historia del Siglo de Oro español)," *Boletín de la Unión de Intelectuales Españoles* 4, no. 26 (1947), 5–10, 5.

60 In "Cervantes y un momento crucial de la Historia de España" (*Cuadernos Americanos* 4 [1948]: 152–60), Pedro Bosch Gimpera states that "[E]n aquel imperio ... no hay un lugar para él, Cervantes" (159), it was Philip II who "selló la ruina de la preponderancia marítima española" (155).

61 Bosch Gimpera continues saying that Philip II "selló la ruina de la preponderancia marítima española" (155), "hundido en su montaña de expedientes, apenas si se entera cuando le hablan de sus súbditos esclavizados en Africa" (158). His badly conceived or administered state ends up filing for bankruptcy "([e]l estado mal construido y mal administrado" that "iba a hacer bancarrota" [156]).

62 War, for Azaña, could never be the main form of international policy: "A foreign policy does not consist of creating war or preparing for conflict, nor of establishing alliances. It entails something bigger and more important ... a cooperation in peaceful, moral, and humanitarian campaigns. And that kind of struggle is where Spain has the strict obligation to show its true colors, its real personality." (*La política internacional no consiste en concertar guerras, ni en preparar guerras, ni en concertar aliazas. Consiste en mucho más y más importante ... la cooperación en obras de paz, de valor moral y humanitario. Y en esta contienda internacional es donde España tiene la obligación estricta de tener personalidad propia, suya*) (*OC*, Vol. 4, 65). The president did not reject all war, however; he found resistance against invasion justified (as in

Spain in 1808) and believed that the balance between national defense and the preservation of individual liberties (when fighting for such collective defense) was deeply challenging but always feasible.

63 In the original:

> España ... es víctima de una propaganda política iniciada en pleno siglo XVI. Entonces había en España una política triunfante, dominadora en toda Europa, que imponía su sello relativamente español y profundamente católico, con tendencia, casi con triunfos de universalidad. ....Esta política creó su propaganda, creó su dotrina. No se hacía entonces en periódicos, naturalmente, pero se hacía a través de las obras de los teólogos, de los filósofos, de los poetas, de los pintores, por todos los medios de publicidad, para formar las conciencias que tenían a su alcance. Pasó la politica que fundó el régimen aquel; pasó el imperialismo español, ...pero no ha desaparecido la propaganda; la doctrina ha subsistido año tras año .... *los hombres de mi generación ....hemos tenido que arrancar de nosotros el sedimento de viciosas propagandas que conduce a la muerte por su anacronismo, por su falsedad, y su ineficacia.* (Emphasis added, Azaña, *OC*, Vol. 5, 166)

64 "Apatía embrutecedora ... de los gabinetes de regencia suficiente valor cívico [que] propusiera a tiempo y con buen modo la emancipación, no la venta ni la cesión, de aquellos países" (*OC*, Vol. 7, 38).

65 José Manuel Gallegos Rocafull, *El pensamiento mexicano en los siglos XVI y XVII* (Universidad Nacional Autónoma de México, Facultad de Filosofía y Letras, 1974), 17–18; see also Eugenio Imaz Echeverría, *Utopías del Renacimiento* (Fondo de Cultura Económica, 1941).

66 "La mayoría pensaba que a Cuba se le tenía que haber dado la libertad" (Ciges, 150).

67 "El único [provecho] al que podíamos aspirar: mercados favorable; repúblicas amigas o alidas, tratados de propiedad literaria e industrial y de arbitraje" (Azaña, *OC*, Vol. 7, 38).

68 "[L]o que hace falta son convenientes tratados de comercio," "juiciosos y sensatos" rather than "los poetas y parlanchines a la hora del los brindis confraternantes." "El florete aduanero," *El Sol*, July 24, 1927, 3.

69 Ibid.

70 (Azaña, *OC*, Vol. 7, 38). Azaña was unsparing in his assessment that the Spanish Empire offered a powerful cautionary tale on the dangers of absolutism: In 1910, he urged, "Let's remember where we come from, politically speaking, what we have left behind but is still not too far from us, *the abysm of despotism* that we had fled and to which we had been chained" (Recordemos todos de dónde venimos políticamente, de dónde hemos salido políticamente, lo cerca que estamos aún *del averno del despotismo del* que nos hemos fugado y al cual [nos] hemos encadenado [ibid., Vol. 4, 52]).

71 Even these terms, Spanish and nation, were "highly charged" concepts in this context, since as Daniel Aguirre Otaiza has explored, "discussing the very definition of nation could and did have disastrous repercussions." *This*

Ghostly Poetry: Reading Spanish Republican Exiles between Literary History and Poetic Memory (University of Toronto Press, 2020), 21.

72   "Nosotros, republicanos españoles, descendientes legítimos de los 'populares' o 'comuneros' del siglo XVI": This is how Anselmo Carretero opens the main text of his article "Tradición de nuestro pueblo. Don Quijote, los Indios de la Nueva España, y la Junta Santa de Avila," *LE* 6 (1947), 8.

73   The quote is from Araquistáin's "1521–1931," appearing in *El Sol* on April 15, 1931. See Chapter 1. Oscar Rodríguez Barreira, *Poder y actitudes sociales durante la postguerra en Almería (1939–1953)*. Thesis (University of Almería, 2007), 123, n.8, thoroughly documents this allusion to the Republican flag and thought. Azaña had drawn this connection countless times before: "Castile had raised in arms, with its revolutionary troops," he reminded readers in 1931, stating that "its revolutionary diaries cannot be read without emotion, because they already identify some of the political issues that at the beginning of this Republic stood still unresolved" [Castilla se había levantado en armas, con sus cuartos revolucionarios .... [sus] actas [revolucionarias] no se pueden leer sin emoción, porque anticipan algunos temas políticos que al advenimiento de la República estaban sin resolver.] (*OC*, Vol. 5, 154–68, 166).

74   In Spanish:

> La nueva España que quería crear la República había de ser la continuadora de una "tradición corregida por la razón," que no la del imperio, que no representa la verdadera España .... Esa España hay que buscarla debajo de la superestructura del imperio romano-visigodo-leonés-trastámara-habsburgo-borbónico-falangista—que no es España, y lo mismo que con él [el imperio] *los pueblos no pueden dialogar, los auténticos españoles tampoco.* (*LE* 2 [1946], 11)

75   "Castilla, como España, como América había sido víctima del despotismo de sus monarcas," Bosch Gimpera, *LE* 2 (1946), 11.

76   "Los Austrias reprimen a sangre y fuego; rompen, cercenan, dilapidan; abren las venas de España en una serie de guerras catastróficas; pisotean y deshonran la obra gigantesca de nuestro pueblo en América," José Ramón Arana, "Voces, ecos, sombras," *LE* 3 (1947). Republished in Las Españas. *Historia de una revista de exilio (1946–1963)*, Valender and Rojo Leyva 566–79, 569.

77   The assertion constantly made by Republican thinkers and historians, both in Spain and in exile, during the 1930, 1940s, and 1950s, could not be echoed in Spain during the dictatorship, but it resurfaced powerfully—if framed within national boundaries—during the transition to democracy in the late 1970s. See Enrique Berzal de la Rosa *Los comuneros: de la realidad al mito* (Sílex, 2008), 306–7, and Mariano Esteban de la Vega, "La creación simbólica de la Comunidad Autónoma de Castilla y León," in *Castilla en España: historia y representaciones* (Ediciones Universidad de Salamanca, 2014), 329–52, 351.

78   In Spanish:

> Al derrotar al movimiento democrático en 1521, España venció anticipadamente a sus colonias como entidades políticas viables. De

allí la terrible dificultad de Hispanoamérica a partir de la Independencia: nuestras luchas por la descolonización han debido combatir, por así decirlo, un colonizaje al cuadrado: fuimos, al cabo, colonias de una colonia. Pues la Metrópolis que nos regía pronto se convirtió en las Indias de Europa. (Fuentes, *Cervantes o la crítica de la lectura* [Centro de Estudios Cervantinos, 1994], 63)

79 Ibid., 62. Fuentes had novelized these events, the 1521 fall of Tenochittlán, and the Comuneros rebellion in his novel *Terra Nostra* (Joaquín Mortiz, 1975). See, for example, Kerstin Oloff, "*Terra Nostra*, and the Rewriting of the Modern Subject: Archetypes, Myth, and Selfhood," *Latin American Research Review* 46, no. 3 (2011), 3–20.

80 Fuentes, *Terra Nostra*, 67–8.

81 Ibid., 60.

82 Ibid.

83 Ibid.

84 Carretero, "Tradición," 8.

85 Cascardi cites the Cannon discussion on *DQ* I. 47, *Cervantes, Literature, and the Discourse of Politics* (University of Toronto Press, 2012), 30.

86 Carretero ("Tradición," 8), provides a succinct and powerful example.

87 Carretero proudly reproduces the 1520 *comunero* resolution that demanded the liberation of American slaves by the conquistadors:

> *Que a ninguna persona, de cualquier*
> *clase o condición que fuese se diese en*
> *merced indios para los trabajos de las*
> *minas y para tratarlos como esclavos,*
> *y se liberarán los que se hubieran hecho.*

(To forbid that any person, of any class or condition, be given as a gift for work in the mines or for being treated as slaves. Those already under this condition must be immediately released.)

Cited by Carretero. Ibid.

88 As Fuentes puts it, Cervantes was "supremely aware of the [liberating] energy and deep contradictions of the Renaissance as of the inertia and the rigidity and false assertiveness of the Counter-Reformation," and thus never succumbs to its orthodoxical demands. This is one of the most-frequently praised traits by Latin American writers ([e]ra un hombre supremamente consciente tanto de la energía, el flujo y las contradicciones del Renacimiento, como de la inercia, la rigidez, y la falsa seguridad de la Contrarreforma; Fuentes 1976, 33).

89 Jose Martí, "Seis Conferencias," in *Obras Completas,* Vol. 5 (CEM, Centro de Estudios Martianos, 2011), 119–22, 120.

90 Ibid.

91 "Los sentimientos del señor Ugarte con respecto de España y sus opiniones acerca de la herencia española de América nos parecen justos: cualquier español de buen sentido los aceptará," Manuel Azaña, "Review. Manuel

Ugarte, *El porvenir de la América Española* (Valencia: Editorial Prometeo, 1920)" *OC*, Vol. 2, 46.

92 Luis Araquistáin. The whole quote in Spanish reads: "Ha interesarnos preferentemente la cuestión de nuestras relaciones específicas, y a mejorarlas han de tender nuestros esfuerzos, con prioridad a otros acercamientos menos urgentes y más laboriosos," from "Hacia un nuevo Hispanoamericanismo," *El Sol,* December 13, 1937, http://www.filosofia.org/hem/dep/sol/9271213.htm. Accessed on March 1, 2020.

93 Ibid.

94 He notes that:

> Either when showing contempt or affection, judgments have been too broad and generic, and those who spoke well or badly of Spain forgot that there are many Spains coexisting simultaneously, and that is fairly stupid to judge them equally. Spaniards supporting or criticizing America have made the same mistake, ignoring that there are many Americas, and that even inside each of its Republics, there are many different ones, and many men that do not hold the same opinion, and that it is always foolish to judge them as an entire Hispanic continent, even each of its countries, with the same praise or attack.
>
> Se ha abusado de los afectos—amables u hostiles—y se ha ejercitado poco la inteligencia crítica. En el menosprecio como en estimación, los juicios han sido demasiado globales, demasiado genéricos, sin advertir los que hablan a de España, en bien o en mal, que hay muchas Españas coexistentes, y que es estúpido medirlas a todas con el mismo rasero; error en que han caído también casi siempre los apologistas como los detractores españoles de América, ignorando que hay muchas Américas, y que dentro de cada República, muchas repúblicas y muchos hombres discordes, y que es necesario enjuiciar todo el continente hispánico, y cada país, con la misma lisonja y la misma invectiva. Ibid.

95 "que agrupe o que alíe en espíritu a los hombres de España y América que tengan una aspiración afín de libertad en todas las manifestaciones de la vida," ibid.

96 Like Azaña, Araquistáin tries to shift political and stereotyped misconceptions, transcending purely emotional responses such as a contempt or affection. Progressive politicians and theorists like them demonstrated that an anti-imperial way of thinking encompassed not only a liberal humanist basis for the current or future relations between Spain and its former colonies, but also the active recognition of the past, rather than an idyllic myth colored by *Hispanidad*, which only highlights the long-term resentment in Latin American nations.

97 José Luis Venegas, "Quixotic Correspondences," *Transatlantic Correspondence. Modernity,* 82.

98 Juan Ortega y Medina offers a good summary of their contributions in "La aportación de los historiadores españoles trasterrados a la historiografía mexicana," *Estudios Historia de México* 10 (1986), 255–79.

99   Palerm Vich created and redesigned with it the Specialized Programs at the Universidad Iberoamerica and Metropolitana of Mexico, serving also as a Mexican Deputy at the PanAmerican Union in Washington. He was described by a colleague, Eric Wolf, as a scholar who was "forced to join the Spanish emigration to Mexico in 1939" and ended up publishing widely on colonial Mexico, pre-Hispanic modes of production, and the anthropology of Marxism. Eric R. Wolf, "Angel Palerm Vich 1917–1980. American Anthropologist," *American Anthropological Association* 83, no. 3 (1981), 612–15, 612.

    According to recent characterizations (2014) of Palerm Vich's work, it is "anti-hegemonic but rooted in a national [here Mexican] tradition," which offered an example to future Mexican anthropologists on how to challenge the conventions of the field, "following their own ancestors, their own tradition, and turning it into their own history" (Joan Pujadas, "Historia de la etnología de Angel Palerm: Humanismo y criticism al servicio de una visión postcolonial de la antropología," *Desacatos* 45 [2014], http://www.scielo. org.mx/scielo.php?script=sci_arttext&pid=S1607-050X2014000200013. Accessed on March 1, 2020).

100   Wolf, "Angel Palerm," 614.

101   "Se producía así un cambio de perspectiva. Los escritores españoles tenían a los ojos no sólo articular el problema de España, sino un extenso horizonte de paisajes, y temas nuevos," Arturo Souto Alabarce, "Letras," *El exilio español*, 363–402, 369.

102   Arturo Souto Alabarce, "Letras," *El exilio español*, 363–402, 365.

103   If Castro (in *La peculiaridad lingüística rioplatense y su sentido histórico* (Losada 1941, revised in 1961) censures the "imprecision," and "poverty" of Buenos Aires's Spanish (90), Borges in a demolishing response—"Las alarmas del Dr. A. Castro" (in "Las alarmas del Dr. A. Castro" [1941] in *Otras Inquisiciones* [1952])—claims, for example, that "I have never observed that Spaniards speak better than us (they do speak louder, like all those that ignore doubt)," https://apuntesliterarios.files.wordpress.com/2013/09/ borges_otras_inquisiciones.pdf (Accessed on April 1, 2020). For a detailed understanding of the issues underlying the controversy, see James Fernandez, "Las américas de Don Américo: Castro entre imperio," in *Américo Castro y la revisión de la memoria: el islam en España*, edited by Eduardo Subirats (Ediciones Libertarias/ Prodhufi, 2003), 63–81.

104   Ultimately, Castro's comments about "Argentianian Spanish" were taken not only as an assumption that all people from Spain shared—but furthermore, unequivocally demanded—a linguistic *Hispanidad:*

> [Castro's] book is less a scientific assessment that a personal, passionate, almost impassionate, defense of [the purity of language] that aims for *a reunification* of the Spanish language, *whose unity* Castro considers seriously damaged by the forms of the Argentinian and Uruguayan dialects. It is, *furthermore, a representative illustration of the position that Spaniards usually adopt, when arriving into these lands, whether or not they are philologists.*

> Este libro [de Castro] es mucho menos un ensayo científico que un alegato apasionado, casi pasional, en procura de una reunificacion de la lengua Española, *cuya unidad* Castro considera seriamente lesionado por el modo de hablar de los argentinos y uruguayos. Es, además, un *alegato sumamente representative de la tesitura que suelen adoptar los españoles al llegar a estas tierras, sean o no filológos.*

José Pedro Rona, "Americo Castro's *La peculiaridad lingüística rioplatense y su sentido histórico.* Segunda edición muy renovada. Madrid. Taurus, 1960." Review. *Anuario de Letras, Universidad Autónoma de México*, https://revistas-filologicas.unam.mx/anuario-letras/index.php/al/article/view/1179. Accessed on March 1, 2020.

105 It seems that in the 1940s, the repute that Castro had acquired as a young historian with *El Pensamiento de Cervantes* (1925) had worn off a bit among his fellow countrymen. Salinas and Guillén called him "Segismundo," thinking of him as a prince locked up in an obsessive theoretical cave ("Don Américo-Segismundo, continúa en su laberinto hispano-árabe: *España en su historia,*" January 28, 1946. *Pedro Salinas/Jorge Guillén. Correspondencia* 371–3, 371). In 1946, after a brief visit from the historian, Salinas tells his regular confidante, Guillén, that "Américo," was particularly "rigid and inflexible ... I was really sad to find him like that. He has become increasingly isolated, more distrustful, more reactive to the slightest thing. For the friendship I have with him, I would do whatever I can to remove those demons and that nonsense from his head" "Américo ... firme y roqueño, casi berroqueño .... Te aseguro que me ha dado pena ver así a Castro. Se le nota cada vez más aislado. Más receloso, más sensible a la más mínima cosa .... a mí me mueve a amistad, a hacer lo que pueda dentro de ella porque se le disipen tantos fantasmas y musarañas," Letter from Salinas to Guillén, from October 26, 1946. *Pedro Salinas/Jorge Guillén. Correspondencia*, 402–6, 402–3. If one Spaniard could ever identify whatever position *"Spaniards usually adopt"* about anything, Castro would probably not be it.

106 For example, for Juan Rejano, it was "evident that Mexicans have introduced into the Spanish language—which is so resounding, choppy, and rough—a softness, an intriguing cadence and half-there intonation that the Peninsula simply doesn't have" (Es evidente que los mexicanos ha introducido en el idioma español—idioma rotundo, encrespado, áspero—una suavidad, un dejo insinuante, una especie de tono medio o media tinta que no tiene la Península. [*La esfinge mestiza* 263]). Speaking also of Mexico, Cernuda describes the language quite poetically: "[f]ew or any voices are here unpolished; regardless of the speaker's social status, it is a delicate language. It is a precise expression, a classic lexicon, without vulgar idioms or plebeian intonations" (Pocas o ningunas voces son aquí incultas; por humilde que sea quien habla, es en lenguaje delicado. Un habla precisa, una lengua clásica, sin modismos vulgares, ni entonaciones plebeyas" (*Ocno; Variaciones sobre tema Mexicano,* edited by Jerano Talens [Cátedra, 2020], 31).

107 Moreno Villa expressed a deep interest in developing a new perception of the country and culture that had sheltered him: "I look at it [Mexico] with European eyes, and can make all sorts of wrong assumptions trying to

judge its beauty, because I am sure that stones here must be looked at in the Mexican way, or better still, with Aztec eyes" (*Yo lo miro, con ojos europeos y puedo equivocarme al juzgar su belleza, porque estoy convecido de que las piedras de acá hay que mirarlas a lo mexicano, o mejor dicho, con ojos aztecas*) (*Cornucopia de Mexico*, 62).

108 Ibid.

109 Rafael Alberti, "Encuentro en la Nueva España con Bernal Díaz del Castillo," (1936) in *Prosas encontradas*, edited by Robert Marrat (Seix Barral, 2000), 178–97, 179.

110 Y como para un español, para un poeta sobre todo, le era imposible moverse solo en esta difícil realidad Mexicana, tuve la suerte de encontrarme con él, y acompañado ya de él recorrer parte de estas tierras' (ibid., 179).

111 ¿Por cuánto tiempo todavía, pensaba yo, motivarán esas maravillosas tierras ... poemas tan amargos ... y tantas voces y puños de protesta conocidos y desconocidos? Tierras dominadas, aguas dominadas, cielos dominados. Como antes, botines para la guerra despidada del más fuerte. Norteamerica, 1808–1935. España, España ... Un 1519 se empieza a dibujar, ya oscurecido, por la estela lisa y casi inmóvil que va dejando el barco (ibid., 184).

112 Before the end of the war, Salinas recognized a similar palimpsest in Mexico "Past in the present, or the present of that which is past, that is the perception I get from Mexico" (*Pasado en el presente, o presente de lo pasado, eso es mi impresión mejicana*) (*Pasajero Salinas Pasajero en las Américas* [Fondo de Cultura Económica, 2007], 155).

113 "Felipe II, en la segunda República, tiene más partidarios que cuando gobernaba en El Escorial," Azaña, *OC*, Vol. 5, 166.

114 Ellos, los a sí mismos llamados tradicionalistas, se ponían en la trágica y cómica situación de únicos herederos de esta huella de España en el mundo, y los únicos sabedores de su sentido .... Y así nos hicieron un pasado de pesadilla, que pesaba sobre cada español aplastándole, inutilizándole, haciéndole vivir en perpetuo terror. Pocos españoles habrán dejado de temblar ante la figura de Felipe II, por ejemplo, sintiéndose como "infraganti" de no se sabe qué falta tremenda. (*Los intelectuales y el drama de España* [Anthropos, 1986], 95).

115 Zambrano, *Los inteletuales*, 286.

116 Don Quijote tiene todas las características de un personaje de tragedia ....que no son nunca victoriosos. El héroe vencedor aparece en la épica. El personaje de la tragedia, si al fin vence, lo hace allá en el reino del Hades, más alla de la vida, o en esta vida en la memoria de los hombres .... Mas nunca vence aquí, a los ojos, del todo; nunca vence en su historia. Su victoria es metahistórica. *España, sueño y verdad*. 1965 (Diario Público, 2010), 41.

117 The reconsideration started in the 1930s, and not only in Spanish criticism—in 1931, Franz Kafka's posthumous "The Truth about Sancho Panza" (published in German as "Die Wahrheit über Sancho Pansa) had already identified the squire with Cervantes. The story was translated into English in 1933 and published in *The Great Wall of China. Stories and Reflections* (Shocken Books, 1946). Ruth V. Gross, Richard Gray et al., *A Franz Kafka Encyclopedia* (Greenwood Press, 2005), 290.

118 *DQ* I:10, 12; II: 12.

119 For example, William Worden, "Sancho Panza, Illiterate Literary Critic, and the Unmasking of Generic Conventions in *Don Quixote*," *Comparative Literature Studies* 43, no. 4 (2006), 498–514.

120 "Sancho grosero, Sancho, lleno de buen sentido, crédulo e incrédulo que ve deshacerse ese mismo mundo sin darse cuenta de que él es el mundo nuevo que va a remplazarlo. Sancho es el mundo nuevo y no el Nuevo Mundo. Sancho es la realidad misma," Aub, *Manual de Historia de la literatura española,* Vol. 1 (Mexico DF, 1966), 302–3.

121 For Sancho and political and theory or criticism, see Roselie Hernández, "Furió Ceriol, Sancho Panza and Althusser: Machiavelli's Prince Reconsidered," *Bulletin of the Cervantes Society of America* 32, no. 2 (2012), 11–36; Ryan Schmitz, "Sancho's Courtly Performance: *Discreción* and the Art of Conversation in the Ducal Palace Episodes of *Don Quijote* II," *MLN* (2013), 445–55; Guillermo Fernández Rodríguez-Escalona, "Pensamiento politico y concepción del mundo en Cervantes: El gobierno de la ínsula Barataria," *Bulletin of the Cervantes Society of America* 31, no. 2 (2011): 125–52; Myriam Yvonne Jehenson and Peter N. Dunn, *The Utopian Nexus in Don Quixote* (Vanderbilt University Press, 2006).

122 For example, Graf, "Sancho's por negros que sean los de he de volver blancos o amarillos' (*DQ* 1.29) and Juan de Mariana's *De moneta* of 1605," *Cervantes: Bulleting of the Cervantes Society of America* 32, no. 2 (2011), 23–51; Daniel Nemser, "Governor Sancho and the Politics of Insularity," *Hispanic Review* 78, no. 1 (2010), 1–23; Luis R. Corteguera, "Sancho Panza Wants an Island: Cervantes and the Politics of Peasant Rulers," *Romance Quarterly* 52, no. 4 (2005), 261–70.

123 John Beverly, "Literature, Difference, and Equality. On an Episode of Don Quixote," in *The Failure of Latin America. Postcolonialism in Bad Times* (University of Pittsburgh Press, 2019), 61–74, 72.

124 For Sancho and the idea of pueblo, see Lucio Pabón Núñez, "Sancho, o la exaltación del pueblo Español," *Cuadernos* 197 (1964), 541–80. For examinations of the character in the twentieth century, Verónica Azcue Castillón, "Cervantes, Don Quijote y Sancho Panza en el teatro del exilio," *Bulletin of the Cervantes Society of America* 35, no. 2 (2015), 161–92; Ana Fernández Cebrián and Víctor Pueyo, "Tener y no tener: Lecturas de Sancho Panza en la dictadura de Primo de Rivera (1923–1930)," *Bulletin of the Cervantes Society of America* 33, no. 2 (2013), 199–222.

125 This view of Sancho contrasts with traditionalist analysis. Certainly the squire is, at least initially, read through a parodic model related to "buffoon" stereotypes (Eduardo Urbina, *El sin par Sancho Panza: Parodia y creación* [Anthropos, 1991], 76).

126 Guillén's poem is included in "Dimisión de Sancho" is the second part of *A la altura de las circunstancias* (1963) and published later in *Aire Nuestro, Clamor* (Barral, 1977), 439. See also Gabriel Celaya's (1911–77) beautiful elegy to Sancho to that "Sancho-bueno," "Sancho-pueblo" "A Sancho Panza," http://www.cervantesvirtual.com/obra-visor/antologia-poetica–51/html/00c1e984-82b2-11df-acc7-002185ce6064_2.html).

127 See, among others, Mariana Genoud de Fourcade, "Jorge Guillén: Sancho y la plenitud del ser," in El Quijote *en Buenos Aires. Lecturas Cervantinas en el*

Cuarto Centenario, edited by Alicia Parodi, Julia D'Onofrio, Juan Diego Vila (Instituto De Filología y Literaturas Hispánicas, 2006), 597–602.

128 Some exiles started paying specific attention to this protagonist, such as Vicente Llorens. Spanish authors returned to Cervantes and *Don Quixote* in general rather than to Ricote in particular as an early representative of the long history of dissidents of the country. Members of the Republican diaspora of 1939 regarded themselves as the last representatives of the long and tragic history of exiles represented by Ricote in the Spanish orthodoxy. Other victims were Jews, Erasmists, Moriscos, liberals, Krausists, etc. See Vicente Llorens, "Emigraciones de la España Moderna," *La emigacion republicana,* Vol. 1 *El exilio español de 1939* (Madrid: Taurus, 1976), 25–93. Through what Mainer has named a "literary consciousness of exile" (*Moradores de Sansueña* 18), exiles appeared to see in Ricote "a spiritual brother who had suffered prosecution and had been misinterpreted and marginalized by his fellow Spaniards" ("Cervantes y sus personajes vistos desde el exilio," in *Cervantes y la narrativa moderna. Actas el Coloquio internacional de Brecen,* edited by László Scholz and László Vasas [Desbrecen, 2001], 104–22, 107). Mainer observes that by seeing themselves as part of a longstanding Spanish exile, these writers were able to establish an ongoing dialogue with their present and past, which rather than unrooting them further from Spain, kept them intimately connected to the country and its history. For a complete conceptualization of the topos of exile with regard to Ricote, see Julia Domínguez, "El laberinto mental del exilio en *Don Quijote*: el testimonio del morisco Ricote," *Hispania* 92, no. 2 (2009), 183–92. For a panoramic view of the theme, see Henry Kamen *The Disinherited: Exile and the Making.*

129 Emphasis added, *DQ* 2: 54, 813 ([A]gora *conozco* y *experimento* lo que suele decirse: que es dulce el amor de la *patria* [*IH* 2. 54: 451]), cited in Domínguez 184. For epistemological approaches see Daniel Lorca "The Epistemic and Emotive Foundations of Sancho," *Bulletin of the Cervantes Society of America* 35, no. 2 (2015), 77–102, and Piñero Díaz, Buenaventura. "Visión del mundo en El Quijote a través de Sancho Panza," in *Cervantes: Su obra y su mundo,* edited by Manuel Criado del Val (EDI-6, 1981), 539–53.

130 "[P]refiere la buena esperanza a la posesión ruin," (Azaña "Cervantes y la invención del Quijote," 64).

131 Forced to acknowledge the obvious historical charge of the "ínsula" episode, Maravall, for example, minimizes its political weight, arguing that Cervantes only voices "isolated political commentaries" (rather than a "judgment") and that those commentaries do not amount to "anything more than an [isolated] piece of the general, histórico-political interpretation of *Quixote*" (no será más que una pieza que se articula dentro de una interpretación histórico-política general del *Quijote* [*El humanism en las armas* 19]).

132 "Urge reconstruir a la persona española," *LE* 5 (1947), 8.

133 "Volvamos a Sancho, que partiendo de él conquistaremos a don Quijote. Integremos al héroe, escindido por duques y barberos, clérigos, y bachilleres. Edifiquemos con Sancho y Don Quijote un heroísmo integral, un humanismo integral, o, lo que es lo mismo, creemos un humanismo español. Indaguemos por nuestras esencias, y, una vez halladas, gobernémolas bien. 'Mejor es

gobernar bien que ampliar el imperio,'" "Sobre el Quijotismo de Sancho
Panza," *LE* 5 (1947), 8.

134 The whole quote in Spanish reads: "Nuestro íntimo deseo—por lo menos
el mío—es que cuando volvamos a España digna y libre, llevemos entre las
manos ese Quijote, hecho aquí, en America, por hermanada colaboración de
americanos y españoles" (Salinas, *Quijote y lectura,* 119).

Epilogue

1 Cascardi, "Beyond Castro," 138–59, 139.
2 Faber, "US Hispanism," *Anglo-American Hispanists,* 49.
3 "Yo no hablo con nadie, absolutamente. Por lo demás, no encontraría con
quién, porque tocar el tema de la política internacional o de la Guerra, es
congelar la expresión del interlocutor y taparle la boca" ([November 1, 1950]
Pedro Salinas/Jorge Guillén. Correspondencia, 547).
4 Joan Ramon Resina, "Cold War Hispanism and the New Deal of Cultural
Studies," in *Spain Beyond Spain: Modernity, Literary History, and National
Identity,* edited by Brad Epps and Luis Fernández Cifuentes (Lewisburg, PA:
Bucknell University Press, 2005), 70–108, 72, and Faber, "US Hispanism,"
Anglo-American Hispanists, 71.
5 Lucille Kerr and Alejandro Herrero-Olaizola, introduction to *Teaching the
Latin American Boom* (New York: MLA, 2015), 7–19, 9.

REFERENCES

Abad Nebot, Francisco. "El 'Centro de estudios históricos' de la 'Junta para ampliación de estudios' (1907–1938)." *Cauce* 30 (2007): 7–39. https://cvc.cervantes.es/literatura/cauce/pdf/cauce30/cauce30_02.pdf.

Abellán, José Luis. *El exilio como constante y como categoría*. Madrid: Biblioteca Nueva, 2001.

Abellán, José Luis. *El exilio español de 1939*. Madrid: Taurus, 1977.

Abellán, Manuel L. *Censura y literaturas peninsulares*. Amsterdam: Rodopi, 1987.

Aguado, Afrodisio. *El Imperio de España*. Afrodisio Galiciana: Biblioteca Digital de Galicia, 1941.

Aguilar Piñal, Francisco. "El Anti-Quijote (1805)." In *Desviaciones lúdicas en la crítica cervantina: primer Convivo Internacional de "Locos Amenos,"* edited by Antonio Bernat Vistarini and José María Casasayas, 125–38. Salamanca: Ediciones Universidad de Salamanca, 2000.

Aguilera, Francisco. "Further Additions to the Cervantes Collection." *Hispania* 30 (1947): 85–8.

Aguirre Otezia, Daniel. *This Ghostly Poetry: Reading Spanish Republican Exiles between Literary History and Poetic Memory*. Toronto: University of Toronto Press, 2020.

Alameda, José. *El exilio español en México, 1939–1982*. Mexico City: Fondo de Cultura Económica-Salvat, 1982.

Alberti, Rafael. *Federico García Lorca, poeta y amigo*. Granada: Editoriales Andaluzas Unidas, 1984.

Alberti, Rafael. *Prosas encontradas*. Edited by Robert Marrast. Barcelona: Seix Barral, 2000.

Alcalá Galán, Mercedes, Antonio Cortijo Ocaña, and Francisco Layna Ranz, eds. "'Si ya por atrevido no sale con las manos en la cabeza': el legado poético del *Persiles* cuatrocientos años después." *eHumanista/Cervantes* 5 (2016).

Alcalá-Zamora, Niceto. *El pensamiento de "El Quijote" visto por un abogado*. Buenos Aires: G. Kraft, 1947.

Almarcha Nuñez-Herrador, Maria Esther, and Isidro Sanchez Sanchez. "La Mancha y basta." In *La ruta de Don Quijote*, edited by Azorín, 9–36. Ciudad Real: Artelibro-Rafael Amorós, 2005.

Altolaguirre, Manuel. *Las islas invitadas*. 1944. Reprint. Madrid: Castalia, 1973.

Altolaguirre, Manuel. *Nuevos poemas de las islas invitadas*. 1946. Reprint. Sevilla: Renacimiento, 2008.

Altolaguirre, Manuel. *Presente de la lírica mexicana*. México: El ciervo herido, 1946.

Álvarez Junco, José. "History, Politics, and Culture, 1875–1936." In *The Cambridge Companion to Modern Spanish Culture*, edited by David Thatcher Gies, 67–85. New York: Cambridge University Press, 1999.

Amorós, Andrés, and Antonio Fernández Torres. *Ignacio Sánchez Mejías: el hombre de la Edad de Plata*. Córdoba: Almuzara, 2010.

Andújar, Manuel, and José Ramón Arana. "Editorial." *Las Españas: revista literaria* 5 (1947): 1.

Andújar, Manuel, and José Ramón Arana, eds. *Las Españas*. 1946–56. Reprint. Madrid: Fundación Pablo Iglesias and Jaime Vera, 2002.

Ángel García, Miguel. "Confrontaciones: Ayala y los poetas del 27." *Mélanges de la Casa de Velázquez* 49, no. 1 (2019): 245–67.

Araquistáin, Luis. "Un gran ciclo histórico, 1521–1931." *El Sol*, April 15, 1931.

Araquistáin, Luis. "Hacia un nuevo Hispanoamericanismo." *El Sol*, December 13, 1937.

Araquistáin, Luis. *La revolución mejicana: sus orígenes, sus hombres, su obra*. 1929. Reprint, Madrid: Biblioteca del hombre moderno, 2006.

Ardila, J. A. G. *The Cervantean Heritage: Reception and Influence of Cervantes in Britain*. London: Legenda, 2009.

Armstrong-Roche, Michael. *Cervantes' Epic Novel: Empire, Religion, and the Dream Life of Heroes in Persiles*. Toronto: University of Toronto Press, 2009.

Arrarás, Joaquín. "Crónica del IV Aniversario de Cervantes." *Revista de filología española* 32 (1948): 537–92.

Aub, Max. *De Max Aub a Cervantes*. 1955. Reprint, Segorbe: Fundación Max Aub, 1999.

Aub, Max. *Manual de historia de la literatura española*. 1966. Reprinted. Madrid: Akal, 1974.

Aub, Max. *Max Aub y la vanguardia teatral: escritos sobre teatro, 1928–1938*. Edited by Manuel Aznar Soler. Barcelona: Aula de Teatre, Servi D'Extensió Universitària, Universitat de València, 1993.

Aub, Max. *Mis páginas mejores*. Madrid: Editorial Gredos, 1966.

Aub, Max. *Pruebas*. Madrid: Editorial Ciencia Nueva, 1967.

Aub, Max. *La verdadera historia de la muerte de Francisco Franco, y otros cuentos*. Mexico City: Libro Mex, 1960.

Azaña, Manuel. *La invención del "Quijote": y otros ensayos*. Madrid: Espasa-Calpe, 1934.

Azaña, Manuel. *Obras completas*. Edited by Juliá Santos. 7 vols. Madrid: Centro de Estudios Políticos y Constitucionales, 2007.

Azcue Castillón, Verónica. "Cervantes, Don Quijote y Sancho Panza en el teatro del exilio." *Bulletin of the Cervantes Society of America* 35, no. 2 (2015): 161–92.

Aznar Soler, Manuel. *Escritores, editoriales y revistas del exilio republicano de 1939*. Seville: Editorial Renacimiento, 2006.

Aznar Soler, Manuel. *Los laberintos del exilio: diecisiete estudios sobre la obra literaria de Max Aub*. Seville: Renacimiento, 2003.

Aznar Soler, Manuel. *Pensamiento literario y compromiso antifascista de la inteligencia española republicana*. Barcelona: Laia, 1978.

Aznar Soler, Manuel. *República literaria y revolución: (1920–1939)*. Sevilla: Renacimiento, 2010.

Azorín. *Con el permiso de los cervantistas*. Madrid: Biblioteca Nueva, 1948.

Azorín. "El Caudillo y Cervantes." *ABC*, November 6, 1942. http://www. cervantesvirtual.com/obra-visor/articulos-de-azorin-publicados-en-el-abc-seleccion–0/html/00237ff6-82b2-11df-acc7-002185ce6064_2.html#I_27.

Azorín. *La ruta de Don Quijote*. Edited by H. Ramsden. Manchester: Manchester University Press, 1966.

Babelon, Jean. "Cervantes y el ocaso de los conquistadores." *Revista de filología española* 32 (1948): 206–12.

Balcells, José Maria, José Antonio Perez Bowie, and Jose Luis Abellán, eds. *El exilio cultural de la guerra civil (1936–1939)*. Salamanca: Universidad de Salamanca, 2001.

Bardon, Maurice. *"Don Quichotte" en France au XVIIe et au XVIIIe siècle, 1605–1815*. Paris: H. Champion, 1931.

Bass, Laura R. "Introduction: 'The *Comedia* and Cultural Control: The Legacy of José Antonio Maravall.'" *Bulletin of the Comediantes* 65, no. 1 (2013): 1–13. https://doi.org/10.1353/boc.2013.0012.

Bataillon, Marcel. "Cervantes penseur, d'après le livre d'Américo Castro." *Revue de littérature comparée* 8 (1928): 318–38.

Bataillon, Marcel. *Érasme et l'Espagne; recherches sur l'histoire spirituelle du XVIe siècle*. Paris: E. Droz, 1937.

Bataillon, Marcel. *Erasmo y el erasmismo*. Edited by Francisco Rico. Translated by Carlos Pujol. Barcelona: Editorial Crítica, 1977.

Bataillon, Marcel. *Erasmo y España: estudios sobre la historia espiritual del siglo XVI*. Mexico City: Fondo de Cultura Económica, 1950.

Batista, Perdomo. "Orígenes del cervantismo: el descubrimiento de la «patria» de Cervantes y las polémicas lingüístico-literarias de la época." *Anales Cervantinos* 51 (2019): 251–76. http://analescervantinos.revistas.csic.es/index.php/analescervantinos/article/view/455.

Bédé, Jean-Albert, and William B. Edgerton, eds. *Columbia Dictionary of Modern European Literature*. New York: Guildford, 1980.

Bell, Aubrey. "Cervantes and the Renaissance." *Hispanic Review* 2, no. 2 (1934): 89–101.

Berzal de la Rosa, Enrique. *Los comuneros: de la realidad al mito*. Madrid: Silex, 2008.

Beverley, John. "Barroco de estado: Góngora y el gongorismo." In *Del Lazarillo al sandinismo: estudios sobre la función ideológica de la literatura española e hispanoamericana*, 77–97. Ideologies and Literature, 1987.

Beverley, John. *The Failure of Latin America: Postcolonialism in Bad Times*. Pittsburgh: Pittsburgh University Press, 2019.

Beverley, John. "Going Baroque? (Baroque Literature in Spain)." *Boundary* 215, no. 3 (1988): 27–39.

Beverley, John. *Una modernidad obsoleta: estudios sobre el barroco*. Los Teques: Fondo editorial A.L.E.M., 1997.

Bibliografía del Quijote por unidades narrativas y materiales de la novela. Alcaláde Henares: Centro de Estudios Cervantinos, 2008. http://cervantes.tamu.edu/V2/Bibliografias/biblquijot/A.htm.

Bonaddio, Federico, ed. *A Companion to Federico García Lorca*. Woodbridge: Tamesis, 2010.

Borges, Jorge Luis. *Obras completas: 1923–1972*. Edited by Carlos V. Frías. Buenos Aires: Emecé Editores, 1974.

Borges, Jorge Luis. *Otras inquisiciones*. Buenos Aires: Sur, 1952. https:// apuntesliterarios.files. wordpress.com/2013/09/borges_otras_inquisiciones.pdf.

Boruchoff, David. "Cervantes y las leyes de reprensión cristiana." *Hispanic Review* 63, no. 1 (1995): 39–55.

Bosch Gimpera, Pedro. "Cervantes y un momento crucial de la Historia de España." *Cuadernos Americanos* 4 (1948): 152–60.

Bosch Gimpera, Pedro. "Dos Españas." *Las Españas: revista literaria* 2 (1946): 1 and 12.

Botti, Alfronso. "Qué es y dónde va el hispanismo historiográfico." In *Memoria del hispanismo: miradas sobre la cultura* española, edited by Joaquín Alvarez Barrientos, 149–56. Madrid: Siglo XXI de España Editores, 2015.

Bou, Enric. Afterword to *Love Poems by Pedro Salinas: My Voice because of You, and Letter Poems to Katherine*, by Pedro Salinas, 199. Translated by Willis Barnstone. Chicago: University of Chicago Press, 2010.

Bowen, Wayne H. *Spain during World War II*. Columbia: University of Missouri Press, 2006.

Bowen, Wayne H. *Truman, Franco's Spain, and the Cold War*. Columbia: Missouri University Press, 2017.

Boyd, Carolyn. *Historia Patria: Politics, History, and National Identity in Spain, 1875–1975*. Princeton, NJ: Princeton University Press, 1997.

Boyd, Stephen F., ed. *A Companion to Cervantes's Novelas Ejemplares*. Woodbridge: Tamesis, 2010.

Boyden, James. "Antonio Maravall." In *Encyclopedia of Historians and Historical Writing*, edited by Kelly Boyd, 761–2. Vol. 2. London: Fitzroy Dearborn, 1999.

Brice Heath, Shirley. "Critical Factor in Literacy Development." In *Literacy, Society, and Schooling: A Reader*, edited by Suzanne De Castell, Allan Luke, and Kieran Egan, 209–29. Cambridge: Cambridge University Press, 1985.

Briggs, Philip J. *Making American Foreign Policy: President-Congress Relations from the Second World War to the Post-Cold War Era*. Lanham, MD: Rowman & Littlefield, 1994.

Britt-Arredondo, Christopher. *Quixotism: The Imaginative Denial of Spain's Loss of Empire*. Albany: State University of New York Press, 2004.

Brownlee, Marina S., ed. *Cervantes' Persiles and the Travails of Romance*. Toronto: University of Toronto Press, 2019.

Brydan, David. *Franco's Internationalists: Social Experts and Spain's Search for Legitimacy*. Oxford: Oxford University Press, 2019.

Buckley, Ramón, and John Crispin. *Los vanguardistas españoles, 1925–1935*. Madrid: Alianza Editorial, 1977.

Bueno, Alex. "Valle de los Caídos." In *Memory and Cultural History of the Spanish Civil War: Realms of Oblivion*, edited by Aurora Morcillo, 51–110. Leiden: Brill, 2014.

Buñuel, Luis. *My Last Sigh*. New York: Vintage Books, 1983.

Burckhardt, Jacob. "Northrop Frye 1912–1991." In *Twentieth-Century Literature Criticism: Excerpts from Criticism of the Works of Novelists, Poets, Playwrights, Short Story Writers & Other Creative Writers Who Died between 1900 & 1999*, edited by Thomas J. Schoenberg and Lawrence J. Trudeau, 138–264. Detroit: Cengage Gale, 2005.

Byrd, Suzanne Wade. *La Fuente Ovejuna de Federico García Lorca*. Madrid: Pliegos, 1984.

Cahill, Kevin M. *To Bear Witness: A Journey of Healing and Solidarity, Updated, Revised, and Expanded Edition*. Oxford: Fordham University Press, 2013.

Calabrese, Omar. *Neo-Baroque: A Sign of the Times*. Translated by Charles Lambert. Princeton, NJ: Princeton University Press, 1992.

Calderón de la Barca, Pedro, and Evangelina Rodríguez. *Los cabellos de Absalón*. Madrid: Espasa-Calpe, 1989.

Calvo Serer, Rafael. *Teoría de la restauración*. Madrid: Ediciones Rialp, 1952.

Cámara Villar, Gregorio. *Fernando de los Ríos: discursos parlamentarios*. Madrid: Congreso de los Diputados, 1999.

Cano Ballesta, Juan. "Miguel y Federico: la amistad que no creció." *Información* (May 5, 1992): 6.

Cano Ballesta, Juan. "Peripecias de una amistad: Lorca y Miguél Hernández." *Cuadernos Hispanoamericanos* 433–4 (1986): 211–20.

Cano Ballesta, Juan. *La poesía española entre pureza y revolución (1930–1936)*. Madrid: Gredos, 1972.

Cano Ballesta, Juan. *Voces airadas: la otra cara de la Generación del 27*. Madrid: Cátedra, 2013.

Carlos Rovira, José. "Lorca-Hernández: crónica de un desencuentro." In *Federico Garcìa Lorca e il suo tempo, atti del congresso internazionale, Parma, 27–29 aprile 1998*, edited by Laura Dolfi, 137–50. Rome: Bulzoni, 1999.

Carpentier, Alejor. "Questions Concerning the Contemporary Latin American Novel." In *Baroque New Worlds: Representation, Transculturation, Counterconquest*, edited by Lois P. Zamora and Monika Kaup, 259–64. Durham, NC: Duke University Press, 2010.

Carretero, Anselmo. "Tradición de nuestro pueblo. Don Quijote, los Indios de la Nueva España, y la Junta Santa de Avila." *Las Españas: revista literaria* 6 (1947): 8.

Cascardi, Anthony. "Beyond Castro and Maravall: Interpellation, Mimesis, and Hegemony of Spanish Culture." In *Ideologies of Hispanism*, edited by Mabel Moraña, 138–59. Nashville, TN: Vanderbilt University Press, 2005.

Castillo, David R., and William Egginton. *Medialogies: Reading Reality in the Age of Inflationary Media*. New York: Bloomsbury Academic, 2017.

Castillo Lanca, Marta. "Las herejías literarias de García Lorca desde la estética franquista." *Lancha Boletín de Arte* 30–1 (2010): 301–25.

Castro, Américo. *De la España que aún no conocía*. Mexico City: Finisterre, 1972.

Castro, Américo. *El pensamiento de Cervantes*. Madrid: Hernando, 1925.

Castro, Américo. *Hacia Cervantes*. Madrid: Taurus, 1967.

Castro, Américo. *La peculiaridad lingüística rioplatense y su sentido histórico*. Buenos Aires: Editorial Losada, 1941.

Caudet, Francisco. *Hipótesis sobre el exilio republicano de 1939*. Madrid: Fundación universitaria española, 1997.

Celaya, Gabriel. "A Sancho Panza." *Cantos Iberos*. 1955. http://www.cervantesvirtual.com/obra-visor/antologia-poetica–51/html/00c1e984-82b2-11df-acc7-002185ce6064_2.html.

Celorio, Gonzalo. "From the Baroque to the Neobaroque." In *Baroque New Worlds: Representation, Transculturation, Counterconquest*, edited by Lois

P. Zamora and Monika Kaup, 487–507. Durham, NC: Duke University Press, 2010.

Cerezo Galán, Pedro, José María Jover Zamora, Pedro Laín Entralgo, Julián Marías, and Ramón Menéndez Pidal, eds. *La Edad de Plata de la cultura española (1898–1936)*. Madrid: Espasa-Calpe, 1993.

Cernuda, Luis. *Estudios sobre poesía española contemporánea*. Madrid: Guadarrama, 1957.

Cernuda, Luis. *Obra completa*. 3 vols. Edited by Derek Harris and Luis Maristany. Madrid: Siruela, 2002.

Cernuda, Luis. *Ocnos. Variaciones sobre tema mexicano*. México: Porrúa y Obregón, 1952.

Cernuda, Luis. *Poesía y literatura*. Barcelona: Editorial Seix Barral, 1960.

Cerutti, Mario. "Propietarios y empresarios españoles en La Laguna (1870–1910)." *Historia Mexicana* 48, no. 4 (1999): 825–70.

Cervantes Saavedra, Miguel de. *Don Quixote*. Translated by Edith Grossman. New York: HarperCollins, 2003.

Cervantes Saavedra, Miguel de. *Don Quijote de la Mancha*. Edited by Adalbert Hämel. Halle: Max Niemeyer, 1925.

Cervantes Saavedra, Miguel de. *El ingenioso hidalgo don Quijote de la Mancha*. Edited by Francisco Rodríguez Marín. Madrid: s.n., 1927.

Cervantes Saavedra, Miguel de. *El ingenioso hidalgo don Quijote de la Mancha*. Edited by L. A. Murillo. Madrid: Castalia, 1978.

Cervantes Saavedra, Miguel de. *Los trabajos de Persiles y Sigismunda*. Edited by Juan Bautista Avalle-Arce. Madrid: Castalia, 1986.

Cervantes Saavedra, Miguel de. *Los trabajos de Persiles y Sigismunda*. Edited by Laura Fernández, Ignacio García Aguilar, and Carlos Romero Muñoz, introduction by Isabel Lozano-Renieblas. Madrid: Real Academia Española, 2018.

Cervantes Saavedra, Miguel de. *The Trials of Persiles and Sigismunda: A Northern Story*. Translated by Celia Richmond Weller and Clark A. Colahan. Indianapolis, IN: Hackett Publishing Company, 1989.

Chesterton, G. K. *The Collected Works of G. K. Chesterton*. Vol. 1. Edited by David Dooley. San Francisco: Ignatius Press, 1986.

Childers, William. "Baroque Quixote: New World Writing and the Collapse of the Heroic Ideal." In *Baroque New Worlds, Representation, Transculturation, Counterconquest*, edited by Lois P. Zamora and Monika Kaup, 415–49. Durham, NC: Duke University Press, 2010.

Childers, William. *Transnational Cervantes*. Toronto: University of Toronto Press, 2006.

Ciges Aparicio, Manuel. *España bajo la dinastía de los Borbones 1701–1931*. Madrid: Aguilar, 1932.

Claret Miranda, Jaume. *El atroz desmoche: la destrucción de la Universidad española por el franquismo, 1936–1945*. Barcelona: Crítica, 2006.

Clemencín, Diego. *El comentario de Clemencín*. Barcelona: Imprenta-Escuela de la Casa Provincial de Caridad de Barcelona, 1944.

Close, Anthony J. "Don Quixote's Love for Dulcinea: A Study of Cervantine Irony." *Bulletin of Hispanic Studies* 50, no. 3 (1973): 237–55. https://doi.org/10.1080/1 475382732000350237.

Close, Anthony J. *The Romantic Approach to Don Quixote: A Critical History of the Romantic Tradition in Quixote Criticism*. Cambridge: Cambridge University Press, 1978.

Close, Anthony J. "Sobre delirios filosóficos y aproximaciones ortodoxas." In *Desviaciones lúdicas en la crítica cervantina, primer Convivo Internacional de "Locos Amenos,"* edited by Antonio Bernat Vistarini and José María Casasayas, 53–70. Salamanca: Ediciones Universidad de Salamanca, 2000.

Close, Anthony J. "Theory versus the Humanist Tradition Stemming from Américo Castro." In *Cervantes and His Postmodern Constituencies*, edited by Anne Cruz and Carroll Johnson, 1–21. New York: Garland, 1999.

Conte, Rafael. "Con permiso de los cervantistas." *El País*, November 6, 2004. https://elpais.com/diario/2004/11/06/babelia/1099701555_850215.html.

Corteguera, Luis R. "Sancho Panza Wants an Island: Cervantes and the Politics of Peasant Rulers." *Romance Quarterly* 52, no. 4 (2005): 261–70.

Cortés Ibáñez, Emilia. *Zenobia Camprubí y la Edad de Plata de la cultura española*. Seville: Universidad Internacional de Andalucía, 2010.

Costa y Martínez, Joaquín. *Crisis política de España (doble llave al sepulcro del Cid)*. Madrid: Biblioteca Costa, 1914.

Costa y Martínez, Joaquín. *Reconstitución y europeización de España: programa para un partido nacional*. Madrid: Imprenta de San Francisco de Sales, 1900.

Crooks, Esther J. *The Influence of Cervantes in France in the Seventeenth Century*. Baltimore: Johns Hopkins Press, 1931.

Croxton, Derek. *Westphalia: The Last Christian Peace*. New York: Palgrave, 2013.

Cruz, Anne J., and Carroll B. Johnson, eds. *Cervantes and His Postmodern Constituencies*. New York: Routledge, 1998.

Cuño Bonito, Justo. "Reforma y contrarreforma de la enseñanza primaria durante la II República Española y el ascenso del Fascismo (1932–1943)." *Revista Historia de la Educación Latinoamericana* 15, no. 21 (2013): 89–106.

Dadson, Trevor J. *Breve esplendor de mal distinta lumbre: estudios sobre poesía española contemporánea*. Seville: Renacimiento, 2005.

De Armas Wilson, Diana. *Cervantes, the Novel, and the New World*. Oxford: Oxford University Press, 2000.

De Armas Wilson, Diana. "Rethinking Cervantine Utopias: Some No (Good) Places in Renaissance England and Spain." *Echoes and Inscriptions. Comparative Approaches to Early Modern Spanish Literatures* Edited by Barbara Simerka and Christopher B. Weimer, 191–209. Lewisburg, PA: Bucknell University Press, 2000.

De Campos, Haroldo. "The Rule of Anthropophagy: Europe under the Sign of Devoration." In *Baroque New Worlds: Representation, Transculturation, Counterconquest*, edited by Lois P. Zamora and Monika Kaup, 319–40. Durham, NC: Duke University Press, 2010.

"Decreto del 17 de enero de 1947 por el que se crean las comisiones que han de preparar los actos conmemorativos del centenario de Cervantes." *Revista Nacional de Educación* 69 (1947): 104–5.

De la Torre, Matilde. *Don Quijote, rey de España*. 1928. Reprint, Santander: Universidad de Cantabria Press, 2010.

De Llera Esteban, Luis. *Ortega y la Edad de Plata de la Literatura Española 1914–1936*. Roma: Bulzoni, 1991.

Delgado, Manuel, and Alice Jan Poust. *Lorca, Buñuel, Dalí: Art and Theory.* Lewisburg, PA: Bucknell University Press, 2001.

De Lollis, Cesare. *Cervantes reazionario.* Rome: Fratelli Treves, 1924.

Del Río, Ángel. "Quijotismo y Cervantismo: el devenir de un símbolo." *Revista De Estudios Hispánicos* 1, no. 3 (1928): 241–67. https://revistas.upr.edu/index.php/reh/article/view/1270/1090.

De Meneses, Filipe Ribeiro. *Franco and the Spanish Civil War.* Abingdon: Taylor and Francis, 2003.

Díaz Fernández, José. *Prosas.* Madrid: Fundación Santander Central Hispano, 2006.

Díaz Fernández, José, and José Manuel López de Abiada. *El nuevo romanticismo: polémica de arte, política y literatura.* Madrid: J. Esteban, 1985.

Diaz-Plaja, Guillermo. *Don Quijote en el país de Martín Fierro.* Madrid: Ediciones de Cultura Hispánica, 1952.

Diego, Gerardo. *Gerardo Diego y el III centenario de Góngora: correspondencia inédita.* Edited by Gabriele Morelli and Luis de Góngora Y Argote. Valencia: Pre-Textos, 2001.

Diego, Gerardo. *Lola: amiga y suplemento de Carmen.* Vol. 2. Sigüenza: De Rodrigo, 1927.

Diego, Gerardo. *Obras completas, I.* Edited by Francisco Javier Díez de Revenga. Madrid: Alfaguara, 1996.

Díez Canedo, Enrique. *Letras de América: estudios sobre las literaturas continentales.* México: El Colegio de México, 1944.

Díez de Revenga, Francisco Javier. *Panorama crítico de la generación del 27.* Madrid: Editorial Castalia, 1987.

D'Olwer, Luis Nicolau. "Cervantes o la comprensión." *Las Españas: revista literaria* 5 (1947): 3.

Domenchina, Juan José. "Apostillas." *Las Españas: revista literaria* 5 (1947): 5.

Domenchina, Juan José. *Poesías escogidas; ciclo de mocedad, 1916–1921.* Madrid: Ediciones Mateu, 1922.

Domínguez, Julia. "El laberinto mental del exilio en *Don Quijote*: el testimonio del morisco Ricote." *Hispania* 92, no. 2 (2009): 183–92.

Douglas, Frances. "Contemporary Spanish Literature." *Hispania* 16, no. 4 (1933): 447–54.

Duarte-Abadía, Bibiana, and Rutgerd Boelens. "Colonizing Rural Waters: The Politics of Hydro-Territorial Transformation in the Guadalhorce Valley, Málaga, Spain." *Water International* 44, no. 2 (2019): 148–68. https://doi.org/10.1080/02508060.2019.1578080.

Ealham, Chris, and Michael Richards, eds. *The Splintering of Spain: Cultural History and the Spanish Civil War, 1936–1939.* Cambridge: Cambridge University Press, 2005.

Egginton, William. "The Baroque as a Problem of Thought." *PMLA* 124, no. 1 (2009): 143–9.

Egginton, William. "Reason's Baroque House (Cervantes, Master Architect)." In *Reason and Its Others: Italy, Spain, and the New World*, edited by David R. Castillo and Massimo Lollini, 186–203. 1st ed. Nashville, TN: Vanderbilt University Press, 2006.

Eguía Ruiz, Constancio. *Los causantes de la tragedia hispana: un gran crimen de los intelectuales españoles*. Buenos Aires: Editorial Difusión, 1938.

Ehrilicher, Hanno, and Stephen Schereckenberg, eds. *El Siglo de Oro en la España contemporánea*. Madrid: Iberoamericana, 2011.

Einstein, Carl. *A Mythology of Forms: Selected Writings on Art*. Translated by Charles Werner Haxthausen. Chicago: University of Chicago Press, 2019.

Elliott, John H. "The Decline of Spain." *Past & Present* 20 (1961): 52–75.

Elliott, John H. *History in the Making*. New Haven, CT: Yale University Press, 2012.

El Saffar, Ruth. "*Cervantes and the Romantic Approach to 'Don Quixote'* by Anthony Close." Review. *MLN* 94, no. 2 (1979): 399–405. https://doi.org/10.2307/2906755.

Enríquez Calleja, Isidoro. "Figuras de España. Emilia Pardo Bazán." *Las Españas: revista literaria* 2 (1946): 9, 12.

Espinosa, Aurelio. *The Empire of the Cities: Emperor Charles V, the Comunero Revolt, and the Transformation of the Spanish System*. Leiden: Brill, 2009.

Etherington, Ben. *Literary Primitivism*. Stanford: Stanford University Press, 2018.

Ezpeleta, Antonio. *Las historias literarias de los escritores de la generación del 27*. Madrid: Arco, 2008.

Faber, Sebastiaan. *Anglo-American Hispanists and the Spanish Civil War: Hispanophilia, Commitment, and Discipline*. New York: Palgrave Macmillan, 2008.

Faber, Sebastiaan. *Exile and Cultural Hegemony: Spanish Intellectuals in Mexico, 1939–1975*. Nashville, TN: Vanderbilt University Press, 2002.

Fagen, Patricia W. *Exiles and Citizens: Spanish Republicans in Mexico*. Austin, TX: University of Texas Press, 1973.

Fagen, Patricia W. *Transterrados y ciudadanos: los republicanos españoles en México*. Mexico City: Fondo de Cultura Económica, 1975.

Feng, Aileen A. *Writing Beloveds: Humanist Petrarchism and the Politics of Gender*. Toronto: University of Toronto Press, 2017.

Fernández Cebrián, Ana, and Víctor Pueyo. "Tener y no tener: Lecturas de Sancho Panza en la dictadura de Primo de Rivera (1923–1930)." *Bulletin of the Cervantes Society of America* 33, no. 2 (2013): 199–222.

Fernández, James. "Las américas de Don Américo: Castro entre imperio." In *Américo Castro y la revisión de la memoria: el islam en España*, edited by Eduardo Subirats, 63–81. Madrid: Libertarias/Prodhufi, 2003.

Fernández Menéndez, José María. "La generación del 36 ante el Quijote." *Revista de la Universidad de Oviedo, Facultad de Filosofía y Letras* 59 (1949): 85–106.

Fernández Nadal, Carmen María. *La política exterior de la monarquía de Carlos II: el Consejo de Estado y la Embajada en Londres, 1665–1700*. Gijón: Ateneo Jovellanos de Gijón, 2009.

Finello, Dominick. "Notes on Nineteenth-Century *Quijote* Scholarship." *Cervantes: Bulletin of the Cervantes Society of America* 7, no. 1 (1987): 59–69.

Fischer, Susan L. *Reading Performance: Spanish Golden Age Theater and Shakespeare on the Modern Stage*. Woodbridge: Tamesis, 2009.

Fischer, Susan L. "'This Thing of Darkness I/Acknowledge Mine': Segismundo, Prospero, and Shadow." In *The Prince in the Tower: Perceptions of La vida es sueño*, edited by Frederick de Armas, 147–64. Cranbury, NJ: Associated University Presses, 1993.

Fitzmaurice-Kelly, James. *A History of Spanish Literature*. New York: D. Appleton, 1921.

Fitzmaurice-Kelly, James. *The Life of Miguel de Cervantes Saavedra: A Biographical, Literary and Historical Study*. London: Chapman and Hall, 1892.

Flaccomio, Rosaria. *La fortuna del Don Quijote en italia nei secoli XVII e XVIII e il Don Chisciotti di G. Meli*. Palermo: Santi Andò e Figli, 1900.

Flores, Ángel, and M. J. Bernardete, eds. *Cervantes across the Centuries: A Quadricentennial Volume*. New York: Dryden Press, 1947.

Forcione, Alban K. *Cervantes and the Humanist Vision: A Study of Four Exemplary Novels*. 1982. Reprint, Princeton, NJ: Princeton University Press, 2017.

Ford, J. D. M., and Ruth Lansing. *Cervantes: A Tentative Bibliography of His Works and of the Biographical and Critical Material Concerning Him*. Cambridge, MA: Harvard University Press, 1931.

Foucault, Michel. *Discipline and Punish: The Birth of the Prison*. New York: Pantheon Books, 1977.

Frutos, Eugenio. "Ettore Zuani ataca a Giménez Caballero y difama a España." *El español. Semanario de la política y el espíritu* 232 (1947). April 5.

Fuentes, Carlos. *Cervantes, o la crítica de la lectura*. Alcalá de Henares: Centro de Estudios Cervantinos, 1994.

Fuentes, Carlos. *Terra nostra*. Mexico City: Editorial Joaquín Mortiz, 1975.

Gallego, Ferran. "El fascismo español y el mito de don Quijote. Una revisión." *eHumanista/Cervantes* 3 (2014): 396–41.

Gallegos Rocafull, José Manuel. *El pensamiento mexicano en los siglos XVI y XVII*. Mexico City: Universidad Nacional Autónoma de México, Facultad de Filosofía y Letras, 1974.

Gamboa Ojeda, Leticia. "De 'indios' y 'gachupines': Las fobias en las fábricas textiles de Puebla." *Tiempos de América: revista de historia, cultura y territorio* 3 (1999): 85–98. https://www.raco.cat/index.php/TiemposAmerica/article/view/105047.

Ganivet, Angel. *Idearium español*. Madrid: Librería General de Victoriano Suárez, 1905.

Gaos, Vicente. *Cervantes: novelista, dramaturgo, poeta*. Barcelona: Planeta, 1979.

Gaos, Vicente. *Claves de literatura española*. Madrid: Guadarrama, 1971.

Gaos, Vicente. *Pensamiento de lengua española*. Mexico City: Editorial Stylo, 1945.

García de Andoin, Carlos. "El erasmismo de Fernando de los Ríos." *Bulletin d'Histoire Contemporaine de l'Espagne* 51 (2017): 173–95.

García García, Bernardo José, and Antonio Álvarez-Ossorio Alvariño, eds. *Vísperas de sucesión: Europa y la monarquía de Carlos II*. Madrid: Fundación Carlos de Amberes, 2015.

García Puertas, Manuel. *Cervantes y la crisis del Renacimiento español*. Montevideo: Universidad de la República, Facultad de humanidades y ciencias, 1962.

García Santo-Tomás, Enrique. *Modernidad bajo sospecha: Salas Barbadillo y la cultura material del siglo XVII*. Madrid: Anejos de Revista de Literatura, 2008.

Gayangos, Pascual de. *Libros de caballerías*. Madrid: M. Rivadeneyra, 1857.

Geist, Anthony. *La poética de la generación del 27 y las revistas literarias: de la vanguardia al compromiso (1918–1936)*. Madrid: Guadarrama, 1980.

Genoud de Fourcade, Mariana. "Jorge Guillén: Sancho y la plenitud del ser." In *El Quijote en Buenos Aires. Lecturas Cervantinas en el Cuarto Centenario*, edited by Alicia Parodi, Julia D'Onofrio, and Juan Diego Vila, 597–602. Buenos Aires: Instituto de Filología y Literaturas Hispánicas, 2006.

Gies, David Thatcher, ed. *The Cambridge History of Spanish Literature*. Cambridge: Cambridge University Press, 2009.

Gifra-Adroher, Pere. *Between History and Romance: Travel Writing on Spain in the Early Nineteenth-Century United States*. Madison, NJ: Fairleigh Dickinson University Press, 2000.

Gil Cremades, Juan José. *El reformismo español. Krausismo, escuela histórica, neotomismo*. Esplugues de Llobregat: Ediciones Ariel, 1969.

Gili Gaya, Samuel. *Galatea o el perfecto y verdadero amor*. Madrid: [s.n.], 1948.

Giménez Caballero, Ernesto. *Don Quijote ante el mundo (y ante mí)*. San Juan, PR: Inter American University Press, 1979.

Giménez Caballero, Ernesto. *España nuestra: el libro de las juventudes españolas*. Madrid: Vicesecretaría de Educación Popular, 1943.

Giménez Caballero, Ernesto, ed. *La Gaceta literaria: ibérica-americana-internacional; letras, arte, ciencia; periódico quincenal, II*. Madrid: E. Giménez Caballero, 1927.

Giménez Caballero, Ernesto. *Genio de España: Exaltaciones a una resurrección nacional y del mundo*. Barcelona: Jerarquía, 1939.

Giménez Caballero, Ernesto. "Un peligro nacional: la vuelta de Don Quijote." *La Gaceta Literaria* 122 (February 1932): 3–6.

Giménez Caballero, Ernesto. "Visitas literarias. Gerardo Diego, poeta fascista." *El Sol*, July 26, 1927, 10.

Giménez Caballero, Ernesto, and José Carlos Mainer. *Casticismo, nacionalismo y vanguardia: (Antología, 1927–1935)*. Santander: Fundación Santander Central Hispano, 2005.

Giner Pantoja, José María. "Los amigos del Museo del Prado." *Bulletin de la Unión de Intelectuales Españoles* 4, no. 28–29 (1947). 1–2.

González Boixo, José Carlos. "El meridiano intelectual de Hispanoamérica: polémica suscitada en 1927 por La Gaceta Literaria." *Cuadernos Hispanoamericanos* 459 (1988): 166–71.

González Calleja, Eduardo. "La prensa carlista y falangista durante la Segunda República y la Guerra Civil (1931–1937)." *El argonauta español* 9 (2012): 1–37.

González de Garay Fernández, María Teresa, and Juan Aguilera Sastre, eds. *El exilio literario de 1939*. Logroño: Universidad de la Rioja, 2001.

González Fernández, José. "Volvamos a lo humano." *Post-Guerra* 10 (1928): 17–18.

Goytisolo, Juan. *Forbidden Territory and Realms of Strife: The Memoirs of Juan Goytisolo*. London: Verso, 2003.

Graf, E. C. *Cervantes and Modernity: Four Essays on Don Quijote*. Lewisburg, PA: Bucknell University Press, 2007.

Graf, E. C. "Sancho's 'por negros que sean los de he de volver blancos o amarillos' (*DQ* 1.29) and Juan de Mariana's *De moneta* of 1605." *Bulletin of the Cervantes Society of America* 31, no. 2 (2011): 23–51.

Graff, Harvey J. "The Legacies of Literacy: Continuities and Contradictions in Western Societies and Cultures." In *Literacy, Society, and Schooling: A Reader*, edited by Suzanne De Castell, Allan Luke, and Kieran Egan, 61–86. Cambridge: Cambridge University Press, 1985.

Graff, Harvey J. *The Literacy Myth: Literacy and Social Structure in the Nineteenth-Century City*. New York: Academic Press, 1979.

Graff, Harvey J. "The Literacy Myth at Thirty." *Journal of Social History* 43, no. 3 (2010): 635–61.

Graham, Helen. *The Spanish Republic at War, 1936–1939*. Cambridge: Cambridge University Press, 2002.

Grandmontagne, Francisco. "El florete aduanero." *El Sol*, July 24, 1927.

Gray, Richard T., Ruth V. Gross, Rolf J. Goebel, and Clayton Koelb. *A Franz Kafka Encyclopedia*. Westport, CT: Greenwood Press, 2005.

Greer, Margaret. "Thine and Mine: The Spanish 'Golden Age' and Early Modern Studies." *PMLA* 126, no. 1 (2011): 217–24.

Gregori, Eduardo, and Juan Herrero Senés. *Avant-Garde Cultural Practices in Spain (1914–1936): The Challenge of Modernity*. Leiden: Brill, 2016.

Guillén, Jorge. *Aire nuestro: Clamor*. Barcelona: Barral, 1977.

Guillén, Jorge. *A la altura de las circunstancias*. Buenos Aires: Sudamericana, 1963.

Guillén, Jorge. "Góngora, el cordobés." *La Gaceta Literaria* 11 (1927): 2.

Gutiérrez, Carlos. "Bibliografía del cervantismo finisecular (1880–1910)." In *Cuatro estudios de literatura*, edited by Pedro Ojeda Escudero, 97–149. Valladolid: Grammalea, 1995.

Gutiérrez, Carlos. *La espada, el rayo y la pluma: Quevedo y los campos literario y de poder*. West Lafayette, IN: Purdue University Press, 2005.

Harrison, Joseph. *An Economic History of Modern Spain*. Manchester: Manchester University Press, 1978.

Hatzfeld, Helmut A. "Thirty Years of Cervantes Criticism." *Hispania* 30, no. 3 (1947): 321–8. https://doi.org/10.2307/333406.

Heng, Geraldine. *The Invention of Race in the European Middle Ages*. New York: Cambridge University Press, 2018.

Hermida Ruiz, Aurora. "Secreta palinodia: la 'Contrautopía' de José Antonio Maravall como descargo de conciencia." *Bulletin of Hispanic Studies* 78, no. 4 (2001): 503–36. https://doi.org/10.3828/bhs.78.4.503.

Hernández, Roselie. "Furió Ceriol, Sancho Panza and Althusser: Machiavelli's Prince Reconsidered." *Bulletin of the Cervantes Society of America* 32, no. 2 (2012): 11–36.

Hernando, Miguel Angel. *Prosa vanguardista en la generación del 27: Gecé y La Gaceta literaria*. Madrid: Prensa Española, 1975.

Herrera Lasso, Ana Lía. "Una élite dentro de la élite: el Casino Español de México entre el porfiriato y la revolución (1875–1915)." *Secuencia* 42 (1998): 177–205.

Herrero, Miguel. *El ingenioso hidalgo Don Quijote de la Mancha*. Hispánica, 1939.

Herzberger, David K. *Narrating the Past: Fiction and Historiography in Postwar Spain*. Durham, NC: Duke University Press, 1995.

Hess, Carol A. *Sacred Passions: The Life and Music of Manuel de Falla.* Oxford: Oxford University Press, 2005.

Highfill, Juli. *Modernism and Its Merchandise: The Spanish Avant-Garde and Material Culture, 1920–1930.* University Park: Pennsylvania State University Press, 2014.

Hirsch, Edward. *A Poet's Glossary.* Boston: Houghton Mifflin Harcourt, 2014.

Holguín, Sandie Eleanor. *Creating Spaniards: Culture and National Identity in Republican Spain.* Madison: University of Wisconsin Press, 2002.

Howard, Jean. "The New Historicism in Renaissance Studies." In *Renaissance Historicism: Selections from English Literary Renaissance,* edited by Arthur F. Kinney and Dan S. Collins, 3–33. Amherst: University of Massachusetts Press, 1987.

Hoyos Puente, Jorge de. *¡Viva la inteligencia!: el legado de la cultura institucionista en el exilio republicano de 1939.* Madrid: Biblioteca Nueva, 2016.

Huerta Calvo, Javier. "Cervantes y Lorca: La Barraca." *Don Galán: revista de investigación teatral* 5 (2015): 13–23.

Hutchinson, Steven. "Perlas críticas surgidas a la luz del patrioterismo aplicado al *Quijote.*" In *Desviaciones lúdicas en la crítica cervantina, primer Convivio Internacional de "Locos Amenos,"* edited by Antonio Bernat Vistarini and José María Casasayas, 281–90. Salamanca: Ediciones Universidad de Salamanca, 2000.

Ibañez Martín, José. *Símbolos hispánicos del Quijote.* Madrid: [s.n.], 1947.

Imaz Echeverría, Eugenio, *Thomas More, Tommaso Campanella, and Francis Bacon. Utopías del Renacimiento.* Mexico City: Fondo de Cultura Económica, 1941.

Jarnés, Benjamín "Quevedo, figura actual" *Las Españas: revista literaria* 1 (1946): 1, 8.

Jehenson, Myriam Yvonne, and Peter Norman Dunn. *The Utopian Nexus in "Don Quixote."* Nashville, TN: Vanderbilt University Press, 2006.

Jiménez Fraud, Alberto, and Luis García de Valdeavellano. *La Residencia de Estudiantes: Visita a Maquiavelo.* Esplugues de Llobregat: Ariel, 1972.

Jiménez Torres, David. *Ramiro de Maeztu and England: Imaginaries, Realities and Repercussions of a Cultural Encounter.* Melton: Boydell & Brewer, 2016.

Johnson, Roberta. "From the Generation of 1898 to the Vanguard." In *The Cambridge Companion to the Spanish Novel from 1600 to the Present,* edited by Harriet S. Turner and Adelaida López, 155–71. New York: Cambridge University Press, 2003.

Kafka, Franz. *The Great Wall of China: Stories and Reflections.* New York: Schocken Books, 1946.

Kagan, Richard. *Spain in America: The Origins of Hispanism in the United States.* Urbana: University of Illinois Press, 2002.

Kallendorf, Hilaire, ed. *A Companion to the Spanish Renaissance.* Boston: Brill, 2019.

Kallendorf, Hilaire. *Sins of the Fathers: Moral Economies in Early Modern Spain.* Toronto: University of Toronto Press, 2013.

Kamen, Henry. "The Decline of Spain: A Historical Myth?" *Past & Present* 81 (1978): 24–50.

Kamen, Henry. *The Disinherited: Exile and the Making of Spanish Culture, 1492–1975*. New York: Harper Perennial, 2008.

Kamen, Henry. *Inquisition and Society in Spain in the Sixteenth and Seventeenth Centuries*. Bloomington: Indiana University Press, 1985.

Kamen, Henry. *The War of Succession in Spain, 1700–15*. Bloomington: Indiana University Press, 1969.

Kasten, Carey. *The Cultural Politics of Twentieth-Century Spanish Theatre: Representing the Auto Sacramental*. Lewisburg, PA: Bucknell University Press, 2012.

Kenny, Michael. "Spanish Expatriates in Mexico." *Anthropological Quarterly* 35, no. 4 (1962): 169–80.

Kerr, Lucille, and Alejandro Herrero-Olaizola, eds. *Teaching the Latin American Boom*. New York: Modern Language Association of America, 2015.

Kirkpatrick, Susan. *Mujer, modernismo y vanguardia en España: (1898–1931)*. Madrid: Cátedra, 2003.

Klemperer, Victor. "Gibt es eine spanische Renaissance?" *Logos: International Zeitschrift für Philosophie der Kultur* 16 (1927): 129–61.

Krauel, Javier. *Imperial Emotions: Cultural Responses to Myths of Empire in Fin-de-Siècle Spain*. Liverpool: Liverpool University Press, 2013.

Laguna, Ana María G. *Cervantes and the Pictorial Imagination: A Study on the Power of Images and Images of Power in Works by Cervantes*. Lewisburg, PA: Bucknell University Press, 2009.

Laguna, Ana María G. "Eroticism in Unexpected Places: Equine Love in Don Quixote." In *Sex and Gender in Cervantes/Sexo y género en Cervantes. Ensayos en honor de Adrienne Laskier Martin*, edited by Esther Fernández Rodríguez and Mercedes Alcalá Galán, 113–32. Kassel: Reichenberger, 2019.

Laguna, Ana María G. "*Life Is a Dream* and the Fractures of Reason." *MLN* 129, no. 2 (2014): 238–54.

Laguna, Ana María, and John Beusterien, eds. *Goodbye Eros: Recasting Forms and Norms of Love in the Age of Cervantes*. Toronto: University of Toronto Press, 2020.

Lahuerta, Juan J. *Dalí, Lorca y la Residencia de Estudiantes*. Madrid: Sociedad Estatal de Conmemoraciones Culturales, 2010.

Laín Entralgo, Pedro. *Descargo de conciencia, 1930–1960*. Barcelona: Barral Editores, 1976.

Laín Entralgo, Pedro. *España como problema*. Madrid: Aguilar, 1956.

Lambert, Gregg. *The Return of the Baroque in Modern Culture*. London: Continuum, 2004.

Landavazo, Marco Antonio. "Para una historia social de la violencia insurgente: el odio al gachupín." *Historia Mexicana* 59, no. 1 (July–September 2009): 195–225.

Lawrence, Mark. *The Spanish Civil Wars: A Comparative History of the First Carlist War and the Conflict of the 1930s*. London: Bloomsbury, 2017.

Layna Ranz, Francisco. "*Don Quixote* y el error americano. Matilde de la Torre revisa la historia y la política españolas en los preliminares de la Guerra Civil." In *Cervantes Transatlántico/Transatlantic Cervantes*, edited by Francisco Ramírez Santacruz and Pedro Angel Palou, 15–32. New York: Peter Lang, 2019.

Ledesma Ramos, Ramiro. *Discurso a las juventudes de España.* 1939. Reprint, Madrid: Ediciones F.E, 1942.

Ledesma Ramos, Ramiro. "Grandezas de Unamuno." *La conquista del estado* 2 (March 1931): 1. http://filosofia.org/hem/193/lce/lce021a.htm.

Lezama Lima, José. "Baroque Curiosity." In *Baroque New Worlds: Representation, Transculturation, Counterconquest,* edited by Lois P. Zamora and Monika Kaup, 212–40. Durham, NC: Duke University Press, 2010.

Lezra, Jacques. *"Contra todos los fueros de la muerte": El suceso cervantino.* Adrogué, Argentina: La Cebra, 2016.

Lida, Clara. "Los españoles en el México independiente: 1821–1950. Un estado de la cuestión." *Historia Mexicana* 56, no. 2 (2006): 613–50.

Llera Esteban, Luis de. *Ortega y la edad de plata de la literatura española (1914–1936).* Rome: Bulzoni, 1991.

Llera Esteban, Luis de. *El último exilio español en América: grandeza y miseria de una formidable aventura.* Madrid: Mapfre, 1996.

Lloréns, Vicente. *La emigración republicana.* Madrid: Taurus, 1976.

López Morillas, Juan. *El krausismo español: perfil de una aventura intelectual.* Mexico City: Fondo de Cultura Económica, 1956.

López Morillas, Juan. *The Krausist Movement and Ideological Change in Spain, 1854–1874.* Translated by Frances M. López-Morillas. Cambridge: Cambridge University Press, 1981.

Lorca, Daniel. "The Epistemic and Emotive Foundations of Sancho." *Bulletin of the Cervantes Society of America* 35, no. 2 (2015): 77–102.

Lorca, Federico García. *Obras completas.* Edited by Arturo del Hoyo. Madrid: Aguilar, 1964.

Lozano Renieblas, Isabel. *Cervantes y el mundo del Persiles.* Alcalá de Henares: Centro de Estudios Cervantinos, 1998.

Luelmo, Julio. "La estirpe caballeresca que destruyó Alonso Quijano El Bueno." *Nuestro Tiempo* 5 (1952): 57–68.

Luelmo, Julio. "Los valores renacentistas en la obra de Cervantes." *Las Españas* 5 (1947): 8.

Lyons, John D., ed. *The Oxford Handbook of the Baroque.* New York: Oxford University Press, 2019.

Machado, Antonio. "Carta a David Vigodsky." *Hora de España* 4 (April 1937): 5–10.

MacKay, Ruth. "The Maravall Problem: A Historical Inquiry." *Bulletin of the Comediantes* 65, no. 1 (2013): 45–56. https://doi.org/10.1353/boc.2013.0000.

Maeztu, Ramiro de. *Don Quijote, don Juan y la Celestina: Ensayos en simpatía.* Madrid: Espasa-Calpe, 1939.

Mainer, José Carlos. "Cervantes (y sus personajes), vistos desde el exilio." In *Cervantes y la narrativa moderna,* edited by László Scholz and László Vasas, 104–22. Debrecen, Hungary: University of Debrecen, 2001.

Mainer, José Carlos. *La Edad de Plata (1902–1931): Ensayo de interpretación de un proceso cultural.* Barcelona: Ediciones Asenet, 1975.

Mainer, José Carlos. *La Edad de Plata (1902–1939): Ensayo de interpretación de un proceso cultural.* Madrid: Cátedra, 1981.

Mainer, José Carlos. *Historia de la literatura española. 1900–1939.* Vol. 6. Barcelona: Crítica, 2010.

Mainer, José Carlos. *Modernismo y 98*. Barcelona: Editorial Crítica, 1994.

Mainer, José Carlos. *Moradores de Sansueña: lecturas cervantinas de los exiliados republicanos de 1939*. Valladolid: Universidad de Valladolid, Servicio de Publicaciones e Intercambio Editorial, 2006.

Mainer, José Carlos. "Of Periodizations and Polemics." In "Repositioning Modernity, Modernism, and the Avant-Garde in Spain: A Transatlantic Debate at the Residencia de Estudiantes," *Romance Quarterly* 66, no. 4 (2019): 159–72. https://doi.org/10.1080/08831157.2019.1677413.

Maldonado de Guevara, Francisco. *La maiestas cesárea en el Quijote*. Madrid: [s.n.], 1948.

Malo de Molina, José Luis, and Pablo Martín-Aceña, eds. *The Spanish Financial System: Growth and Development since 1900*. Basingstoke: Palgrave Macmillan, 2011.

Mangini González, Shirley. *Las modernas de Madrid: las grandes intelectuales españolas de la vanguardia*. Barcelona: Ediciones Península, 2001.

Maravall, José Antonio. *Carlos V y el pensamiento político del Renacimiento*. Madrid: Instituto de Estudios Políticos, 1960.

Maravall, José Antonio. *Las comunidades de Castilla. Una primera revolución moderna*. Madrid: Revista de Occidente, 1963.

Maravall, José Antonio. *Culture of the Baroque: Analysis of a Historical Structure*. Minneapolis: University of Minnesota Press, 1986.

Maravall, José Antonio. "Las etapas del pensamiento político de Carlos V." *Revista de estudios políticos* 100 (1958): 95–146.

Maravall, José Antonio. *El humanismo de las armas en Don Quijote*. Madrid: Instituto de Etudios Políticos, 1948.

Maravall, José Antonio. *Utopia and Counterutopia in the "Quixote."* Detroit: Wayne State University Press, 1991.

Marcilhacy, David. "La Hispanidad bajo el franquismo: el americanismo al servicio de un proyecto nacionalista." In *Imaginarios y representaciones de España durante el Franquismo*, edited by Xosé M. Núñez Seixas and Stéphane Michonneau, 73–102. Madrid: Casa de Velázquez, 2014.

Marín García de Robles, José Pedro, and Alvaro Moreno Egido. "Los expedientes de revisión de depuración del Magisterio español en el Archivo Central de Educación." Archivo Central de la Secretaría de Estado de Educación (ACME). http://www.mecd.gob.es/servicios-al-ciudadano-mecd/dms/mecd/servicios-al-ciudadano-mecd/archivo-central/educar-archivos/comision-depuracion/Revision-depuracion.pdf. Accessed on November 27, 2019.

Mariscal, George. *Contradictory Subjects: Quevedo, Cervantes, and Seventeenth-Century Spanish Culture*. Ithaca, NY: Cornell University Press, 1991.

Márquez Villanueva, Francisco. "Erasmo y Cervantes, una vez más." *Cervantes: Bulletin of the Cervantes Society of America* 4, no. 2 (1984): 123–37.

Marrero, Vicente. *La Guerra Española y el trust de cerebros*. Madrid: Ediciones Punta Europa, 1961.

Marsé, Juan. *La muchacha de las bragas de oro: novela*. Barcelona: Planeta, 1978.

Martí, José. "Seis Conferencias." In *Obras completas*, 5: 119–22. Havana: Centro de Estudios Martianos, 2011.

Martin, Adrienne Laskier. *Cervantes and the Burlesque Sonnet*. Berkeley, CA: University of California Press, 1991.

Martín Baez, Argentinian Antonio. "Entrevista." In *El exilio español en México, 1939–1982*, edited by José Alameda, 896–900. Mexico City: Fondo de Cultura Económica-Salvat, 1982.

Martín Ezpeleta, Antonio. *Las historias literarias de los escritores de la Generación del 27*. Madrid: Arco/Libros, 2008.

Martín Rogero, Nieves. "El uso del Quijote en el aula. Revisión histórica de ediciones escolares y paratextos didácticos." *OCNOS* 3 (2007): 77–90.

Martínez Ruiz, José. *Con permiso de los cervantistas*. Madrid: Biblioteca Nueva, 1948.

Mendelson, Jordana. *Documenting Spain: Artists, Exhibition Culture, and the Modern Nation, 1929–1939*. University Park: Pennsylvania State University Press, 2005.

Menéndez Pelayo, Marcelino. *Historia de los heterodoxos Españoles*. Madrid: Libréria Católica de San José, 1881.

Mitchell, Timothy. *Flamenco Deep Song*. New Haven, CT: Yale University Press, 1994.

Monferrer Catalán, Luis. *Odisea en Albión: los republicanos españoles exiliados en Gran Bretaña, 1936–1977*. Madrid: Ediciones de la Torre, 2007.

Montero Reguera, José. *Cervantismos de ayer y hoy: capítulos de historia cultural hispánica*. San Vicente del Raspeig: Universidad de Alicante, 2011.

Montilla, Francisca. *Selección de libros escolares de lectura*. Madrid: Consejo Superior de Investigaciones Científicas, 1954.

Moradiellos, Enrique. *Franco: Anatomy of a Dictator*. London: I.B. Tauris, 2018.

Moraña, Mabel. *Ideologies of Hispanism*. Nashville, TN: Vanderbilt University Press, 2005.

Moreno Luzón, Javier. *Modernizing the Nation: Spain during the Reign of Alfonso XIII, 1902–1931*. Brighton: Sussex Academic Press, 2012.

Moreno Luzón, Javier. "The Restoration: 1874–1914." In *The History of Modern Spain: Chronologies, Themes, Individuals*, edited by Adrian Shubert and José Alvarez Junco, 46–63. London: Bloomsbury Academic, 2018.

Moreno Villa, José. *Nueva cornucopia mexicana*. México: La casa de España en México, 1940.

Morente Valero, Francisco. *La escuela y el estado nuevo: la depuración del magisterio nacional, 1936–1943*. Valladolid: Ambito, 1997.

Moss, Grant D. *Political Poetry in the Wake of the Second Spanish Republic: Rafael Alberti, Pablo Neruda, and Nicolás Guillén*. London: Lexington Books, 2018.

Murga Castro, Idoia. *Escenografía de la danza en la Edad de Plata (1916–1936)*. Madrid: Consejo Superior de Investigaciones Científicas, 2009.

Naharro Calderón, Jose María. "Twentieth-Century Literature in Exile." In *The Cambridge History of Spanish Literature*, edited by David Thatcher Gies, 620–7. Cambridge: Cambridge University Press, 2009.

Navarro, Aaron W. *Political Intelligence and the Creation of Modern Mexico, 1938–1954*. University Park: Pennsylvania State University Press, 2010.

Navas Ocaña, María Isabel. *España y las vanguardias*. Almería: Universidad de Almería, Almeria: Servicio de Publicaciones, 1997.

Nemser, Daniel. "Governor Sancho and the Politics of Insularity." *Hispanic Review* 78, no. 1 (2010): 1–23.

Nesvig, Martin Austin. *Ideology and Inquisition: The World of the Censors in Early Mexico*. New Haven, CT: Yale University Press, 2009.

Ocampo, Francisco, Nicholas Spadaccini, and Luis Martín-Estudillo. "Debating Hispanic Studies: Reflections on Our Disciplines. Introduction." *Hispanic Issues* 1, no. 1 (2006): 23–9. http://hdl.handle.net/11299/182513.

Oelschläger, Victor. "More Cervantine Bibliography." *Hispania* 33, no. 2 (1950): 144–50.

Ojeda Revah, Mario. *Mexico and the Spanish Civil War: Political Repercussions for the Republican Cause*. Eastbourne: Sussex Academic Press, 2016.

Oloff, Kerstin. "*Terra Nostra* and the Rewriting of the Modern Subject: Archetypes, Myth, and Selfhood." *Latin American Research Review* 46, no. 3 (2011): 3–20.

Onnekink, David. *War and Religion after Westphalia, 1648–1713*. London: Taylor and Francis, 2016.

Orringer, Nelson R. *Lorca in Tune with Falla: Literary and Musical Interludes*. Toronto: University of Toronto Press, 2014.

Ortega y Gasset, José. *Meditaciones del Quijote: meditación preliminar, meditación primera*. Madrid: Residencia de Estudiantes, 1914.

Ortega y Medina, Juan. "La aportación de los historiadores españoles trasterrados a la historiografía mexicana." *Estudios Historia moderna y contemporánea de México* 10 (1986): 255–79.

Otero, Roberto. *Lejos de España: encuentros y conversaciones con Picasso*. Barcelona: Dopesa, 1975.

Pabón Núñez, Lucio. "Sancho, o la exaltación del pueblo Español." *Cuadernos* 197 (1964): 541–80.

Pardo Bazán, Emilia. "Los pedágogos del Renacimiento: Erasmo, Rabelais y Montaigne." *Boletín de la Institución libre de enseñanza* 13 (1917): 129–32.

Pasamar Alzuria, Gonzalo. *Apologia and Criticism: Historians and the History of Spain, 1500–2000*. Oxford: Peter Lang, 2010.

Pasamar Alzuria, Gonzalo. *Historiografía e ideología en la posguerra Española: la ruptura de la tradición liberal*. Zaragoza: Prensas Universitarias de Zaragoza, 1991.

Pastor Comín, Juan José, and Ángel Gregorio Cano Vela. "*Don Quijote*" en el aula: la aventura pedagógica*. Cuenca: Universidad de Castilla-La Mancha, 2006.

Payne, Stanley G. *The Collapse of the Spanish Republic, 1933–1936: Origins of the Civil War*. New Haven, CT: Yale University Press, 2006.

Payne, Stanley G. *Fascism in Spain, 1923–1977*. Madison: University of Wisconsin Press, 1999.

Payne, Stanley G. *Franco and Hitler: Spain, Germany, and World War II*. New Haven, CT: Yale University Press, 2008.

Payne, Stanley G. *The Franco Regime, 1936–1975*. Madison: University of Wisconsin Press, 1987.

Payne, Stanley G. *A History of Spain and Portugal*. Madison: University of Wisconsin Press, 1973.

Payne, Stanley G., and Javier Tusell. *La guerra civil: una nueva visión del conflicto que dividió España*. Madrid: Temas de Hoy, 1996.

Pemartín, José. *Qué es "lo nuevo" … Consideraciones sobre el momento español presente*. Santander: Cultura española, 1938.

Pérez, Dionisio. *El enigma de Joaquín Costa: ¿revolucionario? ¿oligarquista?* Madrid: Compañía ibero-americana de Publicaciones, 1930.

Pérez, Dionisio. "Resurrección de Cervantes en el Mundo." *ABC*, December 16, 1931.

Pérez, Janet, and Maureen Ihrie, eds. *The Feminist Encyclopedia of Spanish Literature*. Westport, CT: Greenwood Press, 2002.

Pérez Fuentes, Pilar. "La emigración española a América en los siglos XIX y XX." Ministerio de Trabajo y asuntos sociales (Entre dos orillas), 2009. http://ies-valledelhenares.centros.castillalamancha.es/sites/ies-valledelhenares.centros.castillalamancha.es/files/descargas/emigracion_espanola_a_america_0.pdf

Pérez-Magallón, Jesús. *Cervantes, monumento de la nación: problemas de identidad y cultura*. Madrid: Cátedra, 2015.

Pérez Moral, Lourdes. "Entre la politización y la instrucción: el giennense don Ángel Cruz Rueda 1930–1942." *Boletin del Instituto de Estudios Giennenses* 195 (2005): 213–24.

Pérez Vejo, Tomás. "España en el imaginario mexicano. El choque del exilio." In *De Madrid a México: el exilio español y su impacto sobre el pensamiento, la ciencia y el sistema educativo mexicano*, edited by Silvia Figueroa Zamudio and Agustín Sánchez Andrés, 23–93. Morelia: Universidad Michoacana de San Nicoláas de Hidalgo, 2001.

Perrault, Pierre. *Critique du livre de Dom Quichotte de la Manche*. Edited by Maurice Bardon. Paris: Les Presses modernes, 1930.

Peyrot Marcos, Beatriz. "Isabel Esteban Nieto." *Maestras Republicanas* (blog), March 7, 2013. http://maestrasrepublicanas.blogspot.com.es/2013_03_07_archive.html.

Phillips, Carla Rahn. "Time and Duration: A Model for the Economy of Early Modern Spain." *The American Historical Review* 92, no. 3 (1987): 531–62.

Picasso, Pablo. *El entierro del Conde de Orgaz: ilustrado con 12 grabados al cobre*. Barcelona: Gustavo Gili and Ediciones Cometa, 1969.

Picasso, Pablo. *Gongora*. Translated by Alan S. Trueblood. New York: G. Braziller, 1985.

Pike, Frederick B. *Hispanismo, 1898–1936: Spanish Conservatives and Liberals and Their Relations with Spanish America*. Notre Dame: University of Notre Dame Press, 1971.

Piña, Francisco. "El hambre de Camilo J. Cela." *Las Españas: revista literaria* 13 (1949): 11–12.

Piñero Díaz, Buenaventura. "Visión del mundo en *El Quijote* a través de Sancho Panza." In *Cervantes: su obra y su mundo*, edited by Manuel Criado Del Val, 539–53. Madrid: EDI-6, 1981.

Poch Noguer, José. *Don Miguel de Cervantes Saavedra*. Gerona: Dalmau Carles, 1936.

Poggioli, Renato. *The Theory of the Avant-Garde*. Translated by Gerald Fitzgerald. Cambridge, MA: Belknap Press of Harvard University Press, 1968.

Posada, Adolfo. *Breve historia del krausismo español*. Oviedo: Universidad de Oviedo, Servicio de Publicaciones, 1981.

Pradera, Víctor. *El estado nuevo*. Madrid: Editorial Española, 1937.

Preston, Paul. *The Politics of Revenge: Fascism and the Military in Twentieth-Century Spain*. London: Routledge, 1995.

Preston, Paul. *Revolution and War in Spain, 1931–1939*. London: Routledge, 1984.

Preston, Paul. *The Spanish Holocaust: Inquisition and Extermination in Twentieth-Century Spain*. New York: W. W. Norton, 2013.

Prieto de Paula, Ángel L., and María del Mar Langa Pizarro. *Manual de literatura española actual*. Madrid: Editorial Castalia, 2011.

Puente, Jorge. "Los estudios del exilio republicano de 1939: una mirada personal." *Dictatorship and Democracies* 5 (2017): 232–85. https://www.researchgate.net/publication/328978212_Los_estudios_del_exilio_republicano_de_1939_a_revision_una_mirada_personal.

Puig-Espert, Francisco. "Grandeza y miseria de un pueblo (Contribución a la historia del Siglo de Oro español)." *Boletín de la Unión de Intelectuales Españoles* 4, no. 26 (1947): 5–10.

Pujadas, Joan. "*Historia de la etnología* de Ángel Palerm: humanismo y criticismo al servicio de una visión postcolonial de la antropología." *Desacatos* 45 (2014). http://www.scielo.org.mx/scielo.php?script=sci_arttext&pid=S1607-050X2014000200013.

Pulido Tirado, Genara. "El Quijote en el pensamiento literario de los exiliados españoles del 39." In *El Quijote y el pensamiento teórico-literario: actas del congreso internacional celebrado en Madrid los días 20 al 24 de junio de 2005*, edited by Miguel Ángel Garrido Gallardo and Luis Alburquerque, 447–68. Madrid: Consejo Superior de Investigaciones Científicas, 2008.

Qualia, Charles B. "Cervantes, Soldier and Humanist." *The South Central Bulletin* 4, no.1 (1949): 1–11.

Rafart I Planas, Claustre. *Picasso's Las Meninas*. Barcelona: Editorial Meteora, 2001.

Ramírez Santacruz, Francisco, and Pedro Angel Palou, eds. *Cervantes Transatlántico/Transatlantic Cervantes*. New York: Peter Lang, 2019.

Ramos Ortega, Manuel. *Las revistas literarias en España entre la "edad de plata" y el medio siglo: una aproximación histórica*. Madrid: Ediciones de la Torre, 2001.

Ramos Ortega, Manuel, and José Ma Barrera López, eds. *Revistas literarias españolas del siglo XX (1919–1975)*. Madrid: Ollero y Ramos, 2005.

Read, Peter. *Picasso and Apollinaire: The Persistence of Memory*. Berkeley, CA: University of California Press, 2008.

Rebolledo, José Enrique. "Sobre el quijotismo de Sancho Panza." *Las Españas: revista literaria* 5 (1947): 8.

Redondo, Agustín. "La recepción del [sic] Erasmo y España de Bataillon (1937–1950)." In *Erasmo y España. 75 años de la obra de Marcel Bataillon (1937–2012)*, edited by Eliseo Serrano, 17–52. Zaragoza: Institución Fernando el Católico, 2015.

Regàs, Rosa. "Creo que hemos tenido una educación siniestra." *El País*, May 14, 2013. https://elpais.com/elpais/2013/05/13/eps/1368455992_855263.html.

Reguera, José Montero. *Quijote y la crítica contemporánea*. Alcalá de Henares: Centro de Estudios Cervantinos, 1997.

Reher, David Sven. *Perspectives on the Family in Spain, Past and Present*. New York: Clarendon Press, 1997.

Rejano, Juan. *La esfinge mestiza: crónica menor de México*. Mexico City: Leyenda, 1948.

Resina, Joan Ramon. "Cold War Hispanism and the New Deal of Cultural Studies." In *Spain Beyond Spain: Modernity, Literary History, and National Identity*, edited by Brad Epps and Luis Fernández Cifuentes, 70–108. Lewisburg, PA: Bucknell University Press, 2005.

Resina, Joan Ramon. "A Spectre Is Haunting Spain: The Spirit of the Land in the Wake of the Disaster." *Journal of Spanish Cultural Studies* 2, no. 2 (2001): 169–86.

Revilla, Manuel de la. *Obras de D. Manuel de la Revilla*. Edited by Antonio Cánovas Del Castillo and U. González Serrano. Madrid: Imprenta central de V. Saiz, 1883.

Ribagorda, Álvaro. *Caminos de la modernidad: espacios e instituciones culturales de la Edad de Plata (1898–1936)*. Madrid: Biblioteca Nueva, 2009.

Ridruejo, Dionisio. *Memorias de una imaginación: papeles escogidos e inéditos*. Madrid: Clan, 1993.

Riley, E.C. "Cervantes and the Cynics (*El licenciado Vidriera* and *El coloquio de los perros*)." *Bulletin of Hispanic Studies* 53, no. 3 (1976): 189–99. https://doi.org/10.1080/1475382762000353189.

Robbins, Jeremy. "Renaissance and Baroque: Continuity and Transformation in Early Modern Spain." In *The Cambridge History of Spanish Literature*, edited by David Thatcher Gies, 137–49. Cambridge: Cambridge University Press, 2004.

Rodríguez Barreira, Óscar J. *Poder y actitudes sociales durante la postguerra en Almería (1939–1953)*. Almería: Editorial Universidad de Almería, 2007.

Rodríguez Escalona, Guillermo Fernández. "Pensamiento politico y concepción del mundo en Cervantes: el gobierno de la ínsula Barataria." *Bulletin of the Cervantes Society of America* 31, no. 2 (2011): 125–52.

Rodriguéz Marcos, Javier. "Amor y odio en la Generación del 27." *El País*, April 22, 2012.

Rodríguez Puértolas, Julio. *Historia de la literatura fascista española*. Madrid: Akal, 2008.

Rodríguez Solás, David. "La Barraca, 1933: el giro lopiano de García Lorca." *Anuario Lope de Vega* 22 (2016): 200–16. http://dx.doi.org/10.5565/rev/anuariolopedevega.148

Rojas Otálora, Jorge Enrique. "El cervantismo." *Literatura, teoría, historia, y crítica* 7 (2005): 293–302.

Romero, Francisco, ed. *Realidad: revista de ideas*. Buenos Aires 1947–49. Sevilla: Renacimiento, 2007.

Rona, José Pedro. "Américo Castro, *La peculiaridad lingüística rioplatense y su sentido histórico*. Segunda edición muy renovada. Madrid, Taurus, 1961." Review. *Anuario de Letras, Universidad Autónoma de México* 4 (1964): 332–7. https://revistas-filologicas.unam.mx/anuario-letras/index.php/al/article/view/1179.

Roniger, Luis, James Naylor Green, and Pablo Yankelevich, eds. *Exile and the Politics of Exclusion in the Americas*. Brighton: Sussex Academic Press, 2012.

Rozas, Juan Manuel. *El 27 como generación*. Santander: Sur, 1978.

Ruiz de Funes, Mariano. "Encuesta sobre la penetración franquista en América." *Las Españas: revista literaria* 10 (1948), 12.

Ruiz de Funes, Mariano. "Un Instituto Hispánico A.M.D.G." *Las Españas: revista literaria* 10 (1948): 12.

Ruta, Maria Caterina. *Memoria del Quijote.* Alcalá de Henares: Centro de Estudios Cervantinos, 2008.

Salinas, Pedro. *Ensayos completos 3.* Edited by Solita Salinas de Marichal. Madrid: Taurus, 1983.

Salinas, Pedro. *Ensayos de literatura hispánica.* Edited by Juan Marichal. Madrid: Aguilar, 1961.

Salinas, Pedro. "La mejor carta de amores de la literatura española." 1952. Reprinted in *La generación del 27 visita a Don Quijote*, edited by Jesús García Sánchez, 39–55. Madrid: Visor, 2005.

Salinas, Pedro. *Obras completas.* 3 vols. Edited by Enric Bou, Monserrat Escarpín Gual, and Andrés Soria Olmedo. Madrid: Cátedra, 2007.

Salinas, Pedro. *Pasajero en las Américas: cartas y ensayos del exilio.* Edited by Enric Bou. Mexico City: Fondo de Cultura Económica, 2007.

Salinas, Pedro. *Quijote y lectura: defensas y fragmentos.* Edited by Enric Bou. Madrid: ELR Ediciones, 2005.

Salinas, Pedro, and Jorge Guillén. *Correspondencia (1923–1951).* Edited by Andrés Soria Olmedo. Barcelona: Tusquets, 1992.

Sánchez Albornoz, Nicolás. *The Economic Modernization of Spain, 1830–1930.* New York: New York University Press, 1987.

Sánchez de Madariaga, Elena, and Consuelo Flecha. *Las maestras de la República.* Madrid: Catarata, 2012.

Sánchez Mazas, Rafael. "A don Angelito, sobre la compasión a Don Quijote." *El español, Semanario de la política y el espíritu* 11–12 (January 1943).

Sánchez Moltó, Vicente. "Una celebración marcada por las postguerras: el IV centenario del nacimiento de Cervantes." *eHumanista/Cervantes* 3 (2014): 465–555.

Sarduy, Severo. "The Baroque and the Neobaroque." In *Baroque New Worlds: Representation, Transculturation, Counterconquest*, edited by Lois P. Zamora and Monika Kaup, 270–91. Durham, NC: Duke University Press, 2010.

Saz Campos, Ismael. *España contra España: los nacionalismos franquistas.* Madrid: Marcial Pons, 2003.

Saz Campos, Ismael. "Entre el fascismo y la tradición. La percepción franquista del Siglo de Oro." In *Tradicionalismo y fascismo europeo*, edited by María Victoria Grillo, 35–53. Buenos Aires: EUDEBA, 1999.

Schammah Gesser, Silvina. *Madrid's Forgotten Avant-Garde: Between Essentialism and Modernity.* Brighton: Sussex Academic Press, 2015.

Schmidt, Rachel Lynn. *Forms of Modernity: Don Quixote and Modern Theories of the Novel.* Toronto: University of Toronto Press, 2011.

Schmidt, Rachel Lynn. "Introduction: A Consideration of Lay Knowledge in Early Modern Spain." *Cervantes: Bulletin of the Cervantes Society of America* 39, no. 1 (2019): 14–28. https://doi.org/10.1353/cer.2019.0003.

Schmitz, Ryan. "Sancho's Courtly Performance: *Discrección* and the Art of Conversation in the Ducal Palace Episodes of *Don Quijote* II." *MLN* 128, no. 2 (2013): 445–55.

Schuler, Friedrich Engelbert. *Mexico Between Hitler and Roosevelt: Mexican Foreign Relations in the Age of Lázaro Cárdenas, 1934–1940.* Albuquerque: University of New Mexico Press, 1998.

Selva, Enrique. *Ernesto Giménez Caballero, entre la vanguardia y el fascismo.* Valencia: Pre-Textos, 2000.

Sender, Ramón José. *Examen de ingenios: los noventayochos; ensayos críticos*. New York: Las Américas, 1961.

Sender, Ramón José. "Hace cuatro siglos de Cervantes." *Las Españas: revista literaria* 4 (1947): 3.

Serrano, Eliseo, ed. *Erasmo y España: 75 años de la obra de marcel Bataillon (1937–2012)*. Zaragoza: Institución Fernando el Católico, 2015.

Shaw, Lisa, and Stephanie Dennison. *Pop Culture Latin America!: Media, Arts, and Lifestyle*. Santa Barbara, CA: ABC-CLIO, 2005.

Silva Herzog, Jesús. "Entrevista." In *El exilio español en México, 1939–1982*, edited by José Alameda, 886–90. Mexico City: Fondo de Cultura Económica-Salvat, 1982.

Sinclair, Alison. *Trafficking Knowledge in Early Twentieth-Century Spain: Centres of Exchange and Cultural Imaginaries*. Woodbridge: Tamesis, 2009.

Sinclair, Alison, and Richard Cleminson. "Alternative Discourses in Early Twentieth-Century Spain: Intellectuals, Dissent and Subcultures of Mind and Body." *Bulletin of Spanish Studies* 81, no. 6 (2004): 687–95. https://doi.org/10.1080/1475382042000272247.

Soufas, Christopher. *The Subject in Question: Early Contemporary Spanish Literature and Modernism*. Washington, DC: Catholic University of America Press, 2007.

Southworth, Herbert Rutledge. *Conspiracy and the Spanish Civil War: The Brainwashing of Francisco Franco*. London: Routledge, 2002.

Southworth, Herbert Rutledge. *El mito de la cruzada de Franco*. Paris: Ruedo Ibérico, 1963.

Souto Alabarce, Arturo. "Letras." In *El exilio español en México, 1939–1982*, edited by José Alameda, 363–402. Mexico City: Fondo de Cultura Económica-Salvat, 1982.

Steiner, Wendy. *Pictures of Romance: Form against Context in Painting and Literature*. Chicago: University of Chicago Press, 1988.

Stevens, Wallace. *The Necessary Angel: Essays on Reality and the Imagination*. New York: Random House, 1951.

Storrs, Christopher. *The Resilience of the Spanish Monarchy, 1665–1700*. Oxford: Oxford University Press, 2006.

Strosetzki, Christoph, ed. *Aspectos actuales del hispanismo mundial: Literatura – Cultura – Lengua*. Berlin: De Gruyter, 2018.

Stroud, Matthew D. "Infallible Texts and Righteous Interpretations: Don Quijote and Religious Fundamentalism." In *Cervantes y su mundo III*, edited by A. Robert Lauer and Kurt Reichenberger, 543–58. Kassel: Edition Reichenberger, 2005.

Suances Marcos, Manuel A. *Historia de la filosofía española contemporánea*. Madrid: Síntesis, 2006.

Sueiro Seoane, Susana. "Spanish Colonialism during Primo de Rivera's Dictatorship." In *Spain and the Mediterranean since 1898*, edited by Raanan Rein, 48–64. London: Routledge, 1999.

Suñé Benages, Juan, and Juan Suñé Fonbuena. *Bibliografía crítica de ediciones del Quijote: impresas desde 1605 hasta 1917*. Edited by J. D. M. Ford and C. T. Keller. Cambridge, MA: Harvard University Press, 1939.

Suñer Ordóñez, Enrique. *Los intelectuales y la tragedia española*. San Sebastián: Editorial Española, 1938.

Tambling, Jeremy. *On Anachronism*. Manchester: Manchester University Press, 2013.

Tapia, Daniel. "Don Quijote desterrado." *Las Españas*: revista literaria 5 (1947): 5.

Tedde de Lorca, Pedro. "De la primera a la segunda Restauración." *Ayer* 21 (1996): 15–49.

Teresa de León, Maria. "El teatro internacional. Teatro de masas." *El Heraldo de Madrid*, July 7, 1933.

Thacker, Jonathan. *Role-Play and the World as Stage in the Comedia*. Liverpool: Liverpool University Press, 2002.

Thomas, Henry. *Las novelas de caballerías españolas y portuguesas: despertar de la novela caballeresca en la Península Ibérica y expansión e influencia en el extranjero*. Translated by Esteban Pujals. Madrid: Consejo Superior de Investigaciones Científicas, 1952.

Thomas, Henry. *Spanish and Portuguese Romances of Chivalry in the Spanish Peninsula, and Its Extensions and Influence Abroad*. Cambridge: Cambridge University Press, 1920.

Torrente Ballester, Gonzalo. "Presencia en América de la España fugitiva." *Tajo*, August 3, 1940.

Torres, Federico. *Miguel de Cervantes*. Serradilla: Sánchez Rodrigo, 1936.

Tortella Casares, Gabriel. *The Development of Modern Spain: An Economic History of the Nineteenth and Twentieth Centuries*. Cambridge, MA: Harvard University Press, 2000.

Trapiello, Andrés. "Leer, vivir?" In *Libros, buquinistas y bibliotecas: crónicas de un transeúnte: Madrid-París*, edited by Azorín and Francisco Fuster García, 5. Madrid: Fórcola, 2014. http://www.elboomeran.com/upload/ficheros/obras/02_azorn_adelanto.pdf.

Trend, J. B. *The Origins of Modern Spain*. London: Constable, 1921.

Ugarte, Manuel. *El porvenir de la América española. La raza, la integridad territorial y moral, la organización interior*. Valencia: Prometeo, 1920.

Ugarte, Michael. *Shifting Ground: Spanish Civil War Exile Literature*. Durham, NC: Duke University Press, 1989.

Unamuno, Miguel de. *Obras completas*. Vol. 3. Edited by Manuel García Blanco. Madrid: Escelicer, 1966.

Unamuno, Miguel de. *Vida de Don Quijote y Sancho*. Madrid: Astral, 1908.

UNESCO. *Interrelations of Cultures: Their Contributions to International Understanding*. Case study. Paris: UNESCO, 1953.

UNESCO. *A New Humanism for the 21st Century*. Press release. 2010. http://www.unesco.org/new/en/media-services/single-view/news/a_new_humanism_for_the_21st_century/.

Urbina, Eduardo. *El sin par Sancho Panza: parodia y creación*. Barcelona: Anthropos, 1991.

Valdés, Juan de, and Lore Terracini. *Diálogo de la lengua*. Modena: Società tipografica modenese, 1957.

Valender, James, and Gabriel Rojo Leyva. *Las Españas: historia de una revista del exilio (1943–1963)*. Mexico City: Colegio de México, Centro de Estudios Lingüísticos y Literarios, 1999.

Vallejo Márquez, Yolanda. "Aproximación al cervantismo decimonónico." *Draco: Revista de literatura española* 5–6 (1993–4): 243–65.

Vandebosch, Dagmar. "Quixotism as a Poetic and National Project in the Early Twentieth-Century Spanish Essay." In *International Don Quixote*, edited by Theo D'Haen and Reindert Dhondt, 15–31. Leiden: Brill, 2009.

Varela, Javier. "El mito de Castilla en la Generación del 98." *Claves de la razón práctica* 70 (1997): 10–16.

Vázquez de Mella, Juan. *El ideal de España, los tres dogmas nacionales*. Madrid: Imprenta Clásica Española, 1915.

Vázquez Montalbán, Manuel. *La aznaridad: por el imperio hacia Dios o por Dios hacia el imperio*. 1st ed. Barcelona: Mondadori, 2003.

Vega, Mariano Esteban de. *Castilla en España: historia y representacione*. Salamanca: Ediciones Universidad de Salamanca, 2014.

Venegas, Jose Luis. *Transatlantic Correspondence: Modernity, Epistolarity, and Literature in Spain and Spanish America, 1898–1992*. Columbus: Ohio State University Press, 2016.

Viestenz, William. *By the Grace of God: Francoist Spain and the Sacred Roots of Political Imagination*. Toronto: University of Toronto Press, 2014.

Villanueva Toledo, María Josefa, and Evelia Vega González. *Los tres centenarios de Cervantes en el siglo XX: fuentes documentales en el Archivo General de la Administración*. Madrid: Ministerio de Educación y Cultura, Secretaría General Técnica, 2005.

Viñao Frago, Antonio. "The History of Literacy in Spain: Evolution, Traits, and Questions." *History of Education Quarterly* 30, no. 4 (1990): 573–99.

Viñas, Ángel. *Los pactos secretos de Franco con estados unidos bases, ayuda económica, recortes de soberania*. Barcelona: Grijalbo, 1981.

Wahnón, Sultana. *Estética y crítica literarias en España: (1940–1950)*. Granada: Universidad de Granada, 1988.

Wantoch, Hans. *Spanien, das Land ohne Renaissance: eine kulturpolitische Studie*. Munich: G. Müller, 1927.

Weber, Alison. "Golden Age or Early Modern: What's in a Name?" *PMLA* 126, no. 1 (2011): 225–32.

Whealey, Robert H. *Hitler and Spain: The Nazi Role in the Spanish Civil War, 1936–1939*. Lexington: University Press of Kentucky, 2015.

Wheeler, Duncan. "Contextualising and Contesting José Antonio Maravall's Theories of Baroque Culture from the Perspective of Modern-Day Performance." *Bulletin of the Comediantes* 65, no. 1 (2013): 15–43. https://doi.org/10.1353/boc.2013.0015.

Wheeler, Duncan. *Golden Age Drama in Contemporary Spain: The Comedia on Page, Stage and Screen*. Cardiff: University of Wales Press, 2012.

Wolf, Eric R. "Ángel Palerm Vich. Obituary. American Anthropologist." *American Anthropological Association* 83, no. 3 (1981): 612–15.

Worden, William. "Sancho Panza, Illiterate Literary Critic, and the Unmasking of Generic Conventions in *Don Quixote*." *Comparative Literature Studies* 43, no. 4 (2006): 498–514.

Yankelevich, Pablo. *México, país refugio: la experiencia de los exilios en el siglo XX*. Mexico City: Plaza y Valdés, 2002.

Zambrano, María. *España, sueño y verdad*. Madrid: Diario Público, 2010.

Zambrano, María. "La reforma del entendimiento español." In *Los intelectuales en el drama de España. Ensayos y notas (1936–1939)*, 100–16. Madrid: Hispamerca, 1977.

Zambrano, María. *Senderos: Los intelectuales en el drama de España. La tumba de Antígona*. Barcelona: Anthropos, 1986.

Zamora, Lois Parkinson, and Monika Kaup, eds. *Baroque New Worlds: Representation, Transculturation, Counterconquest*. Durham, NC: Duke University Press, 2010.

Ziolkowski, Eric Josef. *The Sanctification of Don Quixote: From Hidalgo to Priest*. University Park: Pennsylvania State University Press, 1991.

INDEX

CPSIA information can be obtained
at www.ICGtesting.com
Printed in the USA
LVHW081153240223
740163LV00011B/860